HUMAN RESOURCES MANAGEMENT

A behavioral systems approach

THE IRWIN SERIES IN MANAGEMENT AND
THE BEHAVIORAL SCIENCES

L. L. Cummings and E. Kirby Warren *Consulting Editors*
John F. Mee *Advisory Editor*

HUMAN RESOURCES MANAGEMENT

A behavioral systems approach

LAWRENCE A. KLATT, Ph.D.

ROBERT G. MURDICK, Ph.D.

FRED E. SCHUSTER, D.B.A.

all of
Florida Atlantic University
Boca Raton, Florida

1978

RICHARD D. IRWIN, INC.   Homewood, Illinois   60430
Irwin-Dorsey Limited   Georgetown, Ontario   L7G 4B3

658.3
K63h

ISBN 0-256-02045-0
Library of Congress Catalog Card No. 77–088316
Printed in the United States of America

1 2 3 4 5 6 7 8 9 0 MP 5 4 3 2 1 0 9 8

Preface

This book is both managerial and philosophical in orientation—it is not a handbook or encyclopedia. It is designed for a comprehensive basic course in Human Resources Management (Personnel) which will serve equally the needs of majors in the field who need a broad outlook at their entry point into the field, and majors in all other areas of business who need to become aware of every manager's opportunities and responsibilities in human resources management. The book is thus intended to provide a basis for broadening the appeal and scope of the traditional introductory personnel course.

We take a view that differs from that of traditionalists but one that we think recognizes the tremendous changes that have occurred in the field of management. First, we place the prime responsibility for human resource management on line managers. At the same time, we recognize the very important advisory function of the human resource department, particularly in its role as change agent.

Second, we view the human resource management process as a systems process. There are many authorities in human resource management who are turned off at the concept of taking a systems view of people because of the "human aspect." There is no need for this and we certainly do not slight the human aspect in our view. What we are saying is that a system has objectives and groups of people have objectives; the parts of a system must work together; and appreciation of systems principles leads to more effective achievement of objectives, including worker satisfactions, than does intuitive nonsystematic management.

    We therefore treat human resource management in terms of many traditional topics, but always in relation to each other and in view of management's responsibility.

    We have "forged" this text and our ideas with the help of many reviewers. In particular we wish to thank Andy Divine, Charles A. Meloy, Jon Monat, and Allan Nash. We certainly do not claim that our views represent their views—only that they have helped us shape our thoughts more clearly.

    In addition, many preproduction and administrative chores were involved in our many rewrites. We wish to thank Kerry Ely, Ronald P. Smith, Kay Keehan, and Emily Murdick for helping us to put the pieces together over and over again.

    The authors also wish to thank Elaine Klatt, Emily Murdick, and Elizabeth Schuster for their patience and support during this lengthy project.

January 1978   LAWRENCE A. KLATT
                                               ROBERT G. MURDICK
                                             FRED E. SCHUSTER

Contents

PART II
MANAGING HUMAN RESOURCES: THE TOTAL ORGANIZATION

Business objectives and the human resource system: *The HRS should be unified toward business objectives. HRS objectives are derived from company objectives.* Organization planning: A unifying approach: *The organizational planning function. Traditional approaches to organization structure. Modern organizations—Systems approaches to design. New templates for organizational patterns. Which is the best approach to organization planning?* Human resource needs planning: *Relationship to other parts of the HRS. Relationship to the external environment.* Elements involved in human resource needs planning: *Forecasting. Work force inventories. An interrelated process.*

CASE: COMPANY GROWTH AND GOOD OLE BOYS (AND GIRLS)

Determining necessary job information: *Job analysis. Job descriptions and specifications.* Recruiting qualified candidates: *Internal sources. External sources.* Selecting human resources: *Factors in selection decisions. The selection process. Assessment centers. Evaluation of the selection process.* Legal influences on the staffing process: *Affirmative action programs. Meeting the challenge of equal employment opportunities.*

CASE: KMS INDUSTRIES

What is organization development? *Objectives of organization development. Underlying themes.* Three main approaches to OD. Conducting an effective OD program: *Steps for action research. Intervention techniques.* The impact of OD.

CASE: NTEL, INC.

CASE: TRANSFORMING THE TRANSFORMER COMPANY

The systems view: *System obsolescence. The human resources development concept. The human resources development process. Basic policies for human resources development.* Characteristics of the development process: *Objectives of the process. The process of teaching–learning. Levels of learning. Teaching–learning techni-*

ques. Characteristics of programs. Organizational responsibilities for HRD. How to operate an HRD system: *Forecast future organizational needs for five years. Assess current capabilities, turnover, recruitment plans. Establish long-range HRD objectives. Allocate funds for various programs, and establish a cost accounting system. Develop policies and programs. Measure the system effectiveness and cost. Revise the system.* Problems in the design, implementation, and measurement of training and development.

CASE: A QUESTION OF TRAINING

The role of the reward system: *Balancing financial and nonfinancial rewards. Divide the rewards fairly. Other considerations.* The extrinsic reward system: *Money as the universal reward. Nonfinancial extrinsic rewards.* The intrinsic reward system: *Models of the person.* Requirements of an effective reward system: *Operant conditioning theory. Expectancy and path-goal theories. Equity theory.* Forms of compensation: *Salary. Hourly wages or measured daywork. Piece rates. Sales commissions or bonuses. Productivity bonuses. Plantwide productivity plans. Performance bonuses. Profit-sharing plans. Stock-related supplemental compensation plans.* Noncash benefits: *Statutory benefits. Privately funded benefits.* Recent trends in compensation and benefits.

CASE: THE OLD ORDER CHANGETH (A)

Developing the compensation strategy: *Designing flexible reward systems. Cafeteria compensation. Implementing a flexible system.* Governmental influence on compensation. *The impact of labor market conditions. The impact of a union.* Procedure for developing the compensation system: *Compensation and benefit surveys. Relating survey data to the reward system.* Job evaluation: *The point method. Factor comparison. Ranking. Classification.* The administration of compensation and benefits: *Performance appraisal. Annual salary reviews. Maintaining the system.*

CASE: THE OLD ORDER CHANGETH (B)

The nature of collective bargaining: *Why workers join unions. Historical developments. Union structure. The legal framework for collective bargaining.* The impact of union-management relations on the HRS: *Decision making. Human resource policies and practices. Modifications in the work environment.* Negotiating the contract:

*understand. Summarize. Terminate the discussion constructively.
Follow up.*

CASE: THE CASE OF ANNE GREBLAD

The nature of leadership: *Power. Authority. Leadership defined.*
Theories of leadership: *Trait theories. Leadership styles: The behavioral approach. Situational theories.* The determinants of effective
leadership: *The leader. The followers. Other variables. Implications
of the contingency approach for human resources management.*

CASE: AN ADMINISTRATIVE ASSIGNMENT

The role of performance appraisal: *Roles for line management and
human resource specialists. Uses of appraisals. Hierarchical versus
participative approaches to appraisal. The development of performance appraisal techniques. Management by objectives.* Current
practice in performance appraisal: *Types of plans.* Evaluation of
methods in terms of human resources management objectives: *The
management climate. Length of time in the job.* Relating performance
appraisal to requiting. Step-by-step procedure for the implementation
of a performance appraisal system: *Appraisal. Comparison of performance. Setting nonfinancial rewards. Relating performance to compensation budgets. Taking other managerial actions. Communicating
the final appraisal and the action to be taken.*

CASE: A MATTER OF MONEY

The role of MBO in human resources management: *What is MBO?
MBO and the systems approach. The importance of MBO in human
resources management. MBO and the systems view.* The development and status of the MBO concept. The management by objectives
process: *Organizational goals. Key steps in the MBO process between
the individual and the manager. The criteria for good objectives.*
Implementing management by objectives: *Introducing MBO to the
organization. Where should MBO be applied?*

CASE: MBO ROLE PLAY

CASE: DELTA CORPORATION

Causes of change: *Innovations by subordinates. Changes which the
manager originates. Imposed changes.* The impact of change on the

individual. Stimulating creativity and change: *Factors which impede creativity. Managerial behavior that will stimulate creativity.* Resistance t> change: *Economic reasons. Personal reasons. Social reasons. Political reasons.* Effectively introducing change: *Avoiding resistance t> change. Overcoming resistance to change.*

CASE: ORDER PROCESSING

PART IV
HUMAN RESOURCES IN THE CHANGING ENVIRONMENT

From personnel administration to human resources management: *Fundamental trends. The changing role of human resource specialists.* Social changes: *Women at work. Discrimination at work. The quality of life. Drug abuse, alcoholism, handicapped workers, and ex-convicts. Demography and the energy shortage. Aged workers. Sexuality in the office.* The conditions of employment: *Time. Compensation. The impact of the computer. Objectivity in selecting, promoting, compensating. Health and safety. The quality of working life.* Labor-management relations: *Union membership. Labor issues. The collective bargaining process.* Changes in the economy and problems of productivity: *The decline in the rate of productivity gains. Increasing attention to productivity. Productivity and the quality of working life. The measurement of productivity.* The changing work force—Where have all the robots gone? *The educated work force. Changing value systems. The work ethic and productivity. The shift of the work force to knowledge workers. Mid-life career changing. Underqualified workers.*

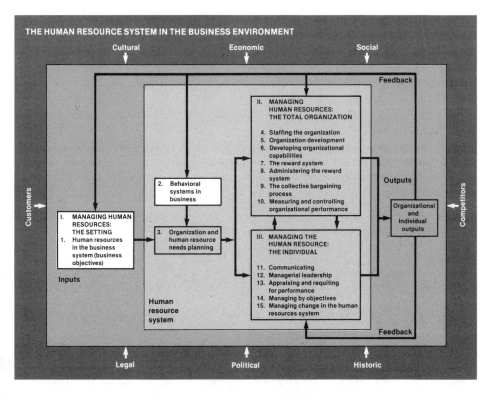

THE HUMAN RESOURCE SYSTEM IN THE BUSINESS ENVIRONMENT

Cultural   Economic   Social

Feedback

II. MANAGING
     HUMAN RESOURCES:
     THE TOTAL ORGANIZATION

4. Staffing the organization
5. Organization development
6. Developing organizational
    capabilities
7. The reward system
8. Administering the reward
    system
9. The collective bargaining
    process
10. Measuring and controlling
    organizational performance

Outputs

2. Behavioral
    systems in
    business

I.   MANAGING HUMAN
     RESOURCES:
     THE SETTING
1.   Human resources
     in the business
     system (business
     objectives)

3. Organization and
    human resource
    needs planning

Organizational
and
individual
outputs

Customers

Competitors

Inputs

Human
resource
system

III. MANAGING THE
      HUMAN RESOURCE:
      THE INDIVIDUAL

11. Communicating
12. Managerial leadership
13. Appraising and requiting
    for performance
14. Managing by objectives
15. Managing change in the human
    resources system

Feedback

Legal   Political   Historic

PART I

**MANAGING
HUMAN RESOURCES:
THE SETTING**

When you have completed studying
HUMAN RESOURCES IN THE BUSINESS SYSTEM
you should be able to:

1. Explain why the management of human resources is so important.
2. Define the role of business in society.
3. List a number of goals which a business may pursue.
4. Define "system."
5. Describe business as a system.
6. Explain how the human resource system fits into the business.
7. Explain the role and function of managers in the human resource system.
8. Explain the changing role of personnel administration in the company.
9. Explain "optimization" and "trade-offs" as applied to human resource systems.

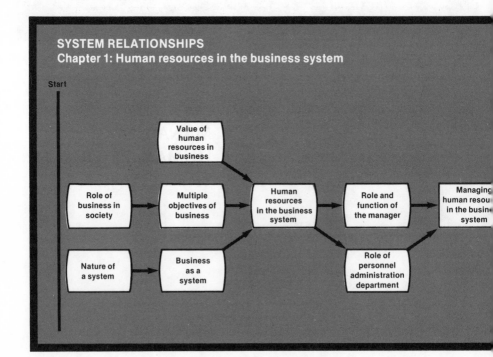

SYSTEM RELATIONSHIPS
Chapter 1: Human resources in the business system

Defective products. Poor service. Don't-give-a-damn employees. Mis-representation of goods and services. Anything to make a buck. Corrupt corporation executives. Shortages of repair parts. Society appears to be disintegrating. The quality of life gets worse every year.

Everyone of us has probably voiced some of the above complaints many times over. What do these complaints have to do with managing human resources in business? Everything! Although we are all complaining about others, we are all *collectively responsible* for such complaints. Many of us are in work situations that do not excite us, stimulate us, make us want to do the best *individual* and *team* jobs that

1

Human resources in the business system

NOTE: The diagram at the left shows the basic concepts of the chapter and their relationships.

we are capable of doing. As both consumers and producers, we are living in an Age of Abundant Discontent.

We have been living up to now in a world in which we could waste material resources and be profligate with human resources. The continued development of technology and sophisticated production equipment fed upon this waste to yield ever-greater production. Suddenly our resources are no longer capable of meeting society's needs if we go on following this route.[1]

The situation facing business, government agencies, and nonprofit institutions today can best be described by modifying some fine words of Admiral Elmo R. Zumwalt, former chief of naval operations, and reapplying them to management instead of the Navy:

> Management of human resources has reached a point where it can no longer drift with the tides and winds of change, totally oblivious to the demands of our youth, the needs of our society, and the dignity of our workers. The problem of management today is not one of discipline but one of enlightened leadership.

ARE PEOPLE AT WORK IMPORTANT?

We believe that the time has come to develop and apply new concepts and understanding to our utilization of human resources. If business could increase the productivity of all workers by only 5 percent, gross national product would be increased by 15 percent. If workers were motivated to the extent that players on a winning football team are, a mind-staggering increase in output and quality would be possible. We are not referring here just to the millions of individual contributors; we are including managers at all levels of the organization as well.

The management of human resources has, of course, been an important field of study for decades. The behavioral sciences are making extremely significant contributions at an accelerating rate to increase our growing knowledge of managing people at work. In fact, behavioral science research reveals a very complex set of influences that affect the attitudes, interpersonal relationships, and productivity of people at work. A systematic understanding of all these variables would make for a much more productive work force and a much more effective management. This text will attempt to provide that systematic understanding by using a systems approach to the study of human resources management. Within this context the firm will be presented as a business system.

Human resources represent a subsystem of the business which dominates all other subsystems of the business. The reason is obvious: humans design and control all other systems. The human resource subsystem thus controls both functional subsystems and other resource subsystems (Exhibit 1–1). Thus, in terms of people, in terms of the functioning of the firm, and in terms of society, we would certainly agree that people at work are very important.

EXHIBIT 1–1
The human resource subsystem controls all other subsystems in a business

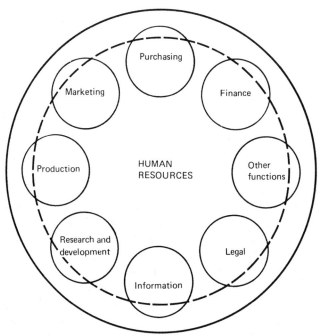

In the systems approach, we try to look at the total picture. Thus, to study the human resource system, we look at the environment of the system first. In this case, we look at the role of the total organization in the environment. The objectives of the total organization will then determine or shape the objectives of all the subsystems of the organization.

THE ROLE OF BUSINESS IN SOCIETY

The question is, do corporate executives, provided they stay within the law, have responsibilities other than to make as much money for their stockholders as possible? And my answer to that is, no, they do not.[2]

Milton Friedman

They [the employees] have a place to stand and a place to sit, and a roof over their heads—which might not be there if it were not for ITT. *I submit that this is our first and most important social responsibility.*[3]

Harold S. Geneen

If in fact the primary or overriding purpose of business is to make a profit, then the free enterprise system should and will be self-destructive.[4]

John Adam, Jr.

A large corporation not only may engage in social responsibility, it had damn well better try to do so.[5]

Paul Samuelson

The role of business in society has often produced heated argument. We should note that not every society has (or favors) privately owned business. The development of private business as an institution has been encouraged in some societies because people believed that this was the best way to produce and distribute goods. In the United States, long a stronghold of Adam Smith's beliefs, modifications are occurring. Over the years, people have been pressing for more government control, or even government ownership, of production and services.

It should be made clear that government ownership and government management are not the same thing. For example, the U.S. government owns land and leases it to private lumber interests. It also owns the Knolls Atomic Power Laboratory, for example, and contracts the management to a private company. On the other hand, governments have established corporations which are managed by nongovernment managers. The government also owns and manages the Postal Service, the Watervliet Arşenal, and other enterprises in competition with private business. Thus it would be theoretically possible for the government to own all property and plant and yet have everything privately managed.

We suggest here that the role of business is to serve society in many ways simultaneously. It serves society best if it produces goods and services desired by society in the form, in the time, and at a price dictated by efficient management of resources. It serves society best if it works toward improving the quality of life. Business serves society best if it *also.* provides satisfaction for the employees who spend such a large portion of their lives at work. (These objectives of business as an institution apply equally to all other productive agencies of society—government, not-for-profit, and so on.)

The problem of business management, then, is to manage human resources in the interests of society, which include the successful perpetuation of the individual business.

THE MULTIPLE OBJECTIVES OF BUSINESS

The fundamental role or general objective of business has been stated above. There may be, however, conflicting subgoals. Achieving one objective fully may mean some sacrifice in achieving other objectives. For example, some objectives business may pursue are:

1. Serving customers well.
2. Satisfying all the needs and desires of every employee.
3. Making the maximum profit for owners (stockholders).
4. Reinvesting profits for growth.
5. Satisfying vendors.
6. Satisfying environmental groups.
7. Satisfying the public's demand for ethical and social responsibility.
8. Growing larger at the expense of competitors.

Let us look at a particular case, the second objective listed. The objective of satisfying employees' desires may conflict with many of the other objectives in the world as it now exists. Employees would like more money at the expense of stockholders, or even at the expense of profit and continuing operation. More employees would like to be vice presidents, say, than the company can endure. Modern production requires that workers, in general, all work the same hours of the day, that is, that their time be structured rather than flexible. This conflicts with individual desires for free time.

As we will see, seeking to balance and integrate conflicting objectives is characteristic of the systems approach. We now need to develop other concepts of systems as the basis for our study of managing human resources.

THE NATURE OF A SYSTEM

The concept of system has been defined and used by many scientists and scholars in such diverse fields as mathematics, cybernetics, sociology, physics, psychology, and management.[6] We are concerned here with empirical or real-world systems as opposed to intangible conceptual systems.

We shall use the word *system* to mean a set of elements or components that are related to each other and that operate on inputs, such as information, physical resources, and people, to achieve common (total-system) objectives. Therefore, a system is a processor which operates on inputs to produce outputs. Some examples of systems are shown in the accompanying table.

System	Inputs: Physical	Inputs: Information	Operations	Outputs
Home heating system	Fuel or electricity	Temperature of air Thermostat setting	Heat and move air	Warm air
Manufacturing business	Materials	Competitive action Market opportunities Government regulations Economic and social data	Convert materials into processed or end products	Products for industry, consumers, or government Information on its products
Logistics system	Vehicle Products	Rates (shipping) Demand Inventories Destinations	Move and store products	Transportation of products Information on product Location and inventory
Personnel	—	Data on inventory of human resources, needs, costs	Compile, aggregate, analyze, report Advise	Reports Advice

Inputs to a system consist of physical or information flow from the *environment*. Flows from the system go back to the environment. Therefore, the *boundary* of a system separates the environment from the system. Exhibit 1–2 shows these system concepts.

The components of a system may be discrete, indivisible units, or they may themselves be smaller systems called subsystems. Thus the definition of a particular system is arbitrary and depends upon the system that the writer wishes to focus on. For example, we may

EXHIBIT 1–2
Model of a system

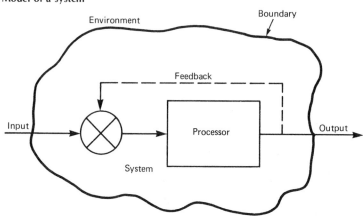

focus on our economic system, on a particular business (system) of interest to us, such as the human resource system, or on the manufacturing system in a particular business.

Good business systems, like good mechanical systems, are controlled by measuring performance against objectives and feeding back the information on the variation as input for the system to act on. Exhibit 1–2 shows this *feedback* by the dashed line. Thus feedback provides a basis for controlling a system's attainment of its objectives.

THE BUSINESS AS A SYSTEM

As we have noted, we may regard the total company as a "system." It is composed of human resources, buildings and equipment, and money. Its purpose is to provide products, services, and information. To accomplish this purpose, it must "process" or convert materials, energy, and information to new forms. The activities of the human resource system are a vital subsystem in the total company.

A business does not exist in solitary confinement but rather is influenced by the world around it. Management wants to make sure that it produces the right products in the right quantities for this outside world. Therefore, we see seven major forecasts that guide the objectives of a business. These forecasts try to describe what will happen with respect to:

1. Customers.	5. Legal change.
2. Competitors.	6. Cultural change.
3. The economy.	7. Social change.
4. Political change.	

We may divide a business in many ways in order to view its subsystems. For a study of functions, such subsystems as marketing, manufacturing, finance, and personnel may be considered in a manufacturing company. If we wish to study the managerial process and resource utilization, however, we would probably consider the business to be composed of the human resource system, the capital asset system, the liquid asset system, the materials system, and the intangible assets system.

This brings us to the subject of this book, the human resource system. It also raises the questions "Why study human resources from a systems viewpoint?" and "Are there other approaches to the study of managing human resources?"

WHY USE A SYSTEMS APPROACH TO THE STUDY OF MANAGING HUMAN RESOURCES?

Previous approaches to the study of managing human resources have split the subject into three separate fields:

1. Managerial processes.
2. Personnel administration.
3. Organizational behavior and development.

Some books on managing deal primarily with the processes or functions carried out by managers. Planning, organizing, staffing, initiating, and controlling are a typical set of functions treated in such books. This approach often minimizes the behavior of individuals and groups in response to the rational managerial approach to the utilization of resources. Further, the practicalities of carrying out those processes that relate to people in actual organizations are glossed over.

The personnel function evolved in response to the need for carrying out the practical and routine activities associated with managing large groups of people. It was only natural that the eventual complexity of the personnel administration function required people with professional training in this function. Hence courses and books appeared which were designed to fulfill this need.

The personnel administration approach has focused on the routine, procedural, record-keeping aspects of human resources management, on the one hand, and on managerial responsibilities that line managers have abdicated or shirked, on the other hand. Thus the traditional personnel administration book does not identify the responsibilities of line managers for human resources management.

The organizational behavior approach evolved as social scientists recognized the need for a scientific basis for statements about people at work. Thus motivation, leadership, and the development of individuals and of the organization as a whole have been the subject of intensive research. The study of organizational behavior has been very useful in helping us to understand why or how people behave. It does not relate the human resource system to the larger problem of setting objectives in terms of total business objectives. It does not relate human resources to functional activities and other resource management or to specific *techniques* for managing human resources. Therefore, we find that we must combine the nonscientific knowledge derived from experience, practice, and logical thought with the scientific evidence from organizational behavior research to present a useful guide for managers.

We have therefore taken the systems approach to the presentation of human resources management because:

1. It requires a clear definition of the total process (system) and objectives of the system.
2. It offers a natural, straightforward method of analysis by permitting division into subsystems and study of the subsystems.
3. It shows the interrelationships among the subsystems of the human resource subsystem.
4. It relates the human resource subsystem to its environment in terms of the inputs, the outputs, and the effects of the inputs and outputs upon the system.
5. It permits the study of managers, individual workers, and groups as subsystems, based upon the extensive research going on in the area of motivation and organizational behavior.
6. It permits examination of the division of work between line managers and the manager of human resources in terms of total system objectives and trade-offs to optimize the achievement of those objectives.

THE HUMAN RESOURCE SYSTEM IN BUSINESS

The human resource system is a unique subsystem of a business because it operates upon all the other subsystems. It is, in effect, the principal subsystem of the business. Whatever in the environment affects the business as a whole also affects the human resource system. In Exhibit 1–3 we have shown several examples of environmental (external) factors and their impact on the business and the human resource system. The human resource system interacts with the environment to change the business operation and *to change itself.*

Let us trace the impact of an environmental change through the business to the human resource system. Under the influence of equal employment opportunity regulations, a firm entered into agreement with the Veterans Administration's Contract Compliance Service to guarantee female employees maternity leave and automatic reinstatement without loss of pay, job status, seniority, or job rights. The environmental influence which led to this agreement impacted the firm's business system in a number of ways. For instance, it is likely that turnover will be reduced, that direct labor costs will be increased, and that the company will attract more female employees. The impact on the human resource system may be that work responsibilities will have to be reassigned temporarily from time to time since about one third of the employees are women. With less turnover, work associations among employees may be strengthened, leading to higher productivity. Some employees will have to be reassigned to different jobs when they return, however, which may have varied affects on their productivity. Thus we may see how the total business actions influence the operation of the human resource system.

As can be seen in Exhibit 1–3, the human resource system receives inputs from the larger business system in the form of business objectives. These objectives lead to organizational plans for the human resource system. One of the major parts of the human resource system, the organizational subsystem, is concerned with modifying the work environment. It deals with the organization as a whole. It in turn consists of various subsystems, such as the staffing and organization structure, the appraisal and reward system, the labor relations system, and the organizational development system. The second major part of the human resource system focuses on the individual as a subsystem. This involves individual development through such means as communication, motivation, leadership, and appraising.

As is further shown in the schematic diagram of Exhibit 1–3, the human resource system results in individual and organizational performance that may be viewed as two separate types of output, individual (need fulfillment, growth, and development) and organiza-

EXHIBIT 1–3
The human resource system in the business environment

THE HUMAN RESOURCE SYSTEM IN THE BUSINESS ENVIRONMENT

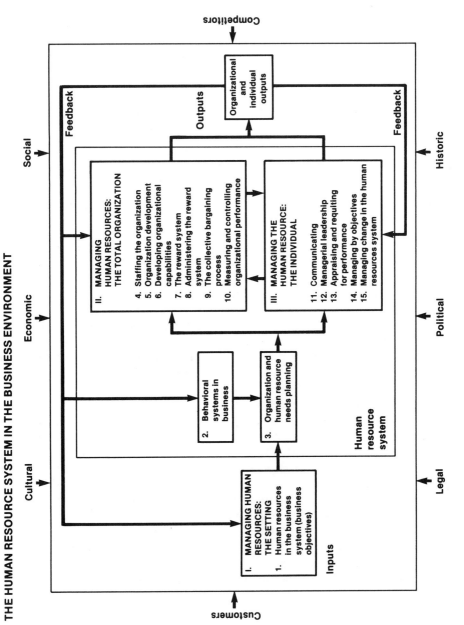

tional (productivity, maintenance, and growth). We shall see in later chapters, however, that it is the manager's job to coordinate these two outputs so that both accomplish the organizational plans, which in turn should achieve the objectives of the total business system.[7] It can also be seen that both the human resource system and the business system operate under the same cultural, economic, social, legal, political, and other constraints.

Because the human resource system controls all other systems in the total business system, the greater the effectiveness and productivity of the human resource system, the more nearly will the business system be optimized. It is for this reason among others that it is so important to improve the management of human resources.

THE ROLE AND FUNCTION OF MANAGERS IN THE HUMAN RESOURCE SYSTEM

When large numbers of people must work together to achieve common objectives, the objectives must somehow be defined and communicated to the entire organization. In a large firm everybody cannot speak at once. Only some of the people in a large firm have the broad knowledge and skills required to set basic goals. Yet everybody in the firm has some important contributions to make toward goal setting. These contributions are (a) technical in terms of expertise and (b) personal in terms of needs. We may view managers as "combiners of information," creators of a unified sense of direction, and developers of human resources.

Basically, a manager is a representative of a group who performs the planning, integrating, and controlling functions for the group as a whole. The manager's role is different from that of other members of the group in that while each individual may plan and control his own activities as a *part* of his job, these activities *are* the job of the manager.

This role of the manager has been stated in very fundamental terms. The breakdown of his activities in terms of managing the human resource subsystem of which he is a part will be covered in subsequent chapters. At this point we mention a most important activity. He is directly responsible for the development and performance of the people in his group, both as individuals and as a group.

THE ROLE OF THE PERSONNEL ADMINISTRATION DEPARTMENT

In the past the personnel administration department has viewed itself as responsible for the recruiting, hiring, staffing, development, transfer, and pay administration of all employees in the company. As keeper of confidential employee records, personnel administration has often been able to extend its authority over the organization. Further, many line managers have, in the past, been glad to abdicate their responsibilities for many aspects of human resources management to the PA department.

Present-day managers have learned of the many problems caused by this dual or shared responsibility for people management. Further, managers are better educated today in behavioral systems. They recognize that they must bear full responsibility for the performance of their people and for the growth of each individual. For these reasons, the PA department is becoming what it should be—a support service and technical adviser to line managers. Members of the PA department should not deal directly with any employee on any matter unless they have permission from the employee's manager.

Recent trends

Two distinct trends in human resources management will be reflected throughout this book. At first glance, these two trends may appear to be contradictory, but we will attempt to show why they are, in fact, quite complementary. One of these trends is the movement of more and more responsibility for the management of human resources out of the hands of the personnel specialist and into the hands of the line manager. The other trend is the increasing opportunity for the human resource specialist to contribute directly to the profitability of the organization.

This latter emphasis on an active, profit-contributing role for human resources managers is primarily a result of recent research in the behavioral sciences, which has opened up new opportunities for increasing the productivity of organizations.

Largely in response to these new opportunities opened up by the behavioral sciences, human resources managers in many progressive organizations are actively involved in redesigning the role, objectives, and structure of the human resources management function. Examination of the human resources management literature over the last several years will quickly confirm that major changes are occurring in the concept of this function and that even more changes are in prospect. For example, Fischer has suggested that the human resources management function is moving rapidly in the following directions: (1) a growing profit orientation and the assumption of a more important role in the management of the business; (2) a shift in emphasis from packaged "personnel programs" to the custom design of staffing systems to fit the specific needs and business objectives of the individual company; (3) the assumption of responsibility for developing the organization rather than just maintaining it (that is, emphasis on planning and developing the company's human resources as opposed to emphasis on keeping records); (4) more direct involvement with the top management of the organization in deploying and developing its human resources.[8]

Through all of these changes in the role and objectives of the human resources management function runs one strong undercurrent which has already been stressed—the need for an integrated systems view which emphasizes the direct relationship between human resources management subsystems and the business objectives of the organization.

Manpower managers as change agents

The field of human resources management is now at the point where a major shift in the direction of the trends indicated above is already occurring. Chief executives increasingly are recognizing that the development and effective utilization of human resources is one of the chief elements of the overall management of the organization, closely linked with the total management process. Thus, rather than being paper shufflers or employee record-keepers, as was too often the case in the past, many personnel managers are assuming a new role as internal change agents. The following comments by Mason Haire of the Massachusetts Institute of Technology are typical of what is being said by many observers:

> We are coming to a time when the management of human resources must take a more prominent place in the firm's decisions. The value and leverage of the resource is simply too great for the kind of reactive response to pressures which has characterized it in the past. . . . As it stands today, the personnel function—or employee relations, or industrial relations, or whatever title is used—is typically not a major mover in the firm. . . . The reactive rather than pro-active tradition is strong in the personnel field. Firms typically pay the standard wage of their industry and neighborhood—a philosophy of compensation that guarantees that we won't do any worse than our friends and competitors, but assures that we won't do any better.[9]

Personnel administration—A changing field

Significantly, the American Society for Personnel Administration, the primary professional organization in the human resources management field, is now considering a change in its name to replace the term *personnel administration* with the term *human resources management*. At this organization's 25th anniversary conference, in 1973, it was estimated that personnel managers will have a 50 percent casualty rate over the next several years unless they develop the new skills needed to handle the major changes now taking place in the profession. At the same meeting, Dr. Herbert Heneman, director of the Industrial Relations Center at the University of Minnesota, and one of the most respected members of the work force management profession, outlined the following changes which he believes are mandated for the work force management function:

1. Push more of the personnel and industrial relations function back into line management where it belongs; help line supervisors do a better job of managing people.
2. Do micro-work force planning for the whole organization.
3. Rediscover employees; push motivation to the forefront.
4. Organize personnel and industrial relations departments around expected goals or outcomes (rather than along functional specialities).

MANAGING HUMAN RESOURCES IN THE BUSINESS SYSTEM

Managing human resources in the business system, therefore, is the responsibility of all managers. Managers are responsible for the development, maintenance, and performance of the human resource system of which they themselves are a part.

The development or construction of the human resource system starts with aggregate resource planning and structure. That is, management must determine how many people with what skills will be required over a number of years in the future. It must estimate total human resource cost and evaluate trade-offs between capital equipment and human labor. (In your economics texts, the term *labor* is used to denote human resources.) Management must also consider human resources in its valuation of the company's assets.

The manager has the responsibility for optimizing his total system, which generally means that all human resource objectives cannot be attained. He must give up some desires and benefits of individuals for the sake of his subsystem and for the sake of the business system as a whole.

The practices of companies have varied widely in the search for optimization of the total system in managing human resources. Let us look at two widely contrasting historical cases. In the first instance, the Kohler Plumbing Supply Company had a violent and bitter relationship with striking employees over a period of eight years, from 1954 to 1962. In contrast, IBM, a real plum for union organizers, has maintained such excellent relationships within its human resource system that unionization has never been a serious challenge.

Studies of companies show wide variability in employee motivation, satisfaction, and productivity. A small company just starting out seems to have a team spirit and camaraderie which often degenerate to bureaucracy, legalisms, and sullen duty as the organization grows.

What changes in management occur to produce this situation? How should human resources be managed in the best interests of the company's survival, society's needs, and the individual employee's needs? How do employees respond in the work subsystems in which they spend most of their lives? The behavioral systems approach to the study of managing human resources is directed toward answering these questions.

SUMMARY

This chapter's objective is to show the structure of our approach to managing human resources from a behavioral systems viewpoint. We have therefore stated in brief form:

1. Improved opportunities for business and society will result from the better utilization of human resources in business.
2. The role that business plays in society is to serve society in many respects, not just economic.
3. Business has multiple, conflicting goals and a human resources manager must balance and integrate resources to achieve those goals.
4. A system is a goal-directed set of elements or subsystems whose subgoals must be subordinated to the total system goals for optimization. A system has inputs, a processor, outputs, and usually a feedback of information with subsequent corrective action.
5. Business, by our definition, is consequently a system and may best be studied as such.
6. Human resources in business comprise a subsystem of the business system. The study of managing human resources should be approached from a systems viewpoint.

7. Managers play a key role in the operation and control of the human resource system. A prescription for managerial behavior in terms of a description of individual and group behavior in business is a prime objective of this book.

8. The role of the personnel administration department has traditionally been distorted in teaching and practice. The PA department's role is to advise and assist managers in the management of human resources, not to substitute for managers.

9. As a result of recent research in the behavioral sciences, progressive organizations are redesigning the role, objectives, and structure of the human resources management function.

10. The success or failure of the business system depends on the success or failure of the human resource system. The upper limit on all other subsystems in business is set by the effectiveness of the human resource system. Some companies excel in human resources management, and others fail miserably. This book should help you to understand why this is so.

QUESTIONS AND PROBLEMS

1. a. Give examples of America's wasted resources.
   b. Do you think we waste human resources? Discuss.

2. Why are people the most important resource in a business?

3. What is the basic characteristic of the systems approach?

4. How is the role of business in society related to the objectives of the human resource system in a particular business?

5. "Business has only one objective—to make the maximum profit for its owners." Discuss this statement in terms of possible objectives of the human resource system.

6. a. What is a system?
   b. In what ways may a business be considered a system?
   c. How can the human resource system be both a "system" and a "subsystem" of a business?

7. Using a concrete example, show how goals in an organization may be suboptimized in order to optimize the total system.

8. Using Exhibit 1–3, discuss how the various environmental constraints may influence the outputs of a business system.

9. Does the true systems approach to studying human resources in business neglect the behavioral variables? Discuss.

10. What kind of knowledge useful for managing human resources does the field of behavioral science provide us with?

11. Identify a change in the environment and trace its impact through the business and the human resource system.

12. Organizations of individuals and each individual may both be considered systems. Why?
13. In what respects are managers "combiners of information"?
14. How does the role of a manager differ from that of other members of the human resource system?
15. Interview the manager of a personnel department in your area. Find out how the role of the personnel department has changed over the past decade.
16. "Managing human resources is a job for the personnel department." Discuss.
17. What is a "change agent"?
18. What is meant by "optimizing" a system's output?

BIBLIOGRAPHY

Beer, Stafford. *Cybernetics and Management.* New York: John Wiley & Sons, 1964.

Blakeney, Roger N., Matteson, Michael T., and Huff, James. "The Personnel Function: A Systemic View." *Public Personnel Management,* January–February 1974.

Coleman, Charles J., and Palmer, David D. "Organization Application of System Theory." *Business Horizons,* December 1973.

French, Wendell. *The Personnel Management Process.* 3d ed. Boston: Houghton Mifflin, 1974.

Fulmer, Robert M. *The New Management.* New York: Macmillan Publishing Co., 1974.

Hall, Arthur D. *A Methodology for Systems Engineering.* New York: D. Van Nostrand, 1962.

Kast, Fremont E., and Rosenzweig, James E. *Organization and Management: A Systems Approach.* New York: McGraw-Hill Book Co., 1970.

Murdick, Robert G., and Ross, Joel E. *Information Systems for Modern Management.* 2d ed. Englewood Cliffs, N.J.: Prentice-Hall, 1975.

Richman, Barry M., and Farmer, Richard N. *Management and Organizations.* New York: Random House, 1975.

Schuster, Fred. "A Systems View of Human Resources Management." *Personnel Administrator,* March–April 1971.

NOTES

[1] Donella H. Meadows et al., *Limits to Growth: A Report on the Club of Rome's Project on the Predicament of Mankind* (New York: Universe Books, 1972). See also "Managing in a Shortage Economy" (special report), *Business Week,* November 10, 1973, pp. 150–63.

[2] "How Business Faces a Hostile Climate," *Business Week,* September 16, 1972, p. 70.

[3] "Accounting and the Road Ahead," a speech made by Harold S. Geneen on May 10, 1972, in Memphis, Tennessee, at the annual meeting of stockholders, International Telephone & Telegraph Co.

[4] John Adam, Jr., "Put Profit in Its Place," *Harvard Business Review*, March–April 1973, p. 150. Copyright © 1973 by the President and Fellows of Harvard College; all rights reserved.

[5] John T. Corson, "Social Responsibility—Time to Take Stock," *Personnel Administrator*, January–February 1972, pp. 39–42. Reprinted with permission; copyright 1972, the American Society for Personnel Administration.

[6] See, for example, Robert G. Murdick and Joel E. Ross, *Information Systems for Modern Management*, 2d ed. (Englewood Cliffs, N.J.: Prentice-Hall, 1975), p. 9; and Ervin Laszlo, "The Meaning and Significance of General System Theory," *Behavioral Science*, January 1975, pp. 20–21.

[7] Ibid.

[8] Frank E. Fischer, "The Personnel Function in Tomorrow's Company," *Personnel*, January–February 1968; William E. Bright, "How One Company Manages Its Human Resources" *Harvard Business Review*, January–February 1976; and Herbert Meyer, "Personnel Directors are the New Corporate Heroes," *Fortune*, February 1976.

[9] Mason Haire, "A New Look at Human Resources," *Industrial Management Review*, Winter 1970, pp. 17–23.

When you have completed studying
BEHAVIORAL SYSTEMS IN BUSINESS
you should be able to:

1. Tell why managers must learn about behavioral systems.
2. Construct a schematic representing the individual worker as a basic behavioral system.
3. Classify and list inputs and outputs of the basic behavioral system.
4. Describe the worker as a processor.
5. Describe the basic needs and motivations of workers.
6. Classify the higher level behavioral systems—the groups of workers—which make up the total organizational system.
7. Identify similarities and differences of classes of workers in the behavioral system.

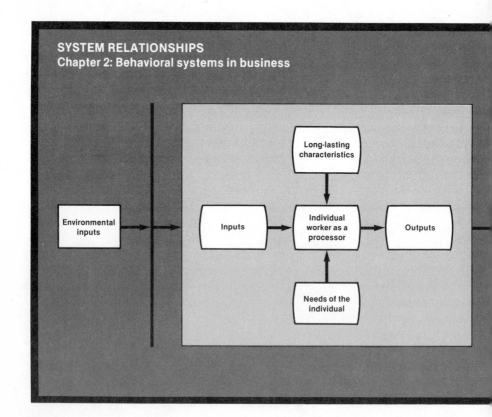

SYSTEM RELATIONSHIPS
Chapter 2: Behavioral systems in business

Managing people both in organized groups and on a one-to-one basis requires a good understanding of behavioral systems.

We have said earlier that an open system, most simply, is composed of inputs from the environment, a processor, and outputs from the processor. A number of such systems are linked together to form the total behavioral system of a business or other agency.

The successful business is an *adapting* system. This means that it changes to respond to the environment. A system which does not adapt dies. The dinosaur and the bankrupt business are examples of such failures to adapt. The

2

Behavioral systems in business

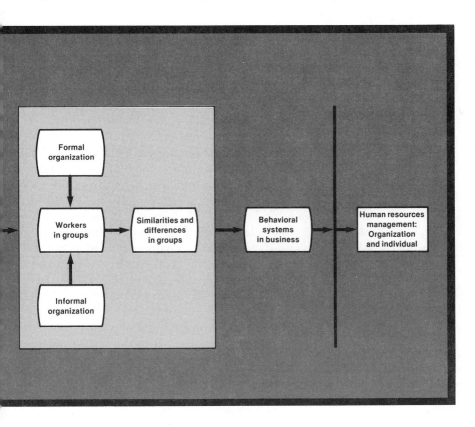

behavioral system is the adaptive system which controls the firm. Each part of the behavioral system, of course, must adapt reasonably well to the needs of the total behavioral system.

The smallest part, or subsystem, in a behavioral system is an individual person. The individual processes inputs to yield outputs. The individual observes the outputs, compares them with his or her goals, and *feeds back* corrections as inputs. Two or more persons operating as a *group* to process inputs and to give outputs directed toward a common goal are also a behavioral system. It is the function of the managers to keep the behavioral subsystems and the total behavioral system operating consistently with their own goals, with related systems, and with the ever-changing environment.

On the basis of the above systems characteristics of organizations, we may conclude that managers:

1. Must understand workers as individuals.
2. Must understand the behavior of workers in groups.
3. Must act as catalysts influencing change in these behavioral systems in order to adapt the business to a changing environment.

In this chapter we will therefore attempt to present the characteristics of individuals as processors and to identify and describe the behavior of groups of workers as systems.

THE BASIC BEHAVIORAL SUBSYSTEM—
THE INDIVIDUAL WORKER

The worker, as a system, processes inputs, according to our definition of a system in Chapter 1. These inputs come both from outside the company and from inside the company, that is, from the environment of the worker-system. The inputs may also be classified as job-related and non-job-related (see Exhibit 2–1). Managers exercise considerable control over a variety of inputs to the worker and hence indirectly over the outputs of the worker-system. A manager exercises this control by creating the work environment or work "climate" and by his/her leadership style. The manager's role in the human resource system is covered in depth in the following chapters.

At the most fundamental level of the systems viewpoint, however, we can identify the three basic *inputs* to the worker as information, physical or material resources, and energy. The basic *outputs* may also be information, material goods, and energy as modified (processed) by the worker-system.

EXHIBIT 2–1

The individual worker as a system (feedback not shown)

Nonjob-related inputs and outputs

Information   Information

Job-related   Job-related
inputs   outputs

Information ⟶   ⟶ Information

Materials ⟶   ⟶ Materials

Energy ⟶   ⟶ Energy

The functioning of the human as a system in the work environment is obviously very complex. Fortunately, we can rely to a great extent on our knowledge of the worker as a *processor* in the total human resource system.

Inputs

Since we may vary the output of a system by changing its inputs, let us examine inputs to the individual worker. Examples of job-related *informational* inputs to the worker are:

1. Description of the company, its organization, and its economic environment.
2. Information on the objectives and goals of the company and of the worker's own unit.
3. Instructions as to what the job is and how it shall be performed, working conditions, hours, and so on.
4. Information on how much freedom the individual has to control *how* the job is performed and to propose changes in the job itself.
5. Reports from other workers or groups.
6. Feedback on job performance in relation to goals and norms.
7. The manager's appraisal of the person's work or request for corrective action.
8. Company policies and procedures.
9. Salary, fringe benefits, recognition, and other rewards.
10. Work location and facilities.
11. Observations of events in the outside world.

Examples of job-related *material or physical* inputs are:

1. Raw materials or subassemblies.
2. Equipment.

3. Reports which the individual must process.
4. Computer tapes or punched cards which the worker must process.

Examples of job-related *energy* inputs are:

1. Light and heat.
2. Power (power conversion devices to make physical work easier).

Other inputs to the worker which are not specifically task-related are:

1. Information from associated workers in a social context, such as during lunch or coffee breaks or on the job.
2. Perceptions of the status, role, and activities of workers in the organization.
3. Perceptions of his/her own role, status, and relationships with other workers.
4. Perceptions of self, values, sentiments, and previous experiences which derive from the worker's position in the surrounding culture.
5. Union viewpoints and activities.
6. General information from the environment outside the company—from reading, listening, and observing.

Outputs

The job-related outputs of a worker may include materials, energy, information, or combinations of these three. For example, a production worker completes the assembly of a custom piece of furniture and notes the applied time on a costing form. The engineer makes a thermal analysis of a new air conditioner design and prepares a report. A manager at a weekly staff meeting gives an oral report of progress on an important program.

Non-job-related outputs, or to be more accurate, outputs not required by the job, are the behavior of the worker, the role played by the worker, and statements made by the worker to other workers. The behavior of the worker includes this person's interactions with other people in the organization.

The worker as a processor

The objective of managers, in the role which they fulfill, is to develop individuals and an organization which optimally achieve the objectives of the entire business. They do this by creating situations in which each individual will perceive that he/she can achieve his own goals *best* by contributing to the objectives of the organization (that is, integration of the goals of the individual and the goals of the organization). As we mentioned in Chapter 1, multiple goals (which may be in conflict) are involved in seeking such an objective. Management may employ three approaches to control the human resource system:

1. Change inputs to individuals: information, energy, and materials.
2. Change the processor: the individual worker.
3. Change the goals of the business to meet the needs of the workers more fully.

It would be nice if we had a simple formula which said, "If we change input X by five units, worker output will double and workers will be 20 percent happier." Instead, we may only list a fairly large number of variables or characteristics of workers which interact in a complex, fuzzy way to operate on inputs and convert them to outputs. Research on individuals and groups of individuals as subsystems in the business organization has been at a very primitive level. We can only examine the results of such research, make a judgment as to the best way to manage a particular organization, and then try it out. There are, however, some rough guidelines which can be employed to use our behavioral knowledge in deciding what actions to take as a manager. We probably can also identify some past and present managerial practices that do *not* work particularly well. This helps to limit our attempts to develop the best system for a particular company in practice.

Long-lasting characteristics

Some characteristics of the individual which influence the individual's behavior as a processor are long-enduring. By this we mean that these characteristics are not easily changed, so that management must either modify company goals, spend considerable effort in changing the characteristics, or remove the worker from that particular system. Such long-enduring characteristics of people are:

1. Value systems.
2. Attitudes.
3. Cultural and educational background.
4. Level of aspiration.

5. Reference group and norms.
6. Level of development in terms of perceived needs and personal "maturity."
7. "Intelligence."
8. Experience or time spent in life or work situations.
9. Perceived role or self-concept.

Everyone has a unique "value system." A *value* is a concept about what is fundamentally good or desirable which the individual holds on to as a guide through life. It is analogous to a written company policy which is rarely modified. The value system is a set of concepts which truly forms a framework for the individual's preferred modes of conduct.[1] Included in this set are "prejudices," or values which other people reject as "unfair." A few values which are commonly held by a number of people in our culture include:

1. Work is good and a reward in itself.
2. We should be honest in our dealings with others.
3. Individual freedom should be limited only by the rights of others.
4. Democracy is intrinsically good.
5. Each of us should control his or her own destiny.
6. All people should have equal rights.

As we can see, any single individual probably has many such values which are held strongly and which prescribe or limit actions. An important idea to note is that there may be conflicts or inconsistencies within the framework of values. For example, "majority rule" based on the value of democracy may infringe on individual freedom (another value).

Attitudes are predispositions to evaluate or respond to some object or aspect of the world in a favorable or unfavorable manner. Workers may have unfavorable attitudes toward their workplace, time study of their work, overtime work, or seniority as a basis for promotion. Attitudes are closely related to value systems.[2]

The cultural and educational background of the individual, the third long-enduring characteristic, represents the things learned and the patterns of behavior acquired from the people around the individual. Language, norms and values, likes and dislikes are characteristics which define a society. As a result of differences in these characteristics, Eskimo, for example, view the world quite differently from Europeans. Similarly, the culture of New Yorkers is different from that of West Virginia miners.[3]

The level of aspiration is the life-goal which an individual sets. Such a goal may change upward or downward over a period of years because of successes or failures.

We all have our "reference group," or people whom we would like to be like. The professor identifies with the teaching community. The shopworker identifies with co-workers, or perhaps the foreman. The construction worker identifies with other construction workers, not Wall Street brokers. We guide our behavior by the norms (that is, standards of behavior), goals, and values of our reference group.

The level of our socioeconomic class refers to the level at which we perceive our needs and our ability to adapt to our situation. If we are uneducated, poor, work for low wages, and are in the lowest socioeconomic class, our needs are apt to be primarily economic. We tend to respond best to authoritarian leadership. At the other extreme, exemplifying a high level of socioeconomic class, we are likely to find the president of a company or a college professor. In these cases we find individuals with considerable control over their work situation. Their economic needs are apt to be relatively fulfilled, and they are more likely to respond to noneconomic factors.

The "intelligence," or reasoning power, of a person apparently changes relatively little through life. An individual's behavior occurs within the limits of his/her intelligence.

Experience is the accumulated time that a person has spent in life situations. Thus an experienced worker would behave differently in the same position from an inexperienced worker. Experience, once attained, is a long-lasting, that is, stable characteristic of an individual.

The self-concept or perceived role is a very important characteristic in behavior. The military has recognized this clearly by the way it has treated recruits. A professional person or an executive drafted from civilian life entered the armed forces with a self-concept as a leader, adviser, and solid citizen to be respected. This self-concept was quickly destroyed in basic training by constant treatment as a menial person, one among thousands. Then the rebuilding of a new self-concept was started. In the business world, self-concepts change very gradually in most cases. We tend to perceive our work role more clearly as time goes by. We behave as we believe someone in that role *should* behave. A person may hold a self-concept of being industrious, respected for integrity, and loyal to the company. To destroy this self-concept completely and suddenly would have a shattering effect upon the individual.

Shorter-term characteristics

The more flexible characteristics of the individual as a processor are:

1. Sentiments, opinions, or beliefs about the company, working conditions, and co-workers.
2. Relationships within the informal work group. (This will be discussed later in the chapter when we view systems composed of two or more individuals.)
3. Relationship with a formal leader or manager as established by the organizational structure.
4. Mental state and physical health on any given day.

Short-term characteristics are more easily influenced by management than long-term characteristics. Let us see how the manager can influence the above characteristics to modify behavior.

MOTIVATION: FROM CHARACTERISTICS TO BEHAVIOR

The previous discussion of characteristics treated what might be called the *limiting* variables of the individual as a system processor. The dynamic force which actuates the individual is called motivation. *Motivation is simply the drive to reduce a tension caused by an unsatisfied need.* Exhibit 2–2 gives an illustration of this state-

EXHIBIT 2–2
Motivation

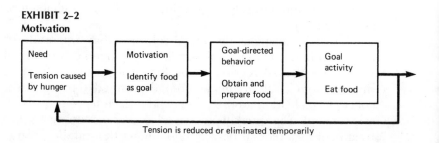

Tension is reduced or eliminated temporarily

ment. If managers were able *to satisfy* all of an individual's needs, the individual would not be motivated to act. Fortunately, new goals and learned needs keep arising. The individual keeps developing higher level and more complex needs as present needs become satisfied.

Summary of basic needs of individuals

Underlying the specific on-the-job needs of people are their life-satisfaction needs. It is important to look at the totality of needs because:

1. Some workers find practically all of their life satisfactions off the job and work primarily to satisfy physical and economic needs.
2. Most workers derive part of their noneconomic life satisfactions on the job.
3. The more needs a worker has an opportunity to satisfy on the job, the more likely the worker is to be highly motivated to perform the job.

A. H. Maslow developed a theory explaining the individual's hierarchy of basic life needs which we may relate to satisfactions on the job and off the job. To some extent, individuals try to satisfy the lower level needs in the hierarchy first. Generally, a particular higher level need does not become potent as a motivator until lower level needs have been satisfied reasonably well.

Starting with the lowest level (first-to-be-satisfied) needs, the hierarchy is:

Physiological: basic physical needs (air, food, water, sex).
Safety: physical and psychological security.
Social: satisfying social relationships with others.
Ego: self-respect and the esteem of others.
Self-actualization: the desire to be all that one can be, to fully utilize one's talents.[4]

In Exhibit 2–3, we have indicated examples of needs for each level of Maslow's hierarchy.

Douglas McGregor's optimistic view of human nature (a view consistent with Maslow's "need hierarchy" theory) led to a different set of beliefs about the nature of people at work (Theory Y) which was consistent with a whole new style of managing by integration and self-control. By "integration" McGregor meant the integration of organizational objectives and individual objectives. Managing by integration and self-control consists of designing work situations in such a way that each individual can achieve his or her personal goals best by contributing to the goals of the organization.

David C. McClelland studied what he considered to be three basic needs of people in organizations. These were the need for

EXHIBIT 2–3
The hierarchy of needs

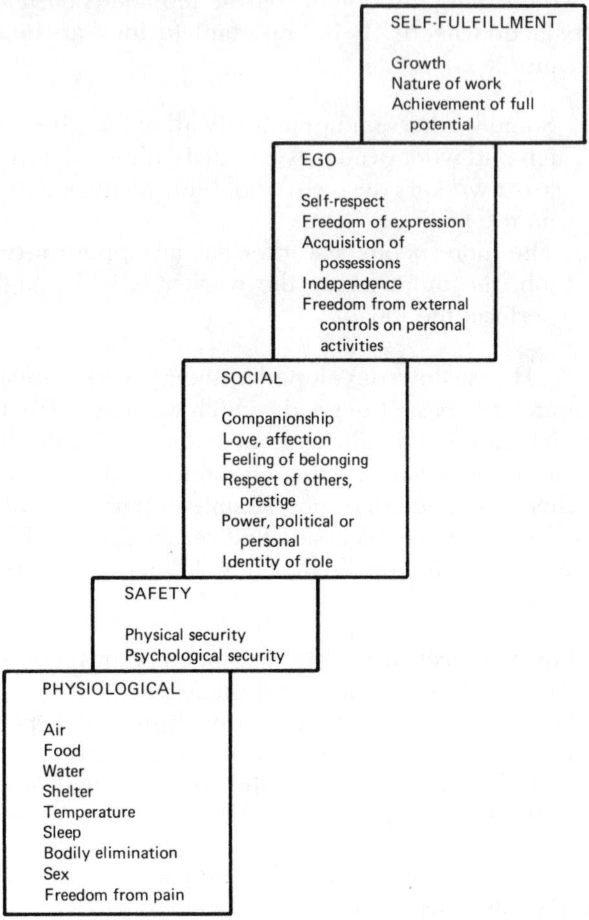

SELF-FULFILLMENT

Growth
Nature of work
Achievement of full
    potential

EGO

Self-respect
Freedom of expression
Acquisition of
    possessions
Independence
Freedom from external
    controls on personal
    activities

SOCIAL

Companionship
Love, affection
Feeling of belonging
Respect of others,
    prestige
Power, political or
    personal
Identity of role

SAFETY

Physical security
Psychological security

PHYSIOLOGICAL

Air
Food
Water
Shelter
Temperature
Sleep
Bodily elimination
Sex
Freedom from pain

achievement, the need for affiliation (friendships), and the need for power.[5] These needs obviously assume that lower level physiological needs have been met.

One important issue is the extent to which a person's total life needs can be satisfied by his or her work. The results obtained from a study of 1,000 production workers in the United States and 1,000 in Japan indicate that culture and organizational systems can produce considerable differences in the satisfactions of workers on the job.

I think of my company as:	United States	Japan
a. The central concern in my life and of greater importance than my personal life	1%	9%
b. A part of my life at least equal in importance to my personal life	22	57
c. A place for me to work with management during work hours, to accomplish mutual goals	54	26
d. Strictly a place to work and entirely separate from my personal life	23	8
	100%	100%

The needs of people at work

According to Frederick Herzberg, people at work have two kinds of needs. The failure to satisfy some environmental needs produces primarily dissatisfaction with the job and a desire to escape from the system. The individual may escape by quitting or obtaining a transfer or may turn to seeking satisfactions outside work or to engaging in dysfunctional activity on the job. Herzberg has called such environmental needs *hygiene factors*. On the other hand, there are needs intrinsic to the work itself. The more these are satisfied, the more workers are motivated toward ever greater achievement. Herzberg called such needs *positive motivators*.

Considerable research has been carried out on Herzberg's theory. Some critics suggest that his methodology is an oversimplification.[7] Others have found that all of the motivators and hygiene factors have been reported as *both* satisfiers and dissatisfiers.[8] From a practical viewpoint, however, Herzberg's concepts have made a tremendous impact on human resource management through the application of "organization development" and job enrichment (see Chapter 5).

Motivation in terms of expectancy of goal achievement

Victor H. Vroom and the coauthors Lyman Porter and Edward Lawler, have developed separate "expectancy" models of motivation.[9] Basically, they view motivation as dependent upon the strength of an individual's desire for a set of goals and the likelihood that a specific type of behavior will lead to the achievement of the individual's goals. These models are consistent with need satisfaction; they merely start with the end needs and work backward to a choice of action by the individual to fulfill them.

EXHIBIT 2–4
The expectancy model of motivation

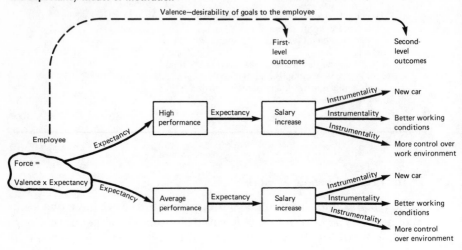

Exhibit 2–4 is a diagram to aid in explaining Vroom's model. Vroom defines motivation as a process governing the choice of a voluntary activity. The model has three components:

1. Valence—the strength of an individual's desire for a particular outcome.
2. Instrumentality—the individual's perception that a first-level outcome will lead to a particular second-level outcome.
3. Expectancy—the individual's perception of the probability that specific outcomes will result from his or her behavior.

In the diagram, the "action area" is the behavior-performance relationship. The worker considers whether his or her best effort will lead to high or average performance. The worker considers the probability that high performance will lead to a good increase in salary and average performance to *some* increase in salary. The worker then considers the relationship between obtaining the increase in salary and achieving desired goals.

The desirability of the second-level outcomes is measured and, by consideration of instrumentalities leading to them, the desirability of the first-level outcomes is determined. We continue to work backward to note that whether the employee works very hard or at a lesser pace is determined by his or her perception that anticipated performance will lead to the desired salary increase. (Vroom is not quite clear about the effort-performance relationship. High effort does not always result in high performance, for example.) In this way we see the strength and direction of motivation depend upon the strength of outcomes and upon the relationship of these outcomes to our actions.

Summary of motivation theory as it relates to the systems approach

If we consider human resources in the aggregate as a system, then we would hope that we could predict and control performance of the system. If we assume that the system is composed of many individuals whose needs and behavior are unstable, unknown, and unpredictable, then we are in bad shape.

To some extent, the theories that have just been described do not wholly support a systems approach to managing human resources. They assume that individuals have different and widely varying needs. These needs vary from time to time, as does the strength of the needs. Further, the behavior of workers is conditioned by their permanent characteristics and by the previous outcomes of their behavior. In addition, for many people work will always be secondary to other interests.

On the other hand, these theories of behavior suggest that most people may be induced to respond to managerial-controlled factors in the work environment. By providing desirable rewards or outcomes for organizationally desirable performance, management may induce *most* workers to respond in a stable and desirable manner.

Our value system requires that we be concerned for the feelings and satisfactions of people apart from our goal of optimal system performance. These theories help us to understand how worker satisfaction relates to performance.

Model of the individual as a systems component

B. F. Skinner is the outstanding proponent of a systems human. He has, on the basis of his research, attempted to discredit the idea of autonomous human beings. Skinner rejects explanations that humans autonomously initiate behavior; the human is a passive processor of inputs. Behavior is determined by its consequences, and management may therefore control the behavior of workers by prompt positive reinforcement of desirable behavior.[10] The concept of needs as an explanation and a predictor of behavior is superfluous.

Despite a fundamental difference in assumptions as to the nature of human beings, the practical applications of Skinner's theories and those of the previously discussed researchers coincide. If management changes the environment and the inputs, the individual will change his or her behavior. For both Skinner and the other researchers, it is necessary to identify the inputs to which the individual will respond.

Whether a worker is viewed as a system processing inputs or as an organism seeking to achieve goals in order to fulfill needs, the manager influences the worker's behavior by altering the work environment and interacting with the worker. This book is concerned with executive action based upon available research for modifying behavior. In general, research indicates that some characteristics are common to all people at work. At the same time there are differences among people which require that they also be dealt with on an individual basis.

HIGHER LEVEL BEHAVIORAL SYSTEMS: WORKERS IN GROUPS

The human resource system (HRS) is not made up solely of individuals as subsystems; rather, it consists of numerous overlapping subsystems. Each individual in the total HRS combines with other individuals to form a variety of behavioral subsystems. Each worker belongs to at least the first two of the subsystems described in the table on page 37.

The need to identify and manage group subsystems

It is readily apparent that managing the HRS requires managing people as individuals. In addition, there must be a system for managing various groups within the total organization. We have structured a major portion of this book around these two concepts.

The identification of groups and differentiation among groups affect such processes as staffing, motivating, communicating, upgrading human resources, managing change, and resolving conflict. Groups vary in degree of permanence and degree of complexity as well as in the goals they seek.[11] The differentiation of groups must be done very carefully. For example, we might mistakenly lump engineers and scientists into the same group and treat them alike. Yet several studies have shown significant differences in the perceptions and needs of people in these professions.[12]

Different groups of managers, such as line managers and staff managers, must be identified and treated differently. These two

Subsystem	Description	Goals
Formal organization	Company-established work relationships, job descriptions, assignments	Communication Functional goals (marketing, production, and so on)
Informal organizations	Groups of workers who have a common interest because of similar work, close location, common outside interests, similar values and norms, and so on	Varied goals relating to both on-job and off-job interests Establishment of better communications, work norms, power, pressure on management or other groups, and so on
Managerial	Groups of managers, usually of like levels in the hierarchy of the formal organization	Establishment of company values and objectives Higher productivity Development of people in the organization Self-advancement and personal power
Professional/Technical	Engineers, accountants, secretaries, aircraft mechanics, nurses, and other licensed or certified groups, or members of professional organizations	Development of discipline skills and remaining abreast of changes
Unions	Associations of workers with a common bond of skill or location	Negotiation with management over working conditions, compensation, benefits

groups frequently engage in power struggles that prevent optimization of the effectiveness of the total HRS. In Chapter 5, we give attention to changing such group behavior.

Since each individual belongs to two or more groups-of-workers subsystems, there is considerable interaction among them. In order to determine how to respond to or modify these subsystems to affect the output of all subsystems, we might show the situation by the simple schematic in Exhibit 2–5, which "uncouples" or separates the subsystems.

The formal organization system

The formal organization is based upon authority derived from owners of the business, from legal statutes in the case of government agencies, or from self-perpetuating boards of trustees in the

EXHIBIT 2–5
System of workers-in-group subsystems

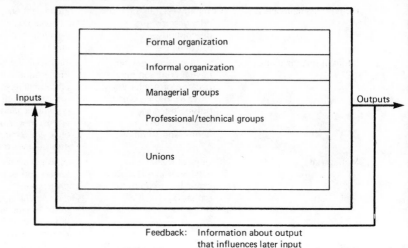

Feedback: Information about output
that influences later input

case of some nonprofit organizations. The primary functions of the formal organization system are to set objectives for the system as a whole and to coordinate the efforts of everyone in the system in working toward those objectives. The formal organization is continually changing, but at any moment in time it may be represented by a chart such as Exhibit 2–6.

The impact of the formal organization on the human resource system as a whole depends on such factors as:

The number of levels of management.

The subdivision of work.

The channels of communication.

The delegation of decision making.

Power.

Control.

The formal organization is a technical system which, too often, is designed without regard to the people who make it function. As Chris Argyris has pointed out, formal organization often places such controls on mature people that they rebel in various subtle ways. This in turn brings about change in the formal organization in order to maintain greater control over the work of individuals so that the formal organization and the aspirations of individuals are in con-

EXHIBIT 2–6
Formal organization chart

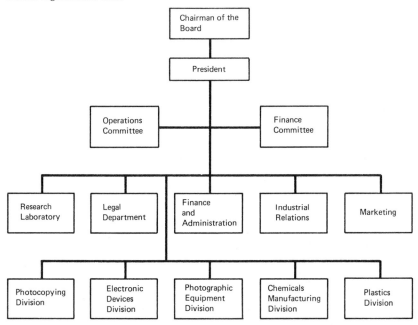

stant conflict. Properly designed, the formal organization should be a positive factor in the total work environment of the individual. This subject is discussed in more detail in Chapter 3.

The informal organization system

The "informal organization system" is actually a number of subsystems ranging from small groups of workers in the same room to perhaps hundreds of workers who are united by some common interest, such as a grievance against management. The informal organization is especially important because it sets norms or standards of behavior for its members (including norms related to productivity) and represents the fastest communication system in the organization. As we have seen in the previous section, the formal organization is that system shown in the management charts. It is a creation of top management. The informal organization, however, is likely to be created by the social relationships existing in the organization. Thus, the informal communications that arise out of these subsystems may be viewed as attempts by workers to interpret their "local" environment, and may take the form of rumors, gossip, or various casual opinions that come to be regarded as fact.[13] Such communications may be heavily distorted due to the beliefs of workers and the tendency of the informal organization system to fill in gaps of information with imagination.

The informal organization is of extreme importance to the human resource system's total effectiveness. The factors which determine the impact of the informal system on inputs are:

1. The norms and goals of the system. (Are these congruent with or in conflict with the objectives of the formal organization?)
2. The communication channels within the system.
3. Conflict resolution within the system.
4. Cohesiveness, or how strongly individuals are bound together in each subsystem.
5. The duration of various groups. (For example, some groups may form and break up as projects are started and terminated.)
6. The status, role, and power of each informal group.
7. The leadership found throughout the informal system.

The informal organization is so important that management should structure the formal organization in a way that will bring informal organization leaders into the decision processes so that the company will gain maximum support from informal groups. This, of course, requires that management identify such groups and their leaders.[14]

Managerial groups

Informal subsystems of managers tend to form because of common goals, desire for informal communication, and desire for power. There are three basic types of informal managerial groups. The first is the group of managers in a common discipline, say, manufacturing or engineering.

The second is the peer group. That is, managers at the same level tend to form a loose group or set of groups. At any particular level, managers from lower levels of the hierarchy are not welcomed to the group and higher level managers don't care to join.

Somewhat in contradiction to the concept of the peer group is the sponsor-protégé system. A high-level manager may provide guidance and support for a number of lower level managers in the organization. In turn, these protégés are a source of information and support within their peer groups. The sponsors and their protégés do not usually socialize (lunch, and so on) at work, but the manager and a single protégé may get together for private family affairs. It is not likely that a high-level manager would meet with a group of protégés.[15]

Professional/technical groups

Professional/technical groups may pose a severe problem to the organization, but at the same time they provide safeguards. A true professional may place loyalty to discipline ahead of company goals. For example, a company may wish to sacrifice the quality of work in the interests of greater quantity. The professional may rebel against compromising the quality of work. Service is no longer professional if it has in any way been dictated by the client or employer.

It is also important to recognize the unique characteristics of the professional and the highly skilled technician. To begin with, the typical member of the group has invested many years in education and training. During those years this person has developed aspirations identified with career. The job then becomes an inherent and vital part of this person's life.[16] One researcher has characterized this group as being "an especially demanding breed of people, bent on individualistic values and requiring more managerial imagination."[17] Similarly, the greater the extent of the professional's academic training, the stronger is the interest in basic, autonomous knowledge-seeking research, and the more difficult it becomes to integrate personal goals with the goals of the overall organization.

Management may find that the human resource system and company goals require that such technical professionals be designated, not as decision makers, but as consultants or researchers for managers or other decision makers in the organization.

Unions

The effects of unions on the human resource system vary so tremendously that different types of formal systems (leadership styles) must be adopted in each situation. The union system includes such variables as:

1. The types of workers that are unionized in the company.
2. The types of workers that outsiders are trying to unionize.
3. The strength of unions in the company.
4. The history of labor-management relations.

5. The number of different unions and their conflicts or cooperation with one another.
6. The type of union leadership—legalistic, power-oriented, degree of maturity, cooperativeness, strength, and so on.

In the case of unions, the human resource system must adapt
greatly to an environmental influence or input. It is not simply a
matter of accommodating company worker interests for the mutual
benefit of each. Fortunately, as union-management relations have
matured, union and business leaders have identified basic common
goals, such as survival of the industry or the company. The effect of
the union on the human resource system is discussed in Chapter 9.

Similarities and differences by classifications of workers

Workers may be classified by the various functions which they
perform. Such classifications are correlated with education, experience, type of intellectual or manual ability, values, and interests. At
the same time, such classifications are also correlated with working
conditions, compensation, the work environment, group formation,
and possibly other factors which are external to the worker. Classes
of workers often represent both formal and informal systems. At the
same time, workers who appear to have a number of similar characteristics may also have really significant different characteristics.
The significant similarities and the significant differences are the
ones which affect the particular subsystem.

For example, if we were to consider a group of semiskilled workers doing office work and a group of semiskilled workers in the shop,
we might notice such similarities as educational level, compensation, level of skill, and working hours. Yet differences in values,
aspirations, role concept, cultural interests, and reference groups
may greatly affect each work group as a system processor. Of course,
it is difficult to generalize since it is possible to find a janitor who is
an opera buff and a top manager who is a cultural know-nothing.

SUMMARY

In the systems approach, we must attempt to describe the elements of the system and the characteristics of these elements. For
the human resource system, we have identified individuals and
certain groups of individuals as subsystems of importance. We are
interested in learning how these subsystems respond to various
inputs. We may modify the inputs in order to obtain the most desir-

able outputs of the human resource system and the total business system.

The subsystems which we identified in this chapter were:

1. The individual worker as a system.
2. Subsystems formed of groups of workers.
    a. The formal organization.
    b. The informal organization.
    c. Managerial groups as subsystems.
    d. Professional and technical groups.
    e. Unions as subsystems.

The fact that every worker is a functioning element in two or more of these subsystems indicates the complexity of the human resource system. It also indicates that optimizing the total business system (the particular company) requires a considerable knowledge of the behavior of people both as individuals and in groups.

The inputs to the individual are job-related and non-job-related. The outputs are similarly job-related and non-job-related. Generally, management has most control over and is most concerned with job-related outputs. Nevertheless, the worker as a processor in the system must be understood in his or her entirety.

As a processor, the worker has certain long-lasting characteristics, such as values, attitudes, and aspirations. Managers may anticipate somewhat stable responses to a particular input when these characteristics dominate in a situation. Unfortunately, much behavior depends upon changing perceived needs, according to most theorists. Attempts have been made by Maslow, McClelland, McGregor, and Herzberg to show that certain classes of needs provide motivation. Vroom, Porter, and Lawler indicate that needs are determined by goals at a given time and by the likelihood that selected behaviors will lead to the achievement of those goals. Skinner says that we cannot know, and therefore should not be concerned with, what goes on in the mind of the individual. He believes that we can condition the individual to respond to inputs in a desired way. Regardless of the model we select, the prescription for the manager is the same: modify the workers' environment to modify behavior.

We find that workers as individuals and groups of workers are different types of processors. Therefore, we have identified groups of workers that must be considered for system control. The behavior of some of these groups, such as unions, will be treated more fully farther on in the book. Here we have emphasized *differences* in groups to point out that groups require special attention.

CASE: THE MOTIVATOR*

When young Tom Babcock was put in charge of a division of a large manufacturing company and told to "turn it around," he spent the first few weeks studying it from afar. He decided that the division was in disastrous shape and that he would need to take many large steps quickly to save it. To be able to do that, he realized that he needed to develop considerable power fast over most of the division's management and staff. He did the following:

1. He gave the division's management two hours' notice of his arrival.
2. He arrived in a limousine with six assistants.
3. He immediately called a meeting of the 40 top managers.
4. He outlined briefly his assessment of the situation, his commitment to turn things around, and the basic direction he wanted things to move in.
5. He fired the four top managers in the room and told them that they had to be out of the building in two hours.
6. He then said that he would personally dedicate himself to sabotaging the career of anyone who tried to block his efforts to save the division.
7. He ended the 60-minute meeting by announcing that his assistants would set up appointments for him with each of the remaining 36 top managers, starting at 7 A.M. the next morning.

Throughout the critical six-month period that followed, the top managers who remained at the division generally cooperated energetically with Mr. Babcock.

Discuss the above true-life case in terms of the motivation theories in this chapter.

QUESTIONS AND PROBLEMS

1. Explain how the individual person is a "system."
2. In what ways is the behavioral system the *adaptive* system controlling the firm?
3. What is the relationship between job-related and non-job-related outputs of the worker? Is one more important than the other?
4. Give specific examples of possible approaches which management may employ to control the human resource system.

---

5. What is a value? Show how a particular value system may influence the manager's ability to manage.

6. In what ways can a "reference group" affect the worker's behavior as a processor?

7. Why are sentiments, opinions, and beliefs about the company classified as flexible characteristics of the individual as a processor? Does this mean that they can be changed by management?

8. Explain the concept of motivation. Be sure to differentiate between a hygiene factor and a positive motivator.

9. Give several examples of horizontal versus vertical loading of a job. How is the latter related to Herzberg's theory?

10. Of what practical value is A. H. Maslow's hierarchy of needs theory?

11. Using an organization that you currently are a member of, show how you are also a member of at least two organized subsystems within that organization's human resource system. Can you think of any instance in which the goals of a subsystem may have conflicted with another system in that organization?

12. In what ways does the formal organization affect the human resource system?

13. What is meant by the informal organization system? Can management influence the informal organization? Explain your answer, using specific examples.

14. Explain how each of the following subsystems have an impact on the goals of the human resource system: managerial groups, professional/technical groups, unions.

15. Write a short speech to be delivered to a group of managers on "how optimizing the total business system of a firm requires considerable knowledge of the behavior of people, both as individuals and in groups."

BIBLIOGRAPHY

Behling, Orlando, and Schriesheim, Chester. *Organizational Behavior: Theory, Research and Application*. Boston: Allyn and Bacon, 1976.

Bridges, E. M., et al. "Effects of Hierarchical Differentiations on Group Productivity, Efficiency, and Risk Taking." *Administrative Science Quarterly*, January 1968.

Brown, Martha A. "Values—A Necessary but Neglected Ingredient of Motivation on the Job." *Academy of Management Review*, October 1976.

Chartier, Robert. "Managing the Knowledge Employee." *Personnel Journal*, August 1968.

Connor, Patrick E., and Becker, Boris W. "Values and the Organization: Suggestions for Research." *Academy of Management Journal*, September 1975.

Ericson, Richard F. "The Impact of Cybernetic Information Technology on Management Value Systems." *Management Science*, October 1969.

Flippo, E. B. *Management: A Behavioral Approach*. Boston: Allyn and Bacon, 1970.

Gibson, James I., Ivancevich, John M., and Donnelly, James, Jr. *Organizations: Structure, Processes, Behavior*. Dallas: Business Publications, 1973.

Guth, William D., and Tagiuri, Renato. "Personal Values and Corporate Strategy." *Harvard Business Review*, September –October 1965.

Herzberg, Frederick. *Work and the Nature of Man*. New York: World Publishing Co., 1966.

Homans, G. C. *The Human Group*. New York: Harcourt, Brace & World, 1950.

Klatt, Lawrence A. "Maximizing the Potential of Scientific Personnel." *Business Studies*, Fall 1971.

Klatt, Lawrence A., and Kurtz, David L. "The 'Grapevine' as a Management Tool." *Akron Business and Economic Review*, Winter 1970.

Kluckhohn, Clyde K., and Murray, Henry A. *Personality in Nature, Society, and Culture*. New York: Knopf, 1953.

Martin, Norman H. "Thinking Ahead—Power Tactics." *Harvard Business Review*, November–December 1956.

Maslow, A. H. "A Theory of Human Motivation," *Psychological Review*, 1943. Reprinted in Robert A. Sutermeister (ed.). *People and Productivity*. 2d ed. New York: McGraw-Hill Book Co., 1969.

Schoderbek, Peter P., Kefalas, Asterios G., and Schoderbek, Charles G. *Management Systems: Conceptual Considerations*. Dallas: Business Publications, 1975.

Steers, Richard M., and Porter, Lyman W. *Motivation and Work Behavior*. New York: McGraw-Hill Book Co., 1975.

Whitehill, A. M., and Takesawa, S. *The Other Worker*. Honolulu: East-West Center Press, 1968.

NOTES

[1] See, for example, Martha A. Brown, "Values—A Necessary but Neglected Ingredient of Motivation on the Job," *Academy of Management Review*, October 1976.

[2] Daniel Katz, "The Functional Approach to the Study of Attitudes," *Public Opinion Quarterly*, Summer 1960. See also William C. Scott and Terence R. Mitchell, *Organization Theory* (Homewood, Ill.: Richard D. Irwin, 1976), chap. 7, "Attitudes."

[3] Clyde K. Kluckhohn and Henry A. Murray, *Personality in Nature, Society, and Culture* (New York: Knopf, 1953).

[4] A. H. Maslow, "A Theory of Human Motivation," *Psychological Review*, July 1943. Reprinted in Robert A. Sutermeister (ed.), *People and Productivity*, 3d ed. (New York: McGraw-Hill Book Co., 1976).

[5] David C. McClelland, *The Achieving Society* (New York: Van Nostrand Reinhold, 1961).

[6] A. M. Whitehill and S. Takesawa, *The Other Worker*, copyright © 1968 by East-West Center Press. Adapted by permission of The University Press of Hawaii.

[7] M. D. Dunnette, J. P. Campbell, and M. D. Hakel, "Factors Contributing to Job Satisfaction and Job Dissatisfaction in Six Occupational Groups," *Organizational Behavior and Human Performance*, May 1967.

[8] Victor H. Vroom, *Work and Motivation* (New York: John Wiley & Sons, 1964).

[9] Ibid.; Lyman W. Porter and Edward E. Lawler, III, *Managerial Attitudes and Performance* (Homewood, Ill.: Richard D. Irwin, 1968); and Richard M. Steers and Lyman W. Porter, *Motivation and Work Behavior* (New York: McGraw-Hill Book Co., 1975), pp. 192–98.

[10] B. F. Skinner, *Beyond Freedom and Dignity* (New York: Knopf, 1971). See also David K. Hart and William G. Scott, "The Optimal Image of Man for Systems Theory," *Academy of Management Journal*, December 1972.

[11] For a review of various perspectives and theories of groups, see chap. 1, "What is an Organization?" in J. Eugene Haas and Thomas E. Drabek, *Complex Organizations: A Sociological Perspective* (New York: Macmillan Co., 1973). See also, William G. Scott and Terrence R. Mitchell, *Organization Theory: A Structural and Behavioral Analysis* (Homewood, Ill.: Richard D. Irwin, 1976), part 2, "Individual and Group Behavior."

[12] M. K. Badawy, "Organizational Designs for Scientists and Engineers: Some Research Findings and Their Implications for Managers," *IEEE Transactions in Engineering Management*, November 1975.

[13] See Lawrence A. Klatt and David L. Kurtz, "The 'Grapevine' as a Management Tool," *Akron Business and Economic Review*, Winter 1970.

[14] For a brief summary of research on informal groups, see chap. 10, "Groups and Committees," in Gary Dessler, *Organization and Management* (Englewood Cliffs, N.J.: Prentice-Hall, 1976).

[15] For example, see Norman H. Martin, "Thinking Ahead—Power Tactics," *Harvard Business Review*, November–December 1956.

[16] Lawrence A. Klatt, "Maximizing the Potential of Scientific Personnel," *Business Studies*, Fall 1971.

[17] Robert Chartier, "Managing the Knowledge Employee," *Personnel Journal*, August 1968, p. 559.

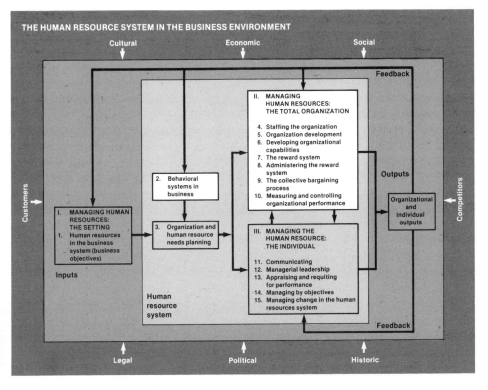

THE HUMAN RESOURCE SYSTEM IN THE BUSINESS ENVIRONMENT

Cultural   Economic   Social

Feedback

II. MANAGING
    HUMAN RESOURCES:
    THE TOTAL ORGANIZATION

    4. Staffing the organization
    5. Organization development
    6. Developing organizational
       capabilities
    7. The reward system
    8. Administering the reward
       system
    9. The collective bargaining
       process
    10. Measuring and controlling
        organizational performance

2. Behavioral
   systems in
   business

Outputs

Customers

Competitors

I. MANAGING HUMAN
   RESOURCES:
   THE SETTING
1. Human resources
   in the business
   system (business
   objectives)

Inputs

3. Organization and
   human resource
   needs planning

III. MANAGING THE
     HUMAN RESOURCE:
     THE INDIVIDUAL

11. Communicating
12. Managerial leadership
13. Appraising and requiting
    for performance
14. Managing by objectives
15. Managing change in the human
    resources system

Organizational
and
individual
outputs

Human
resource
system

Feedback

Legal   Political   Historic

PART II

MANAGING
HUMAN
RESOURCES:
THE TOTAL
ORGANIZATION

When you have completed studying
ORGANIZATION AND HUMAN RESOURCE NEEDS PLANNING
you should be able to:

1. Describe the overall format for developing the objectives and the organizational plans for a human resource system.
2. Explain what organizational planning is and how it relates to the management of human resources.
3. Answer the question "How should organization planning be carried out?"
4. Identify the various approaches to structuring an organization.
5. Describe the best approach to organization planning.
6. Discuss how organization planning and human resource needs planning are interrelated and interacting in the HRS.
7. Describe the essential elements involved in human resource needs planning.
8. Show how the external environment influences a firm's planning for human resources.

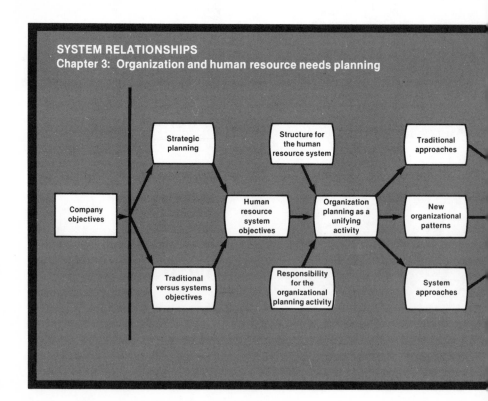

SYSTEM RELATIONSHIPS
Chapter 3: Organization and human resource needs planning

In the previous chapters we have discussed the nature of systems and developed the basic concepts of the human resource system and the underlying behavioral systems. In this chapter we shall see how the formal structure of the human resource system is developed. The process of structuring the human resource system to develop, modify, and ultimately achieve company objectives is called *organization planning*. Once management has carried out its organization planning, it is ready to take systematic steps to match the needs of its plans with human resources. This process is known as *human resource needs planning*.

3

Organization and human resource needs planning

If you don't know where you're going, it doesn't matter how you get there.

Anonymous

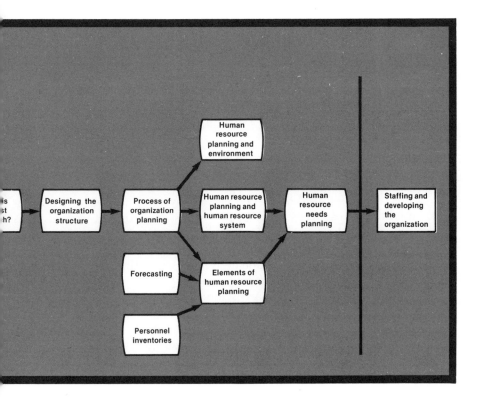

In other words, given clear-cut company objectives, organization planning provides the structural arrangements between the members of the organization and between the members and their work. Once management has carried out its organization planning, human resource needs planning provides for the right people in the right number at the right time, performing activities which give the individual and the organization maximum benefit. In essence, then, organization and human resource needs planning and interrelated processes that give a unified sense of direction to the human resource system. This chapter will discuss how this planning is carried out in order to meet business objectives.

To put the subject material within the context of the system approach, we might note that the planning and development of any system require defining and describing:

1. System objectives.
2. System elements.
3. The structure of the system—that is, the relationships of elements to each other.
4. The process or functioning of the system.

In Chapter 1, we showed how the objectives of the human resource system were derived from business objectives. In Chapter 2, we described the elements of the human resource system. In this chapter, we describe the structure of the HRS and the planning required to bring the structure into being. The remainder of the book deals with the functioning of the HRS in terms of the subsystems shown in Exhibit 1–3 of Chapter 1.

BUSINESS OBJECTIVES AND THE HUMAN RESOURCE SYSTEM

As we noted in the first chapter, the systems approach to managing human resources starts with business objectives as inputs. This means that strategic (long-range) and operating (short-range) objectives must be prepared which link together human resource activities and business function activities (marketing, production, and so on) into a unified sense of direction.

Unless such objectives are made known to all of the people in the company, different people and different organizational components will probably be striving for conflicting goals. For example, the marketing group may be fighting for high-quality custom products while the manufacturing group may be pressing for average-quality standardized products. The difference between the functioning of the company which doesn't plan and the systems action of the company that plans is suggested by Exhibit 3–1. Many studies have also shown that firms that plan are significantly more profitable than those that do not.[1]

EXHIBIT 3–1
Muddle in the "informal planner" company and system in the "formal planner" company

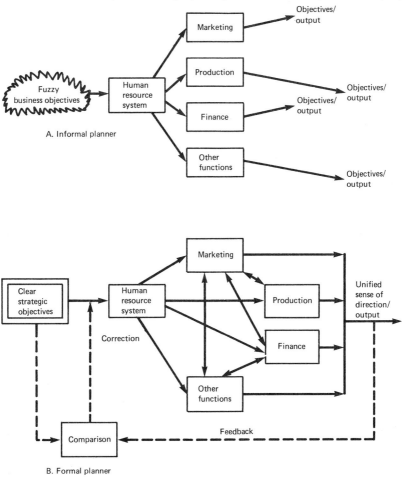

The process of planning in itself forces management to think through the objectives of the firm and the people problems relating to achieving those objectives. For example, a change in strategy usually requires a change in organization structure. That is, a strategy change may require new or different task arrangements which in turn will require different arrangements of people. Without such restructuring, people are apt to continue directing their efforts according to old organizational requirements. It then becomes the function of management to redirect the efforts of employees.

The HRS should be unified toward business objectives

All organizations have objectives. At one extreme, they may be vague, conflicting, and only in the minds of the managers. At the other extreme, they may be clearly defined, published in company manuals, and made available to all employees. Exhibit 3–2 shows

EXHIBIT 3–2
The traditional personnel function

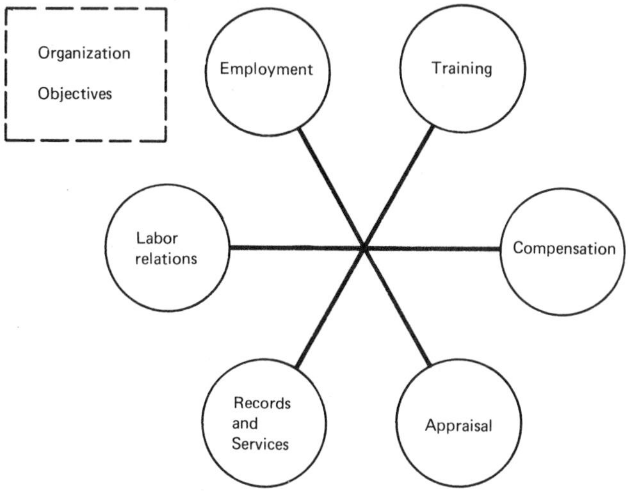

the objectives of an organization as existing somewhere in the background of the human resources management process. But note that there is no clear, direct relationship between the objectives of the organization and the subfunctions of the traditional personnel department. Personnel programs are frequently developed without regard for the objectives of the organization as a whole.

For example, in some firms executives of the human resource staff do not know precisely what the business objectives of the organization are before they are asked to plan hiring programs, training and development programs, compensation programs, and other activities.

Note also that Exhibit 3–2 shows little interconnection among the different subprocesses of personnel management and no logical flow of decision making from one subprocess to another. This illustrates the fact that in many organizations such human resource activities as employment, training and development, and compensation are not managed as a system of related activities. The employment office often recruits new employees in response to requests from line management without really knowing precisely what kind of training and development the employees will later receive. It does not know exactly how each of these new employees fits into the long-range human resource planning.

Similarly, the compensation and benefits organization is concerned with the problems of adjusting compensation and benefits to changing industry trends and internal organization pressures, but is seldom specifically aware of how organization development plans, long-range work force plans, and organization change programs are related to the compensation system. Often, in fact, pay plans are designed without even considering their relationship to benefit plans within a total reward system.

Training departments frequently find themselves planning and conducting a training program primarily because it has been conducted in the past. Such programs may be started because someone has expressed a vague need for such training, or because another company has such a program. No direct relationship between the training program and the specific work force requirements of the organization has been considered in such cases.

Thus, the tendency is for each subfunction to view itself as an independent function, to view its goal as the optimization of its own specific function, and to measure its performance by its own standards of excellence. As a result, each subprocess or department tends toward optimization at the expense of the whole human resources management system. The separate parts are not logically fitted together and balanced with one another as an integrated system pursuing one unified set of objectives directed toward the accomplishment of the organization's overall business objectives.

HRS objectives are derived from company objectives

The strategic objectives of the company should lead to consistent objectives for all activities within the firm, as we have seen in Exhibit 3–1. A couple of examples will suggest how strategic objectives lead to some possible HRS objectives.

Consider one component of strategy, the definition of product scope. If the company decides to engage in a diversification program, HRS objectives which follow relate to staffing, training and development, communication, motivation, and leadership.

Another component of strategy is the future allocation of resources. Should the company replace people with high-cost equipment? Should work be subcontracted? How should funds be distributed among training and other company activities? This component of strategy obviously has a tremendous effect upon the HRS. If funds for the HRS are reduced drastically, staffing objectives, organization development objectives, measurement objectives, and so on, must be developed in terms of the resource constraint.

ORGANIZATION PLANNING: A UNIFYING APPROACH

As we discussed earlier, organization planning is a part of company planning designed to achieve company objectives. It is through organization planning that company objectives are integrated and the structure for the HRS is provided. The planning process as a system is described simply by Exhibit 3–3. The formal

EXHIBIT 3–3
Company objectives and plans as inputs to the human resource system

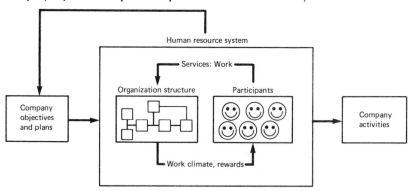

structure interacting with the people in the organization is shown as a subsystem in the block designated as the human resource system. Note how the nature of the organization feeds back to influence company objectives and plans.

The organizational planning function

Although every manager has the responsibility for organizing subordinates into some system of interaction that will accomplish unit goals, the basic overall organizational design has traditionally been the responsibility of the chief executive. However, one study found that many large firms have created organization planning and development departments. Also, medium-sized firms provide for formalized organization planning combined with personnel planning. Frequently, organization planning is developed when there is a change in the management of the company or before a major change in the organization structure.[2]

A study of 244 human resource staff departments revealed that 82 percent had been given general responsibility for organization planning. Another study found that in sessions between chief executives and the human resource staff department, organization planning was one of the most frequently discussed subjects.[3]

Research has been conducted into the goals of departments involved in organization planning and into the reasons for starting organization planning.[4] Usually, one goal was to contribute to corporate objectives by building an effective organization structure and developing an effective management team that would create a healthy organization climate. Major activities in organization planning included more specific duties, such as analyzing the goals of subunits of the firm in order to achieve alignment with overall goals; analyzing the bases of grouping functions in order to determine the actual or prescribed function of a division or a department; or other organizational studies (see Exhibit 3–4). More routine activities included preparing position or job descriptions establishing the organizational manual.

Traditional approaches to organization structure

There exists a large body of knowledge concerning the "best" or most effective ways of organizing the activities and the human resources of a firm. Much of this knowledge dates back to the era of the industrial revolution in this country, during which time businesses began to grow in size, scope, and overall complexity. Without any existing organizational "theories" to guide them in managing their growing businesses, practitioners turned to organizational models in existence at that time—primarily principles being used in the military and the church. As a result, much of

EXHIBIT 3–4
Some specific activities of organization planning

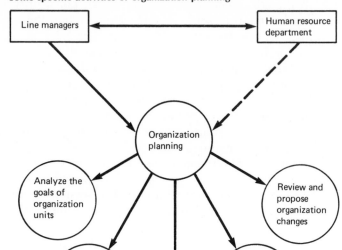

traditional organization planning theory emphasizes the formal structuring of work assignments, with less attention given to the human element. Included in the traditional approach are several "rational" rules or "principles" for designing an organization. These include:

1. Division of labor—complex jobs should be broken down into small specialized jobs for individuals (Exhibit 3–5).
2. Unity of command—a person should have one, and only one, boss (Exhibit 3–6).
3. Scalar chain—there must be a clear line of authority from the top manager of the company to individuals at the lowest level (Exhibit 3–7).
4. Span of control—the number of people reporting to a particular manager is called the manager's span of control (Exhibit 3–8). The larger the number of people reporting, the more contacts

the manager must have with subordinates, and the more difficult it is to coordinate work.

5. Hierarchical structure—the first four principles lead to a clearly defined hierarchical (pyramid) type of organization structure (Exhibit 3–9).

6. Line and staff—the line organization is directly concerned with achieving the objectives of the company, for example, making and selling a product. Staff provides specialized advice, service, or technical control. Exhibit 3–9 shows line responsibilities and staff responsibilities.

EXHIBIT 3–5
Division of labor in making pins

Cuts wire　　　　Sharpens point　　　　Puts on head

EXHIBIT 3–6
One manager per person

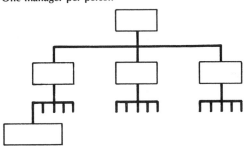

EXHIBIT 3–7
Clear line of authority from top to bottom

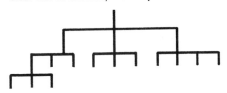

EXHIBIT 3–8
Span of control with an organization of 31 people

A. Flat organization with span of five

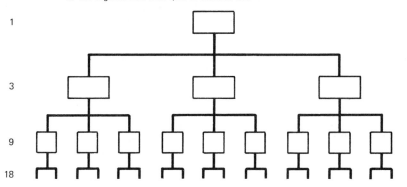

B. Tall organization with span of three or less

Designing an organization by application of the traditional approach has the following disadvantages:

1. The structure ignores the behavior of people in groups.
2. Its formal and rigid lines of communication actually hinder rapid communication.
3. It discourages innovation and initiative.
4. It pays the job and not the jobholder.
5. It tends to rely on coercion to maintain control.
6. Its tight control produces immature behavior and dependency.
7. It prevents the organization from responding promptly to the rapidly changing environment.

The major arguments in favor of following the traditional approach are:

1. It has worked in the past.
2. It appears to be overwhelmingly accepted by businesses despite their lip service to modern theories.
3. It is easily understood and applied.

Although considerable research has been conducted with regard to organization structure, the findings are often inconsistent.[5] One explanation is that studies aimed at examining the same phenomenon have not always used the same definition of terms or identical measurement techniques. The reader interested in knowing more about the relationship of various characteristics of organization structure to members' attitudes and behaviors is advised to look at a recent study conducted by Cummings and Berger.[6] The two researchers base their answers on data obtained from 50 studies conducted over the past ten years.

EXHIBIT 3–9
Hierarchical line-staff structure of General Electric Company

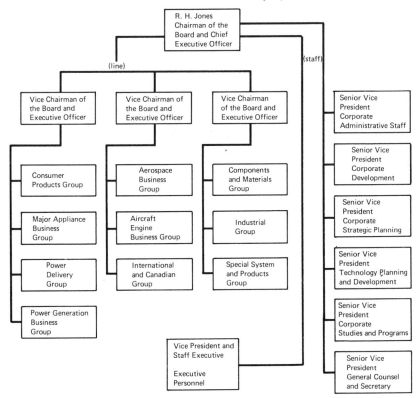

Inconsistency in research findings apparently arises also because the best structure for an organization is dependent (contingent) on the specifics of a particular situation. This means that there is no such thing as the "ideal" or best structure. For example, recent research by Lorsch and Morse has shown that the critical element in the effectiveness of an organization is not its particular structure, but rather the "fit" between the task it performs, the personalities of its members, and its organization structure.[7]

In the manufacturing plants studied by Lorsch and Morse, tasks were short term, repetitive, and predictable. Employees also preferred stronger direction from superiors. As a result, in the most effective plants there was a traditional organization design which provided tight, hierarchical control and coordination, well established routines, and measurement of short-term results.

On the other hand, in the research laboratories studied, scientists and managers had a higher tolerance for ambiguity; preferred to work alone without close supervision; and the tasks were highly uncertain, with results achieved over a long time span. Under these conditions in the laboratories, the most effective organizations were those with a loose and flat structure, allowing a great deal of autonomy and influence for individual scientists. These, and other related research studies, have led to what is called a contingency theory of organization.

Modern organizations—Systems approaches to design

The size and complexity of many modern companies have increased tremendously over the years. Consider General Electric Company with about 300,000 employees, General Motors with over 375,000 employees in the United States alone, or AT&T with 931,000 employees. Many companies are so large that they do not even know how many different products they make and sell. How can such companies organize to make people feel that their contributions are needed and important? How can they organize into work groups requiring hundreds of skills to complete a task or produce a product?

The answer to these questions is being sought by considering the organization as a system composed of many subsystems. Research on cybernetics (feedback control) and related studies of work and social system have suggested new approaches to motivate people and organize their activities.

Two systems approaches are the work flow concept and the work group concept. In the work flow concept, design of the organization is based on operations and the processing of inputs. In the work group concept, design of the organization is based on motivating subsystems of people to perform tasks.

Work flow subsystems. As Chapple and Sayles have stated, "Because people, not lines in a chart, are the major concern, the elimination of points of stress within the flow should be the first consideration of organization design."[8] They recommend the identification of segments of work flows, each of which could logically be put under a single supervisor.

As we have seen, the typical formal organization structure is centered on vertical, superior-subordinate relationships. Organization planners are now beginning to stress the behavior of managers and employees who are in different functional areas yet depend on one another. This relationship exists when different departments or groups of workers all contribute to the same final product and the output of one department becomes the input for the next (see Exhibit 3–10A).

In this work flow structure the outputs from one stage have to be carefully balanced as inputs to the next stage to prevent shortages and/or surpluses. This is usually accomplished through intensive lateral communication among the managers of all the departments. If planning and communication are adequate, work will flow throughout the system.

To illustrate with an actual case, consider the ABC Corporation which manufactures sofas that are sold to retail outlets. Every order taken by a salesperson was processed by several different groups of employees at the home office. These groups included merchandise clerks, billing clerks, credit clerks, and inventory checkers. Accordingly each "functional" group of employees (billing, merchandising, and so on) worked under a separate manager. This meant that each customer order moved through four different departments and two divisions, as seen in Exhibit 3–10B.

The result was periodic chaos and constant conflict among employees. Passing the buck for delays and lost orders became standard operating procedure. Higher management was spending considerable time in settling disputes between departments and between divisions.

After management analyzed the flow of work, the functions were reorganized as shown in Exhibit 3–10C. Now all employees processing orders are under a single general manager who has only two first-line supervisors, each responsible for the same activity in a different geographic area. The sales, warehouse, and credit managers now have a lateral rather than a supervising relationship to the

EXHIBIT 3–10

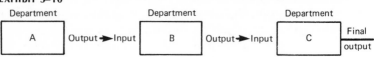

A. Work flow relationship

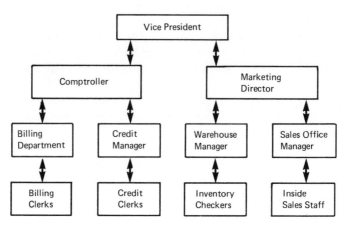

B. Work flow before reorganization

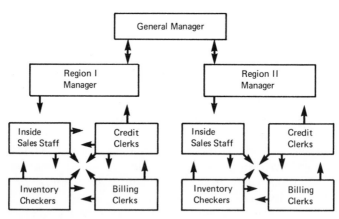

C. Work flow after reorganization

office manager. No longer is it necessary to take complaints up the line through two or three levels of management. Since most disputes are now worked out face-to-face with the work group, output has increased significantly. In essence, these activities of the company are now organized into two almost autonomous regions, each of which can function by itself. Furthermore, the inclusive work teams within each region allow for handling of problems on a one-to-one basis, thus reducing conflict.

Work group subsystems. In organizing by work group subsystems, all groups assigned to any functions or tasks in an organization consist of identical elements, without regard to the simplicity, complexity, period of time, or scope of the work to be conducted. The work group always consists of (a) the leader, (b) specialists to perform the primary assignments, and (c) support staffs to assist with the specific duties necessary for the primary assignments.

Accordingly, specialties essential to perform the work are determined by breaking down business objectives into functions and ultimately into individualized tasks. Emphasis is placed on determining the abilities of each individual and relating them to priority-ranked objectives and functions so that every individual is assigned either as a leader, a specialist, or a support staff member as required to meet predetermined goals.

Although members of the organization are likely to belong to a relatively permanent work group, according to the work group concept any individual may belong to more than one work group at any time. In fact, an individual may lead one group, be a specialist in another, and offer support services to other groups. This is not likely to occur for production workers, but it is not uncommon for professional-type workers, such as accountants, engineers, and analysts.

New templates for organizational patterns

The application of the systems approach leads to some complex patterns of relationships. For one thing, all elements must be connected by a control system. This usually means that one dimension of the organizational pattern follows a hierarchical scalar chain as posed by traditional theory. Let us examine several organizational patterns based upon system concepts.

The matrix organization in two dimensions was developed as an extension of line-staff organizations to achieve better planning and control. It relates functional activities and project (or product) activities. In one dimension, planning and control are established for such basic functions as marketing, engineering, manufacturing, and finance. In the other dimension, project managers cut across the functional areas for their individual products. This is achieved by assigning personnel from each of the functional departments to each project. These people will report to the project manager for program guidance and to their own managers for technical guidance. In some instances, people working on a project may be moved temporarily into an area physically close to the project manager.

The drawback of matrix management is spelled out in traditional "principles"—a person should report to only one manager. The advantage of matrix management is organizational stability, in that every employee has a "home" in the functional group despite varied temporary assignments to projects. At the same time, the planning, pressure, and control of the project-type organization are present to induce high achievement. The arrangement of the organiza-

EXHIBIT 3–11
Matrix organization

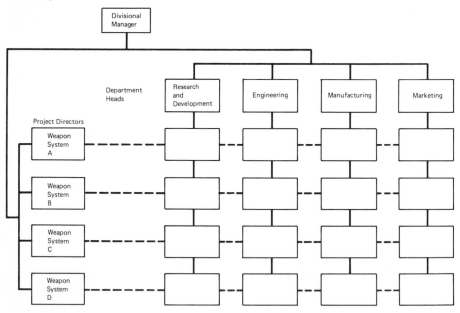

tional pattern shown in Exhibit 3–11 indicates the reason for the term *matrix*. The growth of matrix patterns to include three dimensions is illustrated by Dow Corning's organization, shown in Exhibit 3–12.

EXHIBIT 3–12
Three-dimensional areas

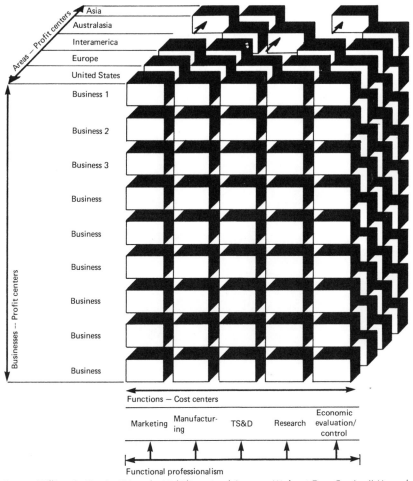

Source: William C. Goggin, "How the Multidimensional Structure Works at Dow Corning," *Harvard Business Review,* January–February, 1973, p. 17. Copyright © 1973 by the President and Fellows of Harvard College; all rights reserved.

Richard Rumelt studied the structure of the *Fortune* 500 firms during a 19-year time span. The simple functional pattern declined from use in 69 percent of the firms to use in about 12 percent. Although all of the firms had functional patterns at some level, the predominant organizational patterns were complex to match complex organizational objectives. Exhibit 3–13 shows changing patterns such as geographic, holding company, product divisional, and functional/subsidiary. This last is a hybrid in which the principal

EXHIBIT 3–13
Changing patterns

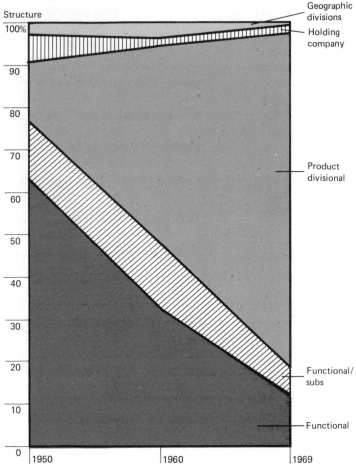

business is managed directly by top management and other, smaller, diversified business is managed by product divisions or subsidiaries.

Peter Drucker identifies another complex system organizational pattern as "simulated decentralization."[9] He states that this is often appropriate for a company which is too big to be functionally organized and too integrated (as opposed to conglomerates) to be genuinely decentralized. It sets up one function, one phase in a process, or one segment of the organization as if it were a distinct business with genuine profit and loss responsibility. It incorporates such accounting functions as transfer prices, capital costs, and overhead allocations as if they were realities in the marketplace.

Drucker has suggested three ways to determine the kind of structure needed for a particular business: *activities analysis, decision analysis,* and *relations analysis.* That is, Drucker suggests that a business be examined to establish its real activities rather than on the basis of preconceived generalized headings, such as "production" or "selling." He stresses that by rigorous activities analysis, management can find out what work has to be performed, what work belongs together, and how each activity should be emphasized in the organizational structure. Accordingly, decision analysis determines what kinds of decisions are needed, where in the organization they should be made, and how each manager should be involved in them. Relations analysis involves finding out the contribution each manager must make to programs, with whom he works, and what contribution other managers must make to him.

Which is the best approach to organization planning?

Research in the general area of organization theory has demonstrated the limitations of the many different approaches to organization planning. Widely used traditional approaches, for example, do not give enough emphasis to the problem of interrelationships or integration of activity. Therefore, most modern organization theorists tend to view organizations as a system of mutually interdependent and interacting parts and variables.

What this means is that the "best" approach to organization planning depends upon the specific standards of effectiveness you choose to use. Ideally, of course, the best approach is the one which provides the most effective and satisfying way to accomplish organizational goals with the human resources available. This, however, is easier said than done.

For example, not only could a given large firm be organized in several hundred different ways, but the same individual would probably *not* organize any two firms in the same way. One reason is that the structure must be matched to the tasks; that is, structure follows strategy, and strategies vary and change. Second, the staffing, and hence the behavioral system, changes with time. In addition, organization planning is influenced by many factors other than the abstract ideal of what is "best." Customs, people, the value systems of executives, technology, and labor relations are just a few of the forces that must be considered.

To further illustrate, organization planning seldom takes place at "day one" of a new business. In almost every case, the need for organization plans is felt by a firm which is already in business. Thus, the planner must work with what already exists and can seldom afford to make changes so drastic as to replace the total current organization. Objectively set plans may suggest replacing all top management, writing new job descriptions, decentralizing the structure, and hiring new employees. Needless to say, these changes would be too drastic and some sort of compromise plan would have to be substituted for the "ideal." In fact, when involved in organization planning, we should ask, "Do our plans allow enough room for compromise and for differences?"

HUMAN RESOURCE NEEDS PLANNING

Once management has formulated its organization plans, it is ready to match the needs of those plans with human resources. An organization cannot rely upon locating talented personnel at the time it is needed. Systematic steps must be taken to have the right people in the right number at the right time, performing activities which give the individual and the organization maximum benefit. Earlier we have referred to this process as *human resource needs planning* (many practitioners also refer to it as manpower planning).

By now we have learned that organization planning and HR needs planning are interrelated and interacting in the human resource system. In fact, organization planning takes precedence over and provides direction to HR needs planning. Exhibit 3–14 shows the flow of activities from organization planning to the determining of human resource needs. As may be seen in this figure, human resource needs are ultimately met through employee development or the acquisition of new employees.

Relationship to other parts of the HRS

It is important that human resource planning be integrated with all parts of the human resource system. It should, in fact, be thought of as the function which has the specific task of integrating all other functions of human resource management. To illustrate, as the organization grows, its need for human resources with specialized skills, expertise, and training also grows. The lead time necessary to educate and/or train people in new technology continues to increase. Thus, human resource planning should point up needs in training and development. At the same time, the quality of training

EXHIBIT 3–14
Planning human resource needs

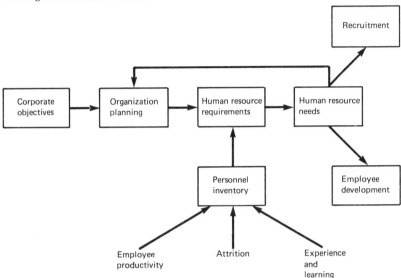

and development will affect the quality of human resources, and this must in turn be considered in human resource plans.

If the firm determines a need to go outside to recruit human resources having the new technology skills, the cost and means of recruiting will have to be considered. The compensation system will also have to be examined in order to provide internal consistency and external competitiveness for all wages and benefits.

The efficient matching of jobs and people, as well as the removal of barriers to mobility within the organization, creates problems that must be considered. Management must remember that human resource planning is more than an attempt to fill the firm's need for human resources. The organization must provide its employees with realistic and satisfying career opportunities. With the proper program, management is able to attract, retain, develop, and utilize talent to meet the future needs of the individual and the organization.

Relationship to the external environment

Aside from human resources developed within the organization, every firm is dependent on the quality and quantity of skills external to it. This means that such things as changing demands for skills and educational levels in the labor market directly affect the staffing process in general and human resource planning in particular. Obsolescence or changing attitudes can create shortages or surpluses of skills in a relatively short time. For example, a recent study conducted by Harvard economist Dr. Richard B. Freeman found that the number of professional and management jobs has not expanded as quickly as the flow of students from four-year colleges. The computer model used in the study forecasts an oversupply of college graduates into the early 1980's. In fact, the model shows that many college graduates, especially liberal arts majors, will end up in nonprofessional, non-managerial jobs. Of course, a major change, such as a massive R&D project comparable to the space program of the 1960s, could change a surplus to a shortage.

Government action at both the federal and local level has had a dramatic impact on HR planning for all firms. Recent laws have been aimed at preventing discrimination in employment on the basis of race, color, religion, sex, national origin, or age. For example, Title VII, Equal Employment Opportunity, of the Civil Rights Act forbids employers to discriminate in hiring or in any of the terms or conditions of employment on the basis of race, religion, sex or national origin. As we shall see, the Equal Employment Opportunity Commission (EEOC) was established to enforce the provisions of the act. This legislation has profoundly influenced the recruiting and selection practices of all organizations, as will be discussed in the next chapter.

The impact of the Civil Rights Act can also be seen in recent out-of-court settlements and court awards. For example, a settlement reached between the EEOC and the American Telephone and Telegraph Company provided for $15 million in back pay to women and minority employees because of discriminatory employment practices. Furthermore, the Bell System companies were required to set goals and timetables for the employment of males in previously all-female job classifications, such as telephone operators and clerks.

Governmental affirmative action programs have the even more ambitious objective of reversing the effects of *past* discrimination and, as might be expected, have an even more direct and visible impact on recruitment and selection practices.

Affirmative action plans required of all bidders on federal contracts under Executive Order J1246 are an important influence on human resources. All government contractors must formulate and submit affirmative action plans which include steps and timetables for guaranteeing job opportunities for females and members of minority groups at all levels in the organization. Often this requires special recruitment efforts to develop pools of minority applicants where none have existed previously.

Businesses have traditionally tended to prefer hiring younger people, thus limiting employment opportunities for older people. To meet this problem, the Age Discrimination in Employment Act of 1967 was passed. The purpose of the act was to promote the

EXHIBIT 3–15
Excerpts from an affirmative action directive to department heads in a state university

Recruitment efforts will be directed at securing applications from qualified minority and female applicants. Appointments will not be made to instructional or professional positions until a good faith effort has been made to secure the services of a woman or a person of minority identification, and until such effort can be adequately demonstrated. Public announcements and advertisements of position vacancies will be placed in local, regional, or national media, journals or professional publications, or communications to professional societies . . . .

H. AFFIRMATIVE ACTION INDICATIONS

Recruiting

1. Utilize minority group persons in:
    a. Your Administrative or Personnel Office, as staff and as interviewers.
    b. Your recruiting visits to high schools, colleges, job fairs, and similar agencies.
2. Establish contacts in the minority and women's communities. The key to good contacts is credibility—credibility between your department and the contact, credibility between the contact and the minority and women's communities, and credibility among women's groups and organizations.
    a. Contact the nationally known minority groups or women's organizations.
    b. Contact community organizations—school committees, churches, local centers. In some places, these lesser-known groups have closer contact with the people than the organizations with national reputation.
    c. If experience shows no group is an adequate contact, seek out individuals and leaders who are well known—ministers, doctors, barbers, beauticians.
    d. If these sources fail, seek out the leaders of community demonstrations. Do not be deterred by radical rhetoric; some of these leaders may have more credibility than better-known groups.
    e. Invite minority and women leaders to visit, tour, and/or lecture to your department.
    f. Make an effort to bring minority group members and women into your vacancy information system and equalize their opportunities.

When you have a job opening,

    a. Advertise it in minority and women's community media (newspapers, magazines, radio and TV stations). Utilize these media as regularly as you use other forms of advertising. Always use the phrase, "An Equal

EXHIBIT 3–15 *(continued)*

Opportunity Employer." Also, indicate that "we welcome applications from minorities and women."

   b. Notify employment agencies with a large clientele of minority group persons.

   c. Make clear to non-specialized agencies that applicants will be rated on merit only, and encourage them to send minority group and women applicants.

   d. Encourage minority and women employees to refer their friends.

DO NOT:

1. Rely predominantly or exclusively on word-of-mouth referral.
2. Rely predominantly on walk-ins, especially if you are located in an all-white area.
3. Rely on qualifications which are not job-related and tend to "screen out" applicants rather than "screen in" qualified minority group persons and women.
4. Continue restricting positions by sex, unless there is a bona fide occupational qualification involved.

Applications

Accept applications from minorities and women whether or not you have an opening. Keep the applications on file; consult them when openings develop. (Minority group persons and women must be built into the system of employment. While white males may hear of future openings by word-of-mouth from present employees, minority group persons and women most often do not.)

Interview

When you interview applicants, be certain that

   a. Interviewers understand and carry out your equal employment policies.

   b. Interviewers are not biased by dress and grooming styles which are unique to certain ethnic or age groups.

   c. Interviewing staff is appropriately representative of group being sought in affirmative action efforts.

Employment Standards

Qualifications should reflect what the applicant needs to get the job done. Do not lose potentially good workers because you have artificially high standards.

   a. Eliminate requirements for diplomas and degrees where neither is needed for proper position or job function.

   b. Eliminate or be flexible about experience requirements when the job can be quickly learned, and reduce experience requirements which are excessive.

   c. Review a person on the basis of his or her previous success record and promise, as well as academic achievement.

   d. Assume that women do not permit marital status to affect their acceptance of employment.

   e. Assume that minorities are willing to live and work in a predominantly white community.

   f. Assume that wives of current employees are qualifiable according to standards set forth in the State Personnel Policies.

   g. Apply all of the same considerations and equalizations for minorities and women to employment of minority and women students.

employment of older persons based upon ability rather than age. Accordingly, any human resource plans must consider both hiring and retaining employees of advanced age. In summary, the above discussion should strongly indicate that human resource planning is not only vitally interrelated with other parts of the human resource system but that it must be conducted within the constraints set down by the outside world. An example of these constraints is shown in Exhibit 3–15.

ELEMENTS INVOLVED IN HUMAN RESOURCE NEEDS PLANNING

An essential element of all work force planning is a forecast to anticipate future human resource needs. Equally important is an *inventory* or *audit* of human resources now in the organization to ascertain the availability of needed skills for current and future job vacancies. Only when this is accomplished can the necessary plans and programs for acquiring and developing managers and employees be completed.

Forecasting

The methods or techniques used in forecasting vary from simple, informal "educated guesses" to sophisticated statistical techniques and mathematical models which utilize computer analysis. For example, a rather simple approach relies on the experience and judgment of the forecasters, who act either individually or in groups. Using a group approach, members present all the facts they know about the subject and the information is assembled and reviewed until a consensus forecast is reached.

Some of the quantitative approaches use a trend-projection method whereby past trends are extrapolated into the future. This method, which assumes that the past is a good predictor of the future, is satisfactory in stable businesses. For firms facing extreme growth or decline and firms in unstable industries, trend projections become limited in usefulness. Other quantitative approaches attempt to relate the need for human resources to one or more internal or external factors, using regression analysis. (The reader unfamiliar with trend or regression analysis may wish to consult a basic statistics book.)

One expert suggests a method for stable industries which first projects the firm's labor productivity rate for the future and then divides productivity per employee into projected future output. Productivity can be measured in several ways, such as by dividing sales by the number of employees. To measure trends in productivity, you can start with the past rate of productivity and then adjust the rate upward for any likely causes of increased productivity, such as investment in new equipment. It should be obvious, however, that what is the best method for one organization is not necessarily the best method for another organization.

Exhibit 3–16 summarizes the forecasting techniques by time period used in 181 of the largest U.S. corporations. According to this

EXHIBIT 3–16
Personnel forecasting techniques by time period (181 organizations using forecasting techniques)

Technique	Short range (6–12 months)	Inter-mediate range (1–5 years)	Long range (5+ years)
Inventories of available talent	65.7%	45.3%	34.3%
Counts of vacant positions	65.2	19.9	12.2
Estimates of losses (turnover, retirement, etc.)	45.9	54.7	43.1
Analysis of operating and project plans	35.9	42.0	34.3
Productivity analysis and projections	17.7	16.6	12.7
Computer analysis of manpower needs			
Markov (probability) analysis	1.1	3.3	1.1
Other mathematical methods	3.9	5.5	3.9
Other (trend analyses, industry guidelines, etc.)	11.0	12.7	11.0

Note: The above percentages reflect the fact that many participants report the use of two or more of the techniques.
Source: Reprinted from *Corporate Manpower Planning: A Study of Manpower Planning Practices in 220 Major U.S. Business Organizations* (Philadelphia: Tower, Perrin, Forster and Crosby, Inc., 1971).

study, we can see that the basic forecasting techniques are widely used, especially for shorter range plans. While interest in more advanced techniques such as trend analyses and computer modeling appears to be high among human resource forecasters, their actual use is rare. We expect that the future will find greater acceptance of these more complex techniques.

Work force inventories

Skills and work force inventories help to answer questions ranging from broad planning issues to immediate placement problems. Broad planning requires information on the overall profile of the current work force, whereas immediate placement requires information on individuals.

A skills or work force inventory generally includes demographic information, such as age, sex, present position, work history, education, date of employment, promotion potential, and training or development needs. The inventory should also show the number and classifications of employees at present and potentially qualified for transfer to other jobs or departments.

If such information is computerized, it becomes possible to answer quickly such questions as: How many employees, and in what jobs, will be retiring next year? Who among our employees is qualified to be a widget designer? How many employees have the potential for promotion to first-line supervisors? You can see that a work force inventory is a carefully thought out but relatively simple tool. In concept, it is simply a list of employees and their strengths and weaknesses as summarized from various skills inventories. Yet it is an extremely valuable tool for work force planning.

Some firms use separate inventory systems for managerial employees. Regardless of the type of system used, the important element is the information collected for presentation to top management, usually in the form of a management personnel replacement chart (see Exhibit 3–17). By showing the age, promotion potential, and performance appraisal of each job's incumbent and replacements, such a chart becomes a valuable tool for top management to use in preparing management recruitment and development programs.

If they are given skills inventories of the present human resources in the firm and forecasts of the firm's future human resource needs, as well as information on turnover, work force planners can analyze these data to arrive at an estimate of work force needs. When a lack of necessary skills and a loss of personnel through attrition show a need for more or different human resources in the future, management knows that recruitment or training programs are a necessity.

An interrelated process

Although we have discussed forecasting and inventories as separate elements, human resource needs planning should be viewed as an interrelated and continuous process. That means it is more than a clerical function which attempts to answer such questions as "How many employees do we need for our next quarter?" As illustrated in Exhibit 3–18, human resource planning requires an in-depth knowledge of how the human resource system operates, with emphasis on the flow (supply and demand) of people into, through, and out of the organization.

Exhibit 3–17
Management personnel replacement chart

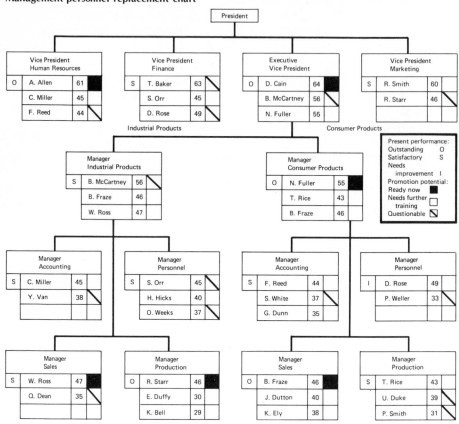

On the supply side, human resource needs planning requires accurate and current information regarding both qualitative and quantitative factors, such as skills inventories and public policy toward human resources. On the demand side, attention must be given to such factors as productivity, technological changes, and sales forecasts. Supply and demand must be continuously balanced within the framework of organizational goals and priorities.

It should be apparent that success in the use of the organizational patterns or structure resulting from organization planning will depend to a great extent on the individuals assigned to the resulting positions. If the human resource needs of a firm are planned in concert with formal organization planning, a meaningful and effective structure is more likely.[10] In a sense, then, human resource planning is really *applied* organization planning.

EXHIBIT 3–18
A human resource planning system

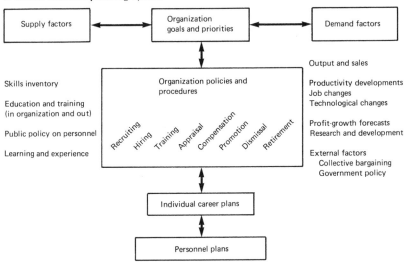

Source: Based on Felician F. Foltman, *Manpower Information for Effective Management, part 2. Skills Inventories and Manpower Planning* (Ithaca: New York State School of Industrial and Labor Relations, Cornell University, 1973), p. 27.

In the next chapter we shall see that human resource planning is an integral part of the staffing process and is directly related to other parts of the human resource system, such as recruiting, selection, and training.

SUMMARY

We have seen that the systems approach to managing human resources starts with business objectives as inputs. This means that strategic (long-range) and operating (short-range) objectives must be prepared which link together human resource activities and business function activities (such as marketing and production) into a system with a unified sense of direction. Through organization planning these objectives are integrated and the structure for the HRS is provided.

More specifically, organization planning was discussed as the vehicle for specifying the purposeful integration of the existing framework, the guiding principles of technology, and the overall goals of the firm. Accordingly, it sets a target for organizational change, especially regarding structure and staffing. It was noted, however, that although organization planning may encompass many activities, its primary purpose is to divide the total task to be performed by the organization into manageable and efficient units and to provide proper integration for these units, according to predetermined business objectives.

There is a large body of knowledge concerning the "best" or most effective ways of organizing the activities and the human resources of a firm. Much of the traditional approaches emphasized the structure and functions of the organization, with less attention given to the human element. Accordingly, certain "principles" were developed which served as guidelines for the managing function.

The complexities of modern business, as well as research findings in the behavioral sciences, have led to different views as to how to organize the activities needed to meet organizational goals. For example, the organizational systems models do not use traditional hierarchy as a basic principle. As we have seen in our discussion of the work flow and work group concepts, activities are organized and a structure is designed which will be best suited to achieve given goals.

Each of the different approaches to organization planning could result in a completely different organization design or structure. A complex business, in fact, could be organized according to literally hundreds of different forms. At one extreme are relatively simple structures consisting of a so-called line organization. At the opposite extreme is the complex matrix organization, often referred to as project organization.

Which is the best approach to organization planning? Research in the area of organization theory and behavior suggests that the answer depends upon the standard of effectiveness you choose to use. The best approach is the one which provides the most effective and satisfying way for accomplishing organizational goals with the human resources available.

We have also seen that an organization cannot rely upon locating personnel at the time it is needed. Systematic steps must be taken to have the right people in the right number at the right time, performing activities which give the individual and the organization maximum benefit. This is known as human resource needs planning. An essential element of this planning is a forecast to anticipate future human resource needs. Equally important are work force inventories. Given inventories of the present human resources in the firm and forecasts of the firm's future human resource needs, along with turnover rates, HR planners can arrive at an estimate of HR needs.

Of course, using the systems approach, organization planning and human resource needs must be integrated with all parts of the human resource system and must be conducted within the constraints of the outside world. We have seen, for example, that such things as the labor market and civil rights legislation have had a dramatic effect on human resource planning in all organizations.

CASE: COMPANY GROWTH AND GOOD OLE BOYS (AND GIRLS)

The Honeygood Company was born in the electronic age. As a manufacturer of modems and control computers, primarily, it was on a fast growth track. It employed about 800 people and had annual sales of about $30 million in 1978. At that time, it had no organization chart and management operated very informally.

The company was highly personality-oriented. The chairman of the company, Larry Gooing, exclaimed, "Organization charts? I hate them!" He and the president of the company, Ms. Intel Lect, a graduate of MIT, had adjoining offices looking out over an office area where informality was the custom.

If an organization chart of the Honeygood Company were drawn, it would look like that shown in the accompanying illustration.

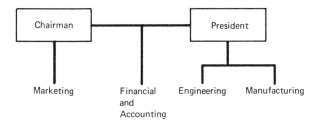

Despite the informality, the chairman and the president agreed that the company should expand in its areas of strength by adding certain computer hardware products to its line over the next five years. They estimated that sales would double and that the number of employees would increase to about 1,500.

Because of the informality, there were only two layers of management. Since the span of managers was large, coordination, control, and feedback of information about problems were slow. The manager of finance and accounting had been pressing for the development of an improved organization structure, human resource planning, and a management information and control system to prepare for the future.

Ms. Intel Lect has agreed that there may be a limit to informality when it comes to long-range planning. You have been hired as a consultant to prepare organization and human resource plans for Honeygood.

QUESTIONS AND PROBLEMS

1. Using a concrete example, show the relationship among business objectives, organization planning, human resource needs planning, and the human resource system.

2. Do you believe that it is possible to develop programs and methods for managing human resources without a thorough study of strategic planning? Give reasons for your belief.

3. Compare the traditional role of company objectives in managing human resources with the systems view of objectives.

4. In what ways do objectives determine the "best" type of organization for a business?

5. What is the primary purpose of organization planning? What are some major and routine activities included in organization planning?

6. Compare and contrast the traditional and the systems approaches to structuring an organization.

7. Draw an organization chart for a church, business, or government agency in which you have been active. To what extent does the organization follow the "principles" of organization discussed in this chapter? In what ways does it violate the "principles"?

8. The matrix organization violates the chain-of-command principle. What are the theoretical and practical reasons for such a violation?

9. List several guides for deciding what activities to group together in departments.

10. Using a concrete example, explain what is meant by the statement "Organizational systems models do not use hierarchy as a basic principle."

11. Explain the difference between the work flow and the work group approaches to organization planning.

12. Why don't all businesses adopt the one best organization structure so that we would find all organization structures alike?

13. Show how organization planning is not only a necessary part of starting a new business but continues to exert a unifying and never-ending influence upon the human resource system.

14. Using a concrete example, show the relationship between organization planning and human resource needs planning.

15. What important factors need to be considered in human resource planning?

16. In what ways have federal and state equal employment opportunity laws caused organizations to alter their human resource policies and practices?

17. Outline a procedure to be followed by a large insurance company in forecasting and planning for its human resource needs. Would this procedure be the same for a medium-sized construction firm?

BIBLIOGRAPHY

Barrett, Jon H. *Individual Goals and Organizational Objectives.* Ann Arbor: Institute for Social Research, University of Michigan, 1970.

Beer, Michael, and Huse, Edgar F. "A Systems Approach to Organization Development." *Journal of Applied Behavioral Science,* 1972.

Bogart, Dodd H. "Changing Views of Organization." *Technological Forecasting and Social Change,* 1973.

Burack, E. H. and McNichols, T. J. *Human Resource Planning: Technology, Policy, Change.* Kent, Ohio: Comparative Administration Research Institute, Kent State University, 1973.

Burack, Elmer H., and Walker, James W. *Manpower Planning and Programming.* Boston: Allyn and Bacon, 1973.

Cummings, Larry, and Berger, Chris J. "Organization Structure: How Does It Influence Attitudes and Performance?", *Organization Dynamics,* Autumn 1976.

Drandell, M. "A Composite Forecasting Methodology for Manpower Planning Utilizing Objective and Subjective Criteria." *Academy of Management Journal,* September 1975.

Drucker, Peter F. *Management: Tasks, Responsibilities, Practices.* New York: Harper & Row, 1973.

Galbraith, Jay R. *Organization Design.* Reading, Mass.: Addison-Wesley, 1977.

Glueck, William F. *Organization Planning and Development.* New York: American Management Association, 1971.

Goggin, William C. "How the Multidimensional Structure Works at Dow Corning." *Harvard Business Review,* January–February 1974.

"Group Management to Control Diversity. *Business Week,* September 15, 1975.

Hinrichs, John R. "Restructuring the Organization for Tomorrow's Needs." *Personnel,* March–April 1974.

McKelvey, Bill, and Kilman, Ralph. "Organization Design." *Administrative Science Quarterly,* March 1975.

Morse, John L., and Lorsch, Jay W. "Beyond Theory Y." *Harvard Business Review,* May–June 1970.

Newman, Derek. *Organization Design.* London: Edward Arnold, 1973.

"New Templates for Today's Organizations." *Harvard Business Review,* January–February 1974.

Patten, Thomas H., Jr. *Manpower Planning and the Development of Human Resources.* New York: John Wiley & Sons, 1971.

Scott, Bruce R. "The Industrial State: Old Myths and New Realities." *Harvard Business Review,* March–April 1973.

Seese, Dorothy Ann. "The Management of Work." *Journal of Systems Management,* September 1971.

Shank, John K., Miblock, Edward G., and Sandalls, William T., Jr. "Balance 'Creativity' and 'Practicality' in Formal Planning." *Harvard Business Review,* January–February 1973.

Shetty, Y. K., and Carlisle, Howard M. "A Contingency Model of Organization Design." *California Management Review,* Fall 1972.

Skibbins, Gerald J. *Organizational Evolution.* New York: AMACOM, 1974.

Sokolik, Stanley L. *The Personnel Process: Line and Staff Dimensions in Managing People at Work.* Scranton, Pa.: Intext, 1970.

Stainer, Gareth. *Manpower Planning: The Management of Human Resources.* London: Heinemann, 1971.

Stieglitz, Harold. "On Concepts of Corporate Structure." *Conference Board Record,* February 1974.

Walker, J. N. "Evaluating the Practical Effectiveness of Human Resource Planning Applications." *Human Resource Management,* Spring 1974).

Walker, J. W. "Models in Manpower Planning." *Business Horizons,* April 1971.

Weisblat, D. I., and Stucki, J. C. "Goal-Oriented Organization at Upjohn." *Research Management,* January 1974.

Wikstrom, W. S. *Manpower Planning: Evolving Systems.* New York: Conference Board, 1971.

NOTES

[1] David M. Herold, "Long-Range Planning and Organizational Performance: A Cross-Valuation Study," *Academy of Management Journal,* March 1972; Zafar A. Malik and Delmar W. Karger, "Does Long-Range Planning Improve Company Performance?" *Management Review,* September 1975; Patrick H. Irwin, "Romulus and Remus: Two Studies in Corporate Planning," *Management Review,* October 1976; and Sidney Schoeffler, Robert D. Buzzell, and Donald F. Heany, "The Impact of Strategic Planning on Profit Performance," *Harvard Business Review,* March–April 1974.

[2] W. F. Glueck, *Organization Planning and Development* (New York: American Management Association, 1971).

[3] Dalton E. McFarland, *Company Officers Assess the Personnel Function,* AMA Research Study 79 (New York: American Management Association, 1967).

[4] Glueck, *Organization Planning and Development;* and W. L. Brockhaus, "Planning for Chance with Organization Charts," *Business Horizons,* June 1974.

[5] Bill McKelvey and Ralph Kilman, "Organization Design," *Administrative Science Quarterly,* March 1975; Larry Cummings and Ali M. El Salmi, "The Impact of Role Diversity, Job Level, and Organizational Size on Managerial Satisfaction," *Administrative Science Quarterly,* 1971; and Andrew Grimes et al., "Matrix Model: A Selective Empirical Test," *Academy of Management Journal,* March 1972.

[6] Larry Cummings and Chris J. Berger, "Organization Structure: How Does It Influence Attitudes and Performance?" *Organizational Dynamics,* Autumn 1976.

[7] Jay Lorsch and John Morse. *Organizations and Their Members: A Contingency Approach* (New York: Harper and Row, 1974).

[8] Elliott V. Chapple and Leonard R. Sayles, *The Measurement of Management* (New York: Macmillan Co., 1961).

[9] Peter F. Drucker, 'New Templates for Today's Organization," *Harvard Business Review,* January–February 1974.

[10] Stanley L. Sokolik, *The Personnel Process* (Scranton, Pa.: International Textbook Co., 1970), chap. 6, "Organization and Manpower Planning."

When you have completed studying
STAFFING THE ORGANIZATION
you should be able to:

1. Explain how to obtain the necessary job information in order to staff an organization.
2. Define the elements of an effective recruitment and selection system.
3. Discuss the relationship between human resource planning, job analysis, recruitment, and selection.
4. Identify the key steps involved in the selection process.
5. Suggest ways to evaluate the selection process.
6. Discuss the problems of government regulations in the areas of affirmative action and equal employment opportunity.

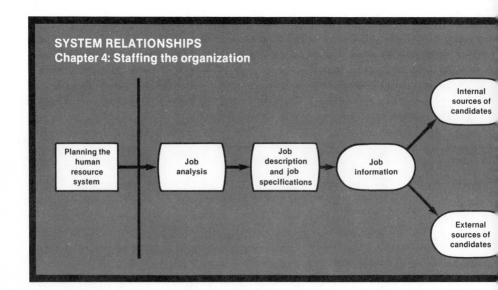

SYSTEM RELATIONSHIPS
Chapter 4: Staffing the organization

Planning the human resource system → Job analysis → Job description and job specifications → Job information → Internal sources of candidates / External sources of candidates

The effectiveness of an organization at any level depends upon the skills of employees who are striving for a common purpose. The objective of the staffing process is to locate and acquire the human resources necessary to fulfill organizational and human resource plans. The staffing process, then, may be viewed as a flow of activities which results in the continuous staffing of organizational positions at all levels. In some industries a particularly difficult part of this job is the smooth and timely staffing of new and radically different jobs as they are created.

We have seen in the previous chapter that in order to carry out this process, management must plan human resource needs to determine the skills

4

Staffing the organization

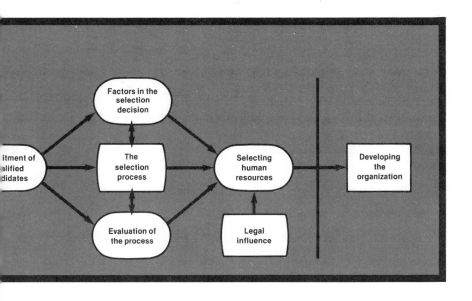

"That's odd! I thought the output waveform equals $\dfrac{1}{2\pi}\displaystyle\int_{-\infty}^{-\infty}\dfrac{\exp{(j\omega t)}}{\alpha+j\omega}\,d\omega$."

From *Infosystems*, February 1975, p. 24.

that will be necessary to meet the organizational goals. As seen in Exhibit 4-1, recruitment, selection, placement, and development programs result from these human resource plans. In a broader sense, the total staffing process encompasses the flow of human resources

EXHIBIT 4-1
The staffing process

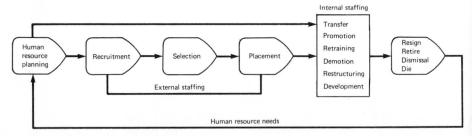

into, within, and out of the enterprise. In this chapter we shall see how this process takes place in an organization. It should be noted, therefore, that organization planning and human resource needs planning are interrelated and provide the input for the staffing process.

The concept of job analysis, which will be discussed first, provides a logical link between the previous chapter on planning and the techniques and functions of the staffing process described in this chapter. Although entire books have been devoted to job analysis, we have been highly selective in our treatment of the topic. The reader interested in further study of job analysis may wish to consult one of the books listed at the end of the chapter.

DETERMINING NECESSARY JOB INFORMATION

It is important to have available a current job description and specification for every job in the firm. The job description serves as a source of basic information for many human resource activities. In fact, most decisions regarding such things as selection, training, promotion, work loads, and compensation require that relevant duties, tasks, and employee requirements be made explicit for each organizational position. Let us look at how we acquire and analyze this relevant information.

Job analysis

For staffing purposes a *job* is defined as a collection or aggregation of tasks, duties, and responsibilities that is viewed as a reasonable assignment to an individual employee. Job titles frequently give misleading impressions of the actual content of a job. (The "traffic-flow engineer" at a local theater was an usher.)

Job analysis is the procedure by which jobs are studied to determine what tasks and responsibilities they include, their relationship to other jobs, the personal capabilities required for satisfactory performance, and the conditions under which work is performed. In a small business or a rapidly growing one, the boundaries of each job may be fuzzy. In these cases, questions such as the following must be asked: Are the duties rigid, or can they be reassigned to other employees as needed? For the essential duties of the job, does the employee need special training, or can the duties be taught on the job?

In smaller firms, management usually conducts job analysis somewhat informally in conjunction with the employees involved. However, most large companies use trained job analysts. The most popular approaches used in studying a job are questionnaires, interviews, observation, and written narratives. The U.S. Training and Employment Service (USTES) of the Department of Labor is more involved in job analysis than any other organization. A job analysis schedule, including a completed job description, used by the USTES is shown in Exhibit 4–2. The specific directions for con-

EXHIBIT 4–2
Job analysis schedule

U.S. Department of Labor

Estab. & Sched. No. ___071–3120–423___

JOB ANALYSIS SCHEDULE

1. Estab. Job Title ___INFORMATION DESK CLERK, receptionist–clerk___

2. Ind. Assign. ___ret. tr.___

3. SIC Code(s) and Title(s) ___5311 Department Stores___

Code 237.568

WTA Group Information Gathering, Dispensing, Verifying, and Related Work p. 258

DOT Title

Ind. Desig.

4. **JOB SUMMARY:**

Answers inquiries and gives directions to customers, authorizes cashing of customers' checks, records and returns lost charge cards, sorts and reviews new credit applications, and requisitions supplies, working at Information Desk in department store Credit Office.

5. **WORK PERFORMED RATINGS:**

	(D)	(P)	T
Worker Functions	Data	People	Things
	5	6	7

Work Field ___282-Information Giving   231 Recording___

M.P.S.M.S. ___890-Business Service___

6. **WORKER TRAITS RATINGS:**

GED   1   2 (3) 4   5   6

SVP   1   2 (3) 4   5   6   7   8   9

Aptitudes   G _3_ V _3_ N _3_ S _4_ P _4_ Q _3_ K _4_ F _3_ M _4_ E _5_ C _5_

Temperaments   D   F   I   J (M)(P) R   S   T (V)

Interests   1a (1b)(2a) 2b   3a   3b   4a   4b   5a   5b

Phys. Demands (S) L   M   H   V   2   3 (4)(5) 6

Environ. Cond. (I) O   B   2   3   4   5   6   7

EXHIBIT 4-2 *(continued)*

7. General Education

    a. Elementary ___8___ High School ___none___ Courses _____

    b. College ___none___ Courses _____

8. Vocational Preparation

    a. College ___none___ Courses _____

    b. Vocational Education ___none___ Courses _____

    c. Apprenticeship ___none___ _____

    d. Inplant Training ___none___ _____

    e. On-the-Job Training ___3 to 5 weeks by Credit Interviewer___

    f. Performance on Other Jobs ___none___ _____

9. Experience ___none___ _____

10. Orientation ___1 week___ _____

11. Licenses, etc. ___none___ _____

12. Relation to Other Jobs and Workers

    Promotion: From ___this is an entry job___ To ___CREDIT INTERVIEWER___

    Transfers: From ___none___ To ___none___

    Supervision Received ___CREDIT MANAGER___

    Supervision Given ___none___

13. Machines, Tools, Equipment, and Work Aids
    Impressing Device - Small Hand-operated device, of similar construction
    to stapler with a nonmoving base and a moveable upper arm containing
    rollers which inked Impressing Device (con) are moved by a
    lever in the upper arm. Charge card is placed in a grove in the base,
    stand-up print facing up, and paper or bill positioned over card, then
    the upper arm is brought down and lever depressed to bring inked rollers
    over paper to make impress of card's print.

14. Materials and Products

    none

EXHIBIT 4–2 *(continued)*

15. Description of Tasks:

1. Answers inquiries and gives direction to customers: Greets customers at Information Desk and ascertains reason for visit to Credit Office. Sends customer to Credit Interviewer to open credit account, to Cashier to pay bills, to Adjustment Department to obtain correction of error in billing. Directs customer to other store departments on request, referring to store directory. (50%)

2. Authorizes cashing of checks: Authorizes cashing of personal or payroll checks (up to a specified amount) by customers desiring to make payment on credit account. Requests identification, such as driver's license or charge card, from customers, and examines check to verify date, amount, signature, and endorsement. Initials check, and sends customer to Cashier. Refers customer presenting Stale Date Check to bank. (5%)

3. Performs routine clerical tasks in the processing of mailed change of address requests: Fills out Change of Address form, based on customer's letter, and submits to Head Authorizer for processing. Files customer's letter. Contacts customer to obtain delivery address if omitted from letter. (10%)

4. Answers telephone calls from customers reporting lost or stolen charge cards and arranges details of cancellation of former card and replacement: Obtains all possible details from customer regarding lost or stolen card, and requests letter of confirmation. Notifies Authorizer immediately to prevent fraudulent use of missing card. Orders replacement card for customer when confirming letter is received. (10%)

5. Records charge cards which have inadvertantly been left in sales departments and returns them to customer: Stamps imprint of card on sheet of paper, using Imprinting Device. Dates sheet and retains for own records. Fills out form, posting data such as customer's name and address and date card was returned, and submits to Authorizer.

EXHIBIT 4–2 *(concluded)*

Makes impression of card on face of envelope, inserts card in envelope, and mails to customer. (5%)

6. Sorts and records new credit applications daily: Separates regular Charge Account applications from Budget Accounts. Breaks down Charge Account applications into local and out-of-town applications and arranges applications alphabetically within groups. Counts number of applications in each group and records in Daily Record Book. Binds each group of applications with rubber band, and transmits to Tabulating Room. (10%)

7. Prepares requisitions and stores supplies: Copies amounts of supplies requested by Credit Department personnel onto requisition forms. Submits forms to Purchasing Officer or Supply Room. Receives supplies and places them on shelves in department store storeroom. (10%)

16. Definition of Terms

    Stale Date Checks — More than 30 days old

17. General Comments

18. Analyst A. Yessarian   Date 7/25/77 Editor M. Major   Date 7/26/77

    Reviewed By John Milton   Title, Org. Credit Manager

    National Office Reviewer W. Irving

EXHIBIT 4–3
Sample job description

Secretary IV

Distinguishing characteristics of work

This is varied and highly responsible secretarial and administrative work as the assistant to a high-level administrator, an agency head, academic dean, major department head, or senior attorney.

An employee in a position allocated to this class performs a variety of secretarial, clerical, and administrative duties requring an extensive working knowledge of the organization and program under the supervisor's jurisdiction. Work involves performing functions that are varied in subject matter and level of difficulty and range from performance of standardized clerical assignments to performance of administrative duties which would otherwise require the administrator's personal attention. Work also includes relieving the supervisor of administrative detail and office management functions.

Work is performed under general supervision, and only assigned projects which are highly technical or confidential are given close attention by the supervisor.

Examples of work performed

(Note: These examples are intended only as illustrations of the various types of work performed in positions allocated to this class. The omission of specific statements of duties does not exclude them from the position if the work is similar, related, or a logical assignment to the position.)

Takes and transcribes dictation or transcribes from dictating equipment subject matter that may vary from simple correspondence to legal, medical, engineering, or other technical subject matter.

Serves as personal assistant to a high-level administrative official by planning, initiating, and carrying to completion clerical, secretarial, and administrative activities.

Develops material for supervisor's use in public speaking engagements.

Attends conferences to take notes, or is briefed on meetings immediately after they take place in order to know what amendments were made and what developments have occurred in matters that concern the supervisor.

Makes arrangements for conferences, including space, time, and place; informs participants of topics to be discussed; and may provide them with background information.

Assists in and coordinates the preparation of operating and legislative budgets; examines budget documents to ensure that they comply with state regulations.

Receives and routes telephone calls, answering questions which may involve the interpretation of policies and procedures.

Serves as office receptionist; greets, announces, and routes visitors.

Performs related work as required.

ducting a job analysis and for preparing the job analysis schedule, given in the USTES *Handbook for Analyzing Jobs*, will not be discussed here.

Job descriptions and specifications

Information furnished through job analysis is written into the record in the form of job descriptions and job specifications. A *job description* describes what the job is, what the specific duties and responsibilities are, and what general work conditions are involved. It frequently states where the job is performed and how the duties are carried out. A *job specification* describes the type of person best suited to fill the position in terms of education, skills, experience, and other personal characteristics. In other words, the job description sets forth duties; the job specification translates those duties into the qualifications necessary to perform them. Exhibit 4–3 is a sample job description; Exhibit 4–4 is a sample job specification.

It is important to be realistic in setting job specifications. Although we may feel that every job in the organization requires a "superman," if we fill a lower level job offering no chance for ad-

EXHIBIT 4–4
Sample job specification

Secretary IV

Minimum training and experience

Graduation from a standard high school and three years of secretarial and/or clerical experience.

Successfully completed studies beyond the high school level may be substituted for the required experience at a rate of 720 classroom hours or 30 semester hours per year.

Possession of Certified Professional Secretary Certificate may be substituted for the required experience.

An equivalency diploma issued by a state department of education or by the U.S. Armed Forces Institute, or a qualifying score on the Division of Personnel Educational Attainment Comparison Test may be substituted for high school graduation.

Necessary special requirements

Ability to type at a rate of 35 correct words a minute.

Ability to take and transcribe dictation at the rate of 80 words a minute is required for designated positions allocated to this class.

---

vancement with an overqualified person, it will be a waste of time and money. The employee will probably become dissatisfied and quit. Therefore, educational and experience requirements should be carefully matched to the job.

RECRUITING QUALIFIED CANDIDATES

Recruitment involves identifying and attracting candidates for current and future jobs. It is a process of developing and maintaining adequate sources for filling human resource needs. The greater the number and variety of sources of personnel, the greater the chance of finding the right individual for the job. Recruitment may be relatively simple, as when the small retail store finds someone to "help out" during the busy season. In a large firm, on the other hand, recruitment may be a complex and expensive activity involving promotions from within as well as advertising, placing orders with employment offices, visiting schools and colleges, attending professional meetings, and conducting research to evaluate these sources and activities.

Since candidates for a given job can only come by movement within the organization or by recruitment from outside, every business faces these questions: When, and to what extent, do we fill our vacancies from within? When do we go outside?

Internal sources

Even if an organization wanted to fill every vacant job with an employee hired from outside, it must rely upon internal sources for filling a number of its jobs. Although many jobs are similar from one organization to another, some jobs require specialized knowledge that can be obtained only within a particular firm. For example, a firm's secret chemical process or solid-state technology may require the use of certain employees who are experienced in that process or technology. Therefore, the realities of the staffing process may require firms to select from within.

Promoting from within is a widely accepted and long-established policy in most organizations. In some companies, such a policy is set forth in the collective bargaining agreement negotiated with a labor union.

Several reasons have been given for filling a job from within whenever possible. The justifications for this policy include the following:

1. It results in better qualified employees. We are in a better position to assess the skills of an employee who has been performing satisfactorily over a period of years, than those of a person who is brought in from the outside.
2. It lowers costs. It is usually less costly to transfer or promote an employee (even one who needs additional training) than to lure away an outsider from his or her present employer. In addition, the recruitment and selection process is simplified if there are only a few entry jobs and if the education and skill requirements for these are lower.
3. It serves as a motivator. The employee who feels that he or she can get ahead by working harder is more likely to strive to succeed.

There are three basic methods of filling job vacancies internally: transferring an employee from a similar job somewhere else in the company; promoting an employee from a lower level job; and upgrading the employee now holding the job. The last method is accomplished by increasing the educational or skill level of the employee.

We should keep in mind, however, that an exclusive promotion-from-within policy can create "inbreeding" and prevent the infusion of new ideas and knowledge. A policy of recruiting from within also assumes, perhaps mistakenly, that the persons in the firm have the aptitudes, interest, and potential for moving ahead.

External sources

If necessary talents cannot be found within the firm, we must look for outside candidates. Some firms look for "new blood" outside their own organization in order to keep the human resource system from growing stagnant. Other firms have found it cheaper and quicker to hire highly trained specialists and professionals rather than to train and develop their own employees.

The particular sources and means by which workers are recruited vary widely, depending upon the types of jobs involved, the local labor market, and economic conditions. For example, during a business boom, when labor is scarce, more aggressive recruiting techniques may be required than those used during periods of high unemployment when "walk-in" applicants are likely to satisfy the bulk of a firm's human resource needs.

Effective hiring requires having a large enough number of applicants from among which to select the most suitable recruits. Depending on the job, the number of applicants might range from 3 to 4 for routine clerical and production jobs to 15 or more for management positions.

Among the sources of recruits are:

1. *Present employees.* Whenever possible, present employees should hear about vacancies first. If they are good workers, their recommendations may provide excellent applicants. This is probably the most fruitful source of job applicants for the smaller firm.
2. *Former employees.* Past employees are often acceptable if they left for good reason and under good circumstances. They may also be able to refer the manager to qualified friends.
3. *"Walk-in" applicants.* In a loose labor market there may be a substantial number of qualified applicants in this category.
4. *State employment agencies.* Branch offices of state agencies affiliated with the U.S. Employment Service are located throughout each state. Without charge, these agencies attempt

to place applicants on the basis of education, experience, and extensive testing.

5. *Private employment agencies.* A reliable private agency can be quite useful in locating applicants. Since most such agencies will do initial screening, it is important to supply them with details about the available jobs.

6. *Newspapers and trade magazines.* Advertising in local newspapers is perhaps the most common method of recruitment, especially for production, clerical, and sales personnel. Trade magazines and nationally circulated newspapers, such as the *Wall Street Journal,* are widely used for obtaining technical, managerial, and professional employees.

7. *Schools.* Trade schools, business schools, and universities often maintain a placement service for their students and alumni. Even if an educational institution lacks such a service, teachers are often interested in helping their graduating students get good jobs.

8. *Trade and professional associations.* These and other local organizations often have a placement service. For example, the local sales executives association might be able to help a firm find a qualified sales manager.

9. *Other sources.* Customers and suppliers are in a position to recommend specialized personnel. In some industries, such as the building trades, the hiring hall of the local union has taken over the responsibility of supplying the employer with certain personnel. In addition, the employment of handicapped, ex-convicts, and older workers should be given careful consideration. If properly matched to jobs, such recruits are capable of reliable and superior performance. For information on hiring handicapped workers you can contact your state vocational rehabilitation office.

A growing recent practice of larger corporations and public agencies has been to hire college students during the summer as interns. This allows such organizations to get some work done during the summer while exposing their full-time staff to potential employees. Many of the interns serve as ambassadors back on campus who "spread the word" about career opportunities with the organization. Equally important, the organizations can carefully evaluate the capabilities of the interns as future permanent employees on the basis of actual performance, thus improving their selection judgment.

SELECTING HUMAN RESOURCES

Managers have always been concerned with the problem of selecting "winners" from available candidates. Bypassing a promising prospect or hiring someone who later does not measure up to requirements can be very costly. Further complicating the manager's job of selecting the "right" candidate are the legal and administrative constraints that have come into existence in the past decade.

Every decision to select an individual for employment or promotion suggests a prediction that the candidate will succeed if placed on the job. Selection, therefore, may be viewed as a process of making predictions by matching differences in people to differences in job requirements. The basic objective of human resource selection is to obtain employees who are most likely to meet desirable standards of performance. This holds true regardless of whether the selection process is used to hire new employees for entry-level jobs, to transfer current employees, to assign employees to specialized training programs, to promote employees to higher level jobs, or to hire highly skilled technicians or managers.

Decisions on staffing policy are primarily a function of line management, as are selection and placement decisions. However, the human resource staff department has the responsibility for improving these decisions through competent professional assistance and recommendations. For example, test construction, evaluation, and interpretation are not within the expertise of line managers. Expertise in these areas requires professional training and experience which are usually furnished by the human resource staff department (or by an outside consultant working with the staff department.)

Factors in selection decisions

All organizations make selection decisions. In a smaller business, selection is likely to be done on a rather informal basis. In a large firm, selection may be a very costly, formalized procedure. Regardless of its size, an organization should consider a number of factors when making decisions regarding the selection of human resources.

The selection process is likely to vary according to the type of position to be filled. For example, technical and professional applicants will probably undergo more thorough evaluation to verify their competence than will unskilled laborers. If a firm is new, its approach to staffing is likely to be less structured than that of a well-established firm.

Social pressures frequently play a part in selection decisions. For example, boycotts by minority groups have forced some businesses to disregard their traditional selection policies in an effort to hire more employees in these groups. In a union shop, seniority may be the basic criterion for selecting employees for some jobs, whereas in a nonunion shop skills and abilities may be the sole criteria.

We must also keep in mind that the staffing process in general, and selection in particular, must be tailored to fit the needs of the given organization. This means that consideration must be given to such things as the level and complexity of the job, the organizational costs if the selected employee fails on the job, the length of the required training period, and the cost of the "ideal" selection process. For example, some firms follow the practice of intentionally overhiring with the intent of "weeding out" poor performers during a probationary period. This practice tends to be costly for many reasons, including the expense of turnover and training. To illustrate, one large bank calculated its cost of replacing one teller as follows:

Recruiting	$ 40
Selection (three hours)	30
Medical examination	25
Reference check	15
Training time (one week)	180
Not fully productive for one month (one fourth of monthly salary)	180
Clerical and payroll costs	55
Indirect training costs	140
	$665

We shall also see in this chapter that some traditional selection techniques have been ruled discriminatory. A growing number of court cases have made it clear that any non-job-related employment practice is illegal if such a practice has an adverse impact on minority group members, women, or persons aged 40 to 65. The high legal costs involved in defending company selection practices, plus lack of expertise in validating "job relatedness," have caused some companies to simply discontinue the use of certain selection tools such as tests.

The selection process

As we have suggested, the selection process may vary from a five-minute interview to a highly involved series of evaluations over an extended period of time. In a more complete program, the selection process is based upon careful job analysis, comprehensive human resource planning, and effective recruitment. The steps most likely included in the actual selection process include:

1. Preliminary screening of applicants.
2. Review of application forms.
3. Employment testing.
4. Reference checks.
5. Employment interviews.
6. Physical examinations.

The sequence in which these six steps are applied may vary. You should also keep in mind that each of these steps is a tool or method for collecting information on which to judge whether or not the applicant is qualified for a specific job (see Exhibit 4–5).

Preliminary screening. This initial screening is intended to eliminate obvious misfits in order to reduce the time and cost of actual selection. For example, all applicants might be given a ten-minute screening interview to determine whether they have the necessary education, training, interest, and experience for the job. The interviewer might tell the applicant about the nature of the job opening and minimum requirements.

The preliminary screening is an important step in the selection process since it results in a pass-fail decision. This means that a potentially qualified applicant could get screened out at this point if the initial requirements are improper or if the interviewer is not qualified. The firm should therefore set specific and minimum standards for rejection which can be accurately determined in a brief interview (for example, job requires a college degree in physics).

If the requirements of the company and the qualifications and interests of the applicant appear to match in the initial screening, the individual would be given a more detailed interview. In most cases the applicant would be asked to complete an application form and then move on to another step in the selection process.

Review of application forms. Next to the interview, the application is the most commonly used selection tool. Typically, the application form gathers information about the education, experience, and personal characteristics of the applicant, as illustrated in Exhibit 4–6. Different forms may be used for different kinds of jobs. One form may be used for hourly employees, another for managerial and professional employees, and still another for sales and clerical personnel. Some firms use a short form when an applicant applies for a job with no immediate vacancy and a long form when the applicant will be considered for a current job opening.

EXHIBIT 4–5
The selection process

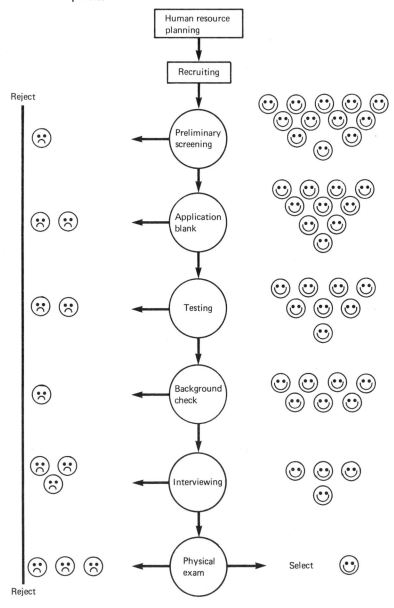

EXHIBIT 4–6
Sample application form

SEARS, ROEBUCK AND CO.

APPLICATION FOR EMPLOYMENT

PLEASE PRINT INFORMATION REQUESTED IN INK.

Date _____

SEARS IS AN EQUAL OPPORTUNITY EMPLOYER and fully subscribes to the principles of Equal Employment Opportunity. Sears has adopted an Affirmative Action Program to ensure that all applicants and employes are considered for hire, promotion and job status, without regard to race, color, religion, national origin, age or sex.

To protect the interests of all concerned, applicants for certain job assignments must pass a physical examination before they are hired. Alternative placement of an applicant who does not meet the physical standards of the job for which he/she was originally considered is permitted.

NOTE: This application will be considered active for 90 days. If you have not been employed within this period and are still interested in employment at Sears, please contact the office where you applied and request that your application be reactivated.

Name _____ Social Security Number _____
     Last   First   Middle   (Please present your Social Security Card for review.)

Address _____
     Number   Street   City   State   Zip Code

County _____   Current phone or nearest phone _____

Previous Address _____
     Number   Street   City   State   Zip Code

If hired, can you furnish proof of age? ☐ YES ☐ NO

U.S. Citizen ☐ YES ☐ NO   or Resident Alien ☐ YES ☐ NO

(Answer only if position for which you are applying requires driving.)
Licensed to drive car?   ☐ YES   ☐ NO
Is license valid in this state?   ☐ YES   ☐ NO

Have you ever been employed by Sears? ☐ YES ☐ NO   If so, when and where last employed? _____ Position _____

Have you a relative in the employ of Sears in the store or unit to which you are applying? _____

A PHYSICAL DISABILITY OR HANDICAP WILL NOT CAUSE REJECTION IF IN SEARS MEDICAL OPINION YOU ARE ABLE TO SATISFACTORILY PERFORM IN THE POSITION FOR WHICH YOU ARE BEING CONSIDERED.

Do you have any physical condition which may limit your ability to perform the job applied for? If so, please give details. _____

EDUCATION	School Attended	No. of Years	Name of School	City/State	Grad-uate?	Course or College Major	Average Grades
	Grammar						
	Jr. High						
	Sr. High						
	Other						
	College					Degree	

MILITARY SERVICE	BRANCH OF SERVICE	DATE ENTERED SERVICE	DATE OF DISCHARGE	SERVICE RELATED DISABILITY	HIGHEST RANK HELD	SERVICE-RELATED SKILLS AND EXPERIENCE APPLICABLE TO CIVILIAN EMPLOYMENT
				YES ☐ NO ☐		

What experience or training have you had other than your work experience, military service and education? (Community activities, hobbies, etc.)

I am interested in the type of work I have checked

Sales _____ Office _____ Mechanical _____ Warehouse _____ Other (Specify) _____

Or

The following specific Job: _____

I am seeking ☐ temporary ☐ permanent employment   I am available for ☐ Part time ☐ Full time work   If part time, indicate maximum hours per week _____

Have you been convicted during the past seven years of a serious crime involving a person's life or property?

NO ☐   YES ☐   If yes, explain. _____

HOURS AVAILABLE FOR WORK	
Sun.	To
Mon.	To
Tues.	To
Wed.	To
Thurs.	To
Fri.	To
Sat.	To

10534 REV. 5-77   (SEE REVERSE SIDE)

EXHIBIT 4-6 *(continued)*

REFERENCES

LIST BELOW YOUR FOUR MOST RECENT EMPLOYERS, BEGINNING WITH THE CURRENT OR MOST RECENT ONE. IF YOU HAVE HAD LESS THAN FOUR EMPLOYERS, USE THE REMAINING SPACES FOR PERSONAL REFERENCES. IF YOU WERE EMPLOYED UNDER A MAIDEN OR OTHER NAME. PLEASE ENTER THAT NAME IN THE RIGHT HAND MARGIN. IF APPLICABLE. ENTER SERVICE IN THE ARMED FORCES ON THE REVERSE SIDE

NAMES AND ADDRESSES OF FORMER EMPLOYERS. BEGINNING WITH THE CURRENT OR MOST RECENT	Nature of Employer's Business	Name of your Supervisor	What kind of work did you do?	Starting Date	Starting Pay	Date of Leaving	Pay at Leaving	Why did you leave? Give details
1				Month		Month		
Name								
Address	Tel. No			Year	Per Week	Year	Per Week	
City State Zip Code								
NOTE State reason for and length of inactivity between present application date and last employer								
2				Month		Month		
Name								
Address	Tel. No			Year	Per Week	Year	Per Week	
City State Zip Code								
NOTE State reason for and length of inactivity between last employer and second last employer								
3				Month		Month		
Name								
Address	Tel. No			Year	Per Week	Year	Per Week	
City State Zip Code								
NOTE State reason for and length of inactivity between second last employer and third last employer								
4				Month		Month		
Name								
Address	Tel. No			Year	Per Week	Year	Per Week	
City State Zip Code								
NOTE State reason for and length of inactivity between third last employer and fourth last employer								

I certify that the information contained in this application is correct to the best of my knowledge and understand that any misstatement or omission of information is grounds for dismissal in accordance with Sears, Roebuck and Co. policy. I authorize the references listed above to give you any and all information concerning my previous employment and any pertinent information they may have, personal or otherwise, and release all parties from all liability for any damage that may result from furnishing same to you. In consideration of my employment, I agree to conform to the rules and regulations of Sears, Roebuck and Co. and my compensation can be terminated with or without notice, at any time, at the option of either the Company or myself. I understand that no unit manager or representative of Sears, Roebuck and Co. other than the President or Vice-President of the Company, has any authority to enter into any agreement for employment for any specified period of time, or to make any agreement contrary to the foregoing. In some states, the law requires that Sears have my written permission before obtaining consumer reports on me, and I hereby authorize Sears to obtain such reports.

Applicant's Signature _____

NOT TO BE FILLED OUT BY APPLICANT

		Tested		(Store will enter dates as required.)	Mailed	Completed
Date of Emp.		Physical examination scheduled for		REFERENCE REQUESTS		
Dept. or Div.	Regular ☐ Part-Time ☐	Physical examination form completed		CONSUMER REPORT		
Job Title				With. Tax (W-4)		
Job Title Code	Job Grade	Review Card prepared	Minor's Work Permit	State With. Tax		
Compensation Arrangement		Timecard prepared	Proof of Birth			
Manager Approving			Training Material Given to Employe			
Employe No.	Rack No.	Unit Name and Number				

INTERVIEWER'S COMMENTS		
Prospect for	1.	
	2.	

Application forms should be tailor-made for a specific firm, and the content of the forms should vary as necessary to cover special job requirements. For low-level jobs where the applicant is likely to have little education and cultural attainment, the form should reflect this in its overall appearance, wording, and instructions. Items referring to race, religion, or national origin should not appear on the application form.

In recent years a growing number of organizations have attempted to determine the validity of their application blank by trying to correlate each item on the form with actual job success. In so doing, a firm may find that some items predict success better than others. These items may then be given more weight than others in selecting employees. To illustrate, a company may find that its successful engineers ranked average in their graduating class and had been active in student organizations. These factors can then be given a definite statistical score when evaluating an application. Since it will take considerable time and effort to develop a *weighted application form,* we would want to develop one only for those jobs which require considerable hiring.

Recent studies have shown weighted application forms to be useful in predicting such diverse factors as creativity and mechanical ingenuity, scientific and engineering performance, and turnover of factory workers.[1] Attempts have been made to market "standard" weighted application forms for use in any company. Research has indicated, however, that ordinary aptitude tests can generally produce better results for less cost.[2]

Employment testing.   Employment tests are usually administered after a preliminary interview has been conducted and the application blank has been examined. Tests have been developed in an effort to find more objective ways of measuring the qualifications of job applicants, as well as for use with employees being considered for transfer or promotion. A properly developed and administered testing program can provide a more objective way of judging job applicants and improve the accuracy of the selection process. Some of the more commonly used tests include the following.

1.   *Performance or achievement tests*—measure how much the job seeker already knows about the job or how well he or she is able to do the job. For example, prospective typists may be asked to type a page or a widget machine operator may be asked questions about the equipment.

2.   *Intelligence tests*—measure the individual's capacity or overall ability to learn. Although such tests have been proven valid

for certain high-level jobs, they have often been misused to screen applicants for jobs that should be measured with performance or aptitude tests. For example, the reasoning factor in the Wonderlic or the Otis tests is not very predictive of ability to be a file clerk. Certain tests (aptitude) of perceptual speed, however, are effective in selecting file clerks.

3. *Aptitude tests*—measure ability to learn specific jobs. These tests may be multi-aptitude or special aptitude. *Multi-aptitude* tests measure a number of traits. For example, the three-hour Differential Aptitude Test is a series of eight tests covering clerical speed, verbal reasoning, abstract reasoning, mechanical reasoning, numerical ability, space relations, spelling, and sentences. *Special* aptitude tests measure specific patterns of abilities necessary to perform certain jobs. For example, mechanical aptitude tests, such as the SRA Mechanical Aptitude, are useful in selecting apprentices for skilled mechanical trades.

4. *Interest tests*—measure the applicant's interest. Although the test results may indicate whether a person likes a particular job, the results are not necessarily related to job success. Therefore, interest tests are primarily used in job or vocational counseling. Examples of interest tests are the Kuder Preference Record and the Strong Vocational Interest Blank.

5. *Personality tests*—attempt to determine how an individual will relate to interpersonal and situational stress. Personality tests are far behind the other types of tests in terms of demonstrated usefulness for selection and placement in industry. Severe criticism of these tests strongly suggests that much more research is needed before they become useful in the selection process. At any rate they should only be administered by a competent psychologist.

Civil rights issues have had a major impact on the use of employment tests. Conflicting rules and guidelines coming from court decisions and federal agencies have confused managers as to what is legal and proper with regard to employment testing. Consequently, a growing number of organizations have dropped their testing programs. A Bureau of National Affairs survey found that 90 percent of the respondents were using tests in 1963, whereas only 55 percent were using them in 1971. Similarly, a 1975 survey conducted by the American Society for Personnel Administration revealed that most firms were confused about their testing responsibilities according to federal guidelines. As a result, over 36 percent said that they did not test at all and most of the others had reduced their testing in the preceding few years.

Recent court decisions have put the burden of proof on the company to show that its tests are predictive of job success. For example, in the case of *Myart* v. *Motorola* a black worker was denied a job because of his low score on an intelligence test. The company was told that it could use the test *if* it could show that the test predicted job success. This is difficult to do since studies have shown that certain tests may not be equally predictive of job success in white and black workers.[3] Test specialists can compute the validity (the extent to which a test is a good indicator or predictor of success in a given job) of a selection instrument in several ways. One way is to find a common factor in the performance of presently successful employees and then to designate it as a predictor. This is known as *concurrent validity*. Another way, called *predictive validity*, is to give tests during the hiring process and then, when the successful employees are identified, to correlate the test or test measures with the successful and unsuccessful employees. A third method, which is more commonly used when the number of persons in similar jobs is very small, is called *synthetic validity*. According to this method, elements of several similar jobs rather than the whole job are used to validate the test.[4]

Opponents of testing claim that tests may discriminate against minorities, are given too much weight in selection decisions, and are often unrelated to job success. On the other hand, if tests are properly developed, administered, and used in conjunction with other selection tools, they can be an important component of the selection process. The reader desiring to learn more about testing is urged to consult the reading materials on testing listed in the bibliography of this chapter. In general, the manager should follow certain guidelines on the effective use of tests, such as:

1. Do not make tests the sole tool for selecting applicants.
2. Use the right tests for the job for which you are hiring.
3. Be sure that a test measures what you want to measure.
4. Try a test on present employees before adopting it.
5. Seek the advice of competent consultants in test selection.

Reference checks.   There is a good deal of variation among firms in the types of references requested, methods of verifying references, and the consistency with which references and applicant data are checked. Although little research has been done on this subject, it appears that most firms have found it useful to learn how the applicant performed on previous jobs.[5] Phoning or interviewing the applicant's past supervisors can be a helpful source of information. Probing is often required since people are very cautious about what they say regarding past employees.

In addition to verifying the accuracy of what the applicant has said in the application form or in an interview, a reference check may disclose further information about the applicant. When conducting a reference check, it is wise to be on the watch for incorrect dates of employment, claims of a higher level of responsibility than that actually held, inflated salary figures, and falsified information about experience or education. Since studies reveal that 90 percent of past employers or supervisors comment favorably when asked to rate a previous employee, there is some doubt as to how much weight should be placed on such ratings. Whenever possible, objective data should be sought, including such information as grades shown in school transcripts and data recorded on personnel records.

Some firms use outside organizations, such as commercial credit-rating companies, to provide information on an individual's work history, character, and financial condition. Such reports are now governed by the Fair Credit Reporting Act, and the applicant must be notified in writing that such information is being sought.

Employment interviews. The employment interview remains the most widely used and the most important tool in the selection process. An effective interview enables the interviewer to learn more about the job applicant's background, interests, and values; it also gives the applicant an opportunity to find out more about the job and the organization.

The different techniques of conducting interviews have been classified in many ways. For example, we might consider an employment interview to be structured, unstructured, or a combination of the two. Although studies have found the structured interview to be more reliable, no single technique or approach is appropriate in all cases.[6] The type of information desired suggests the approach to use.

In the structured interview, we determine in advance the questions and their sequence, based upon the job description and specifications. A form is generally used, whereby we go down a list of questions and record the applicant's replies. Exhibit 4–7 is an illustration of a structured interview guide.

In the unstructured, or nondirective, interview, we have a general topic to discuss and follow no preplanned strategy. The objective is to get the applicants to do the talking, and they have considerable leeway in determining the direction of the discussion and in emphasizing what they feel is important. An unstructured interview might include such questions as "Tell me about yourself" or "What are your career plans?"

Although the interview is almost universally used as a selection

EXHIBIT 4–7
Structured interview guide (sample questions)

Work experience

What is your previous work experience?
What were your duties in your previous jobs?
Why did you leave your previous place of employment?
What kinds of work do you like best? Least?
Why do you want to work for this company?

Education

What is the highest level of education you achieved?
What were your best subjects? What subjects did you do less well?
Have you considered further schooling?
Any special achievements in school?

Career plans

What are your salary requirements?
What are you looking for in a job?
What can you contribute to this company in the way of abilities and experience?
What kind of work would you like to be doing in five years? In ten years?

---

tool, interviewing is an art—not a science. This means that poorly trained interviewers can, and will, make errors. A common mistake is the tendency to stereotype people (for example, "Southerners are slow workers"; "Farm workers are dull"; "Physically handicapped people are unreliable"). Another mistake is to phrase questions in a way that results in unreliable answers (for example, "You do like sales work, don't you?"). On the other hand, research has shown that trained interviewers using sound procedures can and do achieve good results. Managers desiring to improve their interviewing skills will want to read one or more of the many books dealing with employment interviewing. In general, you can improve the quality of your interviewing by observing such principles of interviewing as the following:

1. Formulate the objective of the interview and the questions to be asked before seeing the applicant.
2. Conduct the interview in private, and put the applicant at ease with a few general remarks about the business and the job.
3. Encourage the applicant to talk by asking pertinent questions and listening attentively to the answers.
4. Avoid any suggestion of discrimination. That is, avoid the topics of race, religion, national origin, and political views.
5. Retain control of the interview. Don't be dominant, but keep the interview headed toward the objective.

6. Allow plenty of time, but don't waste it.
7. Record the facts obtained in the interview while they are fresh.

Except when interviewing for the lowest level jobs, it is a good practice, whenever possible, to have the applicant interviewed by at least two persons, preferably on different days. The applicant's prospective supervisor should definitely be one of the interviewers.

Physical examinations. In most firms, the final step in the selection process is a physical examination. Such examinations have not been shown to be highly reliable predictors of future medical problems. However, they are valuable in screening out applicants whose physical qualifications are inadequate to meet the requirements of the job they are being considered for.

Physical examinations are also used to record physical and health problems at the time of hiring in order to protect the firm against unwarranted workers' compensation claims. In a more positive light, progressive companies use physical examinations in an attempt to place persons who are employable but whose physical handicaps require assignment to certain jobs only.

Assessment centers

A relatively new method used for selecting managerial talent is the assessment center. AT&T has formally assessed over 75,000 employees, and numerous other firms, such as IBM, J. C. Penney, General Electric, Standard Oil of New Jersey, and Sears, have established assessment centers. Smaller firms have had some success in utilizing such centers through consultants who provide the service on a fee basis. The use of assessment centers in managerial selection has been described by many writers, including Byham, and Tinkle and Jones.[7]

Assessment centers typically process candidates in groups of 10 to 15, exposing each group to various exercises for one to four days. These exercises may include such standard selection tools as interviews and tests. However, the assessment center takes a "broadband" approach whereby candidates are observed in many settings, including management games and in-basket and problem-solving exercises. Meanwhile, experienced managers observe and note the behavior of each candidate and the patterns of interpersonal relations that develop. Candidates are selected on the basis of the evaluations of these managers.

Studies to date support the assessment center procedure as the most effective and valid method of managerial selection.[8] The most important limitation of the procedure is the high cost.

Evaluation of the selection process

There is little justification for making outlays in selecting human resources without determining how effective the selection process is. However, it is difficult to develop adequate yardsticks by which the selection process can be measured. A decision to select a candidate is based on expected performance as suggested by the various tools used in the selection process. In a sense, then, if these expectations hold true when the candidate is placed in the job, we could conclude that the selection program is valid and effective. It is difficult, however, to isolate all of the other conditions which might be influencing the job performance.

To illustrate, a company inaugurated a new testing program as part of the selection process for new salespeople. In a follow-up study it was found that all of the sales people selected during the first year of the new program had more total sales during their first year than new salespeople had had in earlier years. It was also discovered that turnover among the newly hired salespeople was lower than that of newly hired salespeople in earlier years. The temptation was to immediately attribute these results to the new testing program. However, someone pointed out that sales for all sales personnel had been considerably higher that year. Moreover, that year the firm had recruited from different schools. In addition, the job market was considerably softer for sales people in the industry.

Despite the difficulty in providing proper yardsticks, every firm should make systematic efforts to evaluate the effectiveness of its selection process. Periodic audits, research, and other evaluation techniques are as essential for human resource programs as they are for programs in marketing, production, or any other function. Such evaluation techniques should be directed toward answering this fundamental question, Is the selection process providing the type and quality of human resources specified in human resource plans?

As previously suggested, a key yardstick in our evaluation will be the job performance of newly hired employees. The important indicators will include performance appraisals and results, such as supervisory ratings, attendance records, productivity rates, and length of service. We can then compare these indicators of job success with the predictions recorded at the time of selection. Although comprehensive evaluation procedures are beyond the scope of this book, we can suggest several areas and questions that should be covered in a systematic evaluation of the selection process:

1. Have well-defined selection policies been developed? Are they consistent with public policy?

2. Why are we using the employment standards we have? How are they related to actual performance on the job?
3. Do we maintain accurate records of why each candidate was rejected? ("Not qualified" is not sufficient.) What percentage of those who apply are hired?
4. What contribution does each of the steps in the selection process (interviewing, testing, reference checks, and so on) make to the overall program?
5. How much does each of the steps and tools in the selection process cost?
6. Have these selection tools been properly validated?
7. What percentage of the newly hired is discharged during the probationary period?
8. Is there a correlation between degree of success on the job and the predictions made at the time of selection?
9. Is there an exit interview to help measure how well we are matching people and jobs?

LEGAL INFLUENCES ON THE STAFFING PROCESS

The staffing process is subject to legal scrutiny from several directions. Major legal influences stem from federal, state, and local laws prohibiting employment discrimination because of race, sex, or age. Other legal influences result from privacy rights as protected under consumer credit laws. It should be noted at the outset that the law is more than the words stated in legislation; it also includes how the courts interpret those words, and such interpretation is constantly evolving. The decisions of lower courts, for example, have been reversed by higher courts.

A striking example of court reversal is the *Griggs* v. *Duke Power Company* case. The federal district court and the Fourth Circuit Court of Appeals both upheld the Duke Power Company's position. The U.S. Supreme Court then reversed the lower courts by a vote of 8 to 0. The implication of the Supreme Court decision in this case is that if any employment practice eliminates a higher percentage of minority applicants, or women, or any other group protected by the law, the burden of proof is on the employer to show that the practice is job-related and predicts job performance.

Affirmative action programs

Title VII of the Civil Rights Act is enforced by the Equal Employment Opportunity Commission (EEOC). At first the courts required strict proof of discrimination in hiring practices before ruling against an employer. It had to be shown, for example, that a qualified minority worker did in fact seek a job and that a less qualified white was hired instead. Now the courts are looking to results rather than to the methods by which employees are hired. If a company located in an area with a substantial minority population has a small number of minority employees, the EEOC may inquire into the company's selection process, and the result may well be that the firm will have to take remedial action to ensure the reduction of "inequality." The focus has also shifted from hiring women and minorities at lower level jobs to increasing the proportionate representation of women and minorities at all levels, including management. Remedial action may be costly. In one case, nine steel companies and the steelworkers' union had to give an estimated $31 million in back pay to 45,000 minority and female workers who were determined to have suffered loss of income because of company-union promotion policies that restricted them to lower-paying jobs.

The Office of Federal Contract Compliance is responsible for seeing that employers who receive federal government contracts file an affirmative action plan. If an employer does not have an approved plan, OFCC can institute proceedings to cancel the contract. The employer's plan must have specific steps and timetables to remedy "underutilization" of females and minorities in each job classification.

Meeting the challenge of equal employment opportunities

It is apparent from the above that recent laws, regulations, and court decisions have had a significant impact on the entire staffing process. Equal employment opportunity is now the law of the land. At the same time, as we have seen, it is not always clear when a firm is operating within the law. As a result, a growing number of firms are employing EEO specialists who have an in-depth knowledge of EEO requirements and who keep abreast of court decisions relating to the various EEO laws and regulations. Other firms turn to outside consultants for assistance in operating within the law.

Many of the lower court decisions still have to be resolved by the U.S. Supreme Court. Meanwhile, it is important that the firm develop a positive approach toward an EEO program. Such a program must be viewed as an important and integral part of the firm's total human resource system and not "just another personnel department program." The types of questions management might ask regarding its selection requirements and procedures are presented below from the official handbook of the American Society for Personnel Administration.

Are all job requirements based upon a careful analysis of the job? Are the job descriptions and job requirements in writing? Are the job requirements job related? Could they be defended as such in court? Do the job requirements exceed those of a number of satisfactory incumbents in the job? If so, they can be challenged.

Are there questions on the application form which are not job related and which reject a higher percentage of minority applicants or women? Or which reject on the basis of age? Some of the questions which may be illegal in some states or challenged on a federal basis are: date of birth, age, sex, marital status, citizenship status, draft status, arrest record, number of dependent children, "own your own home," color of eyes and hair, friends or relatives working for the employer, garnishment record, height, weight, maiden name, Mr., Miss, or Mrs., spouse's name, spouse's work, widowed, divorced, or separated? If these items are needed for identification purposes they may be obtained for personnel records after the hire. If the items are not specifically forbidden by law, they may be left on the application, but if they are used in hiring and cause a differential rejection rate, then the burden will be on the employer to show that they are job related. In many cases the use of this data is based on flimsy reasoning which would not stand up in court.

Do you have clearly supportable evidence that interviewers have received training on federal and state law? Have clear instructions been issued to them on hiring? Are their final selection decisions based on clearly supportable job-related job requirements?

Are education requirements clearly supportable? Do you insist on a diploma or a degree when in fact a certain number of years of experience might suffice in lieu of the educational requirement? Are your college-degree requirements clearly job-related? Do your college-degree requirements exceed those of a number of successful incumbents? If so, they may be challenged.

Are your experience requirements reasonable? Are you inclined to favor persons with five years of experience in an area when two years would clearly suffice to make the person qualified?

Are your promotion procedures sufficiently well defined to avoid the possibility of even a semblance of discrimination? Is your procedure in writing? Is there more than one avenue through which a person may be considered? Are employees aware of the requirements for promotion? Can they get information on job openings as they occur? Is there a procedure for review of selection decisions for compliance with legal requirements?

Where performance is a factor in promotion, is the evaluation of performance systematized? Does the person know where he stands? Has he been apprised of the things he may need to do to prepare himself for advancement?

The overriding question in this review of selection procedures is, "Could I successfully defend this procedure in court?"[9]

SUMMARY

The objective of the staffing process is to locate and acquire the human resources necessary to fulfill organizational and human resource plans. We have seen that staffing is a process involving a flow of activities which results in continuously meeting the firm's human resource needs.

In order to staff an organization we must have a current job description and specification for every job in the firm. In fact, both job descriptions and job specifications provide basic information for all HR planning and later become necessary for selecting the right candidate for the right job. The information necessary for job descriptions and specifications is furnished through job analysis.

Candidates to fill job needs must come either by movement within the organization or by recruitment from the outside. Every firm faces the question "When and to what extent do we go outside?" In this chapter we have suggested some guidelines for answering that question. We have also examined several sources for recruiting.

An effective selection program is based upon careful job analysis, comprehensive human resource planning, effective recruitment, and a proven set of evaluation techniques. The actual selection process is likely to include several steps or tools which assist us in deciding whether or not the applicant is qualified for a specific job. The basic objective of the process is to obtain employees who are most likely to meet desirable standards of performance. The assessment center is a more recent method which is receiving growing attention in managerial selection.

A decision to select a candidate is based on expected performance as suggested by the selection process. It is vital, therefore, that we periodically evaluate this process to determine whether it is providing the types and quality of human resources specified in human resource needs plans. In view of recent federal antidiscrimination efforts, we must also examine our staffing program in general and our selection process in particular to see whether our efforts are consistent with public policy.

CASE: KMS INDUSTRIES

KMS Industries is a relatively small but rapidly growing firm with about 400 employees. It is a closely held firm, established about eight years ago by the current president. Although the company has been very profitable, turnover among employees has been a constant problem. In fact, the third person in the past two years to hold the position of sales manager has just submitted his resignation. In the past three years, 12 managers have either quit voluntarily or been asked to resign. Turnover among nonmanagerial employees is about 80 percent higher than the industry average.

Each year the personnel director hires about ten college graduates from universities located in a tri-state area. He has full authority to hire new graduates and will occasionally hire on the spot if an applicant appears to be really outstanding.

Most managerial and technical employees are recruited via employment agencies and advertisements in newspapers and trade publications. The selection tools include an application blank, a personality test, and interviews with the personnel director and with executives responsible for the area in which the applicant will be placed. Mr. Zim, the president, indicated that if the applicant had "shifty eyes" or generated "bad vibrations" during an interview, the company would take a careful look at the applicant and run a reference and credit check.

Mr. Zim made the following additional remarks about the selection of employees, "You don't have to spend a lot of time or money selecting people if you really know what it is you are looking for. I can usually tell in the first five minutes if the applicant is what KMS Industries needs. What we want are clean-cut nice-looking people who are willing to work hard and grow with the company. We don't want any longhair types, prima donnas, or people who are more concerned with our retirement benefits."

The executive vice president was calling a meeting of all top and middle managers to discuss the company's recruitment and selection process. He had just learned through the grapevine that two supervisors were planning to quit next week. He had also heard that a disgruntled female employee was bringing a sex discrimination charge against the company. She claimed that KMS Industries had hired a black male for a managerial job that she said she was qualified to do.

Mr. Murd, the personnel director, thought it might be a good idea to bring in an outside consultant to evaluate the entire KMS staffing process. He had had very little previous background in human resource management and was not entirely satisfied with the way things were going. He felt, for example, that there must be a better way of matching up the right person with the right job than the one KMS was using.

QUESTIONS AND PROBLEMS

1. Distinguish among a job, a job analysis, a job description, and a job specification.

2. Write a job description for a job with which you are familiar. On the basis of your job description, what minimum job specifications would be necessary?

3. For each of the following jobs, list the sources you would utilize to locate suitable candidates: (a) management trainee; (b) tool and die maker; (c) secretary; (d) manager, human resources.

4. "Promotion from within is a good policy, but it results in a stagnant organization." Discuss.

5. Give concrete examples and situations in which it would be advisable to alter the steps in the selection process as discussed in this chapter.

6. What is an employment test? Distinguish between a performance test and an aptitude test.

7. Opponents of testing claim that tests may discriminate against minorities and therefore should be abolished from the selection process. Do you agree? Explain.

8. What kinds of information can be adequately obtained through the employment interview? Suggest several ways in which you could increase your effectiveness as an interviewer.

9. What is an assessment center? How important is it as a selection tool?

10. Arrange to speak with the personnel director of a large company in your city. Discuss how the company evaluates its employee selection process.

11. In what ways does the external environment affect the staffing process in every firm?

12. In what ways have federal and state equal employment opportunity laws caused organizations to alter their human resource policies and practices?

BIBLIOGRAPHY

American Psychological Association. *Principles for the Validation and Use of Personnel Selection Procedures.* Washington, D.C.: APA, 1975.

Black, James M. *How to Get Results from Interviewing.* New York: McGraw-Hill Book Co., 1970.

Bureau of National Affairs, Inc. *Equal Employment Opportunity: Programs and Results.* Personnel Policies Forum Series No. 112, March 1976.

Buros, O. K. (ed.). *The Sixth Mental Measurements Yearbook.* Highland Park, N.J.: Gryphon Press, 1965.

Dunnette, Marvin D. *Personnel Selection and Placement.* Belmont, Calif.: Wadsworth Publishing Co., 1966.

England, George W. *Development and Use of Weighted Application Blanks.* Minneapolis: Industrial Relations Center, University of Minnesota, 1969.

Hawk, R. H. The Recruitment Function. New York: American Management Association, 1967.

Howard, A. "An Assessment of Assessment Centers." *Academy of Management Journal,* March 1974.

Howell, N. L. "Complying with the Fair Credit Reporting Act." *Personnel Administrator* January–February 1972.

Huck, J. R. "Assessment Centers: A Review of the External and Internal Validities." *Personnel Psychology,* Summer 1973, 191–212.

Kraut, A. I. "A Hard Look at Management Assessment Centers and Their Future." *Personnel Journal,* Summer 1972.

Lipsett, Laurence. "Selecting Personnel without Tests." *Personnel Journal,* 51 (1972), 648–654.

Lockwood, Howard C. "Equal Employment Opportunities." In *Staffing Policies and Strategies.* Washington, D.C.: Bureau of National Affairs, Inc., 1974.

Lopez, Felix M., Jr. *Personnel Interviewing.* New York: McGraw-Hill Book Co., 1965.

McCormick, E. J., and De Nise, A. S. "An Alternate Approach to Test Validation." *Personnel Administrator,* January 1976.

Miner, John B., and Miner, Mary Green. "The Logic of Selection." In *Personnel and Industrial Relations.* New York: Macmillan Publishing Co., 1977.

Ruck, Floyd. "The Impact on Employment Procedures of the Supreme Court Decision in the Duke Power case." *Personnel Journal* October 1971.

Sparks, C. Paul. "The Not So Uniform Employee Selection Guidelines." *Personnel Administrator,* February 1977.

Stone, C. Harold, and Puch, Floyd L. "Selection, Interviewing, and Testing." In *Staffing Policies and Strategies.* Washington, D.C.: Bureau of National Affairs, Inc., 1974.

Urban, Thomas F., and Desai, Harsha B. "Both Sides of the Turnover Problem." *Personnel Administrator,* March–April 1972.

U.S. Department of Labor, Manpower Administration. *Handbook for Analyzing Jobs.* Washington, D.C.: U.S. Government Printing Office, 1972.

Yoder, Dale, and Heneman, Herbert G. (eds.). "Staffing Policies and Strategies." In *ASPA Handbook of Personnel and Industrial Relations.* Washington, D.C.: Bureau of National Affairs, Inc., 1974.

NOTES

[1] E. Schaeffer and A. Anastasi, "A Biographical Inventory for Identifying Creativity in Adolescent Boys," *Journal of Applied Psychology,* February 1968; W. A. Owens, "Cognitive, Non-Cognitive, and Environmental Correlates of Mechanical Ingenuity," *Journal of Applied Psychology,* June 1969; and R. L. Ellison, L. R. James, and T. J. Carron, "Prediction of R & D Performance Criteria with Biographical Data," *Journal of Industrial Psychology,* March 1970.

[2] For a good discussion of application forms, see C. Harold Stone and Floyd L.

Puch, "Selection, Interviewing, and Testing," in *Staffing Policies and Strategies* (Washington, D.C.: Bureau of National Affairs, Inc., 1974).

[3] Edward Puda and Lewis Albright, "Racial Differences on Selection Instruments Related to Subsequent Job Performance," *Personnel Psychology*, Spring 1968; see also Charles Sparks, "Validity of Psychological Tests," *Personnel Psychology* Spring 1970.

[4] See John B. Miner and Mary Green Miner, *Personnel and Industrial Relations* (New York: Macmillan Publishing Co., 1977), chap. 10, "The Logic of Selection."

[5] One study was conducted by Allan N. Nash and S. J. Carroll, "A Hard Look at the Reference Check," *Business Horizons*, October 1970.

[6] Orman Wright, "Summary of Research on the Selection Interview since 1964," *Personnel Psychology*, Winter 1969.

[7] William C. Byham, "Assessment Centers for Spotting Future Managers," *Harvard Business Review*, July–August 1970; and G. Tinkle and W. Jones, *Assessing Corporate Talent* (New York: John Wiley & Sons, 1970).

[8] A. I. Kraut, "A Hard Look at Management Assessment Centers and Their Future," *Personnel Journal*, May 1972; and A. Howard, "An Assessment of Assessment Centers." *Academy of Management Journal*, March 1974.

[9] Howard C. Lockwood, "Equal Employment Opportunities," in *Staffing Policies and Strategies*, vol. 1 of the *ASPA Handbook of Personnel and Industrial Relations*, copyright © 1974 by The Bureau of National Affairs, Inc., Washington, D.C. 20037.

When you have completed studying
ORGANIZATION DEVELOPMENT
you should be able to:

1. Describe the origins and objectives of organization development.
2. Define and show the importance of organizational climate.
3. Explain the difference between behavioral and nonbehavioral interventions.
4. Show the relationship between human resources management, OD, and training.
5. Discuss in detail two or more models of organization change.
6. Describe each of the basic steps in action research.
7. Define laboratory training and discuss its objectives.
8. Differentiate the concepts of team building, intergroup training, managerial grid, MBO, and job enrichment.
9. Discuss the future of organization development.

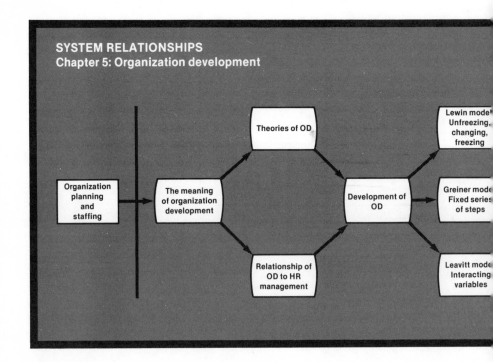

SYSTEM RELATIONSHIPS
Chapter 5: Organization development

"Organization development" may be viewed as a response to McGregor's challenge quoted at the right. Organization development stands for a general approach and a variety of techniques directed toward achieving McGregor's Theory Y type of organization. In such an organization, mutual trust and individual responsibility permit each worker to reach for self-fulfillment in the work climate.

One aim of organization development (OD) is to assist each employee to achieve at his or her full potential. Another aim is to improve working relationships among individuals and groups. This further enhances the functioning of the HRS. From a systems view, then, OD is a means for improving the processing carried out by the

5

Organization development

The limits on human collaboration in the organizational setting are not limits of human nature but of management's ingenuity in discovering how to realize the potential represented by its human resources. [1]

Douglas McGregor

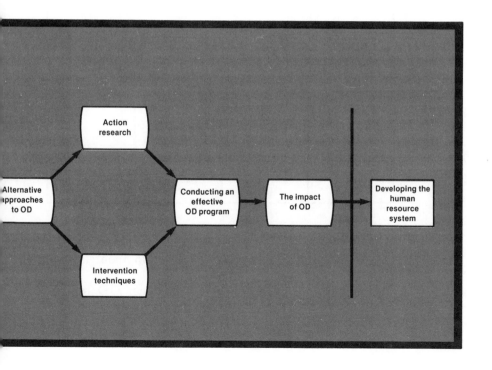

HRS. It does this by modifying the behavior of the organization and its elements.

WHAT IS ORGANIZATION DEVELOPMENT?

OD is a varied set of techniques directed toward improving *organizational* performance. The approach consists of modifying the organizational climate to instill such new behavioral values as openness and trust. Thus, the primary focus of OD is on improving the functioning of a total organization. Once an overall OD strategy has been determined, it *may* be decided that a *part* of this strategy should include the training and development of individuals. Thus, OD is very much a "macro" approach to development as contrasted with individual training and development, which is essentially a "micro" approach.

The relationship of the OD process to human resources management and training and development is shown in Exhibit 5–1.

EXHIBIT 5–1
The partitioning of human resources management

Program for human resources management

Organization development program

Training and education

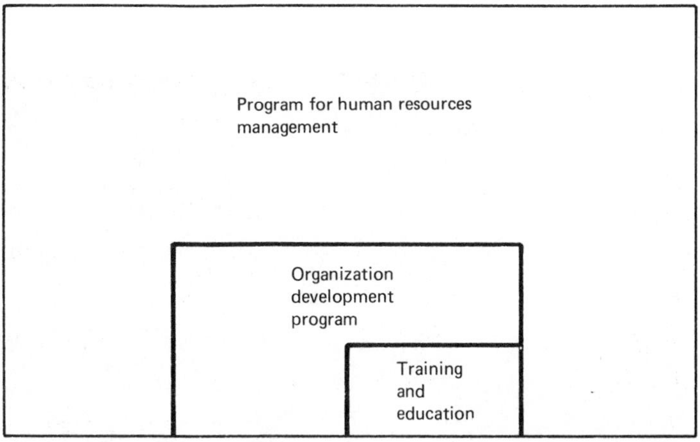

The important subject of training and development is taken up separately in the following chapter.

The principal difference in emphasis between OD and training and development is that OD focuses on the working climate whereas training and development focuses on the individual. The specific differences are summarized in Exhibit 5–2. Further, if we

EXHIBIT 5–2
Comparison of traditional training and the organization change process

Dimension	Traditional training	Organization change process
Unit of focus	The individual	Interpersonal relationships —teams, work units, intergroup relations, superior-subordinate relations
Content of training	Technical and administrative skills	Interpersonal and group membership skills— communication, problem solving, conflict management, helping
Target subjects	Primarily first-line employees and supervisors; managers trained outside organization	All levels; usually initial intervention with upper management in-house
Conception of learning process	Cognitive and rational	Cognitive, rational, emotional-motivational
Teaching style	Subject matter and teacher centered	Participant, immediate experience, problem solving, and subject matter centered
Learning goals	Rationality and efficiency	Awareness, adaptation, and change
View of organization	Discrete functional skill units	Social system

Source: William B. Eddy, "From Training to Organization Change," *Personnel Administration,* January–February 1971, pp. 37–43. Reprinted by permission of the International Personnel Management Association, 1313 East 60th Street, Chicago, Illinois 60637.

explain the meaning of "working climate" more specifically, we will gain a better understanding of the focus of OD.

Just as we live in a climate of weather, we work in a "climate" of other people's behavior and organizational forces. A climate may provide stimulation and motivation which encourages the performance of human resources. It may also contain constraints, blockages, and frustrations which inhibit this performance. The organization climate is intangible like the wind in our weather climate. It is felt but cannot be seen. It affects every member's performance. The organization climate is a composite of many factors, some of which are the managerial style of individual managers and the dominant management style of the organization; the values held by individual managers and reflected in the organization as a whole; and the formal organization (rules, policies, organization structure, the reward system), the informal organization (norms of behavior, beliefs, values, and attitudes of the emergent behavioral system), the communications system, and all other managerial systems.

The organization climate is best thought of as a set of forces within the organization that greatly affect the way people work. These forces influence the motivation and commitment of individuals and groups through their impact on interpersonal and intergroup relationships. In the era of the 1950s and early 1960s preceding the emergence of organization development, it was thought that the climate of most organizations fell far short of encouraging maximum performance by the people in organizations. Thus, organization development was welcomed in the 1960s and early 1970s as a means for acting on an organization to improve its performance.

Objectives of organization development

Various organizations embark on organization development programs in order to achieve a wide variety of specific objectives. However, most of these objectives can be classified in the following way:

1. Improved organizational performance as measured by such indexes as profitability, turnover, innovation, and share of market.
2. Improvement of the organization's adaptation to its environment, including the willingness of members to face up to organizational problems and their effectiveness in consistently reaching creative solutions to those problems.
3. Improvement in internal behavior patterns, including such things as interpersonal and intergroup cooperation, the level of trust and support, owning up to feelings and emotions, openness and completeness of communication, and widespread participation in the planning of organization strategy.

Underlying themes

Although organization development has the appearance of being quite recent, its roots (and some of its techniques) go back to the Hawthorne experiments of the 1920s and early 1930s.[2] These research studies conducted at the Hawthorne Works of the Western Electric Company were among the earliest systematic studies applying the experimental method to the analysis of behavior in organizations. They provided the basis for such concepts of organizational behavior as informal work groups, "emergent behavior," group norms, values and sentiments and the significance of participation in decision making—all still central concepts in the various techniques of organization development.

There are thus two underlying themes which we will keep in mind throughout our discussion of organization development. One of these is the systems approach to developing organizations. The other is commitment to a value system that emphasizes openness, trust, mutual confidence, confrontation, participation, and motivation of the individual through involvement in the decision-making process.

THREE MAIN APPROACHES TO OD

Although there are numerous approaches to or models of organization development, we will discuss the three which have received the most attention in management literature. One of these is the three-step model of Kurt Lewin, consisting of "unfreezing," changing, and "refreezing."[3] In Lewin's model, unfreezing involves readying the organization for change when an apparent challenge or problem makes it clear that change will be required. Changing means going from old behaviors to experimentation with new behaviors to solve the organizational problem. Refreezing consists of reinforcement activities for the new behaviors that will strengthen them and make them a part of the new behavior system of the organization.

A more recent model by Larry Greiner also looks at change from the standpoint of sequential stages or steps in the process. A diagram illustrating Greiner's model is shown as Exhibit 5–3.[4] An important finding of Greiner's research was that for the organization change process to be effective it appeared to be vital that each of the steps or phases occur in the particular sequence indicated in the model. Thus it appeared to be critical that a change process be initiated by outside pressure or stimulus on the top management of the organization, followed by a decision of the top management to take action. The succeeding phases of intervention by a change agent, invention of new solutions, experimentation with new solutions, and reinforcement from positive results appeared to be crucial for the effectiveness of change processes.

Harold J. Leavitt has suggested a somewhat different approach to an organization change model.[5] The emphasis of Leavitt's model is not on the sequential steps or phases of organization change. Rather

EXHIBIT 5–3
The dynamics of successful organization change

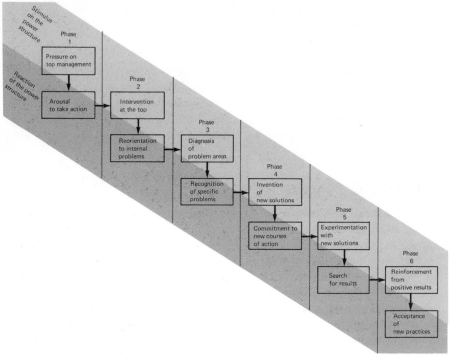

Source: Larry E. Greiner, "Patterns of Organization Change," in Gene W. Dalton, Paul R. Lawrence, and Larry E. Greiner (eds.), *Organizational Change and Development* (Homewood, Ill.: Richard D. Irwin, 1970), p. 222.

it considers the different parts of a system on which change efforts might focus and the interactive nature of those parts. Leavitt views an organization as a system of four interacting variables—task, structure, technology, and people. His model is illustrated in Exhibit 5–4.

There are two important features of Leavitt's model from the practical perspective of a manager. The first is that task, structure, technology, and people are interactive—that is, changing any one of these variables automatically produces change (some of which may be uncontrolled and unwanted) in the other variables. Thus, in planning and implementing change, it is important that the manager focus not only on the specific intended change but also on the effects which that change will have on the other variables. The second is that change can effectively begin with any one of the four

EXHIBIT 5–4
The four interacting variables of an organization

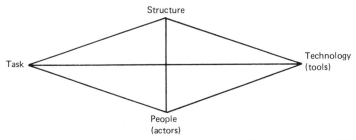

Source: Harold J. Leavitt, *New Perspectives in Organization Research* (New York: John Wiley & Sons, 1964).

EXHIBIT 5–5
OD at General Motors

The theme of worker discontent is a well-documented one: the blue-collar worker sullenly bored on the production line, the middle manager—and sometimes the high executive as well—who sees himself as a lonely figure within a giant, impersonal corporation.

To deal with its "people problems" GM 18 months ago hired 53-year-old Stephen H. Fuller, a former Harvard B-school professor, as vice-president of personnel administration and development.

Fuller's mandate, put most simply, is to develop plans that will better help the world's largest industrial enterprise manage and care for its 808,000 employees.

Traditionally, workers have had little or no say in such matters. . . . This kind of procedure was dramatically altered at the Lakewood (Ga.) plant of the GM Assembly Div. There the emphasis was on better information sharing with employees as part of the OD effort. Each employee—after being given all the information about how the business functions—was encouraged to participate in making decisions regarding his or her own job. To accomplish this, it was necessary to push the decision-making process to the lowest level of the organization, says Frank J. Shotters, who was plant manager at the time. Since then, Shotters has been transferred to Detroit and named director of personnel development, reporting to Fuller.

The workers were also brought in on new model changeover. In many cases, Shotters says, the decisions on rearrangements of the plant work areas, which are part of the changeover, were made after consulting the affected workers. Hourly employees worked with the engineers at the drawing board and were permitted to give their views on how the changes should be made, Shotters says.

A more extensive orientation program was set up for new employees, and first-line supervisors were put through leadership courses that concentrated on encouraging a more open attitude in their dealings with subordinates. Labor grievances dropped nearly 50 percent in two years.

Source: "GM Zeroes In on Employee Discontent," *Business Week*, May 12, 1973, pp. 141–42.

variables. Depending on the manager's diagnosis of the total situation, he or she might elect to start up an organization development effort with interpersonal behavior training of some sort, or to make a purely technological or structural intervention, or to simply modify the tasks.

Exhibit 5–5 contains a brief description of how General Motors put some of these ideas into action. Structure, task, and technology were changed as people were reoriented.

CONDUCTING AN EFFECTIVE OD PROGRAM

Although many specific strategies have been designed to achieve organization development, the "action research model" is the heart of the OD process. Most OD practitioners (despite their many differences regarding specific strategies and interventions) agree that in a genuine OD strategy each of the basic steps of the action research model must take place. These steps are intervention, data gathering, organizational diagnosis, data feedback, and action intervention (Exhibit 5–6). Thus, the considerable disagreement which exists among various OD practitioners centers primarily on the many *techniques* which can be utilized for each of the steps in the basic OD process.

This is particularly true of the action intervention stage, as hundreds of specific intervention techniques have been experimented with by OD practitioners. Many of these intervention strategies have been published, even though in some cases the strategy may have been utilized by only one practitioner or only one organization. Because OD is still in its infancy, there has not been much validation of the various intervention techniques. At this stage, OD is very much an art rather than a science.

Steps for action research

It will be obvious from the above that a detailed discussion of the various techniques utilized for each of the stages in the OD process is beyond the scope of this book. What we will attempt to do is to summarize the important aspects of each of the stages and to discuss briefly some of the most commonly used techniques.

1. **Intervention.** OD begins with the intervention of some agent from outside the organization. Frequently this change agent is a consultant who has no permanent tie to the organization. The advantage of using such a consultant is that the change agent has both objectivity and relative independence from the power struc-

EXHIBIT 5–6
Action research—The key model of OD

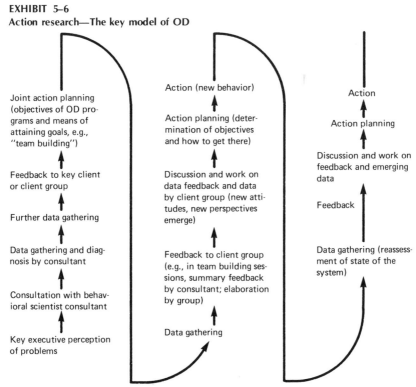

Joint action planning
(objectives of OD pro-
grams and means of
attaining goals, e.g.,
"team building")

↑

Feedback to key client
or client group

↑

Further data gathering

↑

Data gathering and diag-
nosis by consultant

↑

Consultation with behav-
ioral scientist consultant

↑

Key executive perception
of problems

Action (new behavior)

↑

Action planning (deter-
mination of objectives
and how to get there)

↑

Discussion and work on
data feedback and data
by client group (new attitudes, new perspectives
emerge)

↑

Feedback to client group
(e.g., in team building sessions, summary feedback
by consultant; elaboration
by group)

↑

Data gathering

Action

↑

Action planning

↑

Discussion and work on
feedback and emerging
data

↑

Feedback

Data gathering (reassess-
ment of state of the
system)

Source: Wendell French, "Organization Development: Objectives, Assumptions, and Strategies," ©
1969 by the Regents of the University of California. Reprinted from *California Management Review*, vol.
12, no. 2, p. 26, by permission of the Regents.

ture of the organization. Some larger organizations (and this is a
growing trend) have internal change agents. These are relatively
independent staff members at the corporate level who work in the
same manner as external change agents with the various line organizations and divisions of the corporation. In either case, the change
agent usually enters the organization at the invitation of top management in response to some perceived organizational problem (or,
less frequently, a perceived opportunity) related to the ability of
organization members to work cooperatively and effectively.

2. **Data gathering.** The first major task of the change agent is to
gather data for diagnosis of the organization's ability to function
effectively and for the determination of specific problems. There are
two primary methods of data gathering—the interview method and
the survey questionnaire. It is not uncommon for OD practitioners

to combine these two methods; however, some practitioners use one method exclusively.

In the interview method, the top executives of the organization are interviewed individually by the consultant. In virtually all cases this would include at least the chief executive and each of his or her immediate subordinates. Depending on the size of the organization and the time allocated for this step, a sample of the next level of executives might be interviewed. Usually if the first set of interviews has uncovered potential problem areas, executives in these suborganizations or functions receive additional interview attention.

Although practice varies widely, the typical interview consists of a one- to three-hour informal discussion session in which the consultant begins with some very open-ended questions, such as these: "How do you assess the overall effectiveness of this organization?" "Are there any specific obstacles which you believe are holding back the performance of the total organization or some part of the organization or your own performance?" "What frustrations do you experience in this organization, and what things would you like to see changed?" This interviewing is always done with the understanding that the replies of any single individual will be treated in complete confidence. It is also understood that the *problems* identified (particularly those identified by several executives) will be reported back to others in the organization.

In the second method for gathering data, a written questionnaire is given to a group of executives, either alone or in combination with individual interviews. Usually, a larger number of executives participate in a survey questionnaire than would be involved in the use of the interview technique. One advantage of the survey questionnaire technique is that it permits data to be gathered from a much larger range of executives with relatively less expenditure of consultant time. Some experts maintain that the survey questionnaire is more objective and "scientific" than the interview in that each executive respondent is asked exactly the same questions in exactly the same way. Other experts argue that this is, in fact, the major disadvantage of the survey questionnaire—it does not permit individual follow-up by the consultant to probe for the deeper meaning of superficially expressed opinions.

A balanced view recognizes that both the interview technique and the survey questionnaire have unique advantages. The most effective data gathering should probably include both of these techniques.

It could be said that the whole purpose of organization development is to increase both the kinds of data available on the functioning of the organization and the application of these data in the organization. Data gathering attempts to supplement the usual kinds of information about the performance of an organization with information on the climate of the organization, the norms and values of work groups, and people's sentiments and attitudes about such things as management practices, status and power in the organization, communication, and information sharing. Thus, OD focuses both on generating new data about such issues and on encouraging the consideration of such issues as legitimate executive activity.

3. **Organizational diagnosis.** The next stage in the OD process is the preliminary diagnosis of the organizational situation by the consultant in conjunction with the top executive(s). This stage would usually include the informal or formal feedback of some of the data gathered to the top executive(s) along with the consultant's interpretation and/or questions. The primary purpose of the preliminary diagnosis is to enable the consultant to propose the next steps to be taken in the OD process and to obtain the agreement of the organization's leaders for these further steps.

A growing issue in the field of organization development is the recognition of the need for some procedures to assist in the diagnosis of organizational difficulties. It is increasingly being recognized that there would be great benefit from using a standard diagnostic procedure to assist in the initial identification of organizational difficulties. One such approach which has proven quite versatile and helpful is the differentiation and integration model of Lawrence and Lorsch.[6] Another is the conceptual scheme of Arthur Turner (see Exhibit 5–7).[7]

4. **Data feedback and discussion.** The data feedback stage may overlap with the previously discussed stage of preliminary diagnosis. However, it is helpful to separate data feedback for purposes of description. In the data feedback stage, the data obtained from the members of the organization through the combination of interviews and survey research are reported back to groups of executives for their information, discussion, and reaction. Frequently, this data report is in a fairly formal form in which the consultant attempts to summarize the most significant aspects of the data obtained. The consultant may or may not provide interpretation of these data and may or may not raise specific questions for the executives. In any case, at this stage the organization's executives discuss the data leading to the identification of the concerns and issues to be dealt with. The executives are also asked to confront the needs for organization development. They consider various alter-

EXHIBIT 5–7
Work group behavior: Relations between elements of external and internal systems

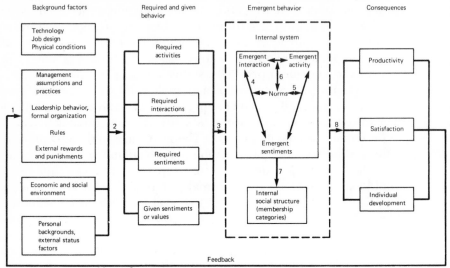

Source: Arthur Turner "A Conceptual Scheme for Describing Work Group Behavior," paper distributed by Intercollegiate Case Clearing House. Copyright © 1961 by the President and Fellows of Harvard College.

native strategies which might be utilized. The primary purposes of the data feedback stage are to ready the organization for further development activities and to plan the specific intervention techniques that will be utilized in the continuing OD effort.

5. **Action intervention.** This stage in the OD process involves the application of one or more specific techniques for organization change. There is a large and rapidly growing inventory of such techniques. Among the most common techniques are laboratory training, sensitivity or T-group training, team building, intergroup building, confrontation, the managerial grid, management by objectives, and job enrichment. In one sense, the action intervention stage may be thought of as the payoff stage of organization development. In fact, many executives incorrectly think that the use of a specific intervention technique is organization development!

Intervention techniques

Most action interventions in OD have traditionally been behaviorally oriented interventions (that is, designed to affect the behavior of individuals and groups). It is, however, perfectly consistent

with the *theory* of organization development to consider much
more structured interventions, such as changes in the organization
structure, work design, technology, or compensation system, as
being a legitimate part of intervention strategy in an overall OD
effort. Let us now examine in more detail some of the most commonly used intervention techniques.

Laboratory training. The most commonly utilized OD intervention technique is laboratory training. Laboratory training is so
named because it is conducted by creating an experimental "laboratory" situation in which people are brought together in groups
to interact in an unstructured environment. The group is challenged
with a "dilemma" for which normal behavior patterns appear to be
inadequate, and it is encouraged to *experiment* with new individual
behaviors and new group interactions in order to resolve the dilemma. Thus, the objective is to create an experimental laboratory
atmosphere in which both individual and group behavioral learning
and development may occur. Laboratory training originated in the
late 1940s and has taken on a variety of specific formats. One principal offshoot of laboratory training is T-group training or sensitivity
training, a specific set of laboratory training techniques originated
by the National Training Laboratory.

The duration of laboratory training may vary from a few hours
("microlabs") to two weeks or more. The most common length of
laboratory programs is probably three to five days of intensive work.
The content of laboratory sessions may also vary widely. Commonly
the leader or trainer announces at the beginning of the sessions that
he or she will take a relatively passive role in the training process—
that is, the leader will attempt to assist the group in learning, but the
group will have control of the agenda and the leader will not direct
the group's processes.

Usually the trainer's introductory remarks will focus the attention of each member of the group on perceiving his or her own
behavior and the behavior of others. The trainer will attempt to
create a nonpunishing environment in which each person's feelings
and reactions to others can be openly expressed to the group as data
for consideration. Although the trainer invariably indicates that
there is no specific agenda, the group members are encouraged to
learn about their own behavior from their experiences in the group.
After these introductory remarks the trainer usually remains silent.

This is perceived as an uncomfortable situation by most group
members and leads to the development of further group behavior
which, with the assistance of the trainer, becomes the focus for
discussion and learning. The role played by the trainer may vary

widely, depending on the trainer, the type of laboratory, the type of group or organization in which the laboratory exists, and the behavior of the participants. Usually, however, the trainer will encourage participants to think about, and then to verbalize, their feelings about the activities of the group.

The major distinction between laboratory training and T-group training is that T-groups focus almost exclusively on the kinds of behavioral interactions just discussed. Laboratory training usually places a heavy emphasis on such activity, but in addition it may include role playing, management games, discussions of theory, and even lectures.

One of the problems of laboratory training is the question of the most effective basis for organizing groups. For example, if "stranger labs" are used, there is the difficulty of translating the learning to interactions with another group of people who have not gone through the same experience. It is clear that much laboratory training has been ineffective for this reason. Thus, the logic goes, it is much better to train a diagonal slice of an organization and best of all to train an actual work group so that the skills learned in the training can be applied more readily on the job.

Although "family groups" seem to provide the greatest potential for the learning and application of new behaviors, for essentially the same reason such groups also pose the greatest dangers to the individuals involved. It is one thing to expose our innermost feelings to those with whom we do not work (and whom we will never see again) and quite another thing to expose those feelings to members of the work group with which we are associated every day. Without doubt, people have been harmed, both psychologically and in terms of their careers, by participation in "family groups." And yet, equally without doubt, in such groups lies the greatest potential of laboratory training.

Unfortunately for the practice of laboratory training, there are no clear-cut reliable data regarding the effectiveness of such training. Proponents of laboratory training point to some demonstrable successes and conclude that it is the most valuable organization development technique yet devised. Opponents of laboratory training point to some undeniable failures and to some serious health problems, including mental breakdowns, attributable to laboratory training.

Two very careful research studies to evaluate such training have been performed by John P. Campbell and Marvin D. Dunnette and by Robert J. House.[8] Significantly, both studies regard the evidence as inconclusive. Campbell and Dunnette state that laboratory training can produce changes in behavior, but they point out emphatically that it has not yet been demonstrated that a tie exists between such changes and job performance. As managers, we might therefore hesitate to invest our company's money in laboratory training programs.

Team building. The idea of team building arose from the belief that the most effective laboratory training would take place among people who actually worked together as a team. Team building is nothing more than the application of the general technique of laboratory training to actual working groups, usually comprising a group of peers and a superior.

The techniques used in team building may run the full gamut of those already discussed in connection with laboratory training—all the way from T-group or sensitivity training through managerial games, exercises, and role playing. Regardless of the techniques employed, team building dwells on improving the ability of the members of the team to work effectively with one another to accomplish the common purpose of the team on the job.

Although the most common application of team building is to a natural work group consisting of a manager and immediate subordinates, team building techniques are also being applied to short-term task teams. This is a very useful application of behavioral science technique, since one of the common problems of a short-term task team is the necessity of developing rather quickly some effective norms to guide the group.

Efforts to improve intergroup relations and effectiveness are a further outgrowth of team building. Such efforts bring together the members of two or more different teams in laboratory training directed toward improving the ability of the teams to work together.

The Managerial Grid®. A specific methodology for team building which has received widespread attention and application in American industry is the managerial grid training of Blake and Mouton.[9] The managerial grid, which is sometimes referred to as "instrumented laboratory training," is a structured version of laboratory training. It consists of a series of carefully planned individual and group exercises designed to develop awareness of individual managerial style, interpersonal competence and group effectiveness.

The managerial grid is in part an attempt to achieve the benefits of sensitivity training or T-group training at reduced risks in terms of individual and/or organizational dysfunction. Thus, instead of focusing on individual perceptions of the behavior of others and giving critical feedback on that behavior, the managerial grid focuses on the observation of behavior in exercises specifically related to work. The feedback given does not refer to the individual's personality but to his or her performance in group exercises. Blake and Mouton feel (and most practitioners agree) that this is a much safer type of laboratory for a family group or a work team. Although the managerial grid is less threatening to individuals, Blake and Mouton feel that it is almost as effective as T-group training.

There is certainly no denying the fact that many of America's leading corporations made a major investment in managerial grid training during the 1960s and early 1970s. At present the managerial grid remains one of the most widely utilized laboratory training techniques.

Using interpersonal and intergroup exercises as the basis of behavioral observation, participants in grid training are encouraged and helped to evaluate their own managerial style. The style of managerial behavior is measured by concern for people and concern for production. Each individual managerial style can be graphed on a chart using these two dimensions as axes. This style can then be discussed in the group and related to the style of other group members as well as to the style of the group as a whole. This graphic representation of managerial style is indicated in Exhibit 5–8.

Management by objectives. Another change strategy or technique which may be used quite effectively with an overall OD effort is management by objectives. As was pointed out earlier, many OD practitioners are concerned about a loose use of terminology in which any MBO program may be referred to as "organization development." Nevertheless, there seems to be agreement that management by objectives may legitimately be considered a specific change strategy to be introduced in the action intervention stage of an OD effort.

There is a growing belief among OD practitioners that MBO can be particularly effective. It ties together the underlying Theory Y philosophy of OD, the behavioral learning of the laboratory training which would precede the implementation of MBO, and a very practical management planning and control technique. This managerial planning and control technique appears work-related and realistic to even the most traditional manager. Because management by objectives will be treated in considerable detail in a later chapter, the mechanics will not be discussed here.

To illustrate the relationship which he sees between MBO and OD, Thomas H. Patten uses the diagram in Exhibit 5–9, which is an adaptation of the "organizational iceberg" suggested earlier by Stanley Herman.[10] Note that in this figure Patten points out the distinction between the older, limited concept of OD which sees

EXHIBIT 5–8
The Managerial Grid®

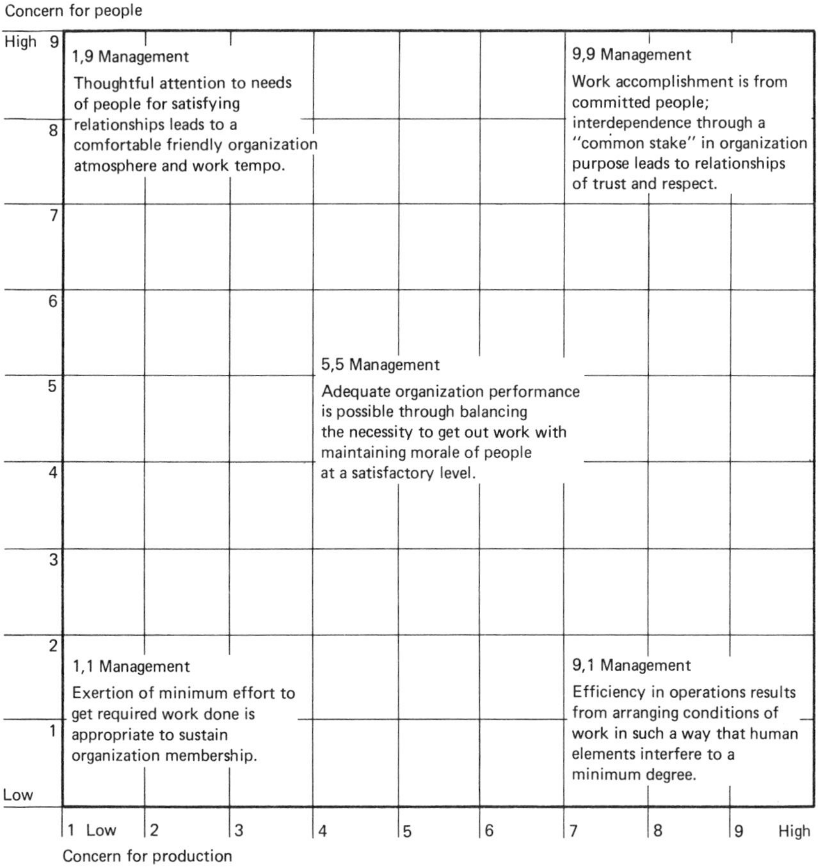
Concern for people
High 9
8
7
6
5
4
3
2
1
Low
1,9 Management
Thoughtful attention to needs of people for satisfying relationships leads to a comfortable friendly organization atmosphere and work tempo.
9,9 Management
Work accomplishment is from committed people; interdependence through a "common stake" in organization purpose leads to relationships of trust and respect.
5,5 Management
Adequate organization performance is possible through balancing the necessity to get out work with maintaining morale of people at a satisfactory level.
1,1 Management
Exertion of minimum effort to get required work done is appropriate to sustain organization membership.
9,1 Management
Efficiency in operations results from arranging conditions of work in such a way that human elements interfere to a minimum degree.
1 Low
2
3
4
5
6
7
8
9 High
Concern for production

Source: R. R. Blake, Jane S. Mouton, L. B. Barnes, and L. E. Greiner, "Breakthrough in Organizational Development," *Harvard Business Review*, November–December 1964, pp. 37–59. Copyright © 1964 by the President and Fellows of Harvard College; all rights reserved.

OD as working only at unconscious levels of behavior, and the newer, more inclusive view of OD. This newer view sees organization development as an overall effort to improve organizational performance which may importantly involve changing perceptions, values, attitudes, and behaviors but may also involve changes in the structure or practices of the formal organization, including such things as MBO and the reward system.

Patten develops the theme that not only are OD, MBO, and the reward system significantly related, but that there is also an optimal

EXHIBIT 5–9
The organizational iceberg

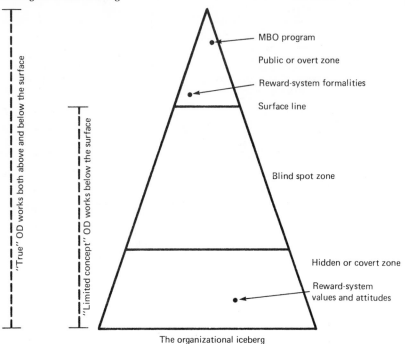

The organizational iceberg

Source: Thomas H. Patten, Jr., "OD—MBO and the Reward System." Reproduced by special permission from O.D.—*Emerging Dimensions and Concepts.* Copyright 1973 by the American Society for Training and Development, Inc.

EXHIBIT 5–10
Schematic diagram of changing organizational culture and employee behavior:
Optimal pattern

OD	MBO	Reward system (RS)
Social-emotional blockages overcome (start with team building)	Rationality limitations overcome (install MBO)	Vary pay, promotion, recognition based upon standard-fulfilling performance directed toward organizational objectives

$$\boxed{1} \longrightarrow \boxed{2} \longrightarrow \boxed{3}$$

Source: Thomas H. Patten, Jr., "O.D.—M.B.O. and the Reward System." Reproduced by special permission from O.D.—*Emerging Dimensions and Concepts.* Copyright 1973 by the American Society for Training and Development, Inc.

sequence in which attention should be given to these specific managerial activities as part of an overall OD effort. The optimal sequence suggested by Patten is OD–MBO–reward system, as illustrated in Exhibit 5–10.

Job enrichment. The last strategy that we will discuss is the systematic attempt to alter the work content of jobs in such a way as to increase the opportunity for motivation. This is done by increasing the difficulty or complexity of the job to provide more challenge, the utilization of more skills and abilities, and more opportunity for achievement and recognition. Thus, as Herzberg has pointed out, job enrichment operates on the same job factors as scientific management or industrial engineering, but for opposite goals.[11] Job enrichment makes work more meaningful to people, rather than making it more scientifically structured for efficiency.

A step-by-step approach to a job enrichment program is:

1. Identify jobs in which (a) attitudes are poor, (b) the "hygiene" factors have become costly, and (c) changes will not be too costly from the industrial engineering standpoint.
2. Take the view that *jobs* can be changed, not just people.
3. Conduct "brainstorming" meetings of key people to develop a list of changes that may enrich jobs.
4. *Eliminate* changes that involve (a) hygiene rather than motivation, (b) generalities rather than specific job changes, (c) job *enlargement* suggestions (horizontal broadening of work).
5. Set up two equivalent groups. In one, introduce the job enrichment changes. In the other (control) group, make no changes. Make before and after tests of job performance and attitudes. (During the first weeks, the new job requirements alone may result in a drop in the case of the job-enriched group.)
6. Expect first-line supervisors to have some anxiety about and hostility to the changes. Work with them to help them rediscover the managerial functions that they should have been performing.

THE IMPACT OF OD

Scientific evidence regarding the effectiveness of OD technology is very hard to come by. In view of the attention which has been focused on OD and its widely heralded potential, it is surprising that so little rigorous research has been done. One paper presented at the 1976 meeting of the Academy of Management observed, "Although organization development (OD) as a change strategy has been widely used, the number of reported attempts to conduct systematic research on the impact or effectiveness of OD has been appallingly slim. Despite repeated calls for systematic research (Bennis, 1969; Raia, 1972; Huse, 1975; Kimberly and Nielsen, 1975), personal testimonies and anecdotal data have continued to dominate the field."[12]

After surveying 37 recently reported studies of OD methods and techniques in order to "bring together previously scattered information and provide future researchers with direction relative to researchable gaps in the field," Tate, Nielsen, and Bacon conclude that "more systematic, longitudinal research on OD is needed."

The plain fact is that very few attempts to objectively evaluate OD technology have yet been made, and even the most rigorous of these studies do not involve satisfactory experimental control. This lack of research is probably due in part to what Newton Margulies calls the "myth of non-researchable variables"—namely, the belief that OD programs are impossible to measure scientifically and that research would interfere with the OD process.[13] The lack of research is also due in part to the relatively long time dimension of OD work (at least five years from initial intervention until measurable results could be expected). This makes it difficult to isolate the effects of experimental variables from those of uncontrolled variables which intervene in any real situation. The lack of research may also result from practitioners' reluctance to step back from intervention activity long enough to observe it objectively, and perhaps even from their unconscious fear that OD might not be able to withstand rigorous scientific evaluation.

Nevertheless, the literature is full of comments (generally positive) by executives and consultants regarding their subjective evaluation of specific OD efforts in a particular organization. Moreover, there are at least a few studies which represent attempts at objective evaluation.

One of these is the study by Blake, Mouton, Barnes, and Greiner of a grid OD effort in a major corporation, called Sigma in the study.[14] The study concluded that OD appeared to have had a powerful positive impact on the organization. It also quoted several executives who perceived a strong tie between the OD effort and improved organizational performance.

Nevertheless, it should be pointed out that although this is one of the most rigorous studies yet performed, it did *not* involve a control group. The effect of other environmental variables on the outcomes will remain unknown. Consequently, the only rigorous conclusion which can be drawn is that the OD effort was followed by improved organizational performance.

A widely quoted study by Paul, Robertson, and Herzberg of a series of job enrichment interventions *did* utilize control groups and also reported positive results.[15] The data in Exhibits 5–11 and 5–12 show that the performance of the experimental groups exceeded that of the control groups.

EXHIBIT 5–11

Percent change in 1968*

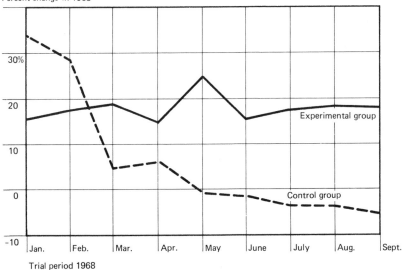

Trial period 1968

* Against corresponding 1967 period, plotted cumulatively.

With regard to the study reflected in Exhibit 5–12, the authors state:

> During the trial period the experimental group increased its sales by almost 19 percent over the same period of the previous year, a gain of over $300,000 in sales value. The control group's sales in the meantime declined by 5 percent. The equivalent change for both groups the previous year had been a decline of 3 percent. The difference in performance between the two groups is statistically significant at the 0.01 level of confidence.[16]

Although control groups were utilized, these studies should be interpreted as *indicative* of OD effectiveness rather than as conclusive evidence of its effectiveness. This is because it is unclear whether the activity measured constituted an OD effort as OD has been defined here and elsewhere or whether it merely constituted a specific organizational intervention.

EXHIBIT 5–12

Mean score

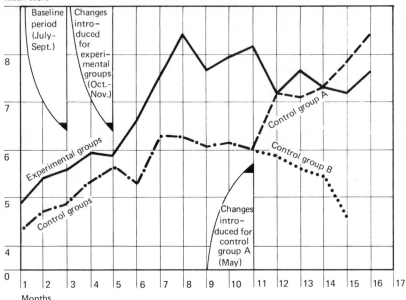

Months

On the other side of the debate, Frank and Hackman have recently reported a carefully controlled and measured OD program which admittedly failed to achieve its objectives.[17] It seems safest to conclude at this point that the evidence regarding the effectiveness of OD is still inconclusive and that much more research work remains to be done.

SUMMARY

Organization development embodies the systems view of the organization's human resources because the major thrust of OD is the improved functioning of the total system. The two underlying themes of this chapter have been:

1. The systems focus on developing the functioning of a total organization (system) as opposed to developing individuals.
2. The commitment to a value system which emphasizes openness, trust, mutual confidence, confrontation, participation, and the motivation of the individual through involvement in the decision-making process.

Although the roots of OD go back to the Hawthorne experiments of the 1920s, most of the processes and techniques which we now call organization development have evolved over the last 15 years. Organization development has been defined as "an effort that is planned, organization-wide, and managed from the top to increase organizational effectiveness and health through planned interventions into the organization's processes, using behavioral science knowledge."[18] Although behavioral intervention techniques have been emphasized in this chapter, the authors believe that it is highly useful to keep in mind that both behavioral and nonbehavioral interventions may legitimately play a part in a concerted OD effort.

Although the specific objectives of organizations may vary, the overall objectives of most OD efforts are improvements in the organization's performance, adaptation to its environment, and internal behavior patterns.

Several models describing the OD process were discussed, and the "action research" model was highlighted as the basic intervention model which runs through all organization development. Action research consists of:

1. Intervention.
2. Data gathering from the organization.
3. Preliminary diagnosis.
4. Data feedback and discussion.
5. Implementation of action strategies.

The decisions to be made and the actions typically taken by the change agent at each of these stages in the OD process were also discussed.

Among the action interventions discussed were the following behavioral and nonbehavioral interventions:

1. Laboratory training.
2. Sensitivity training or T-groups.
3. Team building.
4. Intergroup training.
5. The managerial grid.
6. Management by objectives.
7. Job enrichment.

CASE: NTEL, INC.

NTEL, Inc., is an international firm which employed 13,000 people worldwide in 1978. It consisted of an Industrial Division, a Building Division, a Services and Leisure Division, and a Consumer Products Division. With plants all over the world and rapid expansion continuing, NTEL was having communication problems. As a result, the achievement of profit targets was beginning to slip badly in the various divisions for reasons that had not been precisely identified.

Although top management, headquartered in New York, tried to visit major plants at least once a year, these visits apparently did little to alleviate the problems. Language barriers created further complications, particularly with regard to the efforts of corporate staff executives to develop and obtain adherence to company-wide policies.

Managers (both in the United States and abroad) felt that corporate headquarters management did not understand local problems. Local managements often lamented that "high-level staff lives in an ivory tower."

Further, there was considerable friction over responsibility for local plant decisions. For example, corporate management would often express exasperation with the failure of local management to make a specific decision. At the same time, plant managers and their staffs might complain bitterly about delays in getting the staff approvals from headquarters needed to finalize local decisions.

In order to break through some of these difficulties, the president of NTEL, William Sabastian, had scheduled a meeting of 178 executives, including the top management of the company, to be held in June 1978 in Paris. While preparing his plans for the meeting, he had a long conversation with an old friend, Larry Jones, who headed his own OD consulting firm. As a result, Sabastian asked Jones to help identify NTEL's organizational problems and perhaps suggest some solutions.

CASE: TRANSFORMING THE TRANSFORMER COMPANY

Dr. Al Sklar, president of Transformer International Company, swiveled in his chair at 10:00 P.M. to look out of the window from his 30th-floor office. As he surveyed the expanse of the city skyline glowing with hundreds of thousands of lights, he mused about the role of transformers in supplying the lighting.

Sklar, an outsider, had taken over the helm of the company six months earlier. He had found it to be a conservative, sound engineering company, living off its past reputation. Transformer International was a follower rather than a leader. Before any of its employees took a step, they wanted to be sure that the same step had been taken before by somebody else and had worked. For example, the general approach to design used by the engineers was to study all the available designs and then try to incorporate the best features of each. There was no attempt to develop advanced innovative designs.

Sklar was well aware that technological developments were occurring at a mind-boggling rate in the world around him. He had tried unsuccessfully to persuade his staff that product leadership was essential in the transformer business. As he sat there, he wondered whether Laura Lusk, the new manager of human resources, could help him.

The next day he met with Ms. Lusk to discuss the problem. Together they developed a list of items that needed to be explored just to identify the problem fully:

1. Definition of change variables.
2. The human resource system at TI.
3. The objectives of a change program.
4. Methods of change.
5. Changing individuals and their relationships.
6. Changing group and intergroup relationships.
7. Changing the physical environment.
8. OD.
9. MBO.
10. Management information systems.

At the end of the conference, Sklar asked Ms. Lusk to prepare a practical, cost-effective program which would encourage creativity and innovation in all of the company's activities.

QUESTIONS AND PROBLEMS

1. Discuss the relationship between Theory Y and organization development.
2. Describe the role and function of organization development as a part of the overall human resources management process.
3. Trace the historical development of OD and show its relationship to behavioral science research.
4. Outline a complete OD process for a well-established consumer goods manufacturing company of 5,000 employees that has recently developed serious problems of deteriorating profits, shrinking markets, rising costs, and internal communication difficulties.
5. Differentiate between:
   a. Behavioral and nonbehavioral interventions.
   b. Team building and intergroup training.
   c. Laboratory training and managerial grid training.
   d. Individual training and organization development.

6. Describe each of the basic steps in the action research model.
7. Visit the personnel director of a major firm in your area. Discuss with him or her that firm's approach to organization development and report your findings back to the class.
8. Describe and contrast two models of organization change.
9. What training, experience, and other preparation would you recommend for the director of organization development in a major diversified corporation?

BIBLIOGRAPHY

Beer, M., and Kleisath, S. W.   "The Effects of Managerial Grid Labs on Organizational and Leadership Dimensions." In E. F. Huse et al. *Readings on Behavior in Organizations*. Reading, Mass.: Addison-Wesley, 1975.

Bennis, W. G.   "Unresolved Problems Facing Organizational Development." *Business Quarterly*, October–December 1969.

Bigelow, R. C.   "Changing Classroom Interaction through Organization Development." In R. A. Schmuck and M. B. Miles (eds.). *Organizational Development in Schools*. Palo Alto, Calif.: National Press, 1971.

Blake, R. R., and Mouton, J. S.   "Some Effects of Managerial Grid Training on Union and Management Attitudes toward Supervision." *Journal of Applied Behavioral Science*, October–December 1966.

Blake, R. R., Mouton, J. S., Barnes, L. B., and Greiner, L. E.   "Breakthrough in Organizational Development." *Harvard Business Review*, November 1964.

Bowers, D. G.   "OD Techniques and Their Results in 23 Organizations: The Michigan ICL Study." *Journal of Applied Behavioral Science*, January–February 1973.

Bragg, J. E., and Andrews, I. R.   "Participative Decision Making: An Experimental Study in a Hospital." *Journal of Applied Behavioral Science*, November–December 1973.

Brown, L. D.   "Research Action: Organizational Feedback, Understanding, and Change." *Journal of Applied Behavioral Science*, November–December 1972.

Brown, L. D., Aram, J. D., and Bachner, D. J.   "Interorganizational Information Sharing: A Successful Intervention That Failed." *Journal of Applied Behavioral Science*, 1974.

Campbell, D. T., and Fiske, D. W.   "Convergent and Discriminant Validation by the Multi-trait–Multimethod Matrix." *Psychological Bulletin*, March 1959.

Campbell, John P., and Dunette, Marvin D.   "Effectiveness of T-Group Experiences in Managerial Training and Development," *Psychological Bulletin*, August 1968.

Connor, P. E.   "Values and Assumptions in OD: Some Critical Observations." In *Proceedings of the 35th Annual Meeting of the Academy of Management*, August 1975.

Davis, Keith. *Organizational Behavior: A Book of Readings.* 4th ed. New York: McGraw-Hill Book Co., 1974.

Eddy, William B. "From Training to Organization Change." *Personnel Administration,* January–February 1971.

Ford, R. N. *Motivation through the Work Itself.* New York: American Management Association, 1969.

Frank, L. L., and Hackman, J. R. "A Failure of Job Enrichment: The Case of the Change That Wasn't." *Journal of Applied Behavioral Science,* October–December 1975.

French, Wendell. "Organization Development: Objectives, Assumptions, and Strategies." *California Management Review,* Winter 1969.

Friedlander, F., and Brown, L. D. "Organization Development." *Annual Review of Psychology,* 1974.

Golembiewski, R. T., and Blumberg, A. "Confrontation as a Training Design in Complex Organizations." *Journal of Applied Behavioral Science,* October–December 1967.

Golembiewski, R. T., and Carrigan, S. B. "The Persistence of Laboratory-Induced Changes in Organization Styles." *Administrative Science Quarterly,* September 1970.

Golembiewski, R. T., and Carrigan, S. B. "Planned Change in Organization Style Based on the Laboratory Approach." *Administrative Science Quarterly,* March 1970.

Golembiewski, R. T., Hilles, R., and Kagno, M. S. "A Longitudinal Study of Flex-Time Effects: Some Consequences of an OD Structural Intervention." *Journal of Applied Behavioral Science,* October–December 1974.

Golembiewski, R. T., and Munzenrider, R. "Persistence and Change: A Note on the Long-Term Effects of an Organization Development Program." *Academy of Management Journal,* December 1973.

Greiner, Larry E. "Patterns of Organization Change." In *Organizational Change and Development.* Homewood, Ill.: Richard D. Irwin, 1970.

Greiner, Larry, E. "Red Flags in Organization Development." *Business Horizons,* June 1972.

Hackman, J. R., Oldham, G. R., Janson, R., and Purdy, K. "A New Strategy for Job Enrichment." *California Management Review,* Summer 1975.

Hand, H. H., Estafen, B. D., and Sims, H. P., Jr. "How Effective Is Data Survey and Feedback as a Technique of Organization Development? An Experiment." *Journal of Applied Behavioral Science,* July–September 1975.

Hautaluoma, J. E., and Gavin, J. F. "Effects of Organizational Diagnosis and Intervention on Blue-Collar 'Blues' " *Journal of Applied Behavioral Science,* October–December 1975.

Herzberg, Frederick. "One More Time: How Do You Motivate Employees?" *Harvard Business Review,* January–February 1968.

House, Robert J. "T-Group Education and Leadership Effectiveness: A Review of the Empiric Literature and a Critical Evaluation." *Personnel Psychology,* Spring 1967.

Ivancevich, J. M.   "Changes in Performance in a Management by Objectives Program." *Administrative Science Quarterly,* 1974.

Ivancevich, J. M.   "A Longitudinal Assessment of Management by Objectives." *Administrative Science Quarterly,* 1972.

Kegan, D. L., and Rubenstein, A. H.   "Trust, Effectiveness, and Organizational Development: A Field Study in R & D." *Journal of Applied Behavioral Science,* July–August 1973.

Kimberly, J. R., and Nielsen, W. R.   "Organization Development and Change in Organizational Performance." *Administrative Science Quarterly,* June 1975.

Leavitt, Harold J.   *New Perspectives in Organization Research.* New York: John Wiley & Sons, Inc., 1964.

Luke, R. A., Block, P., Davey, J. M., and Averch, V. R.   "A Structural Approach to Organizational Change." *Journal of Applied Behavioral Science,* September–October, 1973.

McElvaney, C. T., and Miles, M. B.   "The School Psychologist as a Change Agent: Improving a School System through Survey Feedback Methods." In G. B. Gottsegen and M. G. Gottsegen (eds.), *Professional School Psychology, Vol. 3* (New York: Grune & Stratton, 1969).

McGregor, Douglas.   *The Human Side of Enterprise.* New York: McGraw-Hill Book Co., 1960.

McNamar, Richard T.   "Building a Better Executive Team." *California Management Review,* Winter 1973.

Mann, F. C.   "Studying and Creating Change: A Means to Understanding Social Organization." In C. M. Arensberg (ed.). *Research in Industrial Human Relations.* Madison, Wis.: IRRA, 1957.

Margulies, N.   "The Myth and Magic in OD." *Business Horizons,* August 1972.

Margulies, Newton, and Wallace, John.   *Organizational Change; Techniques and Applications.* Glenview, Ill.: Scott, Foresman and Company, 1973.

Margulies, Newton, and Raia, Anthony P.   Organizational Development: Values, Process, and Technology. New York: McGraw-Hill Book Co., 1972.

Marrow, A. J., Bowers, D. G., and Seashore, S. E.   *Management by Participation: Creating a Climate for Personal and Organizational Development.* New York: Harper & Row, 1967.

Maxwell, S. R., and Evans, M. G.   "An Evaluation of Organizational Development: Three Phases of the Managerial Grid." *Journal of Business Administration,* 1973.

Moore, William H.   "Updating the Human Principle." *Financial Executive,* April 1972.

Muczyk, J. P.   "A Controlled Field Experiment Measuring the Impact of MBO on Performance Data." In *Proceedings of the 35th Annual Meeting of the Academy of Management,* August 1975.

Myers, M. Scott, and Myers, Susan S.   "Toward Understanding the Changing Work Ethic." *California Management Review,* Spring 1974.

Nadler, D. A., and Pecorella, P. A.   "Differential Effects of Multiple Interventions in an Organization." *Journal of Applied Behavioral Science,* July–September 1975.

Nielsen, W. R., and Kimberly, J. R. "Designing Assessment Strategies for Organization Development." *Human Resource Management,* June 1976.

Nord, Walter. *Concepts and Controversy in Organizational Behavior.* Pacific Palisades, Calif.: Goodyear Publishing Co., 1972.

Oates, David. "Wood Firm Restores Splintered Morale." *International Management,* March 1974.

Ottemann, R., and Luthans, F. "An Experimental Analysis of the Effectiveness of an Organizational Behavior Modification Program in Industry." In *Proceedings of the 35th Annual Meeting of the Academy of Management.* August 1975.

Pate, L. E. "A Reference List for Change Agents." In J. W. Pfeiffer and J. E. Jones (eds.). *The 1976 Annual Handbook for Group Facilitators* La Jolla, Calif.: University Associates, 1976.

Patten, Thomas H., Jr. *OD—Emerging Dimensions and Concepts.* American Society for Training and Development, 1973.

Patten, Thomas H., Jr. "OD-MBO and the Reward System." In *OD—Emerging Dimensions and Concepts.* American Society for Training and Development, 1973.

Paul, William J., Robertson, Keith, and Herzberg, Frederick. "Job Enrichment Pays Off." *Harvard Business Review,* March–April 1969.

Raia, A. P. "Organizational Development— Some Issues and Challenges." *California Management Review,* Summer 1972.

Schein, Edgar H., and Bennis, Warren G. *Personal and Organizational Change through Group Methods.* New York: John Wiley & Sons, 1966.

Schmuck, R. A., Runkel, P., and Langemeyer, D. "Improving Organizational Problem Solving in a School Faculty." *Journal of Applied Behavioral Science,* October–November 1969.

Seashore, S. E., and Bowers, D. G. "Durability of Organizational Change." *American Psychologist,* March 1970.

Sheflen, K. C., Lawler, E. E., and Hackman, J. R. "Long-Term Impact of Pay Incentive Plans: A Field Experiment Revisited." *Journal of Applied Psychology,* 1971.

Sherwin, Douglas S. "Strategy for Winning Employee Commitment." *Harvard Business Review,* May–June 1972.

Sorcher, M., and Meyer, H. H. "Motivation and Job Performance." *Personnel Administration,* July 1968.

Taylor, J. C. *Technology and Planned Organizational Change.* Ann Arbor: Institute for Social Research, University of Michigan, 1971.

Tosi, Henry L., and Hammer, W. Clay. *Organizational Behavior and Management: A Contingency Approach.* Chicago, St. Clair Press, 1974.

Weisbord, Marvin. "What, Not Again! Manage People Better?" *Think,* IBM, January–February, 1970.

NOTES

[1] Douglas McGregor, *The Human Side of Enterprise.* Copyright © 1960 by McGraw-Hill Inc. Used with permission of McGraw-Hill Book Co.

[2] F. Roethlisberger, and W. J. Dickson, *Management and the Worker* (Cambridge, Mass.: Harvard University Press, 1939).

[3] Kurt Lewin, *Field Theory in Social Science* (New York: Harper & Row, 1951).

[4] Larry E. Greiner, "Patterns of Organization Change", in Gene W. Dalton, Paul R. Lawrence, and Larry E. Gleim (eds.), *Organizational Change and Development* (Homewood, Ill.: Richard D. Irwin, 1970), p. 222.

[5] Harold J. Leavitt, *New Perspectives in Organization Research* (New York: John Wiley & Sons, 1964).

[6] Paul Lawrence and Jay W. Lorsch, *Organization and Environment: Managing Differentiation and Integration* (Boston: Division of Research, Harvard Business School, 1967).

[7] Arthur Turner, *A Conceptual Scheme for Describing Work Group Behavior* (Boston: Intercollegiate Case Clearing House, 1961).

[8] John P. Campbell and Marvin D. Dunnette, "Effectiveness of T-Group Experiences in Managerial Training and Development," *Psychological Bulletin*, August 1968; and Robert J. House, "T-Group Education and Leadership Effectiveness: A Review of the Empiric Literature and a Critical Evaluation," *Personnel Psychology,* Spring 1967.

[9] Robert R. Blake and J. S. Mouton, *The Managerial Grid* (Houston: Gulf Publishing Co., 1964).

[10] Thomas H. Patten, Jr., "OD–MBO and the Reward System," in *OD-Emerging Dimensions and Concepts* (American Society for Training and Development, 1973); and Stanley Herman, "The Shadow of Organization Development," paper presented at Conference on New Technology in Organization Development, New Orleans, February 1974.

[11] Frederick Herzberg "One More Time: How Do You Motivate Employees?" *Harvard Business Review,* January–February 1968.

[12] Larry E. Tate, Warren R. Nielsen, and Paula C. Bacon, "Advances in Research on Organization Development: Toward a Beginning," *Proceedings of the 36th Annual Meeting of the Academy of Management, August 11–14, 1976*, p. 389.

[13] Newton Margulies and Anthony P. Raia, *Organizational Development: Values, Process, and Technology* (New York: McGraw-Hill Book Co., 1972).

[14] R. R. Blake, Jane S. Mouton, L. B. Barnes, and L. E. Greiner, "Breakthrough in Organizational Development," *Harvard Business Review*, November–December 1964.

[15] William J. Paul, Keith Robertson, and Frederick Herzberg, "Job Enrichment Pays Off," *Harvard Business Review*, March–April 1969. Copyright © 1969 by the President and Fellows of Harvard College; all rights reserved.

[16] Ibid.

[17] L. L. Frank and J. R. Hackman, "A Failure of Job Enrichment: The Case of the Change That Wasn't," *Journal of Applied Behavioral Science*, October–December 1975.

[18] Richard Beckhard, *Organizational Development—Strategies and Models* (Reading, Mass.: Addison-Wesley, 1969).

When you have completed studying
DEVELOPING ORGANIZATIONAL CAPABILITIES
you should be able to:

1. Explain the human resources development system and list ten reasons why it makes the company more effective.
2. List policy alternatives to human resources development.
3. Distinguish among training, development, education, and rehabilitation.
4. Diagram the teaching-learning process.
5. Describe the five levels of learning.
6. Describe teaching-learning techniques from a list given.
7. Identify who in the organization is responsible for each aspect of the HRD program.
8. Give a step-by-step procedure for operating an HRD program.

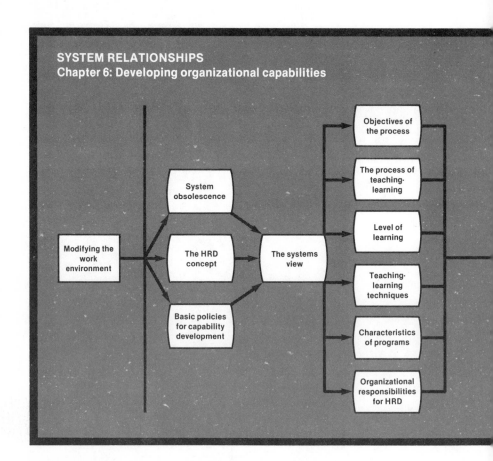

SYSTEM RELATIONSHIPS
Chapter 6: Developing organizational capabilities

Managers are developed, not born.
Highly touted internal management development programs frequently fail to bring up qualified successors.[1]
The General Electric Company spends about $40,000,000 on human resources development programs.
It is practically impossible to define and describe the full dimensions of training in business and industry today.[2]

6

Developing organizational capabilities

Although we lack a lot of information on training, development, and education in business in the United States, we do know that large progres-

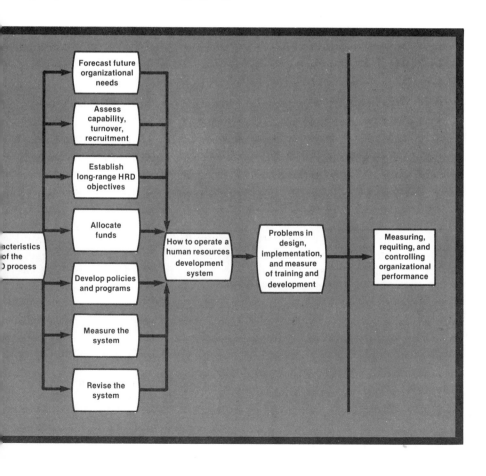

sive companies strongly believe in developing their organizational capabilities by these processes. According to Seymour Lusterman of the Conference Board, companies spent over $2 billion on educating workers in 1975. Of this amount, 70 percent was spent on workers who had already proved their worth to the firms and only 30 percent was spent on new employees.[3]

THE SYSTEMS VIEW

In foregoing chapters we have covered methods for changing the effectiveness and efficiency of the human resource system. These methods have implicitly assumed that the capabilities of people are constant. In other words, we wanted to know how we could do better with the people at hand. Now we want to know how to improve the human resource system by upgrading its individual members to meet greater internal and environmental challenges. This upgrading comes about through involvement in many types of learning experience. The *learning experience* results in a *relatively permanent change* in the behavior of the individual and hence in the behavior of the organizational system.

System obsolescence

When a superior product replaces an old product, the old product is said to be obsolete. The horse and buggy are obsolete for modern cross-country transportation. People may become obsolete, too, if they do not update themselves with regard to new work methods, skills, and knowledge about the environment. An entire organization may become obsolete if it lacks a systematic means for continually developing organizational capabilities. It has been estimated that an engineer's knowledge of his or her field is cut in half every ten years because of the advancement of the field—unless he or she continues to study.

The human resources development concept

According to the human resources development concept, organizational renewal and improvement are possible through planned teaching-learning on a continuous basis. HRD makes the company more effective by reducing problems in such areas as:

1. Staffing for highly skilled positions.
2. High turnover.

3. Lack of management skills.
4. Automation and transfers.
5. Improvement of quality.
6. Improvement of productivity.
7. Reduction of scrap.
8. New product development.
9. Planning and cost control.
10. Job enrichment and employee motivation.

The human resources development process

The human resource system is a processor that acts upon financial and physical resource systems to achieve company objectives. In Exhibit 6–1 we show a portion of the human resource system that

EXHIBIT 6–1
HRD in the staffing process

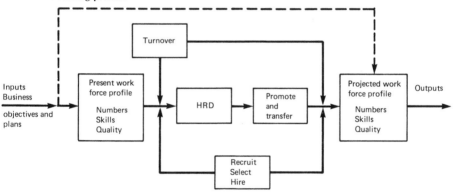

is concerned with improving the system itself. The inputs to the HRD system are business objectives and plans which include projections of the work force required for the planning period. This projected work force profile becomes the objective of the HRD system. If we start with the present work force and the goal for the future, what can happen? For instance, people may quit, retire, die, or be fired. This turnover group must be replaced by hiring new people. Next we put our big training, development, and education program into action to train new employees and upgrade the old-timers. As a result, we are able to promote and transfer people. The holes left by promotion, transfers, and further turnover must again be filled by hiring more people. By this time, the future will have arrived and

EXHIBIT 6–2
The HRD system

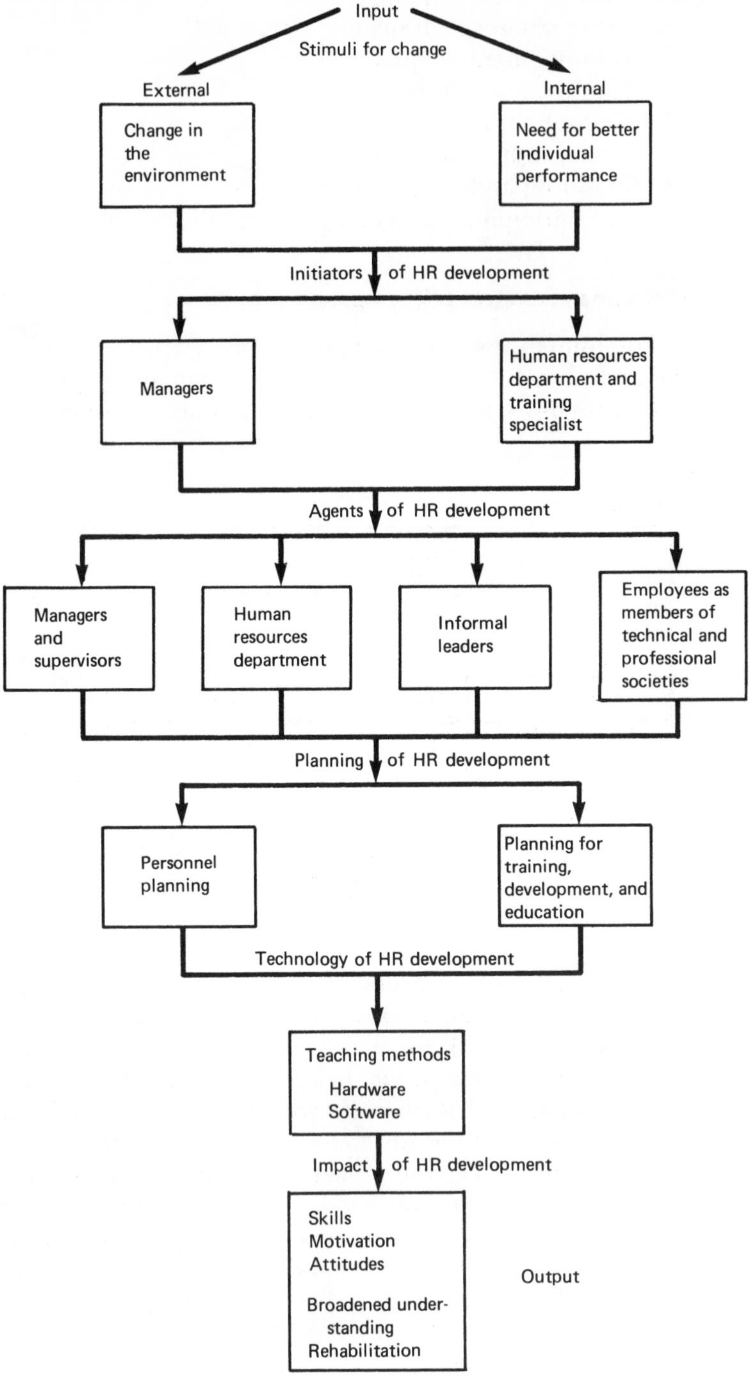

Input

Stimuli for change

External

Internal

| Change in the environment | | Need for better individual performance |

Initiators ↓ of HR development

| Managers | | Human resources department and training specialist |

Agents ↓ of HR development

| Managers and supervisors | Human resources department | Informal leaders | Employees as members of technical and professional societies |

Planning ↓ of HR development

| Personnel planning | | Planning for training, development, and education |

Technology of HR development

| Teaching methods

Hardware
Software |

Impact ↓ of HR development

| Skills
Motivation
Attitudes

Broadened under-
standing
Rehabilitation |

Output

we will have achieved our projected work force profile. The outputs of the work force are, of course, the outputs of the total company.

Now that we have seen how HRD fits into the total human resource system, let us look at the HRD system itself. What happens in HRD? Exhibit 6–2 traces the process from input stimuli to output impact. One basic stimulus is change in the environment which requires that the organization be retrained. Another basic stimulus is the desire of management to improve profits by improving organizational performance.

Once there is a recognized need for HRD, somebody has to initiate it by formally authorizing expenditures of time and money and designating the formal agents of development. Informal agents of development participate by contributing ideas and pressing for HRD. These "informal leaders" and just plain interested employees are shown in the system of Exhibit 6–2. "Agents of HR development" are essentially people who "sell" the rest of the organization on the need for training, development, and education. Once the HRD concept is accepted, management can plan confidently for the acquisition, promotion, and development of employees.

The implementation of development plans requires the selection of teachers; teaching methods or approaches; hardware, such as overhead projectors, TV, and slide projectors; and software, such as outlines, books, audiotapes and work manuals.

The application of the technology of individual development, the teaching-learning process, has as its output changes in individual performance. The desired changes may be improved skills; increased motivation; broadened understanding of the environment; different attitudes toward work, the company, groups within the company, the job, or members of other work groups. One special change may be a result of programs for newly hired disadvantaged or handicapped people, alcoholics, ex-convicts, former drug addicts, or other people with special needs to whom the company may wish to extend help.

Basic policies for human resources development

The human resources department may recommend one of several basic policies to follow with regard to developing the capabilities of the organization's members to meet new challenges. The choice will depend on the value system of the company, on industry practices, and to a great extent on the size of the company. Alternative policies are:

1. Laissez-faire.
2. Encouragement.
3. Joint company-individual commitment.
4. Aggressive company development.
5. Replacement instead of development.

In the first case, the company does nothing about developing its human resources. It assumes that people will prepare themselves and that the good ones will rise to the top. With the proper work

EXHIBIT 6–3

	No. _____473_____
Dravo Corporation and Subsidiaries	Page __1__ of ____1____
Policy Statement	Supersedes
	No. _____
Date Approved _____10-20-75_____	Date: _____

Subject: Continuing Education

It shall be the policy of the company to provide opportunities for individual growth and development which will be in the best interest of the employe and the company. Rapidly changing technology, the dynamic expansion of the company's activities involving new fields of technology, the need for new and improved skills, techniques, and management methods make it necessary to constantly improve and update the respective capabilities of employes.

Recognizing that each individual is primarily responsible for developing his or her own program of self-development, the company, through the following specific policies, provides opportunities for assistance:

Tuition Reimbursement Plan	Policy No. 475–1
Professional and Technical Development	Policy No. 477
Professional Certification or Registration	Policy No. 480–1

In addition to programs offered by various outside educational institutions, a broad range of programs to assist in the development of employes will be provided internally. These programs will be specially designed and planned to meet Dravo needs.

The corporate Personnel Development Department is primarily responsible for the administration and coordination of training activities within the corporation.

Courtesy of Dravo Corporation

climate and a suitable incentive system, this policy may be success-ful in a stable industry where innovations are rare.

The second policy is one of benevolent paternalism. The com-pany may give some courses for employees. It may encourage em-ployees to attend local colleges and record the results in the em-ployees' personnel files. It may send a limited number of people to professional meetings each year. This policy is obviously an un-structured approach to long-range HRD.

The joint company-individual development policy is a planned system. The company establishes development objectives and plans and means for implementing the plans, then matches em-ployee needs to courses or programs offered. A wide range of techniques for development is likely to be used.

Aggressive company development programs are usually found in the large multinational companies. In one such company, the only route to becoming a financial manager was to complete a two- to three-year company program of courses given after working hours. In some high-technology companies, engineers must either take company or university courses every year or risk being released.

Finally we come to a less common policy. A company may de-cide to upgrade through a hiring process rather than a development process. One firm let it be known unofficially that at the end of each year the poorest 10 percent of the professional people would be told to start looking for another job.

Well-managed companies clarify their educational and develop-ment system by means of policies, program catalogs, and forms. To illustrate the nature of these communication devices, we show an example from three different companies. The general policy state-ment of Dravo Corporation, Exhibit 6–3, is backed up by a series of more specific policies. In Exhibit 6–4 we show two pages from the 1977 training and development catalog of Westinghouse Electric Corporation. An application for educational assistance is illustrated by Exhibit 6–5.

CHARACTERISTICS OF THE DEVELOPMENT PROCESS

Before we discuss how to develop and operate an HRD system, we need to examine some basic concepts of the development pro-cess for a better understanding of what is going on.

Objectives of the process

The objective of HRD is to make the business function better, more effectively, and more efficiently. By "function better," we

EXHIBIT 6–4

Marketing Strategy and Business Planning Seminar

Objectives:
To improve the understanding of participants in the formulation of strategy as it applies to business and marketing. A major focus of the seminar will be on long-range strategic planning, that portion of the planning process beyond the annual profit plan. Decisions made, or not made, today often have drastic impact on profits four to five years in the future. More specifically, the participant will achieve a clearer understanding of the meaning of strategy; a knowledge of how to formulate realistic strategies to meet division objective; an appreciation for the "how to" in implementing strategies by day-to-day decisions; and the skill to bring order and discipline to the strategic planning process.

Description:
Case studies, lectures, workshops and discussions are used to develop frameworks and application of the critical strategic planning concepts. Further, the need for marketing strategic plans to be fully integrated with the manufacturing and financial resources is emphasized throughout the course.

Extensive real-life examples will show the effects of conflicting business and marketing strategies and why strategy is completely different from operations. Recent changes in Westinghouse planning and resource allocation are covered, as well as:

Growth Alternatives, Marketing Strategies and Product Line Portfolios

Long-run Price and Cost Experience Curve Relationships

Planning Marketing Strategy: Manufacturing Capacity and Financial Requirements

Marketing Planning and the Concept of Sustainable growth

Integrating International Markets into Long-Range Marketing Strategy: International Product Life Cycle

Marketing Strategy and Contingency Planning

Candidate Selection:
Divisional General Management, Marketing Managers, Product Managers, Sales Managers and Planning Managers, Group and Business Unit Managers. Managers in other functional areas such as Manufacturing and Control should find this seminar useful since strategy development and implementation requires close integration of marketing, manufacturing and financial planning.

Length:
Two and ½ days, starting with evening session.

Management:
R. McClinton
Manager, Marketing Training,
Education Department,
WIN 235-3146

EXHIBIT 6–4 *(continued)*

Women in Business Management Seminar

Objectives:
This course prepares women to:

assume increased responsibility in either managerial or professional roles

participate equally with men in the management of the corporation

grow in their ability to understand and apply management techniques

communicate effectively

handle interpersonal and intergroup relationships

Description:
The opportunities available to women in business are expanding rapidly. This course addresses the many vital subjects to which women have had little exposure. Its primary objective is to help women further develop their business acumen and gain self-confidence in their ability to use it effectively in business careers. Women participating in this three-day course will get an overview of management techniques, motivation, and communication.

Candidate Selection:
Ideal for newly appointed women managers or those about to be promoted as well as women in professional positions.

Length:
Three days. with evening sessions.

Management:
T. A. Cook
Administrator, Functional and Support Training,
Education Department,
WIN 236-7242

Source: *Training and Development Programs 77.*   Courtesy of *Westinghouse Electric Corp.*

EXHIBIT 6–5

TI—2418 0

TEXAS INSTRUMENTS INCORPORATED
EDUCATIONAL ASSISTANCE REQUEST

Please type or print

Complete this form and obtain all approvals (supervisor, cost center manager, Personnel/Training manager) two weeks prior to beginning of course.

Last Name	First	Initial	Empl. No	Div.	C.C.	Dept.	Ext.	M.S.

Title of Course(s)	Course(s) No.	Job Title
		School

Course(s) Begins	Course(s) Ends	Credit Hours	Approximate Total Cost

Explain how this course(s) relates to the improvement of your qualifications_____
Is this course(s) related to your plans for a degree, certificate, diploma or license?_____
If yes, please specify: _____ In what field_____
When do you expect to receive it?_____
Have you filled out a degree plan and turned it in to the Training Department?_____
Will you receive financial assistance for education from other sources?_____
If yes, please designate (G.I. Bill, Hazelwood Act, etc.)_____. How much? _____
Have you received a reimbursement under TI Educational Assistance since January 1 this year?_____
If so, how much? $ _____

Applicant's Signature	Date

Approvals for Educational Assistance

Supervisor's Signature	Date

Cost Center Manager	Date	Level 2 Manager (If required)	Date	Personnel/Training Mgr.	Date

Tager Approval:
This is to certify that the above-named individual will be allowed _____ hours off from work each week to attend Tager classes

Supervisor	Date

Supervisor: If this request is disapproved, state reason & return to Training manager_____

FOR ACCOUNTING PURPOSES ONLY

	Co.	Major	Sub	Major	Amount
Course Grade(s)_____					
Tuition_____					
Books_____					
Other_____					
Total_____					
90% _____ Pay this amount to the above-named individual					

Approved: Personnel/Training Manager

Distribution: White-Accounting; Blue-Training Center; Yellow-Employee/Personnel

---

mean that people find greater satisfaction in their work and are motivated to do their best. There are different phases in achieving this objective:

1. *Training* is directed toward improving performance on the job that the employee is presently doing. For example, a stenog-

rapher may receive training to increase the rate of dictation that he or she can take. A manager may be trained in public speaking so that the speeches he or she gives for the company will be better. Training is used to develop mental or manual skills, to increase knowledge, and to change attitudes. Training is a *job-related* experience.

2. *Development* means preparing an employee for a future but fairly well defined job at a higher level. Development consists of organization-related experience, that is, it is directed toward the future strength of the organization.

3. *Education* is individual-related learning experience. The focus is on improving the breadth of knowledge, the understanding, and the thinking processes of the individual.

4. *Rehabilitation* is experience oriented toward the special skills and attitudes required by some people in order to remain or become useful to society. Some companies, for example, make a special effort to employ and retrain physically handicapped people. Many companies have unpublicized programs for employees who have become alcoholics.

The process of teaching–learning

The human resources department is responsible for staffing company-conducted courses with instructors. If you were the training director, you would want to make sure that all instructors thoroughly understood the teaching-learning process. Learning is not accomplished by ideas in the notes of the instructor being put into the notes of the student without passing through the head of either.

As shown in Exhibit 6–6, there are eight steps in the teaching-learning process. First, the would-be learner must be receptive and motivated to learn. If the organizational climate has not led to this motivation, the burden on the instructor is a heavy one. All instructors should try to reinforce the student's interest in learning, regardless of initial readiness.

EXHIBIT 6–6
The teaching-learning process

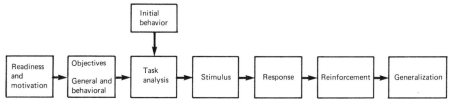

The second step is to prepare objectives for the course. Is the course supposed to train, develop, educate, or rehabilitate? Then, more specifically, what will the instructional objectives be? Robert F. Mager, an authority on instructional objectives, states that such objectives should give:

1. A statement of the desired behavior of the student at the end of the course.
2. The conditions under which the student can perform the desired behavior.
3. The level of achievement he or she will be asked to attain.[4]

Next, the instructor must analyze the student's present level of performance, his or her initial behavior, so that the teaching-learning tasks may be identified. In other words, what does the student need to know or do in order to perform the behavioral objectives?

The instructor prepares the course by developing stimuli that will get the student to respond. For example, you might be asked to read through these steps in the teaching-learning process and then to draw a diagram such as Exhibit 6–6. If your response were a good one, a passing grade would be given to reinforce your behavior. The major reinforcement is passing the entire course. Each time you pass one portion of the course you will know that you are on the way to achieving your goal of getting credit for the whole course.

Finally, in many learning situations, the learner must be able to *generalize* his or her behavior. For example, if you were being taught how to interview a particular job seeker, could you apply the principles you learned whenever you were required to interview another candidate?

Levels of learning

We mentioned above that a complete statement of instructional objectives should include the level of achievement that the student will be asked to attain. It is helpful to illustrate the levels of learning by means of a simplified example. Suppose that we wish to teach the student about leadership. At the lowest level of teaching, we would say that leadership is inducing someone to work toward a predetermined objective. We would explain "induce" and the total idea and require that the student be able to *recall* the meaning of leadership upon request. This level is shown at the bottom step in Exhibit 6–7.

EXHIBIT 6–7
Levels of learning

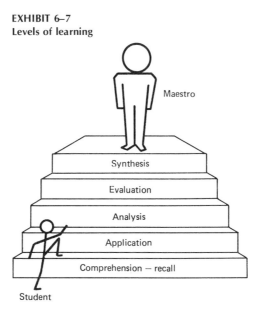

The next level of teaching and learning is the *application* level. We would tell the student what things he or she must do to lead. In other words, the student applies principles.

Analysis means to break up into parts for greater understanding. We would examine the elements of leadership behavior, why such behavior induces people to act, and what research about leadership behavior appears to mean. A student who has a thorough understanding of leadership could *evaluate* the behavior of specific individuals and say which of their actions promoted leadership and which actions were not those of a leader.

Finally, the most difficult level of teaching-learning is the level of *synthesis*. Synthesis is the creation of new ideas and patterns of thought. The instructor cannot give a formula or rule for synthesis for the student to learn; he can only stimulate the student to think independently. Thus a student might arrive at a new description of leadership behavior or originate a new experiment that shows an unsuspected characteristic of leaders.

Teaching–learning techniques

The manager of the Human Resources Department and the training director are both interested in achieving instructional objectives at the lowest cost. The selection of a good technique is based upon the objectives of the instructor, the level of teaching-learning, the backgrounds and maturity of the students, and the available time, facilities, and equipment. There are many teaching techniques, and the training director should, of course, be thoroughly familiar with them. Management should have a general idea of the techniques to the extent summarized in Exhibit 6–8.

Characteristics of programs

A training and development program in industry is usually designed to meet the needs of four different groups: managers, professional employees, semiprofessional employees, and operating personnel, such as general office and factory workers.

In Exhibit 6–8 we have seen how some techniques are especially suitable for one form of program or another. In addition to techniques, however, other characteristics of training and development programs need to be considered. These are:

1. The number of courses.
2. The number of sessions per course.
3. The length of meetings.
4. The time of meetings: on company time, on personal time, or on part of each.
5. The number of students per course and per class.
6. The share of costs borne by employees, if any.
7. Reward or promotion, if any, upon completion.

Because training courses are related to a specific job, they are usually short (several days to several months) and highly structured. Also, because they are directly related to present job performance they are apt to be given on company time and at the company plant.

Professional development courses may range from one-day seminars to two- or three-year accounting, engineering, or manufacturing programs. Although some courses may be given on company time and at the plant, many are given after hours. Tuition refund programs and seminars away from the company plant are common, but the use of company instructors is popular because in this way courses can be focused on company problems. The advantage of sending students outside the company and away from their work is that this gives them fresh outlooks.

Managers may receive training to update them in their functional fields, to develop them for future promotion, or to make their responses to society, the public, and their customers more sophisti-

EXHIBIT 6-8
Teaching techniques

Technique	Description	Suitability	Check points
Lecture	A talk to explain material, with little or no participation by the class in the form of discussion or questions	For large groups For orientation or easy-to-understand material	Unless the preparation is very good, the audience may get lost at some point and miss all of the following ideas. Short lectures and brief applications or quizzes help
Case study	A business problem situation is described in detail, with both relevant and irrelevant information given. The student is required to identify problems, develop alternative solutions, evaluate	For small groups Requires discussion and participation by all participants. The case study method is used to develop skills at analyzing and solving complex unstructured problems and to provide broad simulated experience. It may also be used to develop group decision-making skills	Students may get frustrated because the data are pretty much limited to the case material. Even in real life, however, similar limits are set by time and cost Some students fail to participate unless called upon, and others may dominate the discussion unless controlled Arguments may evolve around opinions rather than analysis of the "facts" of the case
Conferences and seminars	A speaker may lecture, or there may be no speaker, only a conference leader. Knowledge, ideas, and opinions are freely interchanged among all participants	For broadening knowledge, stimulating new ideas, and changing attitudes. "Workshop seminars" may be used to develop skills	Participants may stray from the subject Hardening of attitudes and conflict may occur Seminars away from the company tend to keep politics out of the viewpoints expressed
Tuition reimbursement programs	The company reimburses the employee for part or all of tuition for attending a college or university. Reimbursement may depend on the grade received or on whether the course is part of a degree program	For long-range development where turnover is low For development of managerial talent and professional skills	The program should have some relevance to company human resource needs By agreement with the employer, the employee should give company service for some time after obtaining a degree

EXHIBIT 6–8 *(continued)*

Technique	Description	Suitability	Check points
Programmed instruction and computer-assisted learning	Programmed instruction and, usually, computer-assisted learning are rigid self-learning devices. The student is given material and tested on it immediately before proceeding to new material	For either large or small groups where cost is critical Permits people to study at their own convenience	Appropriate programs must be available. Students may drop out by stretching out their work
Simulation and gaming	A business situation or an entire industry is modeled so that the student may take actions and have the results reported back. Usually the model is stored in a computer	For group projects For developing decision-making skills requiring the integration of many factors	The model should not be too simple, and the required learning of input formats should not be too complex The students may just guess at their input decisions instead of making a good preanalysis Computer reports of results should be returned to students well in advance of subsequent decisions
Video and audio self-development programs	Lectures and rote learning material may be given on video equipment or tape cassettes	For individual study at student's own pace For learning facts For developing skills when responses to the equipment are clear For inspirational purposes, such as in sales training	If the material is not clear, the student will become frustrated and drop out The student's motivation must be strong to carry out a self-development program where reinforcement of motivation may be absent
Remote TV live teaching	Instructor lectures to groups of students at remote classrooms. Usually, two-way voice communication is provided	For a highly skilled lecturer working with groups of students located at widely separated company plants, this is an economical method For courses that require relatively few questions to clarify points	Instructors may outpace students if students do not take the initiative to slow them down Associated written assignments have to be corrected and returned in the period between lectures to be effective

Technique	Description	Uses	Precautions
Laboratory training	A change agent (consultant) devises means for groups of people in an organization to clarify their values, attitudes, and problems to improve understanding, motivation, and the working climate in general	For groups of almost any size For changing an organization's attitudes For increasing organizational problem-solving capabilities	Top management must understand its role and give strong backing to the change agent Considerable time will be required before the impact of laboratory training becomes evident High-level executives may have to devote a good deal of time to such programs
Managerial grid sessions	Six-phase program lasting from three to five years. Starts with upgrading managers' skills, continues to group improvement, improves intergroup relations, goes into corporate planning, develops implementation methods, and ends with an evaluation phase	For rapidly growing and large companies where the considerable investment has time to pay off	Check on progress in achieving objectives Check on turnover of the managers involved
T-group sessions, sensitivity training, group dynamics sessions	Participants are put in situations in which the views, behavior, and personality of each is subjected to examination and critique by the others	For developing better understanding and better perceptions of co-workers	Participants may not be able to stand the stress involved in learning about themselves. They may withdraw from the group or suffer psychological damage Problems arising within the group must be resolved before the group breaks up
Vestibule training	An area away from the production line is set up with machinery similar to that used in production. Trainees are guided and supervised by instructors right at hand	For training machine operators quickly and thoroughly where the high cost involved is worthwhile	The sequence of learning should be carefully established A constant flow of trainees to keep the duplicate machinery in use will help lower costs

EXHIBIT 6–8 (concluded)

Technique	Description	Suitability	Check points
On-the-job training	Employees are instructed and guided while they are working	For not-too-complicated factory jobs For new employees For all employees to some degree To maintain low training costs and uninterrupted work flow	Formal on-the-job training is preferable to informal, trial-and-error learning. A program of supervised learning and measurement should be installed
Job rotation	An employee may be rotated through a series of jobs in different functional areas so that the employee learns all phases of the business	For salespeople so that they will understand the products and production problems better For manager development when the manager is given significant (two–five years) experience in different jobs	The time that a person is assigned to each job should be kept as short as possible since the objective is to broaden the person. The time in a job might be one month for some programs and four or five years for high-level management development
Correspondence courses	Correspondence courses require students to read material on their own or to actually work on equipment which is supplied. Students mail their answers to the company or university that offers the course. In some cases exams must be proctored by local professional teachers	For development of technical/manual skills For training in specialized business subjects, such as accounting For managerial development and broadening (for example, the Alexander Hamilton program)	Students must be highly motivated to study on their own In some cases, students may have friends do the homework. Proctored exams will help reduce this problem

cated and less provincial. The development of managerial talents is a never-ending process that goes on in parallel with managerial experience. The use of seminars for the interchange of ideas, for case study, and for teaching managerial behavior is highly favored. Some companies offer top-level managers educational renewal programs at universities both in the United Sates and abroad. Companies such as Xerox and General Electric have built their own management schools away from the demands of the plant and headquarters (see Exhibit 6–9).

Organizational responsibilities for HRD

Line managers are responsible for the company's short- and long-range development plans. In making such plans, each manager projects the number of people and skills required over the planning period. The human resources department compiles the totals for all managers, evaluates the feasibility of hiring the needed people, and plans the training programs required to supplement the hiring by increasing the present capabilities of the organization.

In very small companies with perhaps 50 employees or less, the owner-manager will probably plan any development programs. In larger companies with a single plant or a single product line, the planning will be carried out by the personnel manager or the training director. Very large companies with separate product divisions conduct both corporate-wide planning and local product division planning for HRD. Each product division has its own training director, and corporate headquarters also has a training director. The somewhat complex relationships are depicted in Exhibit 6–10.

HOW TO OPERATE AN HRD SYSTEM

Theory is relevant to practice, and practice is relevant to the real world. Let us now consider a step-by-step approach to follow if you were a training director setting up a HRD program. We will not go into detail on each step since every development program should be tailored to fit a particular company.

Forecast future organizational needs for five years

With proper planning, product objectives will be forecast year by year for five years ahead. For each product, tasks will be identified in engineering, production, and marketing. For each task, direct labor, materials, indirect labor, and other indirect expense may

EXHIBIT 6–9
Xerox's training center

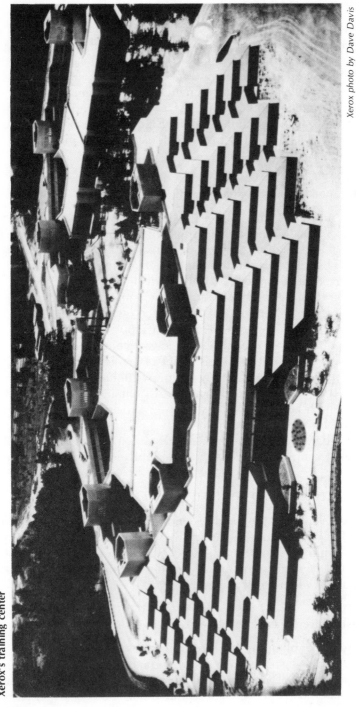

Xerox photo by Dave Davis

On June 2, 1974, the Xerox International Center for Training and Management Development opened its doors to its first students—some 400 Xerox sales and service people.

The Leesburg Center is the culmination of a Xerox dream to offer the very best training and development programs to its people.

When the center is in high gear, technical representatives, sales representatives, computer scientists, managers—more than a thousand students at a time—will be educated in its elaborate facilities on a 2,265-acre site in rural Leesburg, Virginia.

EXHIBIT 6–10
Relationships between corporate services and product departments for human resource development programs and courses

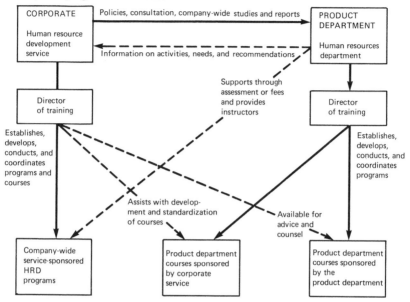

be projected year by year. On this basis the number of people with each skill may be forecast. If tasks cannot be identified for two or more years ahead, a simple curve may be used to forecast work force requirements.

Assess current capabilities, turnover, recruitment plans

"Jim, I was talking with Bill Woodknopf at the party last night, and he told me that all his managers are getting the Vesco 4–D Training Program. Maybe we ought to try it out in our company and see how it goes."

The above incident illustrates the casual way that courses are sometimes introduced into companies and resources wasted. When the company has prepared a projection of its work force needs and skills, its next step is to review where it stands today. Proper HRD management will match capabilities to needs by forecasting (a) losses through turnover, (b) additions from recruiting new personnel, and (c) the development of present personnel by instructional programs.

Although HRD is essentially a line management responsibility, line managers have too little time to develop HRD systems. This being the case, the human resources department typically takes the lead in developing such a system. This is another reason why the human resources department should maintain an inventory of all employees. It should also establish a reporting system so that managers periodically report on projected work force needs and on the instructional needs of all individuals in their organization.

Establish long-range HRD objectives

The long-range HRD objectives should parallel the company's strategy. A brief example is given in the accompanying table.

Company objectives	HRD objectives
Scope: Lubricating oil products in Eastern U.S. markets	Sales, production, and technical personnel Train all groups
Risk: Medium risk in investment of funds	Hire slowly so as to have too few rather than too many. Develop enough managers so that expansion may be carried out rapidly if needed
Competitive edge: Technical quality of product	Specialized programs in technology Tuition refund programs at the graduate level
Specifications (HRD only): 2,250 employees five years hence—1,000 production, 150 marketing, 80 managerial, 20 human resources, 600 technical, 400 supporting services	Provide training and development for 50 percent of employees at the average rate of $1,000/year
Deployment of resources (HRD only): Emphasis on technical and managerial training and development	Same Concentrate on employees under 50 years of age and minority groups

Although it would appear that we should survey the needs of employees in terms of the needs for developing organizational capabilities, the "deployment of resources" limits us. With anticipated sales and cash flow, we must allocate funds among plant, equipment, human resources, and dividends to stockholders. If we increase the number of dollars going to one of these, we must decrease the number of dollars going to another. Therefore, the systems approach tell us that a good *balance* in distributing our funds will probably ensure good growth for the firm. What this leads to is, "Here are X dollars for training and development, Mr. Human Resources Manager. Please set up a long-range program to meet our organizational needs as best you can."

Allocate funds for various programs, and establish a cost accounting system

The training director prepares a list of HRD programs. The funds must be allocated among programs. The cost of a course in a particular program depends upon whether the course has been given previously, the cost for the instructor, classroom and supply costs, the number of student-hours, the teaching technique used, and whether the course is given on company time (and if so, the lost productivity of participants). If the course is away from the plant, fees and travel expenses become factors.

At this point, a cost accounting system should be established to record costs for courses and general administration of HRD. For example, the account number 271 might stand for (2) program for the development of chemists, (7) course on the breakdown properties of fluids, and (1) the cost of the instructor. Everyone, whether in administration, accounting, sales, manufacturing, or services, would report each week on the number of hours charged to any of the HRD accounts. Materials, subcontract, and other expenses, such as long-distance phone calls and travel, would be similarly charged to the proper HRD accounts.

Develop policies and programs

Now that funds have been allocated to programs, we can develop a list of the courses that will make up each program. Remember that some programs may stretch out over several years. Also, a course in a program will only be offered when managers propose a sufficient number of employees as candidates for the course.

Some companies prepare a brochure listing and describing all courses (and the total educational opportunities) offered. In addition, policies must be developed and publicized to employees. Examples of policies might be:

Employees must have one year of service before admission to certain courses.

Tuition refund requires advance approval of the employee's program by his or her manager and the training director.

All courses will be given after work hours. Admission to a course must be based upon the development program worked out by the individual and his or her manager.

All new employees must take the company orientation course.

Any employee may take basic courses that will improve his or her job skills.

Any shop employee who completes the company's manufacturing training program will receive a rate increase of $0.20 per hour.

The training director should make a survey of managers to determine what specific needs for development each manager believes exist. He or she can then shape each program with courses in response to those needs. The proposed set of courses for the coming year should be reviewed by key managers before they are definitely scheduled.

Measure the system effectiveness and cost

From the systems view, evaluation of the teaching-learning system is needed for two reasons. The most important reason is simply to find out how much the teaching-learning system is improving the *total* human resource system relative to inputs—money, people, materials—expended on the teaching-learning system. The second reason for evaluation is to find out how we may improve the teaching-learning system itself. How may we improve programs, instructors, techniques, facilities, course content, and so on?

We may evaluate the teaching-learning activities themselves to find out how each may be improved individually. This is not a *systems* approach, since improving one activity, such as increasing class time, may detract from another activity.

The subject of measurement is not treated in depth here. We will give only some practical approaches to evaluation. From this view we consider the impact of the system by:

1. Evaluation of the employee.
2. Evaluation of the instructor.
3. Evaluation of the administration of the system.

We may evaluate these three factors (a) by comparing before and after measures, (b) by measuring improvement from time to time, or (c) by measuring the performance of employees at the conclusion of the program against the objectives of the program. In Exhibit 6–11, we have summarized some ideas for evaluating the three factors.

One item in Exhibit 6–11, "preparatory and support activities," needs further explanation. This series of questions helps illustrate such activities:

1. Are the teaching-learning program objectives clearly defined?
2. Are the proper kinds and numbers of people assigned to the training director?

3. Are there adequate facilities, space, equipment, and materials?
4. Does the training group receive and utilize periodicals, books, and information relative to advances in industry training?
5. Are the training and development being done on time and as planned?
6. Does the training director publicize training activities and make his or her services understood by the entire organization?

Revise the system

Feedback is information about performance that is related back to the earlier steps in the HRD process. The performance relative to

EXHIBIT 6–11
Evaluation strategies

Focus	Evaluation methods	Who evaluates?
Employee-students		
Mental skills	Achievement tests, before and after	Instructor
	Reports	Instructor
	Work performance appraisal	Manager
Attitudes	Attitude measurement questionnaires	Training director
	Course evaluation	Training director
	Behavioral measures, such as attendance records	Instructor, manager
Manual skills	Work performance appraisal	Manager
	Job performance tests	Foreman or supervisor
	Observation by others	Key employees
	Rating scales	Supervisor
Instructors		
Teaching-learning		
skills	Questionnaire	Students, training director
	Auditing of class sessions	Training director
Effectiveness	Measure of improvement in students or degree of achievement of behavioral objectives	Manager, training director
Training director		
Administration of the		
training program	Measures of organizational performance, before and after	Manager of human resources and line managers
	Observation of preparatory and support activities	Manager of human resources
Value of the program	Cost/benefit analysis	Manager of human resources

EXHIBIT 6–12
T&D Grid©

	Purposes			
	A *Improvement of the individual's performance in his or her present position*	*B* *Improvement of the individual's ability to perform in an upgraded position*	*C* *Improvement of the general performance level of the organization*	*D* *Improvement of the individual independent of his or her job*
Cognitive				
To understand and recall discrete and factual information	1			
To comprehend the meaning of concepts and abstract terminology				
To develop understanding of relationships among combinations of facts, terminology, and concepts				
To improve analytic and problem-solving skills		4		

To improve planning ability—that is, the ability to arrange and work out the details of a plan or idea	3		
To improve imaginative and creative thinking			
Affective			
To change prevailing attitudes, beliefs, and/or sentiments		2	
To improve the individual's behavior in interactions with others			
Psychomotor			
To improve motor, manual, and physical skills			

objectives indicates the kinds of changes that should be made in the HRD system to improve it.

PROBLEMS IN THE DESIGN, IMPLEMENTATION, AND MEASUREMENT OF TRAINING AND DEVELOPMENT

Although the preceding approach to upgrading the organization may appear easy and straightforward to the inexperienced reader, such is not the case. In practical situations, organizations develop their training policies and programs more by muddling through, trial and error, and continual adaptation to changing needs.

From a systems view, we would like to know the cost/effectiveness ratio of many possible alternative programs so that we can choose the one that provides the best trade-off with other parts of the HRS in terms of deployment of resources. This staggering problem is based upon the premise that we can understand the teaching-learning process and can measure it! Educators and psychological researchers have been studying this problem for decades, and many have simply said, "It can't be done."

Recent research by Georgoff and Murdick covered several hundred large corporations and a review of the psychological learning literature.[5] They developed a training and development grid which relates basic individual objectives to organizational objectives. This T&D Grid©, shown in Exhibit 6–12, may be used as a practical tool to identify the priority of individuals' needs. The priorities for an individual which are worked out by counseling may be shown by the rank numbers in Exhibit 6–12. The grid also shows the purposes of each educational course or activity listed after identifying its objectives. When all activities have been listed appropriately on the grid, overlapping, overemphasis, underemphasis, and voids may be revealed.

The above is only one example of the many types of information which only future research can develop. Research on corporate training and development differs from most past educational research which deals with children. The education of adult is called "androgogy," as opposed to "pedagogy," the education of children.

SUMMARY

The development of organizational capabilities is a process performed by a subsystem of the human resource system. We have called this the human resources development system. The system is composed of line managers, the manager of human resources, and the training or development director and staff. The inputs processed are the employees of the company.

Companies adopt a particular basic policy with respect to HRD. It may be: do nothing. Or it may consist of a major integrated systems effort.

In order to understand and apply principles for HRD, we must study some basic concepts. These concepts deal with:

1. The objectives of the HRD process.
2. The process of teaching/learning.
3. The levels of learning.
4. Teaching-learning techniques.
5. The characteristics of programs for manual workers, professional employees, and managers.
6. Organizing for HRD.

Once we have these background concepts in mind, we are ready to lay out a plan for HRD and to execute the plan. In essence, the plan must start with macro objectives, the total organizational needs for development over a two- to five-year period, let us say.

Next we need to establish the amount of money that we will invest in this HRD program.

Within the scope of macro objectives and allocated funds, we establish basic policies for the HRD system. We determine policies for matching the employees to be developed to the funds that are available.

The stage is now set for the detailed development of courses and execution of the program. We plan specific courses for the year ahead, obtain instructors, classrooms, equipment. We schedule class times, in line with our policies. We publicize the courses and obtain definite enrollments approved by employees' managers. We then conduct and monitor the courses.

Every operation or process in business should be measured to determine how well the system involved is working. We may measure the HRD system as a whole, and we may measure "components" in the system. We are interested in system effectiveness, that is, in the degree to which the HRD system is achieving system objectives. We are also interested in the relationship between the benefits and the cost of the system.

CASE: A QUESTION OF TRAINING

First Banktrust of Florida was organized as a multibank holding company in 1972. It has grown to 15 banks located from Miami to Orlando. The rapid growth has made it difficult to find good management. Further, on-the-job training of nonmanagement personnel has not been working well because many positions in banks today require considerable technical knowledge and skills.

The organization of the home office bank is shown in Figure A. Management is considering installing a training section in the Operations Department, as shown in Figure B.

You have just been hired as head of training and asked to present a proposal for a company-wide training program within the next 60 days.

FIGURE A
Bank functional chart

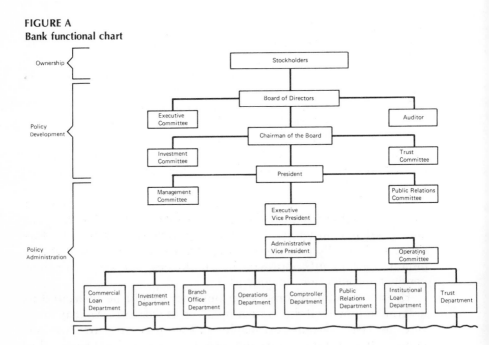

FIGURE B
Operations Department functional chart

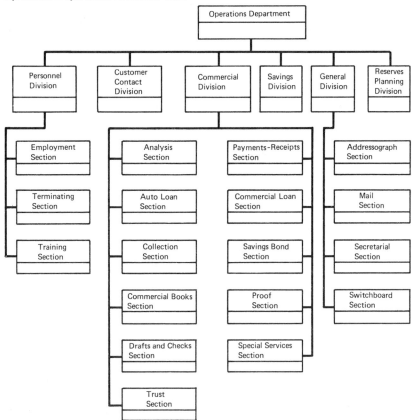

QUESTIONS AND PROBLEMS

1. How does learning affect behavior?

2. If you put a manager on an isolated island for ten years, how do you think he would do if he were put back in his old job?

3. What are some problems that training and development might help solve besides the ten given in the text?

4. a. List some inputs to the HRD system.
   b. List some outputs of the HRD system. (Remember, the HRD system is a *processor* that acts upon people.)

5. How do changes in the environment impel the human resource system to train and develop the people who make up the system?

6. Describe how the manager of human resources might work with the line managers to carry out HRD system planning.

7. As training director, you find that a course in interpersonal communications is planned. Name several possible sources for obtaining an instructor.

8. What do you think are possible effects if a company has no HRD policies or programs?

9. Write a letter to a well-known company asking for information about its training and development programs.

10. *a.* Why might employees find greater satisfaction in their jobs if they are continually being trained and developed by the company?

    b. Do you think that a company might be able to maintain lower turnover, higher morale, greater employee motivation, but lower salaries by keeping employees busy taking courses each year?

11. List the steps in the teaching-learning process. Describe how each step applies to your learning experience with this course so far, or indicate that the step was omitted.

12. What teaching-learning techniques are being used for this course?

13. Visit a local company, perhaps a large retail chain store or a manufacturing company, and obtain information about its management development program. Present your report in class.

14. Assume that you have just been appointed HRD director for a small expanding company. The company has 100 production employees, 13 salespersons, 20 office employees, and 9 managers and supervisors. You report directly to the president. He has asked you to develop an HRD program that will have some good short-term payoffs.

    a. List the steps that you would go through, on the basis of common sense, in setting up such a program. (These would not necessarily be the same steps given in the text.)

    b. List some courses that would seem likely to offer measurable short-term payoffs.

BIBLIOGRAPHY

Bass, Bernard M., and Vaughn, James A. *Training in Industry: The Management of Learning.* Belmont, Calif.: Wadsworth Publishing Co., 1966.

Cone, William F. "Guidelines for Training Specialists," *Training and Development Journal,* January 1974.

Davies, Ivor L.; Hudson, E. "Henry"; Dodd, Bernard; and Hartley, James. *The Organization of Training.* Maidenhead, England: McGraw-Hill, 1973.

Gaylord, John A. "The Development of Skills Training Courses." *Training and Developmental Journal,* April 1974.

Georgoff, David, and Murdick, R. G. A seed grant project. Boca Raton: Florida Atlantic University, 1977.

Kenney, J. P. J., and Donnelly, E. L. *Manpower Training and Development.* London: Harrap, 1972.

Knowles, Malcolm. *The Adult Learner: A Neglected Species.* Houston: Gulf Publishing Co., 1973.

Lusterman, Seymour. "Education for Work." *Conference Board Record,* May 1976.

Mager, Robert F. *Preparing Instructional Objectives.* Palo· Alto, Calif.: Fearon Publishers, 1962.

Miller, Ben. "Closing the Gap in the Training Cycle." *Training and Development Journal,* January 1974.

Nadler, Leonard. *Developing Human Resources.* Houston: Gulf Publishing Co., 1970.

Nadler, Leonard. "Implications of the HRD Concept." *Training and Development Journal,* May 1974.

Ross, Joel E., and Murdick, Robert G. *Management Update: The Answer to Obsolescence.* New York: AMACOM, 1973.

Tracey, William R. *Managing Training and Development Systems.* New York: AMACOM, 1974.

Warren, Malcolm W. *Training for Results: A Systems Approach to the Development of Human Resources in Industry.* Reading, Mass.: Addison-Wesley, 1969.

"Why Companies Go Outside for New Bosses." *Business Week,* February 26, 1972.

Wong, Martin R., and Raulerson, John D. *A Guide to Systematic Instructional Design.* Englewood Cliffs, N.J.: Prentice-Hall, 1974.

NOTES

[1] "Why Companies Go Outside for New Bosses," *Business Week,* February 26, 1972, p. 82.

[2] William R. Tracey, *Managing Training and Development Systems* (New York: AMACOM, 1974), p. 4.

[3] Seymour Lusterman, "Education for Work," *Conference Board Record,* May 1976, p. 39.

[4] Robert F. Mager, *Preparing Instructional Objectives* (Palo Alto, Calif.: Fearon Publishers, 1962).

[5] David Georgoff and R. G. Murdick, a seed grant project, (Boca Raton; Fla.: Florida Atlantic University, 1977).

When you have completed studying
THE REWARD SYSTEM
you should be able to:

1. Describe the crucial relationship of the reward system to the overall human resources management system.
2. Differentiate extrinsic rewards, intrinsic rewards, financial rewards, and nonfinancial rewards.
3. Discuss the concept of equity and recent research related to equity theory.
4. Show how different aspects of the reward system satisfy different levels of needs.
5. Point out the advantages and disadvantages of emphasizing money as the primary or sole element of the reward system.
6. Understand the reasons for the critical linkage between performance and reward if the reward system is to be a motivator.
7. Show why the economic, social, and self-actualizing models of human beings are incomplete, and why a contingency model seems to provide the best basis for a 1980s reward system.
8. Describe the various forms of compensation, including salary, hourly wages, piece rates, commissions and bonuses, productivity plans (Scanlon), profit-sharing plans, and stock-related plans.
9. Describe and differentiate the many kinds of statutory and privately funded benefits.
10. Discuss recent trends in compensation and benefits.

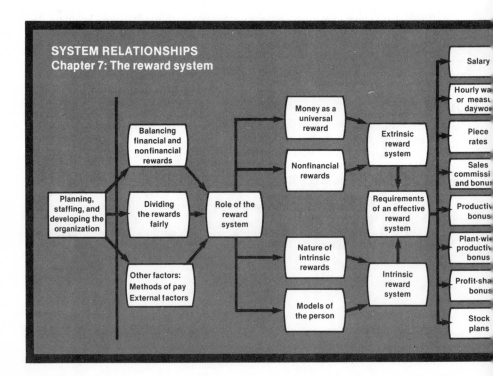

SYSTEM RELATIONSHIPS
Chapter 7: The reward system

THE ROLE OF THE REWARD SYSTEM

7

The reward system

This chapter and the next will deal with a key subsystem of human resources management—the reward system. Like organizational climate, discussed in Chapter 5, the reward system is a crucial element of the work environment. In many ways the reward system is closely related to the organizational climate, since both constitute major elements of the internal environment of the firm. As such, both the organizational climate and the reward system communicate much to each employee about the organization in which he or she is working. Moreover, the reward system determines the basis on which individuals in an organization will be able to

A union official approached a worker who had been showing up with some regularity only four days a week.

"How come you're working four days a week?" the union representative asked the worker.

"Because I can't make enough money in three," was the reply.[1]

Jon Lowell

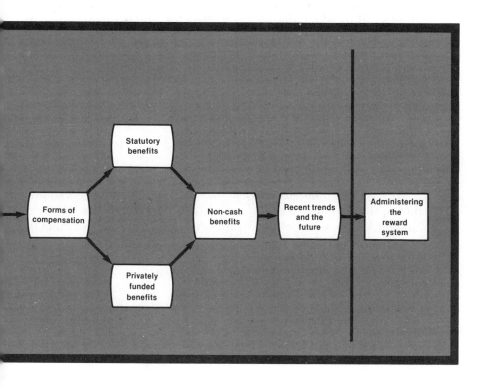

satisfy their personal needs. Since the opportunity to satisfy personal needs is the only basis for the individual's association with the organization, the reward system is a critical element in determining each individual's relationship to the organization.

Balancing financial and nonfinancial rewards

This chapter has been titled "The Reward System" to emphasize the fact that it will consider both nonfinancial and financial aspects of a total reward system. Traditionally, personnel textbooks placed primary emphasis on a compensation and benefits system, with a passing reference (at most) to the fact that nonfinancial rewards are also important. A more recent development has been the overemphasis of intrinsic factors—achievement, recognition, and growth—leaving the implication that money is relatively unimportant. Both of these emphases represent oversimplifications.

Research in the behavioral sciences has demonstrated that most people are not motivated solely by financial rewards. Other needs are important to most people, and for at least a few people, these other needs can be more important than pay. Nevertheless, "good pay" remains very important to most employees. A point emphasized throughout these two chapters is that it is a nonsense question to ask, "Which are more important, financial rewards or nonfinancial rewards?" It would make just as much sense to ask, "Which is more important, the front wheel of a motorcycle or the back wheel?" An effective reward system requires both financial and nonfinancial rewards. Although both are needed, the emphasis should vary, contingent on both situational and individual differences.

Divide the rewards fairly

As has been pointed out by J. Stacy Adams and other researchers, the equity or fairness of pay is just as important to people as its amount.[2] Thus an effective reward system requires not only that the absolute level of compensation paid by an organization compare favorably with that of other organizations; it also requires that the compensation be divided up among the organization's employees in a way that they perceive as equitable.

Another idea that should be emphasized is the importance of applying a contingency approach to the reward system. Traditional approaches to compensation and benefits have started from the assumption that most employees in an organization are essentially

EXHIBIT 7–1

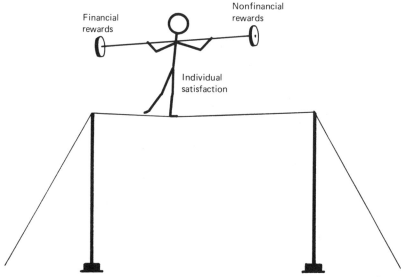

Possible contingent conditions:
a. Tightness of cable.
b. Wind.

alike in their needs, their motivations, and their responses to different types of rewards. A contingency approach assumes, on the other hand, that employees are quite variable—that some respond primarily to extrinsic rewards (pay), that others respond primarily to intrinsic rewards (achievement, etc.), and that still others respond best to a combination of extrinsic and intrinsic rewards. A number of research studies have indicated that both individuals and groups differ in terms of the perceived importance of pay and the effectiveness of money as a motivator.[3] Furthermore, a contingency approach recognizes that although all employees probably seek "equity," there may be many conflicting definitions of "equity," so that what will appear equitable to one employee may not necessarily appear equitable to another.

Other considerations

In a recent article, Larry Cummings has succinctly stated that "three fundamental dimensions . . . underlie the successful designing of a human performance environment:

(1)   valued rewards are offered,

(2)   these rewards are based on productivity, and

(3) employees can directly influence performance and productivity through their efforts."[4]

Other important considerations which play a role in the design of the reward system are methods of wage payments (by time or by output), incentive compensation, the role of government in such matters as the minimum wage and social security, the role of unions, and finally, the appropriate mix of supplementary employee benefits to be provided in addition to cash salary.

The independent considerations mentioned above, which together determine the resulting reward system, are sometimes complementary, but unfortunately they often have a conflicting impact on the reward system. Realistically, then, it is far more accurate to view the reward system at any point in time as the resultant of many (often conflicting) forces rather than as a scientifically determined system, although the latter is obviously the objective toward which the designers of reward systems should always struggle.

THE EXTRINSIC REWARD SYSTEM

The extrinsic reward system refers to all rewards external to the job itself. The extrinsic reward system can also be thought of as that part of the reward system which must be supplied to an individual by a representative of the organization, typically his or her manager. The extrinsic reward system thus consists of both financial and nonfinancial rewards which are meted out to the individual by some representative of the organization, presumably in response to the quality and quantity of his or her performance.

Money as the universal reward

Faced with what has already been described as the highly complex task of designing an effective reward system that consists of many elements, some modern-day managers long for the simpler age of the 20s and 30s when the "reward system" consisted simply of base wages. In that simpler age, about the only decision management had to make about its "reward system" was how much money would have to be paid to hire and retain the workers needed. Some managers may be heard to ask today (and probably many more have thought), "Why can't we simply pay people enough money to satisfy them and forget about all of these other nonfinancial and intrinsic rewards?" It is probably possible to do just that if an organization really wishes to. This is so because of the unique status of money as the universal reward. Money can be exchanged for goods and services to satisfy basic physiological needs. As an economic good it also satisfies security needs. Money, however, has another facet which is sometimes overlooked by behavioral scientists: it is a symbol of achievement. In our American culture we tend to evaluate individuals by the salaries they make and the money they possess. Therefore, compensation is a very powerful symbolic recognition of achievement, success, growth, and (for that matter) personal worth. In this sense, money can serve very nicely as a satisfier of higher level needs.

Thus, it is quite accurate to say, as a few managers have, "All people really need to motivate them is money." To observe that money can satisfy both lower level and higher level needs, however, is by no means to conclude that making money the sole reward is the most cost-effective approach from the organization's standpoint.

There is ample evidence that this would be an enormously expensive solution. As a matter of fact, a number of organizations have unconsciously been pursuing just such a policy. Skyrocketing wage demands which appear to have no end in sight may well result from a situation in which the only possibility for satisfying needs is seen to be higher and higher wages.

Although money can theoretically be used to satisfy all levels of employees' needs, a much less costly strategy involves the effective use of nonfinancial rewards to reduce the total cost of the reward system. There is no doubt that a basic level of financial rewards is a necessary component of the reward system; however, it is equally clear that a second layer of the reward system dealing with the satisfaction of higher level needs can emphasize either financial or nonfinancial rewards.

Nonfinancial extrinsic rewards

Nonfinancial extrinsic rewards comprise the nonfinancial means of recognizing the contributions of individual employees and classes of employees. These means include status symbols, physical working conditions, titles and promotions, control over time at work, public recognition, and informal oral praise.

THE INTRINSIC REWARD SYSTEM

By contrast, the intrinsic reward system consists of those rewards which come from the work itself. An intrinsic reward results from a transaction between an individual and his or her task without the intervention of any third party. The reward comes from the individual's own responses to the performance of the task—a sense of responsibility, a sense of challenge, a sense of mastery or control, a sense of participation, and so on.

Thus extrinsic rewards are determined and delivered by a third party representing the organization, whereas intrinsic rewards are determined by the individual in interaction with the task. We should not lose sight of the fact, however, that both intrinsic and extrinsic rewards are products of the human resources management system. It is not possible for management to stand by and hand out intrinsic rewards. It *is* a responsibility of management to design jobs in such a way that intrinsic rewards are possible for those members of the organization who seek them. This may mean using such techniques as job enrichment to encourage a sense of responsibility in jobs which historically failed to do this; or to encourage a sense of challenge in place of routine; or to provide an opportunity for mastery and control where only a sense of activity has been possible; or to invite participation where only response to directives has been asked for in the past. It seems safe to conclude that virtually all employees seek some intrinsic rewards all of the time and that some employees seek intrinsic rewards to an even greater extent than they seek extrinsic rewards. Thus, it is a primary responsibility of management to identify individuals or groups that might be motivated by intrinsic rewards and then to design jobs in such a way as to give these individuals and groups the maximum opportunity for achieving the intrinsic satisfactions they desire.

Although intrinsic rewards seem to flow from satisfaction of only the highest levels of need, ego need and self-fulfillment need, the extrinsic reward system is related to all levels of need. (See Chapter 2 for discussion of Maslow's hierarchy of needs theory.) Exhibit 7–2 shows the relationship between human needs and the reward system. A better understanding of the basis for intrinsic rewards can be obtained by examining the development of "models of the person."

Models of the person

Behavioral science research has pointed increasingly to the inadequacy of our simplistic models of the person, including the economic model, the social system model, and the self-actualizing model. The research is clearly demonstrating that a more sophisticated model is required. A contingency model thus seems to be the

EXHIBIT 7–2
The reward system

	Extrinsic		Intrinsic
	Financial	*Nonfinancial*	
Lower level needs			
Physiological	Pay (economic value)		
Safety-security	Benefits (security)	Rules and regulations Supervision	
Social		Status	Participation, interaction, status
Higher level needs			
Ego, self-fulfillment	Pay (symbolic value)	Recognition Praise Promotion in *title* New responsibilities New assignment Participation in decisions Challenge Control	Achievement Exploration Mastery Growth Participation Responsibility Autonomy

model of the person around which an effective reward system for the 1980s should be built.

This model hypothesizes that human behavior is not fixed but rather dependent on each situation. Thus, the contingency model assumes that there is no one right solution to any management problem. Rather, the uniquely right solution for each problem is determined by a number of factors, such as the organization (its climate, history, environment, structure, rules and regulations, managerial style, and so on), the nature of the task itself (including the degree to which intrinsic rewards are available), the measurability of performance, and the individual (his or her needs, attitudes, abilities, and preferences with regard to intrinsic versus extrinsic versus mixed rewards).

Specifically, a contingency approach requires that we design, not a static reward system, but rather a flexible system which can vary for different parts of the organization, different tasks, and particularly for different individuals or subsets of individuals within the organization. The process of designing and implementing such a flexible system will be discussed in the next chapter.

REQUIREMENTS OF AN EFFECTIVE REWARD SYSTEM

Now that we have discussed both the intrinsic reward system and the extrinsic reward system in principle, let us examine the critical connection between performance and reward. A considerable body of research shows that for rewards to be effective it is important that the employee perceive a direct relationship between performance and the attainment of the desired reward. This means that the mere establishment of an adequate reward system does not provide the basis for employee motivation. It is equally important that the system be communicated in such a way that each employee perceives that the attainment of desired rewards flows directly from successful performance.

Operant conditioning theory

One of the important lines of research leading to this conclusion is operant conditioning theory, developed by B. F. Skinner.[5] Operant conditioning theory observes that among both animals and human beings behavior which is rewarded tends to be repeated and that behavior which is not rewarded tends not to be repeated (to be "extinguished"). Operant conditioning theory does not require that there be a cognitive connection between the behavior ("operant") and the reward, only a sequential relationship. The theory simply observes that if a particular behavior is exhibited in the presence of certain stimuli and followed by the receipt of a reward, that behavior will tend to be repeated in the future in the presence of similar stimuli.

Expectancy and path-goal theories

A separate, though complementary, line of research leading to the same conclusion is the expectancy theory of Vroom and the path-goal theory of Porter and Lawler.[6] Their research has demonstrated that a number of things are required for any reward system to be effective in eliciting desired behavior from employees:

1. The employee must perceive the existence of the reward, and he must perceive that it is attractive to him.
2. He must perceive accurately what specific behavior on his part will lead to the desired reward.
3. He must perceive that he is capable of that behavior, and he must in fact be capable of that behavior.
4. There must be a direct tie between the behavior and the receipt of the reward, and the employee must perceive that tie.

5. If his performance is to be evaluated by others and the receipt of rewards is to be dependent on such evaluation, he must perceive that the evaluation will be accurately and equitably performed.

Thus, the operant conditioning, expectancy, and path-goal theories all seem to lead to the conclusion that effective reward systems require:

1. An array of intrinsic and extrinsic rewards that are available to individuals on a self-selection basis.
2. A clear statement of the direct relationship between behaviors and anticipated rewards.
3. An accurate performance appraisal system and an effective merit increase plan which assure that performance will be accurately measured and that rewards received will be directly commensurate with objectively measured performance.
4. An effective communication system which makes the existence of item 1, 2, and 3 widely known and understood throughout the organization.

These findings may help to explain the apparently contradictory results of various research studies designed to determine the motivational impact of money. Some studies (notably those of Herzberg et al.) have seemed to indicate that money has little value as a motivator and that it can act primarily as a source of dissatisfaction. On the other hand, over the years a number of research studies have concluded that money can sometimes act as a very powerful motivator.

Perhaps the explanation of these apparently inconsistent findings lies in the notion that the motivational value of money depends upon the individual's perception of the total situation. Where pay is closely tied to achievement and is seen by others in the organization as a form of recognition, it may operate as a very potent motivator indeed. On the other hand, in organizations where there is little perceived relationship between performance and compensation, where pay is not used as an incentive, money may very well have no effect whatsoever as a motivator and may serve only as a potential source of dissatisfaction.

Equity theory

Furthermore, research by J. Stacy Adams has shown that for a reward system to be effective in motivating behavior, it is necessary that employees perceive the system to operate equitably.[7] For this perception to exist "inputs" (which include such factors as age, education, skill, seniority, social status, and effort expended) should relate to "outcomes" (rewards) in the same way for the individual as he perceives them to relate for others. Adams' research has shown that people do, in fact, adjust their input to the perceived equity of their input-output relation as compared to the input-output relation of others.

Because a perception of equity and a perception of direct relationship between performance and reward are necessary for effective motivation, it becomes important that people in an organization be familiar with how the reward system operates and that they have detailed and accurate information on the rewards received by others. A research study by Lawler has shown that the traditional secrecy of pay practices in most organizations is likely to be highly dysfunctional.[8] Specifically, Lawler found that people in an organization who are not told the salaries of other people tend to misperceive reality, not on a random basis, but in a consistent pattern. Because people consistently underestimate the pay of their superiors and overestimate the pay of their subordinates, misperception of pay in an organization tends to severely reduce the motivational effect of the pay system. Thus, another requirement for an effective reward system would seem to be publication of at least ranges of pay for each pay grade and each individual's grade, if not indeed the publication of individual salaries.

Because of the importance and universal use of financial rewards, we will focus next on different forms of compensation and fringe benefits.

FORMS OF COMPENSATION

Although the flexible compensation approach makes cash compensation and "fringe benefits" largely interchangeable, traditionally various forms of pay have been described as compensation and various forms of other benefits as fringe benefits. The many forms of compensation and benefits which make up the typical reward package for top executives are reflected in Exhibit 7–3.

Although there are hundreds of variations, the major categories of cash compensation are as follows.

Salary

Salaried workers are paid a set wage by the week or the month and are expected to work a standard set of hours each week (36–40 hours per week is the most common schedule). Usually salaried workers are not subject to pay loss for absences due to illness (normally up to an annual limit) or even for modest absences for "personal business." For this reason, salaried workers are not usually asked to punch a time clock, although some salaried workers fill out time cards reporting their attendance to the minute.

One implicit assumption of salaried compensation is that the work is of a qualitative nature under the control of the individual so that attention and careful work are of more importance than mere attendance. Another implicit assumption is that salaried individuals can be trusted to deliver a full day's work for a full day's pay without the necessity of close monitoring. There is perhaps even an implicit assumption that most salaried employees are motivated in part by higher level needs.

Normally relatively little variation is anticipated in the work required from persons in salaried jobs so that the company can afford to, in effect, guarantee 40 hours or 36 hours of work each week. Alternatively, it may be felt that the volume of work demanded will vary slightly but that the increased motivation due to salaried status will more than offset the possible savings of paying for a variable number of hours per week in response to demand.

Hourly wages or measured daywork

Hourly wages are a set wage paid for each hour the employee is actually at work or actually works. Sometimes standards of the amount of work expected in a typical hour are established, and this is referred to as measured daywork. Usually hourly workers are required to punch a time clock or to fill out a time record of some sort. Pay at the end of each week or month is computed on the basis of the number of hours worked. Usually no allowance is made for time off for personal business, but often there is allowance for time off due to illness or other specified causes. The primary objective of hourly pay is to provide flexibility for the employer in scheduling hours of work per week.

Over the last 20 years unions have made a number of inroads on this advantage through such devices as supplementary unemployment benefits and the guaranteed annual wage (really a guarantee of a minimum number of hours of work per year). Consequently the flexibility provided by hourly pay has become relatively less advantageous for some employers and there has been a decline in the popularity of hourly wage rates, although this is still the most common method of compensating production workers.

EXHIBIT 7–3
The executive compensation and benefits package

Title	Age	Company business	Company sales ($ millions)	Geographic area	Base salary ($000)
Chairperson	46	Wholesale trade	110	Southeast	65–75
President	48	Manufacturing	125	National	100–150
	64	Manufacturing	200	Southwest	100–150
	57	Petroleum	1,000	Northeast	85–100
	35	Manufacturing	420	Southeast	85–100
	41	Manufacturing	160	National	85–100
	51	Retail trade	300	Far West	75–85
	60	Industrial sales	33	International	65–75
	48	Manufacturing	50	National	65–75
	42	Manufacturing	35	Northeast	55–65
	38	Manufacturing	40	Midwest	55–65
	48	Services	160	International	55–65
	NG*	Metals	100	Northeast	55–65
	55	Manufacturing	84	Far West	55–65
	64	Insurance	60	National	45–55
	44	Manufacturing	78	National	35–45
	66	Manufacturing	50	Midwest	35–45
	55	Manufacturing	25	Midwest	25–35
Executive vice president	53	Manufacturing	4,000+	Northeast	100–150
	60	Manufacturing	490	Midwest	100–150
	59	Retail trade	120	Midwest	65–75
	59	Manufacturing	22	Southeast	45–55
Senior vice president	60	Manufacturing	450	Midwest	85–100
Group vice president	52	Manufacturing	43	Far West	35–45
Vice president—general management	NG*	Manufacturing	1,000+	National	100–150
	48	Insurance	165	National	75–85
	50	Manufacturing	340	Midwest	65–75
	58	Retail trade	500	Northeast	65–75
	52	Manufacturing	120	Midwest	55–65
	47	Real estate	36	Southeast	55–65
	46	Manufacturing	50	Northeast	45–55
	47	Metals	95	Northeast	45–55
	48	Utility	200	Southwest	45–55
	32	Pollution control	87	Northeast	45–55
	43	Manufacturing	32	Northeast	45–55
	50	Retail trade	100	Northeast	35–45
	59	Manufacturing	21	Midwest	35–45
	48	Finance	20	Southeast	35–45
	NG*	Manufacturing	25	Northeast	35–45
	42	Manufacturing	50	Far West	35–45
	48	Manufacturing	36	National	35–45
	NG*	Metals	70	Northeast	35–45
	54	Insurance	500+	Far West	35–45
	58	Manufacturing	50	Midwest	25–35
	34	Manufacturing	100	Southeast	25–35
	49	Utility	150	Southwest	25–35
	48	Insurance	800	Southeast	25–35
	51	Insurance	500+	Far West	25–35
	34	Finance	97	Far West	25–35
	48	Manufacturing	80	Midwest	25–35

* NG—Not given.
Source: *Dun's Review*, September 1974.

Traditionally, hourly wages have been associated primarily with blue-collar work, in contrast to the association of salaried status with white-collar, professional, and managerial work. One disadvantage of hourly pay from the employer's standpoint is its potential for conferring second-class status on hourly workers and thus making

		Other financial benefits					Perquisites			
Bonus	Stock options	Phantom stock	Performance shares	Deferred compensation	Company car	Free physical exam	Club membership	Financial counseling	Low-cost loans	Total compensation ($000)
X	X	X			X	X	X	X		100–150
X	X		X		X	X	X			200+
X	X			X	X		X	X		150–200
	X			X			X			100–150
X	X			X	X	X	X	X		150–200
X	X	X			X	X	X			85–100
	X				X	X	X			100–150
X	X			X			X			75–85
X	X				X	X	X			85–100
X	X		X				X			75–85
X	X				X	X	X			85–100
	X				X	X	X		X	65–75
X	X				X	X	X	X		85–100
					X	X	X			75–85
X	X			X	X		X		X	55–65
X					X					45–55
X										35–45
X	X				X	X	X			45–55
X	X	X				X	X			100–150
X	X					X	X			100–150
X		X				X	X			75–85
X	X			X	X	X	X			55–65
X	X			X	X	X				100–150
X	X				X	X				45–55
X										200+
				X		X	X			85–100
X	X			X		X	X			85–100
	X		X		X	X				100–150
X	X			X	X	X	X			75–85
X						X				75–85
X						X	X			65–75
	X				X	X		X	X	55–65
X					X	X	X			55–65
	X	X							X	75–85
X						X				55–65
X	X					X				35–45
X	X				X	X	X			55–65
X				X			X			35–45
X	X									45–55
X	X			X						45–55
X	X				X	X				65–75
		X				X				55–65
X	X				X					35–45
X	X				X					35–45
X	X	X			X					45–55
				X	X		X			25–35
X	X				X					35–45
										25–35
					X	X			X	25–35
	X				X					35–45

them feel less a part of the organization or less committed to the organization. On the other hand, the flexibility of scheduling hourly workers and paying only for hours worked is still an overriding economic advantage for many firms.

Gillette Safety Razor, IBM, and Texas Instruments have already changed the status of their large hourly work forces to that of salaried employees. Because these are considered "leading firms," this move created considerable attention, and a number of smaller companies have since taken the same step.

It is undoubtedly true that there are other organizations whose situations make them ready for a move to salaried status for all employees. Nevertheless, the contingency approach to reward system design would rule out the automatic application of one compensation method to all employees. Rather, the contingency approach requires a detailed analysis of the specific situation to determine the best arrangement for the particular organization, jobs, and individuals.

Piece rates

Piece rates are one of the many so-called incentive compensation plans. Piece rates provide an incremental payment for each unit of production completed. Usually, piece rates are paid as a bonus on top of an hourly or weekly wage. Piece rates can be paid on the basis of either individual production or group output.

Group piece rates are usually paid when several employees work together on a single product or in situations where considerable cooperation among a group of employees is required for effective performance. It is most common for piece rate plans to provide either a constant or an increasing piece rate after a certain "standard" level of production has been attained, but not to pay a piece rate for units produced up to this standard number. The primary objective of piece rates is to lower unit cost of production for the employer by motivating the employee to maximize output in relation to machine time utilization, overhead costs, and the base wage.

Piece rates for each item of production are usually set by company time study engineers. Since it is vital that piece rates be accurate and up-to-date, the monitoring of piece rates can be a relatively expensive administrative procedure. Furthermore, piece rates may be the subject of frequent and heated debate or negotiation with the union.

Historically, piece rates have been a source of considerable friction between workers and managers, and they appear to have been a common basis for the alienation of workers who, rightly or wrongly, believed that they were being exploited by unfair piece rates.

A considerable amount of research evidence indicates that the effectiveness of various incentive systems can vary greatly, depending on such factors as the preferences of workers, the norms of the work group relative to the restriction of output, whether the task is liked or disliked, and whether the task is simple or complex.[9]

The research also tends to show that the reaction to incentive plans is dependent on personality differences among individuals, including their level of achievement motivation and the reference groups with which they identify.[10] Specifically, individuals high in achievement motivation seem to be less influenced by financial incentives (because they are already motivated), whereas individuals low in achievement motivation respond relatively more strongly to financial incentives; employees from metropolitan areas who have working-class backgrounds and identification tend to be unresponsive to financial incentives, whereas employees with middle-class values and norms and employees who identify strongly with higher occupational groups are relatively more influenced by financial incentives.

Sales commissions or bonuses

The mechanics and the underlying theory of sales commissions or bonuses are virtually identical with that of piece rates. However, piece rates are most commonly associated with production work, whereas sales commissions or bonuses are paid exclusively to salespersons. As with piece rates, sales commissions or bonuses can be paid on every unit sold or only on units beyond a certain minimum. Furthermore, like piece rates, sales commissions can be paid on a level basis per unit, regardless of the number of units sold, or on an increasing rate per unit. It is somewhat more common with sales commissions than with piece rates to make the unit commission the total basis for compensation. This is particularly true in real estate sales.

The objective of sales commissions or bonuses is to maximize sales, and its advantage is similar to that of piece rates in providing pay in direct proportion to the performance of useful work. This relationship may be very significant motivationally, particularly for people who are motivated primarily by extrinsic rewards, because it provides immediate positive feedback each time a sale is completed.

Productivity bonuses

Productivity bonus plans provide wage payments based on units of production which exceed the standard rate or on the completion of tasks in less than the standard time. Productivity bonuses may be paid on either an individual or a group basis. Such bonuses are not nearly as common as piece rates.

Plant-wide productivity plans

Although somewhat related to productivity bonuses, plant-wide productivity plans such as the Scanlon Plan are far more ambitious in their objectives and more complex in their administration. The Scanlon plan provides incentive compensation based on plant performance. Its primary emphasis is to stimulate management-union or management-worker cooperation.

It does this by setting up a series of joint committees consisting of representatives selected by management and by workers at each level in the organization or in each department. These committees review suggestions for the improvement of productivity. Suggestions adopted by the committees are implemented in the organization.

When increases in productive efficiency are realized—that is, when unit labor costs decrease—the employees and the company share the dollar value of the savings according to a predetermined ratio, with a larger amount always going to the workers. The major objectives of the Scanlon plan are to stimulate worker ideas for improving efficiency, to gain the commitment of workers to the objective of efficiency, to improve worker-management relations, and to provide an equitable basis for sharing increases in efficiency.

Performance bonuses

Performance bonuses are similar to productivity bonuses except that they are paid for total performance, including performance which goes beyond mere productivity. Any measurable item of performance can be subject to such bonuses. Thus, performance bonuses can be applied to executive, professional, technical, clerical, white-collar, and blue-collar workers.

Profit-sharing plans

Profit-sharing plans typically provide that a stated percentage of profits will be shared by all employees of the organization or by certain groups in the organization. Profits can be shared on a level percentage basis beginning with the first dollar of profit, but a more popular arrangement is to share an increasing percentage of the profits beyond a certain base. The timing of payment may be current, deferred, or mixed.

Stock-related supplemental compensation plans

There are several variations of supplemental compensation plans related to company stock. These variations include stock purchase plans, stock option plans, phantom stock plans, and performance shares. Stock purchase plans are usually offered to virtually all employees in the company. Although it was once quite common to sell stock to employees at a discount below the market rate, the tax treatment of this practice has changed; hence it is now more common to sell stock at the market rate. Under some forms of stock savings plans a portion of the employee's contribution is partially matched by the company either in additional stock or in cash.

Stock options are granted to an executive at the current market price for the stock, with provision for exercising the option within a limited period of time. Thus, if the company is successful and the stock increases in value, the executive may exercise his option at any time within the stated limits and realize the gain in value between the option date and the exercise date. In order to obtain favorable tax treatment for the transaction, it is necessary that the shares be held for a minimum period of time before resale. Although stock options were extremely popular and considered quite glamorous in the 1960s they are considerably less popular today and are probably still waning in popularity due to severe changes in tax treatment which make them relatively less advantageous than formerly.

A variation of the stock option is the use of phantom stock. Under this arrangement an executive is granted a *mythical* share of stock, thus enabling the executive to avoid the problem of having to lay out the money needed to exercise stock options. At the end of the specified period the executive is simply paid in cash the value of the appreciation of the mythical unit of stock, together with the accumulated dividends.

A fairly recent innovation is the concept of performance shares. Performance shares are granted to an executive as a stock option would be granted. However, the shares are not irrevocably his; they are merely set aside in his name. He must earn his shares by achieving certain performance objectives that are established between him and a performance evaluation committee. At the end of the performance period the committee grants the executive all, some, or

EXHIBIT 7–4
Performance shares are growing in popularity

Dun's Review, January 1973

none of the shares which were set aside, depending on its evaluation of the executive's performance.

Although there is no evidence of such a trend, it is consistent with
the reward system ideas developed in this chapter that performance
shares might be applied gradually to broader segments of the
work force. Performance shares would fit very nicely within the
framework of a contingency-based reward system, since it would
be possible to provide such shares as an optional form of incremental compensation.

NONCASH BENEFITS

We have already discussed the advantages of considering cash
compensation and noncash benefits as parts of a total reward package to facilitate a contingency-based reward system incorporating
the "flexible" approach to compensation and benefits.

There is a second financial reason why this approach seems
highly desirable in the 1970s. Employee benefits were originally
referred to as "fringes" or "fringe benefits" because initially they

EXHIBIT 7–5
Coverage for millions of workers

Business Week, January 12, 1974

represented a small portion of the employer's total compensation cost. Typically, early fringe plans involved pensions, life insurance, and medical insurance, with the employee paying all or a substantial portion of the total cost. Much of the value of these plans came from the actuarial, administrative, and buying power advantages of large group plans as opposed to individual purchase. In general, these advantages were more important than the employer's part in funding the cost of the "fringes."

As is well known, this situation has changed dramatically. Benefits now represent a substantial portion of many employers' total compensation cost. Nevertheless, research studies have shown that most employees vastly underestimate the cost of employer-financed benefits. This means that the employer is getting insufficient credit for these expenditures.

A study conducted by the U.S. Chamber of Commerce showed that in 1973 a sampling of 742 companies paid on the average $3,230 per employee each year for so-called fringe benefits.[11] This figure represented more than 27 percent of the companies' total employment costs. The same study reported that whereas pay for time worked in these firms rose 72 percent during the ten-year period 1963–73, the cost of fringe benefits increased by 126 percent (see Exhibit 7–6).

Benefits are now a substantial portion of total compensation costs (well over 25 percent), and there is every evidence that the

EXHIBIT 7–6
Gains in "fringes" far outpace wages

Average per employee in private industry	1963	1973	Increase
Fringe benefits	$1,431	$3,230	Up 126%
Pay for time worked	5,005	8,623	Up 72%
Total employment cost	6,436	11,853	Up 84%

Note: In 1963, fringe benefits amounted to 22.2 percent of the average firm's employment costs; in 1973, "fringes" made up 27.3 percent of employment costs.
Source: Data, U.S. Chamber of Commerce; chart, reprinted from *U.S. News & World Report.* Copyright 1974 U.S. News & World Report, Inc.

dollar cost and the proportion of total compensation cost represented by benefits are rising rapidly. The $3,230 per employee spent by an average employer for fringe benefits in 1973 (as reported in the U.S. Chamber of Commerce study) was broken down as shown in Exhibit 7–7.

EXHIBIT 7–7
Where the benefits go

Of the $3,230 in fringe benefits per employee in 1973:

Social Security (employer's share)	$527
Pension plans	503
Paid vacations	466
Insurance	457
Paid rest, lunch periods	341
Paid holidays	295
Profit sharing and bonuses	197
Unemployment compensation	117
Paid sick leave	110
Workers' compensation	92
Other benefits	125

Source: Data, U.S. Chamber of Commerce; table, reprinted from *U.S. News & World Report.* Copyright 1974 U.S. News & World Report, Inc.

The primary cause of escalating fringe benefit costs has been the increasing cost of such benefits as social security, pensions, vacations, and insurance. A second cause, however, has been the rapidly mounting list of fringes that have been developed over the last 20 years. A fairly common pattern has been for a new fringe benefit to spring up in only one or two companies or in only one industry as the result of a peculiar situation or a unique union demand, to spread slowly at first to related companies or related industries, and after a few years to spread more rapidly, becoming common throughout industry.

Among the newer benefits receiving attention in 1978 are family counseling for workers' off-the-job problems, dental care, prepaid legal service, free use of employer-owned golf courses, assistance in making out income tax returns, and free psychiatric care. Although each of these items is being discussed in the literature as a novelty, the chances are good that more than one of them will be a standard benefit within the next ten years.

One of the principal advantages of a flexible compensation approach is that it demonstrates that benefits costs are compensation and should be considered as a part of the total reward received for performance. One result of this approach should be heightened awareness of the total value of each employee's compensation and benefits package. Another result might be decreasing pressure for new and more exotic benefits if employees realize that these are a substitute for cash or other benefits.

Statutory benefits

There are two basic types of employee benefits—statutory benefits (those required by law and toward which the employer is legally required to make contributions) and privately funded benefits (those determined unilaterally by the company or as a result of company-union negotiation). Privately funded benefits may be paid for by the employer, by the employee, or by both the employer and the employee.

For most employees the most important statutory benefit is social security. The Social Security Act of 1935, as amended, provides for retirement income, income for survivors, and disability income. Although social security was originally envisaged as a system which would provide a minimal subsistence income, the level of coverage has steadily risen. Today, social security is thought of as the solid base around which most private retirement plans are designed. Under the most recent revision of the Social Security Act, employers and employees each contribute 6.05 percent of the first $17,700 earned annually. Further increases in social security contributions are already scheduled in existing legislation.

Another important feature of the recent revision of the act is the incorporation of automatic cost of living escalators. Under this provision, each time there is an increase in the Bureau of Labor Statistics consumer price index the benefits paid under social security automatically increase. As can be seen, there has been a trend toward the liberalization of social security benefits, and social security is being thought of more and more as the primary basis for retirement income rather than as the basis for a minimal subsistence level.

Another piece of depression legislation, the Federal Unemployment Tax Act of 1935, requires employers of a certain minimum size to pay an unemployment insurance tax. Under the provisions of this act, employees who become unemployed through no fault of their own are eligible for 26 to 52 weeks of compensation. Through a fairly complicated arrangement, much of this act is administered by state governments, with a sizable portion of the employers' contributions going to the states.

Workers' compensation provides payments to workers or their families in the case of job-related accidents, injuries, diseases, or deaths. Although workers' compensation programs exist in all states, they are based on state law rather than federal law. Hence, standards, administrative practices, and costs vary somewhat from state to state. In all states, however, the total cost of workers' compensation is paid by the employer.

Although medical insurance plans and pension plans (other than social security) are not statutory benefits, the federal government in recent years has expressed increasing interest in these two areas. It appears to be entirely possible that either or both of these benefits will become statutory benefits.

Congress has already exerted a major influence on privately funded pension plans through the Employee Retirement Income Security Act of 1974 (ERISA). The enactment of this legislation was widely interpreted as ushering in a new era in which pension plan operation would be subject to increasing government regulation.

ERISA neither forces a company to set up a pension plan nor dictates the size of benefits, but it does set minimum standards for employee pension rights (vesting), the funding of pension obligations, and the administration and investment of pension funds. The pension plans of most large corporations embodied the standards of ERISA prior to its enactment. However, the act will undoubtedly be significant in safeguarding the rights of employees previously covered by inferior plans.

Privately funded benefits

An employer has wide latitude in designing the mechanics of a pension plan within the minimum requirements of ERISA, and within constraints set by the Internal Revenue Service if favorable

"YOU MAY HAVE NOTICED THAT OUR EMPLOYEES AGE RATHER QUICKLY; ON THE OTHER HAND WE HAVE A TERRIFIC PENSION PLAN."

tax treatment is to be obtained. Some pension plans are paid for by the employer, others by the employees. The largest number, however, are paid for through joint employer-employee contributions.

The most common formulas for determining retirement benefits incorporate years of service, level of income (career average or average of highest five or ten years), and age at retirement.

Another common form of privately funded benefits is medical insurance. Typically, medical insurance provides coverage for both the employee and dependents, with at least a portion of the employee's coverage paid for by the employer. Although the employee commonly pays all or part of the cost for the coverage of dependents, the funding of all medical coverage by the employer is becoming more and more common.

The most common form of medical coverage is basic hospitalization insurance of the type offered by Blue Cross–Blue Shield. Major medical insurance to provide supplementary coverage over and above the limits of basic hospitalization and doctor coverage has grown rapidly in popularity.

Another very common privately funded benefit is life insurance, with the employee usually paying all or part of the cost. The amount of coverage allowed is often determined as a multiple of annual salary. In some plans, premiums rise with increasing age, so that each age group is in effect carrying its own weight, whereas in other plans a level premium is charged per dollar of coverage, regardless of age. In general, less attention has been focused on life insurance than has been focused on pensions and medical insurance. This may be due in part to the lack of tradition of full employer payment of premiums.

Although the number of additional privately funded benefits is too great to list here, among the most common are the following:

1. Disability insurance.
2. Supplementary unemployment benefits.
3. Discounts on goods purchased.
4. Vacations.
5. Holidays.
6. Paid sick leave.
7. Other paid leave (personal business, family illness or death, jury duty, military service, and so on).
8. Christmas or other bonuses.
9. Education benefits (tuition refund, time off for education).
10. Perquisites, such as meals, cars, and recreation facilities—most common at the highest levels of the organization as executive status symbols.
11. Service awards or suggestion awards.

RECENT TRENDS IN COMPENSATION AND BENEFITS

The growing significance of benefits as a part of the total reward system has already been discussed. There have undoubtedly been a number of causes for this trend. The initial impetus for the growth of benefits may well have come from the action of the War Labor Board in World War II in granting "fringe" benefit increases at a time when wages were frozen. Employers were quick to add fringe benefits as a way of competing for the scarce work force.

It is equally clear that following the end of World War II union pressure to add fringe benefits played a large role in the rapid development of fringe benefits in the 50s and 60s.

Another influence has been the tax advantages of benefits. For the employer, some benefits represent an immediate tax deduction but a deferred cash flow. Many benefits are advantageous to the employee from a tax standpoint in that they are bought with untaxed dollars rather than with 20 to 30 percent fewer aftertax dollars. In addition, a cost saving is obtained merely through purchasing coverage on a group basis rather than an individual basis. Thus, there are a number of clear economic reasons for allocating a steadily increasing proportion of the compensation and benefits mix to benefits.

There may well also be more subtle and less well recognized social reasons for the popularity of benefits. For one thing, it may reflect a changing life-style and a changing need structure that result from increasing affluence. As basic physiological needs are increasingly met for larger and larger proportions of our population, there may logically be increasing emphasis on the security represented by such benefits as pensions, medical insurance, and life insurance. Further, although benefits are often thought of as satisfying lower level physiological and security needs, many fringe benefits, including some of the ones receiving increased attention, might be said to serve higher level needs. These include educational benefits, increased vacation and holiday time, and such perquisites as the use of golf courses and tennis courts.

Significantly, however, none of these reasons for the increasing popularity of fringe benefits seem to be inconsistent with the notion that a flexible approach to compensation and benefits may be an ideal approach to the design of an effective strategy for human resources management in the 1980s. Such an approach maximizes each individual's opportunity to play a meaningful role in determining the rewards for his or her efforts; and such an approach provides each individual with the opportunity to maximize the utility of his or her total package of rewards, as perceived by the individual.

We foresee an increasing emphasis on the use of compensation to motivate rather than to placate. As we become more knowledgeable about the motivational consequences of pay and pay practices, it seems likely that we will take greater pains to ensure that the organization gets motivational value out of each compensation dollar spent.

This means that we will have to develop performance appraisals that will be perceived as both valid and fair. We will also have to relate such performance appraisals to changes in compensation.

One trend which began in the 1970s is the marked de-emphasis on stock-related plans which award stock (or options) to an executive on a final basis and the increased emphasis on plans (such as performance shares) which award stock contingent on the achievement of specific objectives. This trend reflects a change in thinking at the highest executive levels about how to get the greatest motivational value out of compensation dollars.

Deferred compensation is often financially advantageous to the organization in terms of both tax treatment and cash flows. Because of the differing tax rates which face an individual during his working years versus his retirement years, deferred compensation often looks more attractive than immediate compensation. With increasing affluence, this trade-off should become desirable to more and more people. In addition, as more and more organizations move toward flexible or "cafeteria" compensation, one alternative likely to be requested by employees will be deferred compensation.

The most significant trend over the next 30 years will be the increasing adoption of the contingency-based reward system. Changes in the work force and increasing knowledge about human behavior will require organizations to rethink reward systems. Companies will need to plan a cost-effective combination of extrinsic and intrinsic rewards.

SUMMARY

This chapter has emphasized the role of the reward system as a key subsystem of human resources management. Like organizational climate, the reward system is a crucial element of the work environment. The total reward system consists of both intrinsic aspects (supplied by the work itself) and extrinsic aspects (supplied by the organization), and extrinsic rewards have both financial and nonfinancial elements.

It is important that the reward system be viewed as equitable. That is, each individual in the organization should believe that the rewards he or she receives in relation to effort and contribution are fair as compared to the rewards others receive in relation to their effort and contribution.

Because money is a satisfier of both lower level and higher level needs in our culture, it could serve as the ideal universal reward. As many managers have pointed out, money could suffice as the only element in an organization's reward system—if the organization could afford it. However, making money the only element in the reward system is unlikely to be cost-effective. In most organizations, the effective use of nonfinancial rewards can substantially reduce the cost of the reward system.

The intrinsic reward system consists of those elements of the work itself which provide a sense of achievement, responsibility, challenge, control, and participation—the rewards which may be obtained by the individual through his or her performance of the work.

The financial reward system is made up of two primary components—compensation and benefits (in various forms). Among the forms of compensation described were salary, hourly wages, piece rates, sales commission or bonus, productivity bonus, profit sharing, stock options, phantom stock, and performance shares.

Among the benefits discussed were the statutory benefits of social security, unemployment compensation, and workers' compensation, as well as the privately funded benefits of pensions, life insurance, medical insurance, disability insurance, supplementary unemployment benefits, discounts on goods purchased, vacations, holidays, sick leave and other paid leave, bonuses, educational benefits, perquisites, and suggestion or service awards.

The operant conditioning theory of Skinner, the expectancy theory of Vroom, and the path-goal theory of Lawler were all shown to lead to the conclusion that there must be a critical linkage between performance and reward if a reward system is to be effective in motivating human performance.

Because of the inadequacy of the economic, social, and self-actualizing models of the person, a contingency model is required as the basis for an effective reward system.

CASE: THE OLD ORDER CHANGETH (A)*

The Bygone Daze Company has been in a quiet rut for the past several decades. It manufactures a traditional product that has been on the market for 35 years, and there has never been a problem in sales. As a matter of fact, the company has continually refused to accept orders from new customers. It has had a stock statement on such occasions: "All of our output is committed, and we do not plan to increase production." Over the years, the company has not realized a lot of money, nor has it lost any.

---

* Submitted by Charles A. Meloy, Associate Professor, Saint Peter's College, Jersey City, New Jersey.

The plant is nonunion, and the 800 members of the corporate family have worked side by side—from the top office down to the shipping department—without the question of pay ever becoming a major issue. This was because when employees were hired, they reached an agreement with the personnel officer on the amount of their salary or hourly rate. Notices of increases, which rarely occur, are made by the immediate supervisor to individuals in private.

Since employment is steady, the company is considered to be a good place to work and in this regard has a preferred status. Although the employees are for the most part content in their assignments, the overall attitude throughout the company is one of almost smug indifference.

The compensation program is quite simple. Executives, supervisors, and staff personnel receive a flat salary. Production workers are paid at an hourly rate. Since output is stable, there is overtime only at year-end when inventory is taken. Employees who assist in this work, after hours, receive time and a half.

At Christmastime, each employee from the president down to the janitor receives ten shares of company stock. The stock is traded over the counter and traditionally falls in the $3½ bid and $4 asked range. No dividends have ever been declared.

QUESTIONS AND PROBLEMS

1. Write a five-page library research report summarizing and synthesizing what has been written in major *business* journals in the last three years on the topic "motivation of employees."

2. Visit the personnel director of a local company and discuss with him or her the firm's reward system—intrinsic and extrinsic, financial and nonfinancial.

3. Obtain a copy of a local area wage survey from the library or a local firm. Report to the class on the research methods used and the results.

4. If you were earning $200 a week and a flexible compensation plan allowed you complete freedom to choose, how would you divide up your compensation among different forms of wages and benefits?

5. Compare your answer to 4 with the answers of your classmates. What explains the differences?

6. Write a five-page research paper discussing why it is important for employees to see a direct relationship between their performance and the rewards they receive.

BIBLIOGRAPHY

See listings at end of Chapter 8.

NOTES

[1] "GMAD: Jekyll or Hyde?" *Ward's Auto World*, April 1972, p. 29.

[2] E. E. Lawler III, *Pay and Organizational Effectiveness: A Psychological View* (New York: McGraw-Hill Book Co., 1971); J. S. Adams, "Toward an Understanding of Inequity," *Journal of Abnormal and Social Psychology*, June 1972.

[3] Ibid. See also E. Ghiselli, *Explorations in Managerial Talent* (Pacific Palisades, Calif.: Goodyear Publishing Co., 1971).

[4] Larry L. Cummings, "Strategies for Improving Human Productivity," reprinted with permission of *The Personnel Administrator;* copyright June 1975, The American Society for Personnel Administration.

[5] B. F. Skinner, *Science and Human Behavior* (New York: Macmillan Co., 1953). See also David K. Hart and William G. Scott, "The Optimal Image of Man for Systems Theory," *Academy of Management Journal*, December 1972.

[6] V. Vroom, *Work and Motivation* (New York: John Wiley & Sons, 1964); and L. W. Porter and E. E. Lawler, III, *Managerial Attitudes and Performance* (Homewood, Ill.: Irwin-Dorsey, 1968). See also Orlando Behling and Chester Schriesheim, *Organizational Behavior* (Boston: Allyn and Bacon, 1976), pp. 85–87; and Martin G. Evans, "Extensions of a Path Goal Theory of Motivation," *Journal of Applied Psychology*, 1974.

[7] J. S. Adams, "Toward an Understanding of Inequity," *Journal of Abnormal and Social Psychology*, June 1972.

[8] Lawler, *Pay and Organizational Effectiveness*.

[9] Ibid. See also R. L. Opshal and M. D. Dunnette, "The Role of Financial Compensation in Industrial Motivation," *Psychological Bulletin*, August 1966; F. J. Roethlisberger and W. H. Dickson, Management and the Worker (Cambridge, Mass.: Harvard University Press, 1939); W. F. Whyte, *Money and Motivation* (New York: Harper, 1955); and B. M. Bass, W. P. Hurder, and N. Ellis, "Assessing Human Performance under Stress," unpublished technical report cited in Lawler, *Pay and Organizational Effectiveness*.

[10] J. W. Atkinson and W. R. Reitman, "Performance as a Function of Motive Strength and Expectancy of Goal Attainment," *Journal of Abnormal and Social Psychology*, November 1956; C. L. Hulin and M. R. Blood, "Job Enlargement, Individual Differences, and Worker Responses," *Psychological Bulletin*, January 1968; C. J. French, "Correlates of Success in Retail Selling," *American Journal of Sociology*, 1960; E. E. Lawler III, and J. L. Suttle, "Expectancy Theory and Job Behavior," *Organizational Behavior and Human Performance*, 1973; E. E. Lawler, III, *Motivation in Work Organizations* (Belmont, Calif.: Brooks/Cole, 1973); and John P. Campbell and Robert D. Pritchard, "Motivation Theory in Industrial and Organizational Psychology," in Marvin D. Dunnette (ed.), *Handbook of Industrial and Organizational Psychology* (Chicago: Rand McNally College Publishing Co., 1976).

[11] *U.S. News & World Report*, December 9, 1974, p. 85.

When you have completed studying
ADMINISTERING THE REWARD SYSTEM
you should be able to:

1. Develop the compensation strategy for an organization with which you are familiar.
2. Design a flexible reward system for a particular organization.
3. Discuss fully the cafeteria approach to compensation and benefits.
4. Identify benchmark jobs and use technical guidelines to conduct a compensation and benefits survey.
5. Relate the data from a compensation and benefit survey to an organization's reward system.
6. Use a standard point, factor comparison, ranking, or classification system to write a job description and evaluate the job described.
7. Discuss fully the various steps of the compensation determination process.
8. Describe the impact of unions, the government, and the labor market on compensation and benefits.
9. Describe the role of human resource specialists in updating the reward system through outside surveys and internal reviews.

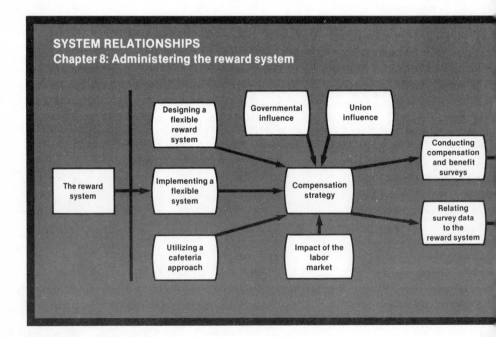

SYSTEM RELATIONSHIPS
Chapter 8: Administering the reward system

8

Administering the reward system

As we have seen in the previous chapter, an effective reward system built on the contingency model must match the organization's history, traditions, managerial climate, formal policies, structure, and so on. Furthermore, the reward system must be fitted to the different tasks (that is, job descriptions). The reward system should also vary in relation to the degree of skill and experience required in the job, the behaviors and attitudes required, the measurability of performance, and the opportunities for intrinsic rewards.

A contingency-based reward system should be adjusted to individuals who are grouped by similar needs. Some individuals will be motivated primar-

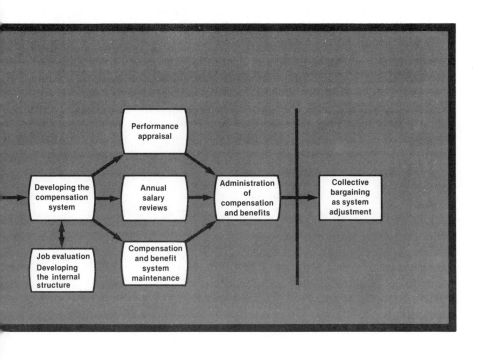

ily by lower level needs—physiological and safety needs; others will be motivated primarily by social needs; and still others will be motivated primarily by ego needs—they will seek opportunities for achievement or creativity, for development, for recognition, and so on. A few individuals may be motivated primarily by self-actualization needs, and will seek opportunities for taking on new and different responsibilities. Finally, individuals vary greatly in the degree to which they seek intrinsic rewards, extrinsic rewards, or a combination of the two.

Designing flexible reward systems

Designing a flexible reward system is far more difficult than designing a uniform reward system. However, all of our evidence about human behavior indicates that such a contingency-based reward system is necessary for the effective management of human resources in the 1980s. As has been pointed out, the motivational structure of people today is more complex than was that of people in earlier periods. In the long run, therefore, it will be a wise investment of time to design a reward system which incorporates the flexibility of a contingency model.

In the typical organization the kind of information needed to design a contingent reward system is simply not available. But this does not mean that such a system cannot be designed. Rather, it means that we must begin the design by obtaining more information than has been obtained in the past about the organization, the jobs, and the individuals in order to have the data necessary to construct the reward system. The required tools, such as survey research techniques, are available in standardized form.

This need to gather more data means that managers who are involved in the design of reward systems will take on more of a research role than they did in the past. Such managers play different roles in the following sequence:

1. The role of researcher to determine the needs and constraints for a reward system within a particular organization, including both the degree and the direction of the flexibility desired.
2. The role of planner in designing a many-faceted reward system that will accommodate as many of the needs and constaints identified in the research as possible.
3. The role of implementer and manager both in introducing the new reward system and in making it effective in terms of the many requirements previously discussed—communication, un-

derstanding, tie between performance and reward, accurate appraisal, equitable internal relationships and so on.

Thus, for jobs that appear to afford little opportunity for intrinsic reward and for individuals (regardless of job) who appear to be motivated primarily by extrinsic reward, the reward system should emphasize extrinsic rewards which are tied directly and proportionately to effective performance. This will necessitate, among other things, a valid and objective appraisal system, differential pay for differential performance, and public recognition of effective performance. For situations in which individuals say that they are motivated by opportunities for intrinsic satisfactions and/or situations in which there are ample opportunities for such intrinsic rewards as exploration, learning, achievement, and mastery, the reward system should certainly offer adequate and equitable pay. But for motivational purposes it might also enhance and spotlight the intrinsic rewards of the job through such means as job enrichment, participation in decision making, and increased feedback on performance.

Cafeteria compensation

A fairly recent development which could facilitate a contingency-based reward system is "flexible compensation" or, as it is sometimes called, "cafeteria compensation". Flexible compensation is a system which gives each individual a number of options as to the form and timing of his or her total compensation package, instead of informing the individual of the company's unilateral decision regarding the portion of total compensation that will be given in the form of cash, a retirement plan, life insurance, health insurance, vacation time, and so on. The employee is told how many compensation cost units have been granted to him, and perhaps also the required minima in such areas as cash compensation, retirement, and health insurance. He is then allowed to use his remaining compensation units to "shop" from among the options offered, much as he would select a meal in a cafeteria.

Advantages of the cafeteria approach. This approach appears to have a number of practical advantages. First of all, it makes possible a contingency-based reward system, since the organization can supply an array of equal-cost alternative rewards and allow each individual (within limits) to select his own. This will, of course, maximize each individual's opportunity to choose rewards which meet his own need structure, attitudes, and preferences. Moreover,

EXHIBIT 8-1
Cafeteria compensation

Under a flexible compensation arrangement, employees choose the specific benefits they want, and the company totals up the dollar amounts until limits are reached.

Source: Thomas E. Wahlrone, "The Cafeteria Approach to Employee Benefits," *Administrative Management*, December 1974.

although the cost to the company remains the same regardless of the combinations chosen, the psychological value of the reward for each individual should be higher since he is getting 100 percent of the rewards which are of greatest value to him and none of the rewards which might represent a cost to the company but be of no value to the employee. Psychologically, this is like giving the employee a raise at no cost to the company. Another value of this approach is that it allows employees to participate in a vital decision which relates to their jobs. This opportunity to play a decision-making role rather than a passive role in a job-related area of vital concern is itself a satisfier of higher level needs, and thus should have its own motivational impact.

The cafeteria approach also makes obvious to each employee the economic value of each fringe benefit which he chooses. In many organizations this is no small matter. A number of research studies have shown that employees often grossly underestimate the cost, and therefore the economic value, of the fringe benefits supplied by their employers. Since they underestimate the cost of the company-supplied fringe benefits, they underestimate the total compensation they receive from the company. The flexible compensation approach makes this unfortunate result virtually impossible.

Limitations of the cafeteria approach. None of the practical constraints and problems that need to be solved in implementing flexible compensation appear to be insurmountable. However, the matter of tax treatment for optional benefits will require careful attention. IRS tax treatment of many types of compensation and benefits has been designed on the assumption that all or a large percentage of the employees in an organization participate on a nondiscriminatory basis in each of the benefits offered. In order to maximize the tax advantages of benefits, therefore, it will be necessary to plan carefully and perhaps to work directly with the IRS in arranging options that will meet the IRS tests for favorable tax treatment.

A particular example is the retirement plan. One IRS requirement for retirement plans that receive favorable tax treatment is nondiscrimination in participation as to both salary and organizational level. Since the IRS applies this test, not to the *opportunity* to participate, but rather to *de facto participation*, care will have to be exercised to prevent the voluntary formation of "discriminatory groups" of participants.

Another area of difficulty is the adverse selection of certain insurance coverages. It will be necessary to provide either minimum levels of coverage for all employees and/or limitations or medical qualifications for coverage to avoid the problem that under voluntary participation only employees anticipating heavy medical expenses would elect the highest levels of medical insurance coverage, and only older employees would elect the highest life insurance coverage. One possible solution to adverse selection of medical insurance would be to require a medical examination for supplementary levels of coverage (though not for the base level); and a possible solution to adverse selection of life insurance would be to charge differential rates based on attained age rather than a standard rate for all employees.

Thus, the practical problems that must be worked out to make flexible compensation operational appear to be solvable. Although little has been reported on this subject, TRW Systems, Cummins Engine, and Educational Testing Service have flexible compensation plans in operation and other companies are working on such plans.

Implementing a flexible system

The mechanics of operating a flexible compensation system are a bit more complex than the principle, but well within our capabilities in the age of computers. The number and complexity of the computations involved made cafeteria compensation impractical until recent years. At present, however, the computations involved are relatively simple as a computer operation. Basically, what is required is to compute the dollar cost equivalents of an array of compensation options which the employer wishes to offer to employees participating in the flexible compensation system. Typically, options and equivalents would be computed for some or all of the following:

Immediate cash.

Deferred cash.

Retirement plan.

Company stock investment plan.

Mutual fund investment plan.

Medical insurance (perhaps with two or three levels of coverage as options).

Long-term disability insurance.

Life insurance.

Vacation time.

Perhaps some local individualized options.

Although it is theoretically possible to compute dollar equivalents for the various forms of compensation and then to let each individual have complete freedom in selecting his mix, this is unlikely to happen in the near future for a number of reasons. One is a sense of corporate responsibility for making sure that an individual does not select so unwisely as to put himself out on a limb. Perhaps more important, significant tax considerations make it impractical to have some benefits totally optional. What is more likely to happen is that the company will specify a certain minimum percentage of compensation to be taken in cash and in each other area, and will then allow optional selection of incremental amounts.

Thomas H. Paine, an authority on compensation, has recommended this four-step procedure for implementing flexible compensation:

1. Establish management policy regarding the role flexibility is to play.

2. Design a balanced program encompassing both basic nonoptional benefits and flexible supplements.
3. Provide an opportunity for employees to be involved in the design of the program.
4. Establish an efficient and responsible administrative system.

The administrative system should include some controls to assist employees in avoiding serious mistakes in choices. For example, Paine recommends that after employees make their choices a computer printout be reported back to them for their review and approval before the choices become final.[1]

The value of involving employees in the design of the flexible compensation program is both motivational (it gives employees an opportunity to participate in an important organizational decision) and functional (a broad cross section of employees will reflect the needs and desires of the total employee group).

Governmental influence on compensation

There are a number of different influences on the organization's compensation policy. Among these are: the prevailing wages in the industry or the geographic area; governmental influence; union leaders' attitudes toward job evaluation, collective bargaining, and the appraisal of individual performance; and the organization's overall objectives and strategy for the reward system.

One factor which should receive more detailed attention is the impact of governmental influence on compensation. We have already mentioned in Chapter 7 that the Employee Retirement Income Security Act of 1974 (ERISA) has exerted a major influence on privately funded pension plans. The most fundamental governmental influence on compensation, however, is that of the Fair Labor Standards Act of 1938, as amended most recently in 1977. This act sets minimum wages which may be paid to employees "engaged in commerce or in the production of goods for commerce." Because the operational definition of the expression "engaged in interstate commerce" has been expanded over the years, the Fair Labor Standards Act applies to the vast majority of jobs in this country.

Under the most recent revision, a minimum wage of $2.65 per hour must be paid to all workers covered by the act. The minimum increases to $2.90 in 1979, $3.10 in 1980, and $3.35 in 1981. For detailed current data, readers should consult the most recent bulletin of the Wage and Hour Public Contracts Division, U.S. Department of Labor.

As mentioned earlier, the impact of the minimum wage law is not limited to its direct influence on the lowest wages paid. It also exerts indirect influence on the total wage structure by making it necessary to raise the pay of all job grades in order to maintain prevailing internal relationships.

Thus, each time an amendment to the Fair Labor Standards Act has raised the minimum wage, the entire wage structure of the country has been affected. Furthermore, there is little doubt that the act has had a direct influence on the rate of unemployment. Each time the minimum allowable wage is raised, it inevitably becomes uneconomic to utilize the services of certain marginally employable people. The result is to increase the rolls of the unemployed, thus creating a social cost which must be balanced against the social gain of raising wages.

The Fair Labor Standards Act also has an impact on compensation practice through its encouragement of guaranteed annual wage plans. If a union-management agreement guarantees pay for no less than 1,840 hours of employment per year (and provides that a higher limit will not be exceeded), the act exempts companies from paying overtime within certain limits. The net effect of this provision is to encourage guaranteed annual wage plans.

Other federal legislation prohibits discrimination in pay practices on the basis of sex, race, or age. The Equal Pay Act of 1963, an amendment to the Fair Labor Standards Act, provides that "no employer . . . shall discriminate . . . between employees on the basis of sex by paying wages . . . at a rate less than the rate at which he pays wages to employees of the opposite sex . . . for equal work on jobs the performance of which requires equal skill, effort, and responsibility, and which are performed under similar working conditions." The Civil Rights Act of 1964 requires that employers act affirmatively to ensure that there is no discrimination in either employment or pay on the basis of race, creed, color, or national origin. Finally, the Age Discrimination in Employment Act of 1967 added age to the prohibited bases of discrimination.

The impact of labor market conditions

Wage determination is a complex process in which many different pressures and forces collide to produce the wage structure. (The term *wage structure* simply refers to the categorization of jobs into a series of job grades and to the relationships of compensation ranges for the grades.) It is not a neat process in which the "true value" of each job and its pay are determined objectively and scientifically.

Moreover, the process is further complicated by the prevailing labor market conditions. Suppose, for example, that a severe shortage of computer programmers and engineers drives the prevailing wage for such jobs to an amount double the wage indicated by a company's job evaluation. The company will simply be unable to hire people with these skills unless it violates the job evaluation plan and pays something approaching the market rate.

Thus, internal compensation relationships and structures are sometimes violated or compromised in order to obtain critically short skills. As long as this is recognized as a practical accommodation to reality, a limited number of exceptions to the firm's compensation structure should cause no alarm.

On the contrary, if employees are given a straightforward explanation of the reason for the exceptions, the vast majority will accept the logic of accommodating to reality. On the other hand, some firms have gotten into serious difficulties by trying to disguise the fact that the system was being violated. Attempts to pretend that the out-of-structure wage can be justified by redefining responsibilities, for example, have a very high probability of being discovered and thus endangering the perceived validity of the total system. Honesty and a realistic assessment of the appraisal system are advisable. If the system is described as a nonscientific effort to juggle as many conflicting determinants as possible in order to come up with what will be recognized as an internally equitable set of relationships, few employees will have difficulty in accommodating to occasional job market irregularities. On the other hand, if the internal structure is advertised as "scientifically accurate and precise," any deviations will be seen immediately as an indication of basic management dishonesty or as a defeat of the system.

The impact of a union

The union may be the most important single external influence on compensation and benefit determination. If the firm is unionized, it can be safely said that a major thrust of the union's efforts will relate to compensation and benefits. Depending on the union-employer relationship, the union's impact may range from advisory influence to virtual control.

The role of compensation and benefit surveys and job evaluation in situations in which compensation and benefits are determined by employer-union collective bargaining vary greatly, depending upon the attitude of the union. Some unions use comparisons within the industry, among industries, or within their geographic area to determine their demands, and base a major part of their negotiating strategy on obtaining equality. Other unions disdain this "follower" role and simply concentrate on seeking "more" in terms of higher compensation, new benefits, or higher benefit levels.

Furthermore, some unions cooperate closely with management in designing and administering job evaluations in order to establish appropriate internal relationships within the salary structure. Other unions disdain job evaluation as a management tool to destroy traditional internal relationships among jobs. Where there is a union, its objectives, traditions, and expectations become additional constraints which must be taken into account in designing the organization's compensation strategy.

PROCEDURE FOR DEVELOPING THE COMPENSATION SYSTEM

The first step in detailing an organization's compensation system is to determine the objectives of the compensation program. These objectives should include consideration of the role which compensation and benefits are expected to play in the total reward system. Specifically, the objectives should consider the appropriate balance between extrinsic and intrinsic rewards. The next step is to determine the appropriate balance between financial and nonfinancial rewards. Given these particular employees, this particular organization, and these particular jobs, a decision must be made concerning the appropriate division of the resources allotted to mandatory cash compensation, mandatory benefits, and optional rewards.

Another basic decision must be made concerning the firm's competitive strategy regarding compensation and benefits. Does the firm wish (and can it afford) to be an industry or area leader? Or does it wish merely to keep up with industry or area averages? Or does it wish to follow a strategy of lagging industry or area compensation and benefits, but to supplement this strategy with greater attention to nonfinancial rewards?

Compensation and benefit surveys

Once the above objectives have been established, the next step is to obtain the needed data for planning purposes. Sometimes these data are available from published industry or area surveys. The results of a survey of top executive compensation are shown in Exhibit 8–2.

Some industry associations conduct annual surveys of compensation and benefits for their members. In some localities the Chamber

EXHIBIT 8–2

The compensation of top executives as a function of company sales

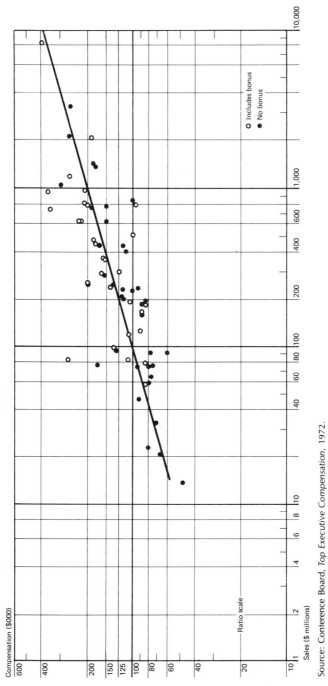

Source: Conference Board, *Top Executive Compensation*, 1972.

of Commerce or another employer group conducts an annual compensation and benefit survey to provide such data. Often, however, no such survey will exist or specific data needs may not be satisfied by the survey. In such instances the organization must conduct its own compensation and benefits survey or employ a consultant to do so.

Fundamentally, the process is simple and straightforward, and it can be discussed in principle here. The first step in conducting a compensation survey is to determine a series of benchmark jobs. These are jobs which have been carefully and completely defined and described in the organization, and are believed to exist in similar form in the other organizations which will participate in the survey. Thus, benchmark jobs provide basic reference points for comparing equivalent jobs in different organizations. After data have been obtained for a series of benchmark jobs, other jobs within the organization can be fitted in between the wage structure of the benchmark jobs, using the internal job evaluation process.

Depending on the constraints, compensation and benefit surveys may be conducted either by mail or in person. In the case of surveys conducted by mail, it is often helpful to follow up receipt of the survey data with a telephone call to discuss unclear details and to confirm the assumed similarity of benchmark jobs, as well as to clear up any other ambiguities.

Relating survey data to the reward system

Once the survey data have been obtained, it is helpful to display them graphically for each benchmark job, showing the minimum pay, the maximum pay, and the median pay for each benchmark job covered in the survey, as well as the relationship between the different benchmark jobs. Such a graph is illustrated in Exhibit 8–3.

The benchmark jobs can then be used to determine a series of job grades or steps and an appropriate salary midpoint and range for each grade. Depending on its objectives and strategy, the organization may wish to set its salary midpoints for each grade at the average (median) of surveyed firms, at 10 percent higher than the average, at 10 percent lower than the average, or perhaps at the average of some subcategory of the total survey.

Whatever the strategy, once the midpoint of the salary range for each benchmark job has been determined, and once the benchmark jobs have been arrayed along a continuum of job grades, then any job in the organization may be related to this wage structure, and

EXHIBIT 8–3
Survey data for benchmark jobs

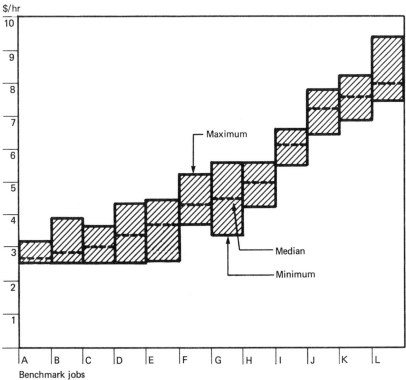

Benchmark jobs

the appropriate salary minimum, maximum, and midpoint for that job may be determined by using a job evaluation system to compare it with the benchmark jobs. The same evaluation system is used to evaluate all of the jobs in the organization. Each job is assigned a grade based on its relative number of evaluation points. Once a grade is assigned to a job, that job has automatically been assigned a salary minimum, maximum, and midpoint, as shown in Exhibit 8–4.

The benefits component should also be determined in relation to the compensation and benefits survey, although usually on a less mathematical basis. Determination of the mix of benefits, the level of each benefit offered, and the funding arrangements will usually be done by evaluating the organization's unique situation and its employees' needs in light of the survey data, rather than by attempting to translate the survey data directly into equivalent practice.

EXHIBIT 8–4
Wage structure

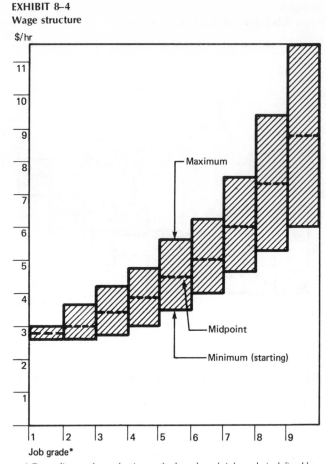

Job grade*

* Depending on the evaluation method used, each job grade is defined by:

1. A range of evaluation points.
2. A series of benchmark job descriptions.
3. A classification description.

JOB EVALUATION

A major task in developing a wage structure is determining the relative worth of each job. This task of determining the relative worth of jobs is called "job evaluation."

The objective of job evaluation is to ensure that internal relationships among the pay of various jobs are appropriate in light of the factors which are considered important *by the members of the given organization*. These factors typically include the effort, training, and experience required; the difficulty, responsibility, and hazards of the job; the value or contribution of the job to the organization; and the organization's traditions of internal job relationships. Thus, the objective of job evaluation is to ensure internal equity *in the eyes of the members of the organization*, not to ensure equity in terms of some "objective" standard external to the organization. Although such a task is impossible as a practical reality, managers have sometimes thought and textbooks have implied that an objective standard of equity was the goal of job evaluation. Job evaluation is still very much an art and by no means a science. Managers lose sight of this fact at their peril.

We have said that the job evaluation reflects *internal* standards of equity and traditional relationships. We have also said that once benchmark jobs are identified, the compensation and benefits survey determines industry or geographic standards for each benchmark job in order to create a wage structure based on the benchmark jobs. It should be pointed out that this process may have laid the groundwork for a serious inconsistency.

Implicit in the process of compensation determination discussed above is the assumption that internal job evaluation will create the same relationships among benchmark jobs that are found in the outside firms participating in the survey. Obviously this may or may not be the case. If we are lucky, our internal relationships will turn out to be rather close to the relationships determined by the survey. However, it is certainly possible that due to unique internal circumstances or traditions some of our benchmark jobs are felt to be worth relatively more than our external surveys say they are worth in other organizations.

There is no standard method for dealing with this dilemma, but it is important to recognize at this point that if such practical problems arise, the only solution is to make a pragmatic judgment. Of course, the external data may help change internal perceptions.

There are four basic methods of job evaluation:

1. The point method.   3. Ranking.
2. Factor comparison.   4. Classification.

Each of these methods begins with a job description (discussed in Chapter 4).

The point method

By far the most common method of job evaluation is the point method. This procedure usually examines four or more job factors

common to the jobs being evaluated and rates each job on a numerical scale in relation to each factor. Thus, points are accumulated for
each factor on the basis of the relative degree to which the job is
seen as possessing that factor.

For example, if the factor to be evaluated were "education,"
grade school or less might be scaled as one point; two years of high
school as two points; high school graduation, three points; two years
of college, four points; four years of college, five points; master's
degree, six points; and Ph.D., seven points. A factor such as "responsibility" might scale several different levels of dollar responsibility, in terms of the value of production or the cost of errors.

The number of factors used may vary from as few as 2 to as many
as 30, although several research studies have shown statistically
that 4 or 5 factors seem to be about as accurate a basis for distinguishing jobs as a higher number. As can be imagined, the factors
used vary widely among different organizations and industries. The
more common factors in use include education, responsibility (for
production, equipment, budget, persons, or safety), skill, experience, outside contacts, supervision, job conditions, physical effort,
mental effort, and creativity.

Whatever the factors in a particular system, the total points for
each job are determined by summing the points assigned for each
factor. Each job can then be related to other jobs on the basis of their
respective total point scores.

Furthermore, the point score can be related to the structure of job
grades and wage ranges previously discussed by assigning a job
grade to each range of points. Exhibit 8–5 illustrates point evaluation in a typical point system.

Factor comparison

The factor comparison method is very similar to the point
method, except that it does not evaluate each of the factors on a
numerical scale. It may use the same factors as those used in the
point method. However, instead of assigning points, the factor comparison method *ranks* benchmark jobs in relation to each other on
each factor at the outset of the process. It is important to include in
this group only jobs that are widely believed to be accurately paid.

Following the ranking of the benchmark jobs on each of the factors, a fairly complex mathematical procedure is utilized to determine how much of the present rate of pay of the jobs is accounted
for by each of the separate factors, that is, the weights of the factors.
After this has been determined, the remaining jobs to be evaluated

are then ranked on each of the factors in relation to the benchmark jobs. When the dollar values of the ranked positions on each factor have been determined, these values are summed to arrive at the dollar value of the total job. The factor comparison method is not as widely used as the point method, principally because it is much more complicated and takes more time to learn and apply. Moreover, the fact that the method is hard to understand may lead to lack of trust in its application.

Ranking

The ranking method is perhaps the simplest method of job evaluation. The various jobs to be evaluated are ranked in relation to each other on a total basis. There is no attempt to determine the significant factors in the jobs or to evaluate the jobs in terms of their subelements. Rather, only a single overall judgment is made regarding the relative worth of each job in relation to the others.

This is, in fact, the most common method of job evaluation in smaller organizations, in which perhaps two secretaries, a typist, and a file clerk must be evaluated. In a small organization in which relatively few jobs are involved and all of the people participating in the evaluation are intimately familiar with the details of all the jobs, this is perhaps a very effective method of evaluation.

However, this method very quickly breaks down when larger groups are involved and there is less knowledge of each of the jobs. Since there are no written guidelines for evaluation, it is obviously important that the ranking of all the jobs be done by the same individual or group so that the subjective basis for ranking can be consistent. Even under the best of conditions, there is always the danger that the individuals doing the ranking may have imperfect knowledge of the jobs or be subject to bias. To some extent this can be overcome by use of job descriptions.

Classification

The classification method of job evaluation is by far the most common method used in civil service systems. In this method before any jobs are examined an a priori assumption is made regarding the number of pay grades to be included in the final structure. Then, following the perusal of many job descriptions, a description is written for each grade or "class" of jobs in the structure.

These descriptions cover such items as the education required, the skill required, job responsibility, and other factors that are pertinent to a particular class of jobs. Thus, a particular job class or grade may be described as requiring a high school education, moderate finger dexterity, light physical exertion (as specifically described), and a moderately high level of judgment.

Once a description of each of the job grades has been written, the descriptions of the jobs to be evaluated are examined. Jobs are classified into the grade or level which has the most closely corresponding description.

Although appearing to be somewhat less "scientific" than the point or factor comparison methods, in many situations this method

EXHIBIT 8–5
Points assigned to factor degrees and range for grades

Factors	1st degree	2d degree	3d degree	4th degree	5th degree	6th degree	7th degree
Training							
1. Education	15	30	45	60	75	100	
2. Experience	20	40	60	80	100	125	150
Initiative							
3. Complexity of duties	15	30	45	60	75	100	
4. Supervision received	5	10	20	40	60		
Responsibility							
5. Errors	5	10	20	40	60	80	
6. Contacts with others	5	10	20	40	60	80	
7. Confidential data	5	10	15	20	25		
Job conditions							
8. Mental or visual demand	5	10	15	20	25		
9. Working conditions	5	10	15	20	25		
Supervision							
10. Character of supervision	5	10	20	40	60	80	
11. Scope of supervision	5	10	20	40	60	80	100

Score range	Grades	Score range	Grades
100 and under	1	311–340	9
101–130	2	341–370	10
131–160	3	371–400	11
161–190	4	401–430	12
191–220	5	431–460	13
221–250	6	461–490	14
251–280	7	491–520	15
281–310	8	521–550	16

EXHIBIT 8–5 *(continued)*

	Job Rating Specifications (clerical, technical, supervisory) COMPTROLLER	Class	Code no.	B–01
			Dept.	Accounting
			Grade	15
			Total points	500

Factors	Substantiating data	Deg.	Pts.
Education	Broad knowledge of general, cost, and payroll accounting theory and practice, budgetary control, and finance. Familiar with business organization and administration, office management and economics, foreign exchange. Equivalent to college education in business administration.	4	60
Experience	Over seven and up to eight years.	6	125
Complexity of duties	Wide variety of budgetary control, accounting, and office management duties and responsibilities, involving general knowledge of related company policies and procedures. Duties require considerable judgment in devising new methods and procedures, modifying standard practices to meet new conditions, making decisions guided by precedent and based on company policies.	4	60
Supervision Received	Under general direction of Treasurer as to policies and general objectives. Rarely refer specific problems to superior for other than policy decisions.	4	40
Errors	Probable error in judgment or supervision may result in incorrect financial data, costs, or inventory information. Considerable accuracy and responsibility involved.	4	40
Contacts with others	Contacts with various company officers, subsidiary companies, and branches, requiring considerable tact and diplomacy to obtain results through influencing others.	4	40
Confidential data	Regularly work with confidential corporate financial data such as balance sheet, profit and loss statements, costs, etc. Disclosure may be detrimental to the company's interests.	4	20
Mental or visual demand	Supervisory and contact duties involve normal mental and visual attention most of the time.	2	10
Working conditions	Usual office working conditions.	1	5
For supervisory positions only			
Character of supervision	General supervision of accounting, payroll; billing, and general office services, with responsibility for results in terms of costs, methods, and personnel.	4	40
Scope of supervision	Responsible for supervising 62 persons, including 9 subordinate supervisors.	5	60
Remarks			

may be just as accurate. Furthermore, this method is relatively easy to understand and therefore appears to be straightforward and "legitimate." Thus, in many organizations it may be easier for employees to accept this method as being "honest."

THE ADMINISTRATION OF COMPENSATION AND BENEFITS

The administration of compensation and benefits has three major facets:

1. The performance appraisal of individuals.
2. Annual salary reviews for each individual.
3. Maintaining the compensation and benefit system through surveys and internal reviews.

Performance appraisal

The wage structure developed for an organization determines a number of job grades or levels. Each of these job grades has a minimum and maximum salary. The job evaluation system determines the salary grade of each job, and thus determines the minimum salary and maximum salary which may be paid to an employee assigned to that job.

Thus, there is a range of possible pay rates for each job which runs from the minimum to the maximum allowed for the job's salary grade. Although the job evaluation system determines the range (that is, the minimum and maximum salary) within which an individual holding a particular job may be paid, it does not in any way determine what specific salary within that range the individual should receive. Depending on the design of the particular system, the individual's compensation within the range for his or her job grade is determined by some combination of seniority (that is, time spent in the job) and individual performance.

A few organizations have compensation systems which provide for automatic progression from the entry level all the way to maximum pay for the job grade on a seniority basis (contingent on minimally acceptable performance). The more common practice is to base advancement within the range on individual performance or to provide advancement to the midpoint of the range on the basis of seniority, with advancement beyond the midpoint determined solely by individual performance.

In the majority of compensation systems, some form of performance appraisal is a major determinant of the individual's specific salary within the range determined for his or her position. Performance appraisal is in itself a highly technical art and a major responsibility of every manager. For this reason, a separate chapter devoted to performance appraisal (Chapter 13) will discuss commonly used alternative approaches and the manager's critical role.

Annual salary reviews

Following the completion of performance appraisals, the manager must review the salary of each subordinate annually in order to determine what increments to award or recommend. In many organizations one portion of the employee's salary increase is determined by his or her manager on the basis of performance, while another portion of the increase is determined by such matters as the cost of living and changes in the structure of the compensation system. Therefore, the manager often determines salary increase recommendations in conjunction with a member of the human resources management staff who provides input on the organization-wide portions of the salary increase.

Generally, salary increases are determined by the following factors, although the weight given to each factor may vary widely from organization to organization or from time to time:

1. Changes in the cost of living as measured by the Bureau of Labor Statistics of the Department of Labor.
2. Adjustments occasioned by changes in the wage structure as a result of changing jobs in the organization or changing relationships between jobs.
3. Adjustments upward of the whole structure as a result of compensation and benefit surveys.
4. Seniority or step adjustments
5. Adjustments related to the individual's performance appraisal ("merit").

Although currently a practice in few organizations, we believe that from a motivational standpoint it is important to make explicit the determinants of the salary increase for each individual (particularly the portion of the increase that is based on individual performance). This is often deliberately avoided in order to "avoid hurting people's feelings," but this omission is a breach of effective human resources management.

Maintaining the system

The third major function in the administration of compensation and benefits is the maintenance of the compensation and benefit system through surveys and internal reviews. Compensation and benefit surveys have already been discussed in the context of developing a wage structure. Benchmark jobs are identified, and the salaries paid to equivalent jobs by competing firms in the industry or the geographic area are determined through surveys.

For most organizations, the best practice will be to take advantage of all published surveys which may be relevant, to study and compare these surveys carefully, and then to conduct their own survey to supplement the published surveys.

In any case, it is probably desirable for most organizations to conduct such a review at least annually, and many organizations will have reviews in progress constantly. The annual survey does not in itself imply a change in the organization's wage structure; it only provides a basis for decision making. Data will also be available regarding changes in the cost of living and in the organization's profitability.

Following comparison of the survey data with the organization's wage structure, a basic policy decision at the highest level (with the advice of the Human Resources Department) must be made about changes in the organization's compensation in response to job market changes reflected in the surveys.

The need for internal review.   Internal reviews must also be conducted constantly to keep job evaluations up-to-date. Although it is important to provide a system for automatically rewriting job descriptions and reevaluating jobs each time a job is changed, many smaller changes that occur constantly tend to be overlooked. Therefore, it is vital that a periodic audit of each job description and job evaluation be conducted to make certain that each continues to be up-to-date.

In addition, it is necessary to review the entire wage structure periodically to make sure that it is sound and appropriately related to the mix of jobs. For example, over time the necessary number of job grades may change. Or the relationship between grades may need to be changed. These things can be determined only by comparing the results of internal job evaluation reviews with the results of compensation and benefit surveys.

From a motivational standpoint it is extremely important for an organization to constantly review its total system of compensation and benefits. Only through such review is it possible to maintain a system that the employees view as "equitable" and that serves as a motivating device.

The role of the specialist.   The process of maintaining the compensation and benefit system is a major piece of work in an organization of any considerable size. Thus, most organizations of more than a few employees will have at least one specialist in compensation and benefits within the Human Resources Department. Larger organizations will have sizable departments of compensation and benefit specialists.

It is the specific assignment of these departments to keep the compensation and benefits system up-to-date through the reviews which have been discussed. In addition, they often advise and assist line managers in matters that concern the compensation and benefits system.

A final part of the internal review which can be highly valuable for management is the periodic involvement of the entire work force in a review of the reward system. One way of achieving this is through an annual questionnaire to all employees asking for their opinions on various facets of the nonfinancial and financial reward systems.

For example, questions might be asked regarding the perceived equity of the general level of wages, the wage structure, performance evaluations, and the relationship of individual pay to individual performance. Additional questions might be asked about the adequacy of the benefits provided or about the adequacy of the optional forms of compensation in a flexible compensation system.

Another procedure is to use groups of employees to review the compensation and benefits system. A very effective approach is to have an employee committee review and discuss the results of an organization-wide questionnaire survey, with an assignment to recommend changes to top management.

SUMMARY

In order to effectively motivate a wide range of employees it is important that a reward system be flexible so that the specifics of the system can vary from individual to individual and situation to situation, contingent on the individual (needs, attitudes, intrinsic versus extrinsic motivation), the task (intrinsic versus extrinsic rewards, measurability), and the organization (climate, history).

In light of our current knowledge regarding human behavior, it is clear that only a contingency-based reward system which takes into account differences among individuals, tasks, and organizations can provide an adequate basis for the motivation of individuals. As an illustration of a contingent reward system, the flexible compensation or "cafeteria" approach was described. This appears to be the best means of providing a maximum degree of individual tailoring in the reward system. From a motivational standpoint, the cafeteria approach also has the advantage of giving the individual additional control over aspects of his work which are highly important to him.

Also discussed was the role of the compensation and benefit specialist in planning and implementing compensation strategy. Among the specific responsibilities of compensation and benefit specialists are the various steps of the compensation determination process, including the writing of job descriptions, job evaluation, conducting compensation and benefit surveys, developing a wage structure for the organization, and constantly updating the total reward system.

CASE: THE OLD ORDER CHANGETH (B)*

Two months ago, the president and founder of the Bygone Daze Company passed away. The tradition and philosophy he established had always been rigidly adhered to (see "The Old Order Changeth (A)" case in Chapter 7). This accounted for the company's policy of limited output—just enough to assure a satisfactory return—and a family of employees who never needed to fear the wolf at the door.

The successor management feels that the time has arrived for Bygone Daze to turn over a new leaf. It plans to expand facilities, to take on new business, and to consider product line additions. The company has already signed long-term contracts with several new customers. This will assure a market for the expanded production. A new advertising and promotion campaign is in the planning stage. A major loan to cover the associated costs has been successfully negotiated, and a liberal line of bank credit has been established. Expansion of the physical plant is already in the drawing board stage and Methods Analysts, Inc., an industrial engineering firm, is working on new systems and procedures for the production and office areas.

The major long-term concern of the new management is the impact of the company expansion on the "corporate family," which will include newly hired personnel. The new management is aware of the need for a revamping of the company's compensation system, and it is also concerned about the need for employee motivation. It has come up with a three-phase program, kept confidential, of course, that summarizes its objectives:

1. Increase output through better personnel cooperation.
2. Establish a corporate pay system that is fair to all (the top executive, supervisors, office and plant employees).
3. Keep the union out.

---

* Submitted by Charles A. Meloy, Associate Professor, Saint Peter's College, Jersey City, New Jersey.

You have been asked to suggest a new compensation program that will help the new management carry out its three major objectives. That is, you are to suggest:

1. How the company should go about establishing a pay system that is fair to all.
2. What employee motivation may be necessary in order to increase output.
3. How a climate may be established that will tend to discourage unionization of the employees.

QUESTIONS AND PROBLEMS

1. Obtain from the library a textbook on job evaluation which contains a complete point plan. Using the plan, do a complete evaluation of a job familiar to you.

2. Evaluate the same job using a classification plan from the same or a different textbook.

3. Write a library research report on "maintaining a compensation and benefit system."

4. Visit the compensation manager of a local firm, and discuss with him or her the organization's procedure for job evaluation. Report your findings to the class.

5. Visit the same firm's benefits manager to obtain information on the firm's fringe benefit program. Report these findings to the class.

6. Write a five-page report on *your* views of the role of the human resource staff regarding the compensation and benefit program.

BIBLIOGRAPHY

Adams, J. S. "Toward an Understanding of Inequity." *Journal of Abnormal and Social Psychology*, April 1972.

Beach, Dale S. *Managing People at Work*. New York: Macmillan Co., 1971.

Behling, Orlando, and Schriesheim, Chester. *Organizational Behavior*. Boston: Allyn and Bacon, 1976.

Campbell, John P., and Pritchard, Robert D. "Motivation Theory in Industrial and Organizational Psychology." In Marvin D. Dunnette (ed.). *Handbook of Industrial and Organizational Psychology* Chicago: Rand McNally College Publishing Co., 1976.

"A Changing Pattern in Allocating Pay Hikes." *Business Week*, June 23, 1975.

Crystal, Graef S. "*The New 10 Commandments—plus 1—of Executive Compensation*." *Financial Executive*, July 1974.

Cummings, Larry L. "Strategies for Improving Human Productivity." *Personnel Administrator*, June 1975.

Evans, Martin G. "Extensions of a Path Goal Theory of Motivation." *Journal of Applied Psychology*, April 1974.

"Executive Compensation: The Ups and Downs Are Sharper." *Business Week,* May 12, 1975.

"Flexible Compensation." *Personnel Management—Policies and Practices,* July 17, 1973.

Ford, R. N. *Motivation through the Work Itself,* New York: American Management Association, 1969.

French, Wendell. *The Personnel Management Process.* Boston: Houghton Mifflin, 1974.

Galbraith, J. R., and Cummings, L. L. "An Empirical Investigation of the Motivational Determinants of Task Performance: Interactive Effects between Instrumentality-Valence and Motivation-Ability." *Organizational Behavior and Human Performance,* August 1967.

Ghiselli, E. E. *Explorations in Managerial Talent.* Pacific Palisades, Calif.: Goodyear Publishing Co., 1971.

Herzberg, F., Mausner, B., and Snyderman, B. *The Motivation to Work.* New York: John Wiley & Sons, 1959.

Hess, Randall K. "Tapping Human Resources: Promise and Pitfalls for Productivity." Unpublished manuscript, Florida Atlantic University, 1977.

"How Much Should You Make?" *Dun's,* September 1974.

Japlonsky, S. F., and De Vries, D. L. "Operant Conditioning Principles Extrapolated to the Theory of Management." *Organizational Behavior and Human Performance,* April 1972.

Jaques, E. *Equitable Payment.* New York: John Wiley & Sons, 1961.

Lawler, E. E., III. *Motivation in Work Organizations.* Belmont, Calif.: Brooks/Cole, 1973.

Lawler, E. E., III. *Pay and Organizational Effectiveness: A Psychological View.* New York: McGraw-Hill Book Co., 1971.

Lawler, E. E., III, and Suttle, J. L. "Expectancy Theory and Job Behavior." *Organizational Behavior and Human Performance,* June 1973.

Megginson, Leon C. *Personnel: A Behavioral Approach to Administration.* Homewood, Ill.: Richard D. Irwin, 1972.

Meyer, Pearl. "The Luring of the President." *Dun's,* April 1974.

Meyer, Pearl. "What Price Presidents?" *Dun's,* January 1974.

Nash, Allan N., and Carroll, Stephen J., Jr. *The Management of Compensation.* Belmont, Calif.: Wadsworth Publishing Co., 1975.

"New Fringe Benefit: Prepaid Legal Service." *Business Week,* January 12, 1974.

Otis, Jay L., and Leukart, Richard H. *Job Evaluation: A Basis for Sound Wage Administration.* Englewood Cliffs, N.J.: Prentice-Hall, 1958.

Paine, Thomas H. "Flexible Compensation Can Work!" *Financial Executive,* February 1974.

"Pension Reform's Expensive." *Business Week,* March 24, 1975.

"Performance Shares: New Style in Executive Pay." *Dun's,* January 1973.

Pigors, Paul, and Myers, Charles A. *Personnel Administration,* New York: McGraw-Hill Book Co., 1969.

Porter, L. W., and Lawler, E. E., III. *Managerial Attitudes and Performance.* Homewood, Ill.: Irwin-Dorsey, 1968.

"Problems in Review." *Harvard Business Review,* July–August 1974.

"The Rich Rewards for Oil's Top Men." *Business Week,* April 14, 1975.

Roche, W. J., and MacKinnon, N. K. "Motivating People with Meaningful Work," *Harvard Business Review,* May–June 1970.

Rock, Milton L. *Handbook of Wage and Salary Administration.* New York: McGraw-Hill Book Co., 1972.

"Sambo's Serves Its Managers an Extra Slice." *Business Week,* January 26, 1974.

"The Secret Executive Perk." *Dun's,* August 1974.

"Should Your Production Workers Be Salaried?" *Industry Week,* January 13, 1975.

Simons, Myron. "The Name of the Game Is Stocks." *Forbes,* June 15, 1975.

Smith, Ephraim P. "Stock as a Means of Executive Compensation." *Personnel Journal,* August 1974.

"The Status of Today's Executive." ASPA–BNA Survey No. 28. *Bulletin to Management.* Washington, D.C.: Bureau of National Affairs, Inc., July 17, 1975.

Swanson, Trevor J., and Devore, John J. "A Structured Approach to Hiring." *Datamation,* May 1974.

"$3,230.00 per Worker—That's What 'Fringes' Average Now." *U.S. News & World Report,* December 9, 1974.

Vroom, V. *Work and Motivation.* New York: John Wiley & Sons, 1964.

Werther, William B., Jr. "A New Direction in Re-Thinking Fringe Benefits." *MSU Business Topics,* Winter 1974.

Yaney, Joseph P. *Personnel Management: Reaching Organizational and Human Goals.* Columbus, Ohio: Charles E. Merrill Publishing Co., 1975.

NOTE

[1] Thomas H. Paine, "Flexible Compensation Can Work!" *Financial Executive,* February 1974.

When you have completed studying
THE COLLECTIVE BARGAINING PROCESS
you should be able to:

1. Describe the collective bargaining process in terms of contract negotiation and administration.
2. Explain why workers join unions and the implication for human resources management.
3. Explain the development and structure of labor unions in this country.
4. Discuss the legal framework for the collective bargaining process in terms of its impact on union-management relations.
5. Describe and explain the impact of union-management relations in the human resource system.
6. With regard to contract negotiations:
   a. Identify various bargaining strategies.
   b. Describe common bargaining issues.
   c. Recommend ways of overcoming impasses.
7. Identify and describe a grievance procedure.
8. Formulate a series of steps for a positive, problem-solving approach to handling grievances.

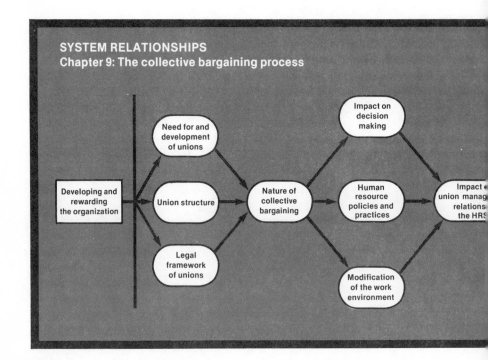

SYSTEM RELATIONSHIPS
Chapter 9: The collective bargaining process

THE NATURE OF COLLECTIVE BARGAINING

9

Collective bargaining involves the joint determination by employees and management of problems related to the human resource system. Collective bargaining embraces a wide variety of issues, such as compensation, retirement, fringe benefits, discipline, layoffs, promotion, and work scheduling. It should be evident, however, that the collective bargaining process does not give rise to these problems. These problems are related to the human resource system and exist in the absence of unionization. If the workers are not represented by a union, management solves the problems on an individual basis—or at least

The collective bargaining process

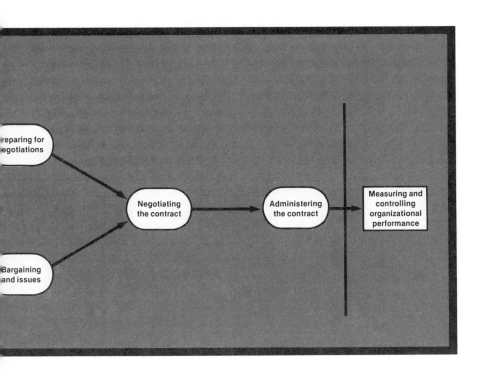

unilaterally. With the arrival of unionization, collective bargaining provides the vehicle by which management and representatives of the workers try to reach collective agreement on solving, and avoiding, problems related to wages, hours, and other conditions of employment. As we shall see in this chapter, the union, though often viewed as a party outside the organization, is very much a part of the human resource system and has a significant impact on the management of human resources.

The collective bargaining process consists primarily of two phases: contract negotiation and contract administration. The *negotiation* phase entails the joint determination of the terms of the labor agreement under which both parties must operate. The *administration* phase encompasses the joint efforts for carrying out and applying the terms already agreed upon. As we shall see, the *grievance* process is the focal point for administration of the labor agreement.

Today, over 20 million U.S. citizens hold union membership. Union members comprise about one fourth of the entire nonagricultural labor force. Thus, we can see that labor unions are a formidable factor and that no human resources manager can act effectively without an understanding of the collective bargaining process and its impact on the human resource system. Perhaps a logical starting point is to ask this basic question: Why do workers join unions?

Why workers join unions

This question has been researched, discussed, and written about by numerous scholars. The fact is that there are almost as many reasons for joining a union as there are union members. At the same time, certain common elements seem to run through these reasons, allowing some degree of categorization. The categories include the following.

1. *Economic reasons*. Higher wages, increased benefits, shorter hours, and improved working conditions are certainly important reasons for joining a union. Whether or not unionization actually produces these results has been debated by labor economists.[1] What is important, however, is that workers perceive the unions as increasing their share of the economic package. During these inflationary times, workers see their paychecks eroding in terms of purchasing power. At the same time, management is becoming more cost-conscious and seeking ways to reduce costs. The natural reaction of the individual worker is to seek out the strength of numbers offered by unionization in order to bargain more effectively with the employer.

2. *Job security.* One basic human need is security. In the work environment, employees find themselves in a dependent relationship relative to their bosses and to what they are likely to view as impersonal organizations. They want to feel that they will have some cushion against economic fluctuations and resulting cutbacks. They want to know that their jobs will exist in the future and that they will be protected against unfair or arbitrary treatment.

3. *Social reasons.* Men and women are social beings. Therefore, workers have a strong need to be accepted by their peers, to belong, and to go along with others. A union meets this need by offering affiliation with peers having common interests. Some unions offer attractive benefits, such as group auto insurance and union-owned recreation facilities. Peer pressure may also cause workers to join unions. A case in point would be the worker who is socially ostracized or even harassed by union members until he or she finally joins. As an interviewee in a study remarked, "They approached you, kept after you, hounded you. To get them off my back, I joined."

4. *Recognition.* Some employees have found that the union structure offers them an opportunity to gain recognition not available to them in the business organization. For example, a worker with little education may serve on a shop committee or even be elected to a position of influence, such as steward or an officer in the local.

5. *Participation.* Many workers, especially at higher levels and in white-collar-type occupations, have explained their union membership in terms of their desire to obtain a voice in decisions which affect them in their working environment. For example, we find schoolteachers organizing to demand a say in textbook selection, class size, and student discipline. To other workers who feel lost in our large, complex, industrial society, the union is viewed as a last hope that they will be able to influence their destiny.

6. *Compulsion.* Aside from social pressure to join a union, some workers become union members simply because the employment contract requires them to do so. In fact, three fourths of all labor contracts in the United States have union shop clauses which require new employees to join the union as a condition of employment after having served a probationary period.

You can see, therefore, that the reasons why employees join a union cannot be reduced to any single, uncomplicated statement. Aside from the case of compulsion, it would appear that unions serve a broad network of employee needs. To the extent that people cannot find opportunities to satisfy those needs in the workplace, they tend to form unions. In fact, some writers have gone so far as to say that the existence of a union is an indictment of management's failure to provide opportunities for need satisfaction at all levels of the organization.

Historical developments

The following brief survey of historical developments will provide some insight into the problems facing labor unions. It will also furnish the necessary background for our later discussions of union structure and collective bargaining.

Early efforts to organize. Craftsmen, such as shoemakers and carpenters, banded together as early as 1791, primarily to protest the existing wage rates. Generally, these organizations were weak and survived for only a short time. A forerunner of the union business agent grew out of the need to check on shops to see whether they were adhering to the union wage scale. Employers attempted to destroy the effectiveness of unions through such tactics as hiring nonunion workers and getting the courts to declare the union illegal.

During the middle and late 1800s the labor movement concentrated on efforts to unify labor groups and to promote social and political reform. A brief-lived organization called the National Labor Union was formed in 1866 to bring together in one body many of the unions and social reform organizations. The rioting and bloodshed which characterized the 1860s and 1870s caused this period to be referred to as the "era of upheaval." In fact, the early period of labor relations in this country is an often-repeated story of inter- and intraunion squabbles, frequent bloody clashes between unions and management, and labor political activity.

In 1869 the Noble Order of the Knights of Labor was founded. Its broad goal was to replace a competitive society by a cooperative one which would give workers the opportunity to enjoy fully the wealth they created. The Knights of Labor relied on political methods and education rather than collective bargaining to promote equal pay for equal work for women, an eight-hour day, the establishment of cooperatives, and public ownership of utilities. Failure to reconcile the interests of its skilled and unskilled workers led to the downfall of the Knights of Labor and the birth of the American Federation of Labor.

Later developments. In 1886 a group of craft unions formed the American Federation of Labor with a philosophy of "pure and simple unionism." Its main goals were higher wages and improved working conditions. The program of the AFL leaders was, therefore, pragmatic. They were out to improve the conditions of the workers they represented, and they represented skilled workers or workers whose strategic position enabled them to command employer recognition.

The AFL's failure to organize mass production industries gave impetus to a movement to issue industrial union charters in the mass production industries. (An industrial union includes all occupations within an industry, such as assemblers, machinists, and die makers in the auto industry.) This issue was heatedly debated at the 1935 AFL convention and led to the formation of a rival group, the CIO (Congress of Industrial Organizations). The CIO's push for industrial unionism in large, mass production industries, such as steel, rubber, and automobiles, met with enthusiastic response from workers. In fact, the CIO grew to such an extent that it became a serious competitor of the AFL.

In the early 1950s, leaders of these two rival organizations realized that organized labor could be strengthened if they joined forces. In 1955 the AFL and the CIO merged and also signed a nonraiding pact that minimized jurisdictional disputes. Today, about four out of every five labor unions are affiliated with the AFL–CIO.

Although we may at first think of unions in terms of factory and service workers, the unionization of white-collar workers, such as office employees, has been growing over the past few decades. In addition, the unionization of professionals has been increasing as they, representing a large portion of the middle class, have been caught in repeated economic squeezes. Professionals who have become unionized include actors, newspaper reporters, engineers, teachers, college professors, government administrators, nurses, medical interns, and law enforcement officers.

With this brief background on the historical development of labor unions, let us consider the structure of labor unions.

Union structure

A knowledge of union structure is essential to dealing with unions. To begin with, there are about 80,000 local unions in this country, most of which are associated with national unions. The entire union structure consists of about 108 national and international organizations. Exhibit 9–1 lists the unions that had 100,000 or more members in 1970. Approximately 85 percent of all union members

EXHIBIT 9–1
National unions and employee associations reporting 100,000 or more members

Unions	Members	Unions	Members
Teamsters		Textile Workers	178,000
(independent)	1,829,000	Iron Workers	178,000
Automobile Workers		Oil, Chemical	175,000
(independent)	1,486,000	Retail, Wholesale	175,000
Steelworkers	1,200,000	Electrical (UE)	
Electrical (IBEW)	922,000	(independent)	163,000
Machinists	865,000	Postal Clerks	162,000
Carpenters	820,000	Bakery	152,000
Retail Clerks	605,000	Transport Workers	150,000
Laborers	580,000	Fire Fighters	146,000
Meat Cutters	494,000	Papermakers	145,000
Hotel	461,000	Bricklayers	143,000
State, County	444,000	Boilermakers	138,000
Ladies' Garment	442,000	Transit Union	132,000
Service Employees	435,000	Printing Pressmen	128,000
Communications		Maintenance of Way	126,000
Workers	422,000	Sheet Metal	120,000
Operating Engineers	393,000	Typographical	112,000
Clothing Workers	386,000	Chemical	
Government (AFGE)	325,000	(independent)	101,000
Plumbers	312,000	Federal Employees	
Electrical (IUE)	300,000	(NFFE)	
Musicians	300,000	(independent)	100,000
Railway Clerks	275,000	Mine Workers	
Transportation Union	263,000	(independent)	—
Rubber	216,000		
Letter Carriers	215,000	*Associations*	*Members*
Painters	210,000		
District 50		Education Assn.	1,100,000
(independent)	210,000	Civil Service (NYS)	190,000
Teachers	205,000	Nurses Assn.	181,000
Pulp, Sulfite	193,000	California	113,000

Source: U.S. Department of Labor, Bureau of Labor Statistics, *Directory of National Unions and Employee Associations, 1971,* Bulletin 1750, Washington, D.C.

belong to a union affiliated with the AFL–CIO. The largest unions affiliated with the AFL–CIO are the United Steelworkers of America (1,200,000 members) and the International Brotherhood of Electrical Workers (922,000). The two largest unions outside the AFL–CIO are the United Auto Workers (1,500,000) and the International Brotherhood of Teamsters (1,850,000).

It should be noted that the AFL–CIO is not a labor union. It is a loosely knit federation of affiliated national, international, and independent local unions. The structure of the AFL–CIO is shown in

EXHIBIT 9-2
Structure of the AFL-CIO

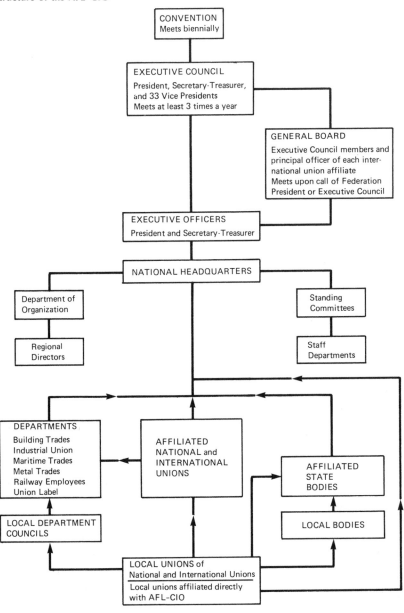

Exhibit 9–2. The AFL–CIO services its affiliates with a wide variety of functions, such as mediating disputes among unions, providing advice and assistance on organizing activities, conducting training for union leaders, supplying information and economic and legal assistance, and lobbying at all governmental levels.

The national (or international) union.[2]   Most national unions are headed by a president, a secretary-treasurer, and one or more vice presidents. The officers are selected either by a convention or by referendum. A convention is the supreme governing body of most unions. The national or parent union regulates the administration of all its local union affiliates.

The national union usually has a large staff of paid professionals, such as attorneys, economists, research specialists, and public relations personnel. The national union typically negotiates a master agreement or a contract with a national firm, such as the UAW contract with the Ford Motor Company, which becomes binding on all locals dealing with that firm. The local must also receive prior approval from the national union for any strike activity. The national union helps locals in many ways, such as providing training for local union leaders, assisting locals in negotiating local contracts, setting up strike funds, and organizing new members.

The local union.   The structure of the entire labor movement is founded on the local union. It is at this level that the manager comes into day-to-day contact with the union. The local has direct control over the rank-and-file worker. The functions of the local are carried out by officials elected directly by the members.

The jurisdiction and the size of locals differ. In most cases the local has jurisdiction over a single plant and its size depends on the plant size. Some locals have as few as 10 to 50 members. Local 600 of the UAW, on the other hand, consists of more than 40,000 members employed at the River Rouge complex of the Ford Motor Company. Craft union locals usually have jurisdiction over their craft in a geographic area. For example, all carpenters in the city of Grand Rapids are organized under one local.

The larger local unions may have one or more full-time officers, such as a president or a business agent. The international representative from the parent union is likely to be quite important in a union without a full-time officer. More commonly, local officials have full-time jobs in addition to their union duties. This is especially true for shop stewards, who are key people in the relationship between the union and its members and between the union and management. As can be seen in Exhibit 9–3, a typical local union consists of a very simple organization, with considerable power residing in the local president.

EXHIBIT 9-3

The legal framework for collective bargaining

The legal environment for the collective bargaining process in the United States has been formulated primarily by two federal laws: the Taft-Hartley Act of 1947, which amended the Wagner Act of 1935, and the Landrum-Griffin Act of 1959. In addition, important decisions of labor agencies, such as the National Labor Relations Board (NLRB), tend to be important sources of labor law. For example, the NLRB's interpretation of the Wagner Act and the Taft-Hartley Act largely determines the practical application of these laws.

The executive branch of government also serves as a source of labor law. To illustrate, in 1962 President Kennedy issued Executive Order No. 10988, which provided a measure of protection for federal employees to engage in collective bargaining. Several states followed this precedent and influenced the growth of public employee unions on the state level.

Most laws and regulations affecting labor relations are quite complicated, and the human resources manager would be best advised to seek an expert for assistance with specific problems. The following general survey, however, will give the reader a basic understanding of the legal framework within which collective bargaining must operate.

The National Labor Relations Act. The basic statute governing union-management relations is the National Labor Relations Act (the Wagner Act of 1935), as amended by the Taft-Hartley Act of 1947. This act guarantees the right of covered workers to bargain collectively concerning wages and working conditions, and further regulates the union-management relationship by prohibiting certain "unfair labor practices." The act also established the National Labor Relations Board, which administers most of its provisions. The NLRB has two major functions.

To begin with, it *administers the procedure by which unions become the certified collective bargaining agents for a group of workers.* To see how this procedure works, consider the case of a union attempting to organize the ABC Company, a nonunion firm. According to the act, the union organizers can attempt to get the workers to sign authorization cards. Thirty percent of the employees must sign such cards before the union can petition the NLRB to hold a representation election. When the petition for an election has been made, the employees are made aware of this fact by the NLRB, which posts Form 666, shown in Exhibit 9–4. This form

EXHIBIT 9–4
NLRB Form 666—notice to employees

briefly describes the employees' rights and states that an election may be held.

During this organization drive, it is illegal for either employers or union organizers to threaten employees. Since it is also illegal to discharge employees for prounion activity, the management of ABC must be certain to document terminations for poor performance during the union campaign in order to avoid charges of an "unfair" labor practice.

Given the necessary signatures, the NLRB will determine the "appropriate" bargaining unit for the employees. When this determination has been made, the NLRB holds a secret-ballot election in which employees select the union which filed the petition, no union, or any other union having the support of 10 percent of the employees. If a union is selected, it is certified and has to be recognized by the ABC Company as the bargaining agent for the employees on wages, hours, and terms and conditions of employment.

The other main function of the NLRB is to prevent labor or management from committing unfair labor practices. The five prohibited unfair labor practices for management are:

1. To interfere with, restrain, or coerce employees in the exercise of their rights to self-organization.
2. To dominate or interfere in the affairs of the union.
3. To discriminate in regard to hire, tenure, or any condition of employment for the purpose of encouraging or discouraging union membership.
4. To discriminate against or discharge an employee because he or she had filed charges or given testimony under the act.
5. To refuse to bargain with chosen representatives of the employees.

Several unfair practices pertain to unions. Unions are prohibited from:

1. Coercing employees in the exercise of their rights or in the selection of a collective bargaining representative.
2. Causing an employer under a union shop agreement to discriminate against employees who were denied admission to the union or were expelled from the union for certain reasons.
3. Engaging in a jurisdictional strike or a secondary boycott.
4. Charging excessive or discriminatory initiation fees to employees covered by a union shop agreement.
5. Causing an employer to pay money or other things of value for services not performed.
6. Refusing to bargain collectively.

The act also allows the president of the United States to seek an injunction for a period of 80 days against strikes and lockouts affecting the nation's health and welfare. Between 1947 and 1972, the act's national emergency provisions were invoked by the president 34 times.

The Landrum-Griffin Act. Also known as the Labor-Management Reporting and Disclosure Act of 1959, the Landrum-Griffin Act has two basic aims: (1) to set minimum standards of democratic procedure, responsibility, and honesty in the conduct of union internal affairs; and (2) to clarify several parts of the Taft-Hartley Act. Accordingly, the act requires employers to file reports on their financial relationship with union leaders and on any payments to persons made for the purpose of influencing employees in the exercise of their rights. The act's passage resulted from the congressional investigation conducted by the McClellan Committee from 1957 through 1959. The investigations produced 58 volumes of testimony, over half of which were devoted to evidence of various types of racketeering and corruption in the Teamsters' Union. A major objective of the act, therefore, was to eliminate crime, racketeering, and corruption in labor unions. To accomplish this, the act has several provisions designed to reduce conflicts of interest and transactions through which unscrupulous union officials and employers might reap financial gains at the expense of employees. For example, unions cannot make direct or indirect loans to officers which result in a total indebtedness of more than $2,000. The word *indirect* is included in the provision to avoid such "back-door" deals as the $25,000 loan made by Jimmy Hoffa's local union to an individual who in turn reloaned it to Hoffa.

The Landrum-Griffin Act spells out the rights of union members, along with the responsibilities of union officers, and safeguards on the use of union funds. The amendments to the Taft-Hartley Act contained in the Landrum-Griffin Act include provisions that tighten the ban on secondary boycotts and prohibit "hot cargo" agreements (agreements in which the employer agrees not to discipline employees for refusing to handle nonunion products, which are termed *hot cargo*).

Thus, we can see that the collective bargaining process does not take place in a vacuum. It is very much influenced by public opinion as reflected in the legal environment. The human resources manager, though not necessarily expected to be a union expert, must have knowledge of unions and their operation, and of basic laws regarding union-management relations.

THE IMPACT OF UNION-MANAGEMENT RELATIONS ON THE HRS

As suggested in our discussion of the legal framework for collective bargaining, an organization drive by the union requires substantial preparation on the part of management. (For example, someone needs to advise management on what can and cannot be done during the campaign.) If the firm has a centralized human resources department, this job is typically given to that department. Exhibit 9–5 illustrates some guidelines given to university administrators during an organization drive in the University System of

Some dos: What university administrators clearly may do

University administrators in the SUS clearly may do any or all of the following:*

Tell employees they are *free* to form, join and participate in a union or *to refrain* from doing so without prejudicing their status as State employees.

Communicate to employees orally or in writing reasons for selecting the **"no agent"** option in any collective bargaining election, provided such communications are consistent with the **don'ts** hereinafter listed.

Convene meetings of employees during working hours (until the 24-hour period preceding an election) to discuss unionization for collective bargaining.

Explain to employees the dues and fees required for union membership, provided that in discussing the dues or fees which any given union requires, accurate figures taken from that union's own publications are referenced.

Provide employees with *accurate* factual data about the unions seeking their support, including affiliations with other state, national or international labor organizations, the salaries of union officials, and strike statistics (in connection with any discussion of strikes, mention should be made of the fact that strikes by public employees are prohibited by both the Florida Constitution and the Public Employees Relations Act and the possible consequences of violating the anti-strike law should be detailed).

Remind employees that signing "union authorization cards" does *not* require them to vote for any union in a subsequent collective bargaining election.

Rebut inaccurate, distorted or misleading union communications with the facts.

Relate past experiences of administrators with particular unions at institutions where an agent has been elected.

Tell employees that proposed union benefits do not occur automatically but must be negotiated—and that the BOR is not required to agree to any proposal or make any concession, provided that it is not stated or implied that the BOR will refuse to bargain any proper subject in good faith.

Some don'ts: What university administrators may not do

University administrators in the SUS may *not* do any of the following:

Promise or grant employees pay increases, promotions, benefits or special favors for not joining a union, opposing unionism or voting against a union. All personnel actions must be made in accordance with existing BOR rules and regulations and taken without regard to the employees' membership or participation in a union, or support for its activities.

Threaten loss of jobs, reduction of income, discontinuance of privileges or benefits presently enjoyed, or otherwise threaten reprisal or force by the use of intimidating language which may influence employees in the exercise of their right to form, join or assist a union or to refrain from doing so; threaten or actually discharge, discipline, transfer, promote or lay employees off because of membership in or activities on behalf of a union; or threaten, *through a third party, any* of the foregoing acts of interference.

Spy on or have a representative spy on or even openly attend union meetings (parking across the street from the place of meeting in order to watch employees entering the meeting has been held to be illegal); or conduct themselves in a way that would indicate to employees that they are being watched to determine whether or not they are participating in union activities.

Discriminate against employees actively supporting the union by intentionally assigning undesirable work to them; transfer employees prejudicially because of union affiliation or active support; or generally engage in any partiality favoring non-union employees over employees active on behalf of the union.

Discipline or penalize employees actively supporting a union for an infraction which non-union employees are permitted to commit without being likewise disciplined.

Make any work assignment for the purpose of causing employees active on behalf of a union to quit their jobs or to give up their union membership.

Intentionally assign work or transfer employees so that those active on behalf of the union are segregated from those it is believed are not interested in supporting a union.

---

* For purposes of this listing, the term *administrators* includes presidents, vice presidents, provosts and deans, together with those persons assisting presidents, vice presidents, provosts and deans in the discharge of their duties, and also includes other university personnel discharging administrative responsibilities.

Florida. Similar efforts must be undertaken to protect the company's rights and to see that the union is not guilty of unfair labor practices. Data may also have to be gathered for NLRB hearings.

It is during this initial stage of unionization that great care must be taken by management to minimize conflict that could jeopardize the collective bargaining at a later date. In some cases it has taken many years for the wounds to heal following especially bitter relations between the company and the union during an organization drive. Once the union is certified, unionization continues to have considerable impact on the human resource system in at least three areas.

Decision making

The mere existence of a union is likely to mean that all management decisions are subject to closer scrutiny and challenge. Granted that in the absence of a union, progressive managers are interested in employee participation and attitudes. But now the union gives the worker a formal method for challenging decisions viewed as within the realm of collective bargaining. Certain decisions once made unilaterally by management, such as those regarding work standards or the subcontracting of work, are now subject to collective bargaining.

Lack of contract knowledge on the part of the supervisor frequently results in time-consuming and costly grievances. To remedy this, some companies have centralized certain human resource decisions and put them in the hands of higher levels of management or trained labor relations specialists. The unfortunate result has been a further downgrading of the first-line supervisor.

Human resource policies and practices

Human resource policies and practices are more likely to be formalized under unionization. This comes about in several ways. The labor contract itself, as well as written statements resulting from handling grievances, formalizes matters related to wages, hours, and the conditions of employment. There is also a tendency on the part of managers to start putting in writing all actions and decisions affecting workers in an effort to protect themselves from later union charges of contract violations. This is illustrated by Exhibit 9–6, which reproduces a page of contract statements dealing with lunch periods and overtime.

A by-product of unionization is the introduction of "outsiders" into the human resource system. For example, one or more profes-

EXHIBIT 9-6
Sample page from a "typical" labor agreement

7.8 Lunch Period Within Five Hours

(a) A lunch period, without pay, of not less than thirty minutes will be allowed employees within their first five hours worked on any shift. Employees who are assigned by Local Management to work beyond their first five hours without a lunch period will be paid one and one-half their regular straight time rate for all time worked beyond the first five hours until they have a lunch period.

(b) This Section will not apply to an employee working on a shift which includes a paid lunch period regardless of whether an actual lunch period is provided.

ARTICLE 8   OVERTIME

8.1   Definition of Regular Straight Time Hourly Rate

The regular straight time hourly rate means an employee's straight time hourly base rate plus his incentive pay and applicable shift premium.

8.2   Hours Worked in Excess of Eight (8)

The Local Management will pay an employee one and one-half times his regular straight time hourly rate for all hours he is required to work over eight (8) a day.

8.3   Hours Worked in Excess of Twelve (12)

The Local Management will pay an employee two times his regular straight time hourly rate for all hours he is required to work over twelve (12) a day.

8.4   Exceptions to Daily Overtime

When an employee is permitted by Local Management to change from one shift to another at his own request, and the new shift starts within the same twenty-four (24) hour period as his preceding shift, overtime provided under Sections 8.2 and 8.3 will not be paid. However, the starting time of the new shift will start a new twenty-four (24) hour period for the purpose of determining overtime.

New employees will become eligible to share in the impartial distribution of overtime after they complete their probationary period of employment. New employees will not be allowed to claim overtime after completing this probationary period to make up for overtime which was worked before they were on the seniority roster.

(c) If it is shown that Management was in error in the distribution of overtime during the two weeks immediately preceding the date of the review of the Foreman's record with the grievance committeeman and that an employee did not properly share in available overtime during such period, Local Management will make an adjustment in future overtime schedules within 60 calendar days after the error has been reported in writing by the committeeman to Management or at the end of the 60 day period compensate the employee for the earnings he would have earned had he been given his proper overtime opportunity.

(d) The Union will cooperate with the Local Management in fulfilling the overtime manhours to meet overtime schedules.

ARTICLE 9   WAGES (Hourly Employees)

The provisions of this Article 9 apply only to hourly employees in the production and maintenance units. Salaries of employees in the salaried units are covered by the provisions of Article 3 (Salaries) of Appendix B of this Agreement.

9.1   1968 Cooperative Can Industry Agreement and Manual

(a) The parties have agreed on the principles and the basic procedures of a cooperative program for describing and classifying hourly jobs covered by this Agreement and for the development and application of related administrative procedures.

These principles and procedures have been incorporated in an Agreement called the 1968 Cooperative Can Industry Agreement and Manual, hereinafter referred to as the Manual. The 1968 Cooperative Can Industry Agreement and

---

sional union officials who are not employees of the firm, such as the business agent or the international representative, may be involved in contract negotiations and the later administration of grievance resolution. Smaller firms will have to rely more on attorneys or labor relations experts. In the event of an impasse in the collective bargaining process, such as inability to agree on a new contract, a third party will be brought in as a mediator or arbitrator.

Finally, it is often argued that as a result of unionization management loses a great deal of flexibility in formulating and carrying out human resource policies. For example, management's discretion is reduced by union demands that policies related to pay, promotion, discipline, transfers, and so on, be written into the contract. On the other hand, such contractual provisions ensure that all workers are treated alike.

Modifications in the work environment

Initially, collective bargaining may place management and the union in adversary roles. The union may attempt to dramatize every company mistake; management may try to undermine the union by showing the workers that the union is unnecessary. Needless to say, such a climate is detrimental to productivity. Take, for example, the need for a change in the work assignment. If the union and management are engaged in a power play, the union will try to protect the status quo and resist any changes. As a result we find meatcutters refusing to handle precut and prepackaged meats; requirements that union electricians stand by to replace burned-out light bulbs; and the use of operating engineers merely to push buttons.

There is a need, therefore, for management to recognize that its own actions and attitudes have an impact on union behavior. Furthermore, management should recognize that unions can make a contribution to cost reduction and productivity improvements. This has been dramatically demonstrated in such cases as the Kaiser Steel Corporation and numerous Scanlon plan agreements whereby the company and the union cooperate to reduce costs and increase efficiency. The important thing, therefore, is for unions and management to work jointly toward replacing conflict with cooperation in the work environment.

NEGOTIATING THE CONTRACT

The more spectacular aspects of labor relations are evident during contract negotiations. At such times, public attention is focused on strikes, pickets, union demands, and employer rejections. Behind the scenes, however, both the unions and management work hard to prepare for negotiations and to develop proposals for handling the problems that will arise in carrying out the agreements negotiated.

The procedures used in negotiating a contract depend on the situation, since there is no one best way. However, there are several common aspects of contract negotiation, which we shall discuss here.

Preparing for negotiations

The amount of preparation depends on the resources available for research and the bargaining requirements of the parties. For example, if the U.S. Steel Corporation is to negotiate with the United Steelworkers, its preparation will be extensive and carefully researched. On the other hand, a small local trucking firm may do very little preparation for negotiating with a local of the Teamsters.

If the parties have already negotiated one or more agreements, the timing of the negotiations may be prescribed by the existing contract. Typically, advance notice must be given 60 days before the contract expires if changes are to be sought in a new agreement.

In preparing for negotiations, management can obtain considerable necessary information from company records. Data regarding grievances, overtime, layoffs, disciplinary action, transfers, and promotions will be useful in formulating a bargaining strategy. A review of the existing agreement will suggest clauses that need to be modified or dropped. Line managers should be polled to get their ideas on contract changes. Because of their close contact with union members, first-line supervisors are in an ideal position to know what complaints the union is likely to voice and what changes in the contract will be sought.

Bargaining

In many cases, the general pattern of the contract will have been determined before the actual bargaining takes place. This is especially true of any wage adjustments sought by the union, as well as the general content of the contract. The union may simply present the employer with a copy of a contract recently negotiated in the industry or by the same union in another industry. But even given the existence of a general pattern, the actual bargaining between the parties will be modified to fit the needs and peculiarities of the firm involved.

The first meeting between labor and management negotiation teams usually establishes the ground rules, procedures, and schedules for future meetings. At the initial meeting the union will often formally present its specific proposals for contract changes. The particular approach to bargaining used by labor or management may follow one of two distinct formats: the *step-by-step approach* or the *total approach*. In the step-by-step approach, each item is treated as a separate issue and is discussed and agreed upon before the negotiators move on to the next item. In the total approach, nothing is considered settled until everything is agreed upon. From a system perspective, this approach is preferred since most issues are interrelated and their impact on the total organization cannot be evaluated in isolation. In most cases, a combination of the two approaches is used.

There have been many attempts to categorize the different types of bargaining relationships that develop between union and management. For example, Benjamin Selekman has described nine such relationships. A few, such as collusion and racketeering, are less common today than they were. The following four suggest the variety of possible relationships:

1. *Containment-aggression.* Management aggressively tries to curtail the union and keep it in check, while the union attempts to usurp management's rights.
2. *Power.* Each party attempts to get every possible advantage from the other, as permitted by the economic situation.
3. *Accommodation.* Tolerance and compromise are practiced by both parties; extreme displays of power are avoided.
4. *Cooperation.* This resembles "accommodation" but is also characterized by mutual concern about the total work environment, such as technological change and productivity.

Walton and McKersie take an approach to bargaining which focuses, not on the *relationship* between the parties, but rather on the *strategy* of the bargaining.[3] They identify the most common bargaining pattern as *distributive* bargaining. This type of bargaining assumes that management and labor have conflicting goals and are trying to get a bigger piece of a given pie. As a result, each party develops a type of "horse-trading" strategy. Another pattern is *integrative* bargaining, in which the goals of labor and management are not seen as conflicting and, as a result, both parties try to develop mutually acceptable solutions to problem areas. The integrative approach may involve the use of special committees for joint research and fact-finding to solve difficult problems. Examples of this approach have included changes in pension and benefit plans, union action to control wildcat strikes, and improvements in the grievance procedure.

Bargaining issues

The collective bargaining agreement is usually a rather lengthy contract which may be drawn up in final form by an attorney. The agreement, or contract, sets forth the basic rules and standards which govern the relationship between the employer and the employees for the duration of the agreement. Negotiations may involve an almost unlimited number of issues, as suggested by Exhibit 9–7, which contains a table of contents from a contract negotiated between a large multiplant employer and a large international union. On the other hand, all bargaining issues may be grouped into the following general categories.

Union security and management rights.   A union tries to protect its position by negotiating a union security clause. The union will

EXHIBIT 9–7
Union contract—Multiplant employer and international union

Table of Contents

push for a union shop whereby all employees are required to join within a specified time after hiring, and to remain members as a condition of employment. A variation is the modified union shop, which exempts certain employee groups from having to join. Substantially less security is afforded the union by an agency shop clause, in which employees pay a fixed monthly amount to the union but are not required to join it. Other union security issues may include the checkoff of union dues and the definition of the bargaining unit.

Many agreements do not contain management rights provisions on the assumption that all rights not specifically bargained away belong to management. Some companies prefer to insert specific areas of action and decision that remain the exclusive prerogative of management, such as the right to discipline for cause and the right to determine the uses to which company assets will be employed.

Wages, hours, and working conditions. These issues provoke perhaps the most debate during negotiations and typically result in the most extensive provisions in the labor agreement. Besides hours of work and direct compensation, discussion will focus on many subissues, such as cost-of-living adjustments, shift differentials, overtime pay, and washup time. Many items related to sanitary working conditions and safety devices and practices, which were once included in negotiations, are not now discussed since they are required of all covered employers under the Occupational Safety and Health Act.

Employee security. The employee is interested in fair treatment and a guarantee of continuity of employment. Unions, therefore, will push for seniority as the determining factor in layoffs, recalls, and promotions. Management takes the position that efficiency will suffer unless it has the right to make such decisions on the basis of ability and performance.

Due process, or the handling of grievances, is another issue under the heading of employee security. There is a need to define what is to be regarded as a grievance and to outline how employee complaints will be handled.

Administration. This category covers issues related to the machinery established to enforce the terms of the agreement and to put due process into effect. Examples include the payment for time spent by stewards involved in handling grievances and the selection and duties of arbitrators.

The duration of the contract and the provisions for renewal are other administrative issues. As might be expected, management pushes for longer contracts in an effort to minimize conflict. Most contracts are in effect for a two- or three-year period.

Impasse resolution

For bargaining issues to be satisfactorily negotiated, an agreement must be reached within the limits that the union and the employer find acceptable. The area within these two limits has been called the *bargaining zone*. As seen in Exhibit 9–8, the solution sought by one party exceeds the tolerance limit of the other party, resulting in a solution outside the bargaining zone. A collective bargaining impasse will occur if the first party refuses to change its demands enough to bring it within the bargaining zone or if the

EXHIBIT 9–8
The tolerance limits that determine the
bargaining zone

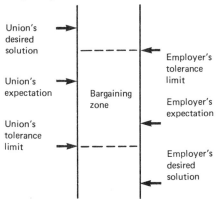

Source: From R. Stagner and H. Rosen, *Psychology
of Union-Management Relations.* Copyright © 1965
by Wadsworth Publishing Company, Inc. Reprinted
by permission of the publisher, Brooks/Cole Publishing Company, Monterey, California.

second party refuses to change its tolerance level to accommodate
the demands of the first party. In order to resolve an impasse, three
things may occur.

Strike or lockout. A strike is the refusal of a group of employees
to perform their jobs. Union leaders may seek a strike authorization
from the workers to strengthen their position if an impasse develops.
Therefore, a strike vote by the rank and file does not necessarily
mean that the rank and file desire a strike or will go out on strike.
More commonly, the strike vote is taken to strengthen the bargaining position of the union negotiators. Sometimes the mere threat to
exercise this strike option is sufficient to win concessions from
management.

A lockout is management's version of a strike; it is the refusal to
allow employees to work. Although the lockout is rarely used today,
it does give the employer a psychological advantage when it is
perceived by the union as a show of economic strength. Since many
states now permit locked-out employees to claim unemployment
benefits, the impact of the lockout has diminished.

Conciliation or mediation. A conciliator or mediator can be very
useful when a breakdown occurs during negotiations. In conciliation, a neutral third party tries to bring the two conflicting parties
together again. He or she attempts to get management or the union

to settle their differences themselves by getting each to see the other's point of view.

Mediation goes a step further than conciliation by offering suggestions in addition to those proposed by management and the union. Mediation, like conciliation, is not compulsory. By offering some new alternatives, however, the mediator gives the conflicting parties the opportunity to retreat from impasse without loss of face.

The Federal Mediation and Conciliation Service (FMCS) was established by the U.S. Congress to assist unions and managements in reaching agreements and avoiding work stoppages. Sometimes the union and management will agree to bring in an outsider, such as a university professor or a local public official.

Arbitration. In mediation, a solution can only be recommended, at which time either or both parties may reject it. In arbitration, both parties agree beforehand to abide by the arbitrator's decision. This means that the arbitrator, in a sense, performs the role of a judge who hears both sides of the issue and then makes a decision. In the public sector, employees are commonly forbidden by law to strike and are required to submit to compulsory arbitration if an impasse cannot be resolved.

As you can see, arbitration, like mediation, introduces an "outside" party into the human resource system. In fact, with arbitration, decisions which directly affect the management of human resources are made by an outside party. This means that management must take care in selecting an arbitrator. At the same time, the arbitrator must be acceptable to the union. Labor attorneys and professors teaching in the area of human resources management frequently serve as arbitrators. The American Arbitration Association and the FMCS supply lists of experienced arbitrators.

ADMINISTRATION OF THE CONTRACT

The final settlement and signing of the contract does not mean that the collective bargaining process is completed until the contract runs out. As we noted at the beginning of this chapter, the collective bargaining process involves the joint determination by employees and management of problems related to the human resource system. In a sense, the contract sets the framework for labor relations in the firm. During the course of the contract period, however, problems develop related to its application and interpretation.

Regardless of the time and effort put into writing the contract, things will come up in which there are differences of opinion regarding its intent. For example, the contract may have a clause dealing with the allocation of overtime. Management may take the position that the day-shift employees have the right to overtime under certain circumstances. A group of workers on the night shift may feel that they have priority for work not completed. Or problems may develop because unanticipated issues or events arise. For example, during an "emergency" management may direct certain workers to do tasks outside their job description. Did the company violate the agreement provision which specified that employees would perform only jobs falling within their job description? As these two examples suggest, nearly every provision in the labor agreement can be the basis for day-to-day problems that must be resolved. Much of the attitude and general nature of the problem-solving efforts involved in contract administration is greatly influenced by the work climate existing in the given human resource system. It is vital, therefore, to remember that the day-to-day dealing with the union and employees is part of the collective bargaining process, which in turn is part of a much broader human resource system with its overall goals and policies.

Thus, we can see that negotiations comprise only a part of the collective bargaining process. It is the *grievance procedure* which provides the mechanism for continuing the process during the life of the contract. Consequently, the company should negotiate a grievance procedure which can be used to settle problems quickly and fairly while allowing management to retain the flexibility necessary to maintain stable and efficient operations.

The grievance procedure: Description and operation

The grievance procedure provides an orderly system through which management and the union can determine whether or not the contract has been violated. As already suggested, however, the grievance procedure serves other purposes. For one thing, it provides for the interpretation of contract provisions. Similarly, the grievance procedure permits management and the union to meet regularly and get a better understanding of each other's problems. In this sense, it also serves as a communication channel from the rank and file to top management. Often overlooked, and of great significance, is the fact that the grievance procedure is frequently a vehicle for continued collective bargaining. For example, if the union can get management to make an exception to settle a grievance, that exception may be made the basis for a union demand in the next contract negotiation. Provisions in the contract under which grievances frequently seem to develop also suggest areas for consideration and possible renegotiation at the next contract talks.

There are different types of grievance procedures. To be effective, a grievance procedure should be designed to promptly deal with and resolve the different kinds of problems which might arise under the agreement. It should also clearly define the method of taking an appeal from one step to the next. The employees, as well as management and the union, should understand the exact process to be followed. Ideally, the contract should contain a no-strike clause whereby all disputes involving the application or interpretation of the agreement will be settled via the grievance procedure and without strikes or other interruptions to operations.

Exhibit 9–9 shows a typical grievance procedure for a larger

EXHIBIT 9–9
The grievance procedure for a large company

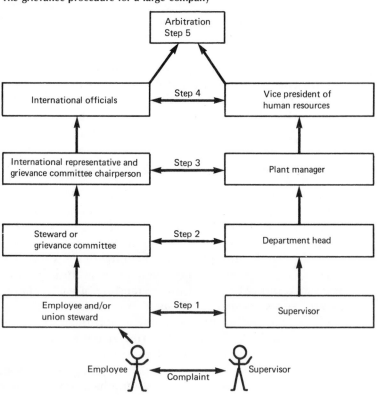

company from the time the grievance is filed until it is settled by arbitration. Such a procedure may operate as follows:

1. Following discussion between the immediate supervisor and the employee and/or the shop steward, a grievance form is filled out and submitted to the immediate supervisor, who writes an answer explaining his or her rationale.
2. If the grievance is not settled, the employee can take the second step. Here the employee, together with the steward or the shop grievance committee, discusses the grievance with the appropriate department head. If the issue is not resolved, it continues to Step 3.
3. The plant manager, with advice and assistance from the human resources department, confers with the chairperson of the shop grievance committee and the international representative.
4. If the grievance is still unsettled, high-ranking union officials from the international will meet with the corporate vice president for human resources in an attempt to resolve the dispute.
5. In the event that the parties fail to reach an agreement, the issue is submitted to an independent arbitrator who renders a binding decision. About 99 percent of all grievances are resolved before going to arbitration.

A positive approach to grievances

An unfortunate side effect of the grievance procedure is that it can develop into a "win-lose" game played by the union and the supervisors. For example, the first-line supervisor may become more concerned about maintaining a good record of "winning" grievances than about working out equitable solutions to the problems or complaints of workers. Similarly, the "loser" in a grievance case may seek redress or retaliation in other ways. Thus we find supervisors who "lost" suddenly carrying out certain rules to the letter when these rules apply to those who filed the grievance. Or if the union lost, work slowdowns or acts of sabotage may occur. Such problems have led some critics to attack the grievance procedure as leading to lower morale and defensive behavior.

On the other hand, if management adopts a positive, problem-solving approach to handling grievances, the difficulties suggested above can be minimized or avoided and the grievance procedure will contribute to reaching organizational goals. The firm sincerely interested in viewing the grievance procedure as a means for ob-

EXHIBIT 9–10
Issues in cases in which arbitrators selected from FMCS panels made awards,
fiscal year 1972

Specific issues*	Frequency of occurrence
Discharge and disciplinary actions	1,226
Incentive rates or standards	77
Job evaluation	387
Seniority†	646
Overtime‡	363
Union officers—superseniority and union business	21
Strike or lockout issues	18
Vacations and vacation pay	132
Holidays and holiday pay	101
Scheduling of work	182
Reporting, call-in, and call-back pay	77
Health and welfare	51
Pensions	21
Other fringe benefits	92
Scope of agreement§	211
Working conditions, including safety	48
Arbitrability of grievance‖	261
Miscellaneous	237

* Compilations based on the number of arbitration awards for which data were available; that is, 3,414 of the 3,432 awards. Some awards involved more than one issue.
† Includes promotion and upgrading (137), layoff, bumping, recall (327), transfer (96), and other matters (86).
‡ Includes pay (172), distribution of overtime (172), and compulsory overtime (19).
§ Includes subcontracting (92); jurisdictional disputes (17); foreman, supervision, and so on (61); mergers, consolidations, accretion, other plants (11).
‖ Includes procedural (141), substantive (68), procedural/substantive (32), and other issues (20).
Source: James Power, "Improving Arbitration: Roles of Parties and Agencies," *Monthly Labor Review*, November 1972, pp. 15–22.

taining a better climate of labor relations may well consider the following:

1. Effective grievance handling does not begin with the filing of a grievance. It begins back at the bargaining table. As we have seen, negotiations constitute the beginning of the collective bargaining process, whereas the grievance procedure provides the vehicle for continuing the process during the contract life. As a result, if the contract is ambiguous or one-sided, it will invite later grievances. If the union has been misled or deceived by management during negotiations, the company can expect the union to seek redress for political purposes via the grievance procedure. Thus management's attitude at the bargaining table will provide the setting for later union-management relations.

2. The number and kinds of grievances are an indicator of prob-

lem areas in the human resource system. Periodically an analysis should be made to pinpoint problem areas either in the contract or in supervision. Most of the grievances filed deal with disciplinary cases, application of the seniority system, and management rights (as suggested by Exhibit 9–10). Unresolved grievances work to the detriment of harmonious labor relations. In fact, some firms have found that contract negotiations had to cease until joint committees were able to resolve the backlog of grievances satisfactorily.

3. It is important to keep in mind that a grievance is a very important matter to the employee. This means that every employee complaint should be taken seriously. Even if the employee complaint has no merit, management should make every effort to hear the employee out and to determine the source of the grievance. Since it is easier to get to the core of the matter with oral investigation, most managers find it advantageous to discuss the employee complaint in an informal manner to the extent possible rather than rely on a legalistic exchange of written documents.

4. First-line supervisors, who are responsible for the day-to-day administration of the labor agreement, are the heart of a positive approach to grievance resolution. Frequently, the human resources department is thoroughly familiar with the contract, whereas the supervisors have only a vague familiarity with its provisions or application. Far too often, supervisors are merely given a copy of the new contract and told to "read it over carefully." There is a critical need to have supervisors receive proper guidance and instruction on interpreting the contract as well as current and past practices in the company's work rules. Supervisors need to know what the company's attitude toward grievance resolutions is, how to handle grievances, and when to seek advice from the human resources department or an immediate superior.

5. Management has a responsibility to impress on supervisors the necessity for taking adequate time from their busy schedules to dispose of grievances satisfactorily. Grievance handling must be viewed as a part of the supervisor's job rather than as an interruption of the job. At the same time, higher echelon management must evaluate each grievance on its own merits and avoid "rubber-stamping" the decision of the manager at the previous step in the grievance machinery, especially if that manager was in error.

SUMMARY

Collective bargaining provides the vehicle by which management and representatives of the workers try to reach collective agreement in solving, and avoiding, problems related to wages, hours, and other conditions of employment. It is essentially a social process for balancing the social pressures of two groups which have a mutual interest in the human resource system.

We have examined some of the reasons why workers join unions. To provide insight into the operations of unions and into interactions of unions with the organization, we have briefly surveyed the historical course of union development as well as the structure of unions. Our discussion of labor laws and regulations has given us a basic understanding of the legal environment in which collective bargaining must operate.

An organization drive by a union requires substantial preparedness on the part of management. Once the union is certified, unionization continues to have considerable impact on the human resource system in at least three major areas: decision making, human resource policies and practices, and the work environment.

The collective bargaining process consists primarily of two related phases: contract negotiation and contract administration. To provide some familiarization with the negotiation phase, we have discussed four of the more important aspects of contract negotiation:

1. Preparing for negotiations.   3. Bargaining issues.
2. Bargaining.   4. Impasse resolution.

Contract administration encompasses the joint efforts of management and the union in carrying out and applying the provisions of the labor agreement. Central to this process is the grievance procedure, which provides an orderly system through which management and the union can resolve disputes. Much of the attitude and the general nature of the problem-solving efforts involved in contract administration is greatly influenced by the work climate existing in the human resource system. It is vital, therefore, to remember that management's day-to-day dealings with the union and employees are part of the collective bargaining process, which in turn is part of the much broader human resource system.

CASE: MANAGEMENT'S RIGHT TO CLOSE THE PLANT*

Company: Texas Rebuilders, Inc.
Union: International Brotherhood of Boilermakers, Iron Shipbuilders, Blacksmiths, Forgers and Helpers, Local 96
Arbitrator: Clyde Emery

---

* Reprinted with permission from Edwin F. Beal et al., *The Practice of Collective Bargaining*, 5th ed. (Homewood, Ill.: Richard D. Irwin, Inc. 1976), pp. 516–17.

The following presentation of the facts in this case was prepared by Clyde Emery, the arbitrator.

The facts of the case

The company is one of six subsidiary corporations, the parent corporation's plant being in Illinois; all are engaged in rebuilding automobile parts. During the first quarter of 1974, sales declined; April, May, and June were the worst sales quarter in company history. It became imperative to reduce inventory and the expense of maintaining it—while avoiding layoff if possible.

In June the parent office directed the subsidiary plants to sound out the union on the possibility of a shorter workweek; during the week of June 17 the plant manager and the director of personnel involved here talked with the union committee about a four-day week. A one-day shutdown on July 5 (to continue the closing on July 4) was also probably considered. The plant manager so recalled and testified; so did the director of personnel; and the warehouse foreman, who had been chief steward at the time of the meeting, after several efforts to remember what was said, recalled that a woman on the union committee had insisted that the employees should be paid if the plant closed down on July 5.

On June 25, 1974, the following notice was posted:

> To: All employees   Subject: July 4th holiday
>
> Thursday, July 4, will be a paid holiday for all eligible employees. The plant will be closed Friday, July 5th. This will not be a paid holiday; however, all employees desiring to take one day of their vacation will be allowed to do so. The determining dates for eligibility for holiday pay (seven hours on the last day before and seven hours on the first day following) will be Wednesday, July 3d, and Monday, July 8th.
>
> I want to wish everyone a safe and enjoyable holiday.
>
> [W.]—Personnel

On July 10 all probationary employees were terminated. The next day, July 11, approximately 50 employees were laid off from the bargaining unit of 325 or 350. (The laid-off employees were recalled about August 1, but only 75 percent returned; some new employees were hired. Then the company and the employees proceeded to have a record month for the plant.)

The union had filed a grievance on July 8 alleging that the July 5 shutdown violated the agreement and seeking one day's pay for the employees. This was the only grievance filed throughout the corporation-wide system. (All of the parent corporation's plants are organized.)

Questions

1. Would it have made a difference if July 4th had fallen on a Wednesday instead of a Thursday in 1974? Could the union in that case have demanded two days' pay? Or if the holiday had fallen on a Monday and had been followed by a shutdown to the following week could the union have demanded four days' pay?
2. The company failed to get the union's agreement to a four-day week but apparently was able to lay off 50 employees without consulting the union. Could the company have gone to a four-day week without the agreement of the union?
3. Are there any limitations on management's right to close down the plant?

QUESTIONS AND PROBLEMS

1. A number of writers and experts suggest that "unions have outlived their usefulness in those progressive companies where enlightened management treats employees like human beings." Discuss.
2. What factors cause workers to join unions? Does the existence of a union mean that management has failed to provide for the satisfaction of employee needs?
3. Briefly trace the highlights of the labor movement in this country. In what ways have the early developments in the movement influenced labor relations as it exists today?
4. Speak to an officer of a local union in your area. Find out what the national union does for the local. Discuss the major problems faced by that local union.
5. Explain how a union becomes "certified" as a bargaining agent for a group of workers.
6. What is an unfair labor practice? Do unfair labor practices pertain more to management or to the union?
7. Show how the collective bargaining process is influenced by public opinion.
8. Discuss how the unionization of a large department store would affect human resources management in that store.
9. Compare and contrast Selekman's categorization of bargaining relationships with that of Walton and McKersie.
10. What issues are usually covered in a labor agreement?
11. With regard to contract negotiations, define and distinguish among conciliation, mediation, and arbitration.
12. What purposes are served by the grievance procedure? Is the principle of a

grievance procedure primarily applicable to unionized employees, or would it apply equally well in a nonunion organization?

13. Discuss the proper role of the first-line supervisor in contract administration. How can the first-line supervisor be made more effective in handling employee grievances?

14. What criteria would you suggest for evaluating the collective bargaining process in a specific organization?

BIBLIOGRAPHY

Beal, Edwin F., Wickersham, Edward D., and Kienast, Philip. *The Practice of Collective Bargaining.* 5th ed. Homewood, Ill.: Richard D. Irwin, 1976.

Bloom, Gordon F., and Northrup, Herbert R. *Economics of Labor Relations.* 8th ed. Homewood, Ill.: Richard D. Irwin, 1977.

Blum, Albert A. (ed.). *White Collar Workers.* New York: Random House, 1971.

Davey, Harold W. *Contemporary Collective Bargaining.* Englewood Cliffs, N.J.: Prentice-Hall, 1972.

Fleming, Robben W. *Labor Arbitration Process.* Urbana: University of Illinois Press, 1965.

Marshall, Howard O., and Marshall, Natalie J. *Collective Bargaining.* New York: Random House, 1971.

Meyer, Arthur S. "Function of the Mediator in Collective Bargaining." *Industrial and Labor Relations Review,* January 1960.

Mueller, Stephan J., and Myers, A. Howard. *Labor Law and Legislation.* 4th ed. Cincinnati: South-Western Publishing Co., 1974.

National Industrial Conference Board. "White Collar Unionization." Studies in Personnel Policy, No. 220, 1970.

Power, James. "Improving Arbitration: Roles of Parties and Agencies." *Monthly Labor Review,* Spring 1970.

Rees, Albert *The Economics of Trade Unions.* Chicago: University of Chicago Press, 1962.

Sayles, Leonard R., and Strauss, George. *The Local Union.* 2d ed. New York: Harcourt, Brace & World, 1967.

Selekman, Benjamin. "Varieties of Labor Relations." *Harvard Business Review,* March 1949.

Sherskin, Michael J., and Boxx, W. Randy. "Building Positive Union-Management Relations." *Personnel Journal,* June 1975.

Sloane, Arthur A., and Whitney, Fred. *Labor Relations.* 3d ed. Englewood Cliffs, N.J.: Prentice-Hall, 1977.

Stagner, Ross, and Rosen, Njalman. *Psychology of Union Management Relations.* Belmont, Calif.: Wadsworth Publishing Co., 1965.

Stevens, Carl M. *Strategy and Collective Bargaining Negotiations.* New York: McGraw-Hill Book Co., 1963.

Taylor, George W., and Whitney, Fred. *Labor Relations Law* 2d ed. Englewood Cliffs, N.J.: Prentice-Hall, 1975.

U.S. Department of Labor, Bureau of Labor Statistics. *A Brief History of the American Labor Movement.* Washington, D.C.: U.S. Government Printing Office, 1970.

U.S. Department of Labor, Bureau of Labor Statistics. *Directory of National Unions and Employee Associations, 1971.* Washington, D.C.: U.S. Government Printing Office, 1972.

Walton, Richard E., and McKersie, Robert B. *A Behavioral Theory of Labor Negotiations.* New York: McGraw-Hill Book Co., 1965.

Wortman, Max S. (ed.). *Critical Issues in Labor Relations.* New York: Macmillan Co., 1969.

NOTES

[1] For example, see Albert Rees, *The Economics of Trade Unions* (Chicago: University of Chicago Press, 1967), pp. 94–96.

[2] Unions are called "international" in the United States because they have locals in Canada.

[3] Richard E. Walton and Robert B. McKersie, *A Behavioral Theory of Labor Negotiations* (New York: McGraw-Hill Book Co., 1965).

When you have completed studying
**MEASURING AND CONTROLLING
ORGANIZATIONAL PERFORMANCE**
you should be able to:

1. Explain the concept of control.
2. Differentiate between the manager's role and the role of the human resources department in organizational control.
3. Identify and describe various measures for organizational control.
4. Define effectiveness and efficiency as dimensions of control.
5. Formulate a series of steps for controlling organizations by indirect means.
6. Formulate a series of steps for controlling an organization by direct means.
7. Formulate a series of steps for controlling an organization by feedback methods.

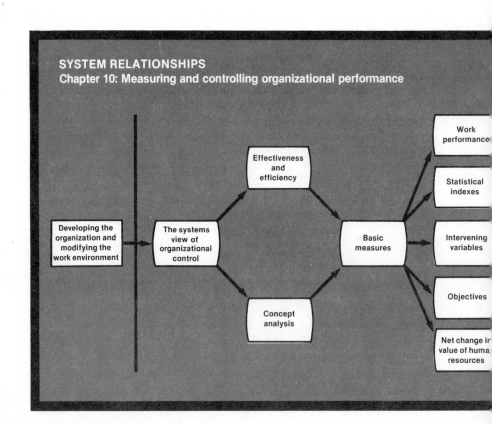

SYSTEM RELATIONSHIPS
Chapter 10: Measuring and controlling organizational performance

Developing the organization and modifying the work environment → The systems view of organizational control → Effectiveness and efficiency / Concept analysis → Basic measures → Work performance / Statistical indexes / Intervening variables / Objectives / Net change in value of human resources

To control is to:

Regulate.

Guide.

Coordinate.

Align performance with a standard.

Restrain.

Screen input or output.

THE SYSTEMS VIEW

Our systems view of human resources in the company suggests that we
look to system concepts for an understanding of control. We have seen that
the human resource system is composed
of various organized groups. Manage-

10

Measuring and controlling organizational performance

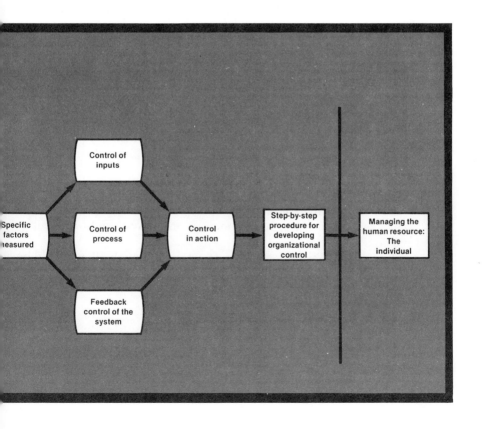

ment must control these groups at each level within the company in order to achieve company objectives. The fact that people control all other systems, such as facilities, equipment, financial, and information systems, makes control of the human resource system most important.

The control process consists of measuring and correcting performance so that goals are accomplished as planned. Controlling is closely related to planning. In fact, control is used to see that plans are being carried out. The control process keeps the manager informed on whether or not things are working out as planned.

This chapter treats control from the *technical* viewpoint. That is, we discuss control in terms of the identification and measurement of the variables which represent the performance of the system. We treat control as modifying inputs and processes. The *implementation* of control concepts involves getting people to modify their behavior and is treated in a number of chapters throughout this book.

In order to control, standards must be determined, performance must be compared to standards, and prompt remedial action must be taken when results are significantly below par. Frequently, simply formalizing the comparison between actual and planned performance challenges the manager to determine the causes of problems and thus enables the manager to remedy performance.

In controlling, it is also important to shorten the time period over which performance is measured. For example, if we wait until the end of the year before measuring absenteeism against our goal, it may be too late to remedy excessive absenteeism.

Desirable characteristics of a control system

Both line managers and the human resources department have major responsibilities for the measurement and control of performance.

A system of performance measurement and evaluation should be:

1. Related to company goals.
2. Based on plans.
3. Based on standards of measurement.
4. Readily understandable by everyone.
5. Limited to key points and events.
6. Objective and quantitative whenever possible.
7. Able to detect variances and problems quickly.
8. Economical.

9. Able to modify organizational behavior for preventive and corrective purposes.

The systems view of organizational control

In the systems view, organizations are processors that cause other parts of the system, such as equipment, to function. The output is measured, and the measurement is sent back to management, which compares it with company objectives. Suppose that an objective were to produce 2,100 units of a product per day but that only 1,900 units were produced. It is important that managers know about this shortage or about any *trend* in output. Exhibit 10–1A shows how the feedback of information enables managers to control the organization subsystems. You can see that when managers find that output is increasing or decreasing, or that output is not in line with the firm's objectives, management either changes or seeks to influence the organization's subsystems. In Exhibit 10–1B, we show how feed-

EXHIBIT 10–1

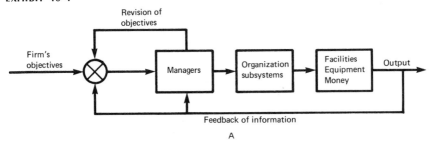

A

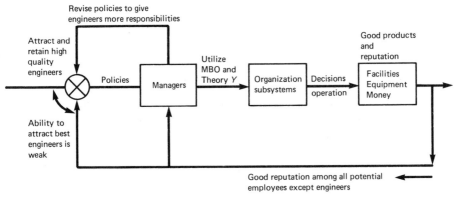

B

back to managers indicates that a company is not meeting a certain objective. The company's policies have been such that high-quality engineers are not attracted. When this information gets back to management, management makes corrective changes in its policies.

We have shown the managers as being separate from the organization components to simplify our explanation at this stage. However, since managers do exercise great influence over the control of the work of organizations, Exhibit 10–1 is a good approximation of reality. Let us consider further the roles of both managers and the human resources department in controlling organizational activities.

The manager's role

Each manager leads and controls an organization subsystem, that is, the group of people who report to him or her. The degree to which a manager exercises either direct or indirect control depends upon the manager's style, the people in the organization, and the situation. The manager is held *accountable* for the performance of his or her organization. This means that he or she may be rewarded, transferred, or removed, depending upon the performance of the organization. Thus the manager has a vital interest in the control procedure.

Control, like other management functions, arises from the need to obtain the best use of scarce resources and to attain the goals of the organization. Although the idea of control may arouse opposition from individuals who like to carry out their work without interference, some degree of control is necessary for the orderly and efficient management of any group of people. The good manager, therefore, controls employees, yet recognizes their dignity by allowing them to participate in matters affecting them. The good manager also makes "results," not the restriction of people, the target for control.

The role of the human resources department

Although the primary responsibility for the control of organizational performance rests with management, the human resources department (HRD) plays a vital supporting role. It trains managers and provides them with expert advice. It recommends policies and procedures which shape the work environment. It implements some policies relating to the organizational environment, such as training programs, health and insurance programs, counseling, and safety programs. The human resources department should work closely with line managers on all activities relating to the development and maintenance of organizational performance.

In addition, the human resources department actively participates in the control process. It gathers data, maintains records, and supplies indexes and advice to managers to assist them in carrying out their control function. For example, data on promotability, discipline, turnover, human asset evaluation, absenteeism, and safety are provided by the HRD.

The essence of a control system

Controlling is a *dynamic* activity because both the long-range and the short-range objectives of a company *change with time*. As a result, for example, of the actions of competitors or new technical developments, short-range objectives may change from month to month. In addition, managers and employees change as human resources are hired, promoted, demoted, or fired. Keeping performance on target with established goals in a dynamic environment requires considerable managerial skill. This process, called "maintaining dynamic equilibrium," is a balancing act in which changes occur continually. Let us see how it is done.

TO CONTROL, WE MUST MEASURE—BUT WHAT?

Before anything can be controlled, we must determine whether performance is or will be in accordance with plans. In order to do this we need to set standards against which to judge results. Because of the variety of company plans, the typical organization will have a multitude of standards for measuring organizational performance. Some of these standards will be tangible and quantitative, and therefore easy to measure. Examples would include the number of units to be produced, total revenues, selling costs, turnover rates, the number of employees of each grade and skill, and the return on investment.

Other standards may be used as a basis for measuring less tangible outputs or processes and thus present a real challenge to human resources management. For example, what is the total cost of human resources to the company? Is the executive development program worth the money it cost? Has the new personnel program adversely affected employee morale? Is the computer group more effective than the R&D group?[1]

We can see from these examples that precise measurement in

some areas or activities is not possible. Even in situations of this kind, however, systematic attempts to measure help make the control process concrete and more effective. Let us now consider some of the "whats" which companies attempt to measure.

Effectiveness and efficiency

Regardless of the measurement approach used, we should consider whether we are measuring effectiveness or efficiency. *Effectiveness* is the degree to which we achieve our objective. Suppose that the American Telephone and Telegraph Company had set as its objective the participation of 120,000 employees in programs specifically designed to expand and enrich the scope of their jobs by the end of 1973. We then note in the company's *Annual Report* (February 12, 1974) under the heading "Human Resources" that 100,000 were actually participating at that time. We would say that the program was 83 percent effective. (Actually, since the objective is not given in the report, it is possible that the program was 100 percent effective.)

The *efficiency* of an organization is the ratio of output to input, or the benefit/cost ratio. There is almost always some waste or loss, and efficiency can never be more than 100 percent. Exhibit 10–2 shows how these two dimensions of measurement work. As we shall see,

EXHIBIT 10–2
Dimensions of organizational measurement

Effectiveness 100%	
Attainment of objectives but at uneconomically high cost New training program goes into action but at twice the budgeted cost	Attainment of objectives with little waste, so Output/Input is close to 1.00 A set of policies on human resources management is developed on time and at budgeted cost
Low attainment of objectives Low Output/Input Human resources department is eight months behind on a computerized employee inventory system despite extra staffing	Low attainment of objectives, but little waste is involved, so Output/Input is close to 1.00 Only 20 percent of the desired number of candidates are recruited, but cost/candidate is low

Efficiency 100%

some of the methods discussed below measure effectiveness, and some measure efficiency.

Concept analysis—A measure of effectiveness

A concept analysis may be the basis for measuring the organization as a system which is a part of a larger organizational system.

The idea of the concept analysis is to determine the degree to which the organization fulfills its function in the total human resource system. In this measurement approach, a series of questions must be developed, such as:

1. What is the strategy of the company?
2. In terms of this strategy, what is the purpose of the organization being measured?
3. What conflicts of functional goals does this organization face relative to the functional goals of other organizations within the company?
4. What constraints and trade-offs are necessary to optimize the organization's activities in the interest of the total company strategy?
5. Is the organization structured to facilitate behavior directed toward achieving organizational objectives?
6. What behavior taking place within the organization is deflecting the organization from its mission?
7. Does the organization place accountability and responsibility properly among its members?

THE SPECIFIC FACTORS MEASURED

Work performance

When we think of measuring company performance we usually think in terms of daily units of output, product quality, profits, or increases in assets. For an organizational subsystem such as marketing, we may think of sales volume per salesperson, cost per sale, or salesperson turnover.

The difficulty in measuring performance, however, develops because performance consists of two inseparable components: quantity and quality. In a very real sense, quantity and quality represent two conflicting goals in terms of the limited time and cost available. For example, given a certain amount of money and time to produce widgets, we can only produce so many widgets without sacrificing quality. Assuming properly trained workers, we can only increase the number of units produced beyond a certain level by sacrificing some quality, or produce higher quality units by reducing the number produced. Thus more quantity and higher quality require more time and/or cost. The point is that performance, which consists of both quantity and quality, is interrelated with the funds and time available. We can see then that controlling is a process that requires a delicate balance among certain "givens" if organizational objectives are to be met.

Statistical measures

Various types of statistics are commonly used to compare the organization's performance to some criteria. This is usually done by collecting certain data, such as the number of people absent or costs per worker, and then analyzing these data by the use of ratios and other comparative methods.

Exhibit 10–3A lists some indexes that are used in measuring the effectiveness or efficiency of organizational performance. It is impor-

EXHIBIT 10–3
A. Indexes for comparison in measuring organizational performance

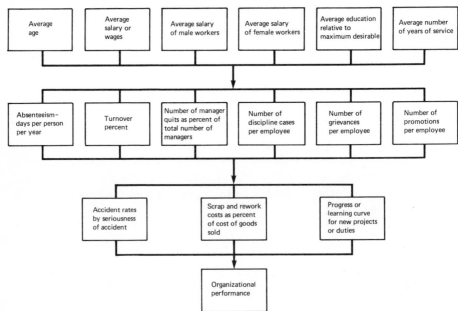

EXHIBIT 10–3 *(continued)*

B. Indexes used to measure organizational performance

*Effectiveness measures**

1. Physical output per worker-hour.
2. Physical output per year for a specific organization.
3. Physical output per manager.
4. Payroll costs per unit of physical output.
5. Number of promotions divided by the number of employees.
6. Reduction in the number of grievances filed.
7. Employee attitude ratings of company work conditions.

Ineffectiveness measures

1. Scrap loss per organization unit.
2. Accidents per organization (number and seriousness).
3. Lost time due to accidents.
4. Number of grievances lost in arbitration.
5. Employee turnover.
6. Lost time due to tardiness.
7. Sabotage incidents per organization unit.
8. Average days of sickness per employee.

Efficiency measures

1. Dollar value of cost reductions per employee.
2. Number of contracts or customers served on schedule and within budgeted costs.
3. Increase in dollars of sales per employee.

Intervening variables in organizational performance

1. Average age of workers, managers, and nonmanagers.
2. Employee job satisfaction as measured by attitude surveys.
3. Length of service of employees by class of work.
4. Employment distribution by sex, race, ethnic group, and manager/nonmanager.
5. Salary and wage structure ratios.
6. Number of employees enrolled in educational programs.
7. Amount company spends per year on education and training per employee.
8. Number of patents per employee.
9. Number of days of leave granted per employee.
10. Number of work-days spent at professional meetings per employee.
11. Quit rate.

  * A survey of literature on effectiveness models is given by Richard M. Steers, "Problems in the Measurement of Organizational Effectiveness," *Administrative Science Quarterly*, December 1975. Most of these models do not provide direct quantitative indexes. Listed are adaptability-feasibility, productivity, satisfaction, profitability, resource acquisition, absence of strain, control over environment, development, efficiency, employee retention, growth, integration, open communications, and survival.

tant to keep in mind that ratios or statistics in themselves never evaluate anything. For example, let us consider turnover, which may be defined as:

$$\frac{\text{Number of people who leave in a month}}{\text{Number of people employed at mid-month}} \times 100$$

If the firm's turnover rate is computed to be 5 percent, is this good or bad? This cannot really be answered without looking at the turnover rates of similar companies in the area or at some industry turnover average (comparative analysis). We would also want to look at our own rate for past periods (historical analysis). If our rate were 5 percent versus 10 percent for the industry, this might suggest that employees who may not be contributing to organizational effectiveness are being retained. Therefore, no turnover at all may well be as bad as "excessive" turnover.

In Exhibit 10–3B, we have listed organizational performance indexes in more detail and have indicated whether they are effectiveness or efficiency indexes.

Intervening variables

Good organizational performance is highly dependent upon an organization's cohesiveness and upon the quality, motivation, and technical competence of its members. "Causal variables" are inputs to the human resource system which provide these factors. Between the inputs and the outputs of the organization, there are characteristics of the organization in action. These are called "intervening variables." Rensis Likert, former director of the Institute for Social Research at the University of Michigan, has made a long and extensive study of the measurement of intervening variables.

Exhibit 10–4 shows Likert's conception of the relationships among input, intervening, and output variables. In this exhibit, System 1 represents an "Exploitive Authoritative" management system, System 2 represents a "Benevolent Authoritative" system, and System 4 represents a "Participative Group." Arrows 1 through 4 indicate how causal variables in the Likert model lead to the associated intervening variables. If the intervening variables are measured and found to be at the favorable end of the scale used, then, as arrows 6, 7, 5, and 10 indicate, the output variables will be favorable. On the other hand, arrows 5, 8, 9, and 11 indicate that intervening variables in authoritative systems lead to undesirable performance or organizational characteristics.

Attitude questionnaires have been developed and used by a number of companies to measure the characteristics of an organization in action. Perhaps the most sophisticated use of attitude questionnaires has been made by Rensis Likert, who incorporates survey feedback methodology in his design for a human control system. Likert's approach is particularly relevant for us because it applies

EXHIBIT 10–4
Simplified diagram of relationships among variables for System 1 or 2 and System 4 operation

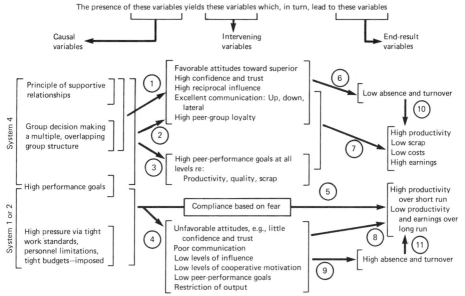

Source: Rensis Likert, *The Human Organization: Its Management and Value* (New York: McGraw-Hill Book Co., 1967), p. 137.

the feedback control methodology we have already discussed to the control of human resources.

Likert's methodology consists essentially of measuring attitudes longitudinally in an organization on a recurring basis, utilizing a highly refined and validated questionnaire. The results of these surveys are fed back to top management, within the framework of Likert's model incorporating systems 1, 2, 3, and 4. This enables the executives to take corrective action with regard to human resources. Thus, Likert's model closely matches the general model for feedback control systems which we detailed earlier.

Likert's methodology is the first explicit application of this general model to human resources. Exhibit 10–5 shows a sample of the Likert Survey Questionnaire and indicates the scaling technique which characterizes his methodology. Exhibit 10–6 shows a sample of items from another questionnaire form.

The Likert model is quite extensive and rich in its implications. We have brought it up only to show input/output concepts which

EXHIBIT 10–5
Likert Survey Questionnaire

Profile of Organizational Characteristics

Instructions:

1. On the lines below each organizational variable (item), please place an *n* at the point which, *in your experience*, describes your organization at the present time (*n* = now). Treat each item as a continuous variable from the extreme at one end to that at the other.

2. In addition, if you have been in your organization one or more years, please also place a *p* on each line at the point which, *in your experience*, describes your organization as it was one to two years ago (*p* = previously).

3. If you were not in your organization one or more years ago, please check here _____ and answer as of the present time, i.e., answer only with an *n*.

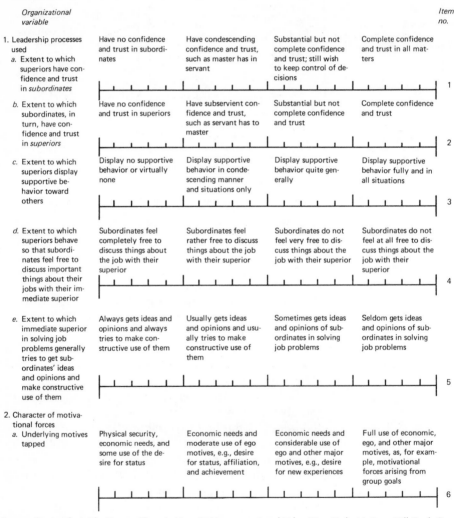

Organizational variable				*Item no.*
1. Leadership processes used *a.* Extent to which superiors have confidence and trust in *subordinates*	Have no confidence and trust in subordinates	Have condescending confidence and trust, such as master has in servant	Substantial but not complete confidence and trust; still wish to keep control of decisions	Complete confidence and trust in all matters
				1
b. Extent to which subordinates, in turn, have confidence and trust in *superiors*	Have no confidence and trust in superiors	Have subservient confidence and trust, such as servant has to master	Substantial but not complete confidence and trust	Complete confidence and trust
				2
c. Extent to which superiors display supportive behavior toward others	Display no supportive behavior or virtually none	Display supportive behavior in condescending manner and situations only	Display supportive behavior quite generally	Display supportive behavior fully and in all situations
				3
d. Extent to which superiors behave so that subordinates feel free to discuss important things about their jobs with their immediate superior	Subordinates feel completely free to discuss things about the job with their superior	Subordinates feel rather free to discuss things about the job with their superior	Subordinates do not feel very free to discuss things about the job with their superior	Subordinates do not feel at all free to discuss things about the job with their superior
				4
e. Extent to which immediate superior in solving job problems generally tries to get subordinates' ideas and opinions and make constructive use of them	Always gets ideas and opinions and always tries to make constructive use of them	Usually gets ideas and opinions and usually tries to make constructive use of them	Sometimes gets ideas and opinions of subordinates in solving job problems	Seldom gets ideas and opinions of subordinates in solving job problems
				5
2. Character of motivational forces *a.* Underlying motives tapped	Physical security, economic needs, and some use of the desire for status	Economic needs and moderate use of ego motives, e.g., desire for status, affiliation, and achievement	Economic needs and considerable use of ego and other major motives, e.g., desire for new experiences	Full use of economic, ego, and other major motives, as, for example, motivational forces arising from group goals
				6

Source: Rensis Likert, *The Human Organization: Its Management and Value* (New York: McGraw-Hill Book Co., 1967).

EXHIBIT 10-6
Some items from an attitude survey form

How much attention has your immediate manager given to helping you with your personal career plans?

There has been no need for such a discussion so far .... ☐ 0

He has helped me considerably in developing my own personal career plans .... ☐ 1

Although my manager has never formally discussed career planning with me, he has nevertheless given me all the opportunity for development and advancement that I could ask for .... ☐ 2

He has discussed the subject with me, but has helped me only a little .... ☐ 3

I need this kind of help, but haven't gotten it from my manager .... ☐ 4

To what extent have you been given sufficient information about ways to qualify yourself for promotional opportunities?

I have no interest in this kind of information ...... ☐ 0

I've received full and sufficient information— all I need .... ☐ 1

I've received quite a bit of information .... ☐ 2

I've received some information but need quite a bit more .... ☐ 3

I've received nowhere near enough information .... ☐ 4

Within this operation, is the right amount of emphasis placed on developing the abilities of people so they will be ready for upgrade or promotion, as contrasted with going out and looking for people who are already fully qualified?

Too much emphasis is put on searching out people who are already fully qualified .... ☐ 1

About the right emphasis is placed on both factors .... ☐ 2

Too much emphasis is put on trying to develop people who are already in the operation .... ☐ 3

The promotion policy here places the *most* emphasis on:

I don't know .... ☐ 0

Performance on the present job .... ☐ 1

Qualifications and background for the new job ... ☐ 2

Length of service .... ☐ 3

Knowing or being known by the right people .... ☐ 4

Other .... ☐ 5

Do you know what you need to do in order to qualify yourself for upgrade or promotion?

I have no interest in qualifying for a promotion .... ☐ 0

I'm quite certain I know exactly how to qualify myself for upgrade or promotion .... ☐ 1

I believe I know fairly well how to qualify myself for upgrade or promotion .... ☐ 2

I don't think I know very well how to qualify myself for upgrade or promotion .... ☐ 3

I don't know at all how to qualify myself for upgrade or promotion .... ☐ 4

To what extent is your opportunity to advance out of your current job limited by a lack of formal training or education?

Without further formal training or education, I can't advance beyond where I am now .... ☐ 1

Without further formal training or education I may advance just a little, but I'll never get a chance at any real promotions ..... ☐ 2

Even without further formal training or education, there

EXHIBIT 10-6 *(concluded)*

is still a fair chance that I can advance and be promoted .... □ 3	formal training or education or not .... □ 5
I believe I can continue to advance easily with only a minimum of added formal training or education (in-house courses, for instance) .... □ 4	How long have you been in your present job assignment—that is, doing the same type of work? (Being upgraded, downgraded, or transferred to another type of work would be a change in job assignment.)
I believe that there is no limit on my opportunity to advance or be promoted, regardless of whether I ever take any further	Less than 6 months .... □ 1
	7 to 18 months .... □ 2
	19 months but less than 3 years .... □ 3
	3 to 5 years .... □ 4
	More than 5 years .... □ 5

are of interest to management for controlling the organization. For a full treatment of the model, the reader should refer to Likert's book.[2]

The net change in the valuation of human resources

Another approach to measuring organizational effectiveness is to evaluate the human resources in terms of dollars and cents. This concept, proposed by Rensis Likert, has been put into practice by Robert L. Woodruff, Jr., vice president—human resources for the R. G. Barry Corporation. According to Woodruff, investments in human resources are made in group processes and team development. The R. G. Barry Corporation started with an outlay-cost approach consisting of:

Recruiting outlay costs.

Acquisition costs of bringing a new person into the company.

Formal training costs.

Familiarization costs.

Investment building experience costs (the development of a capability beyond the normal expected).

Development costs associated with specific technical skills.

The first pro forma balance sheet developed by the company to combine financial and human resources is given in Exhibit 10–7. The change in the value of "net investments in human resources" may be considered to provide a measure of total organizational performance. The same concepts could be carried down through the

EXHIBIT 10-7
The total concept

R. G. BARRY CORPORATION AND SUBSIDIARIES

Pro Forma Balance Sheet

(financial and human resource accounting)

	1969 Financial and human resource	1969 Financial only
Assets		
Total current assets	$10,003,628	$10,003,628
Net property, plant and equipment	1,770,717	1,770,717
Excess of purchase price of subsidiaries over net assets acquired	1,188,704	1,188,704
Net investments in human resources	986,094	—
Other assets	106,783	106,783
	$14,055,926	$13,069,832
Liabilities and stockholders' equity		
Total current liabilities	$ 5,715,708	$ 5,715,708
Long-term debt, excluding current installments	1,935,500	1,935,500
Deferred compensation	62,380	62,380
Deferred federal income taxes as a result of appropriation for human resources	493,047	—
Stockholders' equity:		
Capital stock	879,116	879,116
Additional capital in excess of par value	1,736,253	1,736,253
Retained earnings:		
Financial	2,740,875	2,740,875
Appropriation for human resources	493,047	—
Total stockholders' equity	5,849,291	5,356,244
	$14,055,926	$13,069,832

Statement of Income

	1969 Financial and human resource	1969 Financial only
Net sales	$25,310,588	$25,310,588
Cost of sales	16,275,876	16,275,876
Gross profit	9,034,712	9,034,712
Selling, general, and administrative expenses	6,737,313	6,737,313
Operating income	2,297,399	2,297,399
Other deductions, net	953,177	953,177
Income before federal income taxes	1,344,222	1,344,222
Human resource expenses applicable to future periods	173,569	—
Adjusted income before federal income taxes	1,517,791	1,344,222
Federal income taxes	730,785	644,000
Net Income	$ 787,006	$ 700,222

Source: R. L. Woodruff, Jr., "Human Resource Accounting," *Canadian Chartered Accountant,* September 1970, p. 159. Reprinted with permission from CA magazine, published by The Canadian Institute of Chartered Accountants, Toronto, Canada.

hierarchy of organization components to measure the smallest formal groups in the company.

The variance of performance from objectives

A method which has received increased attention in recent years is the management by objectives approach. In this case, the factor measured is the variance of the performance from the objective. Exhibit 10–8 shows an application of MBO to an organizational

EXHIBIT 10–8
A bank's performance appraisal form for its corporate planning office

	Date _____
Performance Appraisal	Date _____
	Date _____
Name _____	Date _____

PERFORMANCE MEASURES

1. Not Adequate. Not fully up to standard development or other action needed.	2. Fully Adequate. Performance measure satisfactory to all standards.	3. Above Expectancy. Performance consistently exceeds standards Contribution is above expectancy overall.	4. Exceptional Performance is unusual and clearly of superior quality. Contribution is unique and is easily and generally identified and accepted as such.

Accountabilities and Measurements	*Performance Value*			

I. Has the Corporate Planning Office provided the CEO with adequate assistance in:
   a. The formulation of long-range policies, plans, and goals?
   b. Have existing corporate planning manuals been updated on a timely basis?				

II. Have strategic planning needs been adequately defined?				

III. Has the office provided adequate assistance to the CEO in the establishment of:
   a. Environmental assumptions?
   b. High performance standards?				

IV. In connection with corporate performance standards, has the office adequately maintained a profile of our 22 competitive banks?				

V. Has the coordination of long range-plans been:
   a. Effective?
   b. Timely?				

VI. Were the objectives of the annual Planned Growth Conference adequately met?				
VII. Have policies, plans, and goals relative to corporate development (product extension as well as mergers and acquisitions) been adequately defined?				

Source: James K. Brown and Rochelle O'Connor, *Planning and the Corporate Director* (New York: Conference Board, 1974).

group. Accordingly, all goals and activities of any work group are divided into three categories: problem-solving objectives, innovative goals, and routine chores. At the individual level, employees then work with their supervisor to set quantitative and qualitative goals for each work unit and activity. Since this method for measuring the organization usually depends upon measuring all individuals in the organization, we will cover the method in detail in Chapter 14.

George Odiorne suggests three other approaches to evaluating human resources programs. These involve comparing your organizational performance against external standards as follows:

1. Audit your organization by comparing your programs with those of other companies, especially the successful ones.
2. Have an outside authority, such as a consultant, audit your organization.
3. Have a staff department, such as the human resources department, set up all policies, procedures, and rules regarding human resources management. The internal auditor, along with his or her regular duties of checking revenues and expense procedures, audits the degree of compliance with these standards.

Although this method does not follow the internal contingency approach that we have adopted in this book, it is useful in ensuring compliance with legal requirements (such as those of the Equal Employment Opportunity Commission) and union contracts.

THE CONTROL PROCESS

Merely measuring some activity, performance, or output is not controlling. The process of control requires that we take corrective action. Management can use three basic approaches to avoid or limit variations from standards and to take the necessary corrective action when deviations occur.

Control through inputs—Getting it right the first time

Of course, even with perfect inputs, the processor in the system (people) may not turn out the desired output. At any rate, the control process can be made more effective by controlling the inputs of the system. This can be done by:

1. Modifying the formal work environment.
   a. Issuing policies that will guide people toward desired action.

    b. Establish short- and long-range plans which explain who does what, when, and where.

    c. Redesign an organization structure that will establish the interpersonal relationships necessary for achieving the desired results.

2. Modify the staffing process. Control the organization by controlling the quality and mix of new employees. Planned changes in staffing then become a means of controlling organizational inputs.

3. Modify personnel in the job. This is done through training, education, and attitude modification.

4. Modify the mix of limited resources. Management must evaluate the degree to which machinery, computers, or other capital items are substituted for human resources (see Exhibit 10–9).

EXHIBIT 10–9
Allocation of limited resources

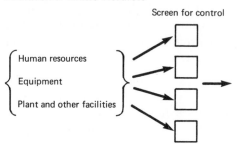

Similarly, by allocating more or less personnel to an organization, or any part of the organization, its effectiveness, efficiency, and structure may be changed.

Control of the process—Keeping on the right track

Beside controlling inputs to the organization, we may control the processes performed by the organization *at the time the processes are performed.* Companies employ three methods for this type of control.

Monitoring the day-to-day processes. Suppose that we look at a specific group, the materials handling section in a company. The function of this group is to move heavy equipment, desks, files, and even portable walls from one point in the plant to another. In order to maintain close control, one large company uses the single-job plan. Instead of giving a group of the handlers a batch of jobs at the beginning of the day, the supervisor gives the group one job and requires the group to report back, with the time spent filled in on a form. Thus the supervisor can monitor each job and can quickly determine whether the group is falling behind the daily work plan.

This real-time monitoring process, as it is called, may be used for many work groups requiring rather close supervision, such as work groups doing clerical jobs in accounting or insurance offices. Of course, such supervision may be very costly in terms of decreased motivation. This is the sort of judgment which makes managing human resources a difficult challenge.

Coordinating—Systems maintenance. Coordinating consists of keeping all members of the organization synchronized by gearing their jobs together. A mob is not coordinated. A crack Marine rifle drill team is a coordinated group.

In order to coordinate a group, companies use a variety of techniques that interconnect jobs and the timing of activities. Examples of these techniques are listed in Exhibit 10–10.

EXHIBIT 10–10
Techniques for coordinating

Oral techniques	*Written techniques*
1. Regular staff meetings.	1. Statements of company objectives and philosophy.
2. Problem review meetings.	
3. General organization and information meetings.	2. Organization charts.
	3. Documented plans.
4. Conferences or technical meetings.	4. Operating and policy manuals.
5. Committee meetings.	5. Program instructions, "work packages," work orders.
6. Task force meetings.	
7. Manager-subordinate daily interviews.	6. Memos, reports, letters, bulletins.
8. The grapevine.	7. Minutes of meetings.
	8. Engineering and manufacturing drawings.
	9. Specifications.

Self-control. As we have seen in an earlier chapter, people are motivated through job enrichment. Giving individuals control over their own work is one means of enriching jobs. An organization as a whole may exercise great control over its work as it progresses through *self-control.* Instead of feeding information about problems up the line and having correctional directives flow down, the organization is given information, adequate time, and higher level support to solve its own problems.

A very crude but clear illustration of this is the Zero Defects programs that some companies have instituted. Zero Defects means doing the job right the first time. When Avandale Mills in Alabama instituted ZD, more than 50 significant improvements in yard and fabric quality, efficiency, and waste reduction occurred in just six months. Communicating the nature, the number, and the cause of defects to workers allowed them to correct and improve their methods.

Feedback control—Getting back on the right track

In feedback control, we wait until we see what happens and then feed back information to see whether what happened matched our input plan. For feedback control, we must first set standards of performance or specific objectives to be accomplished in a given time. We observe the difference (variance, as the accountants say) and then use some technique to modify the organization's behavior and functioning.[3]

If the organization were to be controlled to correct every little deviation from standard, it would be jerked this way and that way. It would be difficult to sustain a well-directed thrust toward the main goals. As an illustration, suppose that a turnover standard were set at 2 percent. If turnover for a three-month period hits 2.3 percent, should management come charging out of its firehouse with engines clanging? No. We would probably set limits, such as 1.5 percent to 2.5 percent. If turnover exceeds these limits in either direction, it is *exceptional*. Management then takes notice only of exceptions so that it is said to "manage by exception."

A common form of feedback control is to *sample* the output. Work sampling is employed, for example, to observe a work group at random times. Conclusions may be drawn, such as "Workers spend 22 percent of their time operating calculating machines and 5 percent of their time at the coffee machine." This information is fed back and compared with standards in plans or with industry data. The organization's behavior is then modified, if necessary, by the methods described in the preceding chapters.

HOW TO PUT ORGANIZATIONAL CONTROL INTO ACTION

Although we have described the various aspects of controlling organization systems, we should summarize the step-by-step approach to put our knowledge to work. Let us suppose that you are the president of a manufacturing company called Heavenly Products, Inc. You believe that if you can get your employees to follow company plans you will achieve control over the company's physical and financial resources. You make the accompanying notes which you have expanded into a full detailed program.

Manager's mental notes

Step 1. I will get together with Jill Sleek, manager of the Human Resources Department and the other managers reporting to me. We will try to identify key organizational systems on the basis of our long-range and short-range plans. I'll give Jill a call and ask her to prepare a list of systems for discussion purposes.

Examples of action taken

Memo

From: I. M. Hoomen
To: Managers of Human Resources, Marketing, Production, Engineering, Financial Accounting, and Auxiliary Services

Let's meet in my office at 8:30 A.M. Tuesday, December 3, for the purpose of developing an organizational control program. We will try to identify key organizational systems on the basis of our recently completed plans. You should keep the entire morning free for this meeting.

Formal organization groups:

   I. Marketing
     A. Sales
     B. Advertising
     C. Marketing research
     D. . . . .
  II. Production
 III. . . . .

We should be sure to include cross-organizational systems of people as well as the formal organization groups.

Cross-organizational groups:

   I. Product planning
  II. Logistics
 III. Capital addition planning
 IV. . . . .

Step 2. Well, I think we have identified the groups of people responsible for major tasks in our company plans. Our next job is to hold another meeting and set some "standard" objectives to fit our plans and "target" objectives that will exceed our plans.

   I. Marketing
    . . . .
  II. Product planning
    Standard objective: Decrease the average time between approval of a new product and market entry to three months.
    Target objective: Decrease the average time between approval of a new product and market entry to two months.

Manager's mental notes	*Examples of action taken*
Step 3. Now that we have the objectives, we should set organizational effectiveness and efficiency measures for each objective.	Objective: Decrease the time for launching a new product. Effectiveness measure of the engineering organization: Perform value analysis and life testing in parallel with the design work. Efficiency measure of the engineering organization: Reduce design costs by 5 percent this year. Statistical (effectiveness) measure of the engineering organization: Number of new product ideas per engineer. Intervening variable measure of the engineering organization: Absenteeism, days/person/year. Concept audit: Are we measuring and controlling the really important areas of engineering performance?
Step 4. That last step was sure a big one. I wonder every once in a while if it is worth it. Then I think how complex our company really is, with all the interlocking systems of people. If every group went in a different direction, or if even one key group got way out of line, what would happen? Our last step is to set up a system of control so that our people can see if they are "out in left field" or if they are staying on the ball.	Marketing objective: Increase sales 10 percent this year. Control of inputs: Salespersons assigned, market information, engineering and production support of shipments, logistical support at regional warehouses. Control of process: Competitors' actions immediately transmitted to salespersons. Cumulative weekly sales this year versus last year supplied promptly to salespersons. New leads reported to salespersons. Training of salespersons on use of time, sales techniques, product benefits, customer characteristics. Coordination of advertising and all salespersons by the sales manager. Feedback control: Information on gaps between objectives and performance that exceed 20 percent of standard is fed to sales manager for corrective action.

SUMMARY

1. The total organization may be considered a system containing many subsystems. The most important subsystems are the groups of people that are formed to carry out company activities. Control or regulation of these subsystems depends upon establishing standards, developing measures, and implementing control processes.

2. Both managers and the human resources department play important roles in developing control systems that will motivate workers and managers.

3. Control depends upon measuring some characteristics of the organization in order to keep performance matching standards. Both the effectiveness and the efficiency of organizational work groups should be measured.

4. Various measures of organizational performance that have been used are:
   a. Quantity, quality, cost, and benefit of work.
   b. Statistical measures, ratios, and indexes related to specific standards.
   c. Intervening variables, that is, variables describing the characteristics of the organizational groups rather than outputs or inputs.
   d. Net dollar change in valuation of the human resources—an accounting approach.
   e. Concept audits—measuring the basic character and purpose of an organization in terms of the total human resource system.
   f. Management by objectives—measuring the degree to which specific objectives of the organization are attained.
   g. Use of an independent auditor as a measuring device.

5. In general, the control process requires organizations to stay within specified variations from standard values. The three approaches to achieve this may be used alone or in combination:
   a. Control the organization by controlling the inputs which "drive" the organization.
   b. Control the "process" of organizational action by monitoring, coordinating, and using on-the-spot control by employees.
   c. Use feedback control by feeding back information about performance that will enable managers to take after-the-fact corrective action.

CASE: FAST FOOD—SLOW CONTROL

Memorandum

To: Ms. Donna Gulin, Director of Human Resource Services
From: Dave Minter, President

Our financial control system tells us that we have problems involving people performance. By the time we get the word, identify the problem, and take corrective action, however, a lot of money has gone down the drain.

I read something about "key performance areas" recently. Could you identify key performance areas for our personnel, develop standards and methods of measurement, and propose a program for the implementation of control?

Donna Gulin recently received her MBA from Florida Atlantic University. Although she had had several years of business experience, this was her first executive position—director of human resource services for the Hercules Hamburger Company. She had held this position only three months when she received the above memo.

Hercules Hamburger Company was a fast-food chain of 30 outlets in southeast Florida. The outlets were owned and managed by the company. The problem areas were personnel turnover, the tendency of managers to let the outlets get run-down in appearance, occasional failures to keep equipment and premises clean, and occasional failure of order-takers to be courteous and prompt in servicing customers.

In addition, it appeared that managers who obtained good locations tended to drift rather than build up business the way managers did at poorer locations. Managers did not always identify with the company objectives of growth and dynamism.

QUESTIONS AND PROBLEMS

1. How are planning and control related?
2. Explain the meaning of "the organization as a processor."
3. Who exercises the ultimate control over a company?
4. What is the manager's role in the control of the organization?
5. What is the role of the human resources department in controlling organizational performance?
6. a. What are the four basic elements in *any* control system?
   b. What are these elements called in an organizational control system?
   c. Name a *specific* element for each of the four general elements listed in organizational control. (Example: Measurable output = Number of units per day.)
7. a. What are the three fundamental outputs that measure organizational performance?
   b. Make up and describe a situation in which you give the *planned* status for these three outputs at some point in time. Now show how it is possible for each of these to be out of phase in the *actual* status at that point in time.
8. a. Compute physical output per person-hour if fixed investment per person-hour = \$3 per person-hour. (Physical output per fixed investment = 20 units per dollar.)

    b. Compute physical output per manager if physical output per number of nonmanagers = 100 units per nonmanager. (Number of nonmanagers per number of managers = 12.6.)

    c. Visit a local store or company. Devise a measure of productivity for this type of business. Obtain the data and compute the index.

9. Write to the director of public relations of a large company and request a copy of an attitude survey, if they have conducted one. Report on the survey in class if you receive a copy.

10. As a group project, seek a local company or a large national company that will cooperate in evaluating human resources. Construct a balance sheet similar to that shown in Exhibit 10–7 for financial resources alone and for financial and human resources combined.

11. Compare MBO and key performance areas as measures of organizational performance.

12. Take a simple organization chart of a real company for major components of the company. For each component, write two or three sentences which you think would serve as a functional organizational description.

13. Select an organization (from work, school, or social group). Develop a series of five to ten specific questions that would serve for a "concept analysis" of the organization.

14. Distinguish between efficiency and effectiveness by making up an example of a work situation.

15. *a.* What is "feedforward control?"

    b. Name variables that may be modified by managers to exercise feedforward control of an organization.

16. Write a brief paper on the process of coordination for organizational control.

17. Describe how a management information system operates to permit organizational self-control.

18. *a.* What is the basis of control by feedback?

    b. What is the effect of the lag in time between measuring output and correcting input?

    c. Give an example of feedback control in an actual organization.

BIBLIOGRAPHY

Clayton, Edward R., and Moore, Laurence J. "PERT vs. GERT." *Journal of Systems Management,* February 1972.

Cunningham, J. Barton. "Approaches to the Evaluation of Organizational Effectiveness." *Academy of Management Review,* July 1977.

De Witt, Frank. "A Technique for Measuring Management Productivity." *Management Review,* June 1970.

Ferguson, Charles R. *Measuring Corporate Strategy.* Homewood, Ill.: Richard D. Irwin, 1974.

"General Electric Company." BC260R2. Cambridge, Mass.: Harvard Business School Intercollegiate Case Clearing House, 1970.

Jauch, R., and Skigen, M. "Human Resource Accounting: A Critical Evaluation." *Management Accounting*, May 1974.

Jones, D. M. C. "Accounting for Human Assets." *Management Decision*, Summer 1973.

Kast, Fremont E., and Rosenzweig, James E. *Organization and Management: A Systems Approach*. New York: McGraw-Hill Book Co., 1970.

Lang, Douglas. "Project Control Comes to Personnel." *Personnel Management* (England), May 1974.

Lawler, Edward E., III, and Rhodes, John Grant. *Information and Control in Organizations*. Pacific Palisades, Calif.: Goodyear Publishing Co., 1976. See chap. 9, "Measuring the Human Organization."

Lewis, Robert L. "Measurement, Reporting, and Appraising Results of Operations with Reference to Goals, Plans, and Budgets." In Max D. Richards and William A. Nielander (eds.). *Readings in Management*. 4th ed. Cincinnati: South-Western Publishing Co., 1974.

Likert, Rensis. *The Human Organization: Its Management and Value*. New York: McGraw-Hill Book Co., 1967.

Likert, Rensis. "Human Organizational Measurements: Key to Financial Success." *Michigan Business Review*, May 1971.

Likert, Rensis. "Human Resource Accounting: Building and Assessing Productive Organizations." *Personnel*, May–June 1973.

Likert, Rensis. "Measuring Organizational Performance." *Harvard Business Review*, March–April 1958.

McSweeney, Edward. "A Score Card for Rating Management." *Business Week*, June 8, 1974.

Murdick, Robert G., and Ross, Joel E. *Information Systems for Modern Management*. 2d ed. Englewood Cliffs, N.J.: Prentice-Hall, 1975.

Ouchi, William G., and Maguire, Mary Ann. "Organizational Control: Two Functions." *Administrative Science Quarterly*, December 1975.

Paine, Frank T., and Naumes, William. *Strategy and Policy Formation*. Philadelphia: W. B. Saunders Co., 1974.

Pugh, D. S. "The Measurement of Organization Structures." *Organizational Dynamics*, Spring 1973.

Pyle, William C. "Monitoring Human Resources—'On Line.'" *Michigan Business Review*, July 1970.

Schoderbek, Peter P., Kefalis, Asterios G., and Schoderbek, Charles G. *Management Systems*. Dallas: Business Publications, 1975. In particular, see chap. 11, "Management Cybernetics: Principles," and chap. 12, "Management Cybernetics: Applications."

Steers, Richard M. "Problems in the Measurement of Organizational Effectiveness." *Administrative Science Quarterly*, December 1975.

Stokes, Paul M. *A Total Systems Approach to Management Control*. New York: American Management Association, 1968.

Tosi, Henry, and Carroll, Stephen J., Jr. "Improving Management by Objectives: A Diagnostic Change Program." *California Management Review,* Fall 1973.

"Where Electronics Speeds Executive Decisions." *Business Week,* August 10, 1974.

NOTES

[1] Edward E. Lawler III and John Grant Rhodes, *Information and Control in Organizations* (Pacific Palisades, Calif.: Goodyear Publishing Co., 1976). See chap. 9, "Measuring the Human Organization."

[2] Rensis Likert, *The Human Organization: Its Management and Value* (New York: McGraw-Hill Book Co., 1967).

[3] For a careful and concise treatment of feedback control, see Peter P. Schoderbek, Asterios G. Kefalis, and Charles G. Schoderbek, *Management Systems* (Dallas: Business Publications, 1975), especially chap. 11, "Management Cybernetics: Principles," and chap. 12, "Management Cybernetics: Applications."

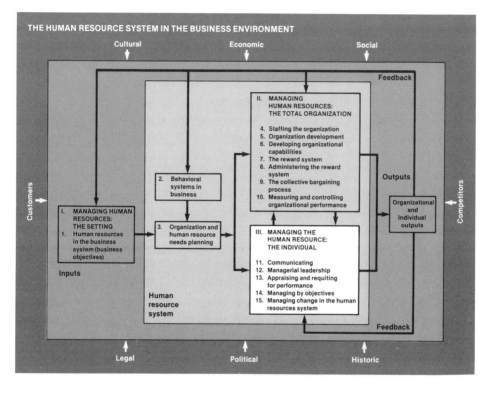

THE HUMAN RESOURCE SYSTEM IN THE BUSINESS ENVIRONMENT

Cultural Economic Social

Feedback

Customers

Inputs

II. MANAGING
HUMAN RESOURCES:
THE TOTAL ORGANIZATION

4. Staffing the organization
5. Organization development
6. Developing organizational capabilities
7. The reward system
8. Administering the reward system
9. The collective bargaining process
10. Measuring and controlling organizational performance

2. Behavioral systems in business

I. MANAGING HUMAN RESOURCES: THE SETTING
1. Human resources in the business system (business objectives)

3. Organization and human resource needs planning

Human resource system

III. MANAGING THE HUMAN RESOURCE: THE INDIVIDUAL

11. Communicating
12. Managerial leadership
13. Appraising and requiting for performance
14. Managing by objectives
15. Managing change in the human resources system

Outputs

Organizational and individual outputs

Competitors

Feedback

Legal Political Historic

PART III

MANAGING THE
HUMAN RESOURCE:
THE INDIVIDUAL

When you have finished studying
COMMUNICATING
you should be able to:

1. Describe the role of communicating in the human resource system.
2. Distinguish between broadcast and interpersonal communication.
3. Give definitions, objectives, and important aspects of communication, information, and messages.
4. List objectives of manager-subordinate communication.
5. Present guidelines for improving interpersonal communication.

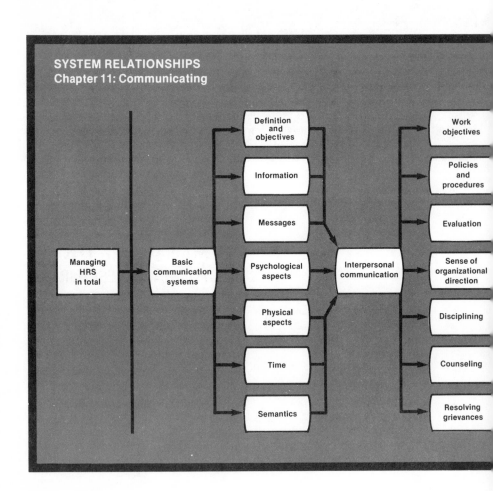

SYSTEM RELATIONSHIPS
Chapter 11: Communicating

President to VPs at monthly staff meeting:

We apparently will have a very profitable year. Due to the cyclone that wiped out our Texas plant, we will suffer a loss in our fertilizer division, however, and will have to transfer the 350 employees there to other locations.

VP to division managers:

Our only loss this year will be in the fertilizer division. Due to a cyclone, at least 350 employees who worked in our Texas plant will have to be moved out.

11

Communicating

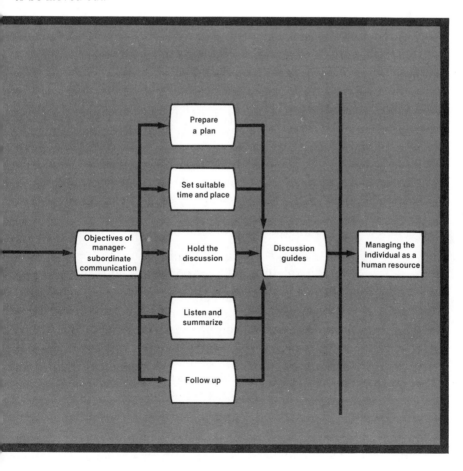

Division manager to department managers:
Losses in our fertilizer division have affected company earnings, and over 400 employees in our Texas plant will have to be laid off.

Department manager to employees:
The company is facing big losses this year, and layoffs of almost 500 employees will take place shortly.

Engineer to accountant:
Looks like a lot of us may get fired. I'm going to find another job while I still have time.

THE ROLE OF COMMUNICATION IN THE HUMAN RESOURCE SYSTEM

The above account illustrates how a breakdown in communication may disrupt the organizational system. Because *a system cannot function without communication* among its parts, we must give intensive efforts to ensuring the appropriate flow of information in the human resource system.

Communication may be treated in depth from the organizational view in terms of formal management information systems, operating information systems, organizational development, and informal communication systems. To a great degree, we have covered these system-wide approaches in previous chapters.

Communication may be also treated at the individual level, notably manager-subordinate relationships, as interpersonal communication. In this chapter we will cover primarily the manager-subordinate communication process. This type of communication is the most common form of communication involved in the implementation of human resource activities. Let us begin by examining the roles of interpersonal communication:

1. Coordination.   3. Leading.
2. Problem solving.   4. Appraising and regulating.

Coordination. When a number of people, especially a large number of people, are working together to achieve common objectives, their efforts must be coordinated. Interpersonal communication is required so that each person may relate his or her work and its timing to the work of others in the organization. Managers are important "communication centers" in the activity of coordination. They are responsible for keeping people informed about objectives, progress, and problems.

Problem solving and innovating. Many problems are solved day in and day out by individuals who apply specialized skills to their jobs. On the other hand, such problems as long-range planning, organization development, engineering projects, or even the stream of "fires" or crises that occur in business are solved by group efforts. In such situations, innovative solutions are stimulated by communication among members of work groups. The communication ranges from the complex and formal (systems, procedures, forms) to the informal and interpersonal.

Leading. To inform and influence subordinates, peers, and superiors, managers must have good communication skills. They must be able to present situations in a light which causes subordinates to be motivated. Leadership will be discussed in subsequent chapters in detail.

Appraising and regulating. Communication provides the means for carrying out the vital tasks of appraising human performance and regulating the performance of the human resource system. Here the role of communication is to feed back information to managers and workers so that they may take any corrective action required.

LINE MANAGERS AND THE HUMAN RESOURCES DEPARTMENT

Line managers are responsible for communicating with their subordinates on work-related topics. Essentially they are responsible for keeping the human resource system operating to perform the myriad of necessary tasks properly.

The human resources department acts as adviser to line managers and as monitor of the communication system. As a crude analogy, it is like a maintenance crew, guarding against breakdowns and working on repairs. It guides line managers on a personal basis and by developing training programs for the improvement of communication. The human resources department also supplements face-to-face communication between the manager and the worker by preparing and issuing policies. These policies represent line managers' views which are common to the organization. The human resources department advises line management on policies, prepares policy statements in clear, appropriate form, secures the approvals of the managers concerned, and issues the statements.

In areas where line managers do not have highly specialized expertise, the communication process is transferred to the human resources department. Examples include psychological counseling, interpreting company-sponsored physical examinations of employees, and handling questions concerning pension benefits.

BASIC COMMUNICATION SYSTEMS

Communication occurs at various system levels within the organization. The communication system which links all the workers in the organization to the ideas and concepts of management is a general "broadcast" system. Most of this system is usually nonpersonal. The same messages must reach many people. The media for broadcast methods are company policies and procedures, the company newspaper, the bulletin board, newsletters, and public announcements. The broadcast system is designed to present objectives and the unifying purpose of the company.

EXHIBIT 11–1
Systems of communication

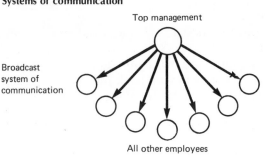

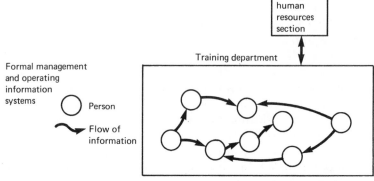

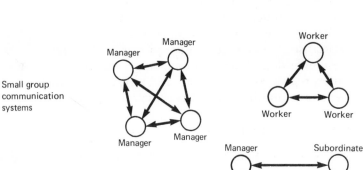

Also at the macro level are the formal information systems. These systems provide for communication among all workers who need specific information in order to do their daily jobs (see Exhibit 11–1).

Both of the above systems are supplemented by small group and interpersonal communication to provide clarification, amplification, and feedback. The lowest system level of communication is the typical two-person manager-subordinate interchange. Such interchanges may be written (memos), telephonic, or face-to-face (see Exhibit 11–1).

Let us now look at a single individual in terms of face-to-face discussion. At the intrapersonal level, we would study the communication system within the individual. This deals with physiological and psychological systems of sensing, interpreting, encoding, and decoding messages; channel capacity; speed of response; and transmitting and receiving meaning.[1]

At the interpersonal level, we see the manager dealing with one or more subordinates or others involved in problem solving. Studies have been made of communication patterns in three-, four-, and five-person task-solving groups. Exhibit 11–2 shows that the man-

EXHIBIT 11–2
Task-solving patterns

Systems of communication	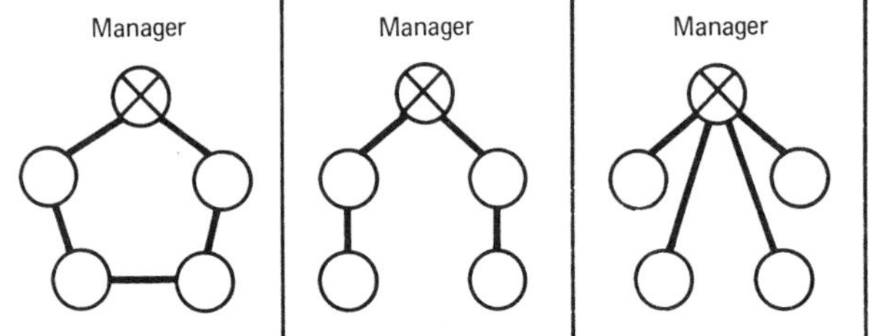 Manager	Manager	Manager
Speed	Slow	Fast	Fast
Accuracy	Poor	Good	Good
Organization	No stable form	Slowly emerging but stable	Almost immediate and stable
Morale	Very good	Poor	Very poor

Source: Adapted from Alex Bavelas and Dermot Barrett, "An Experimental Approach to Organizational Behavior," in Edwin Fleishman (ed.), *Studies in Personnel and Industrial Psychology* (Homewood, Ill.: Dorsey Press, 1961), p. 406.

ager may establish different systems of communication with different characteristics. In addition, if the manager meets with subordinates as a group, interaction between the manager and any single subordinate is greatly influenced by the presence of the others.

Also at the interpersonal level, an entire organization unit may communicate with another organization unit through many individual contacts. For example, engineering may communicate with manufacturing in this way, or accounting with finance. In Exhibit 11–3 you may see the development of interpersonal communication

EXHIBIT 11–3
The development of interpersonal communication

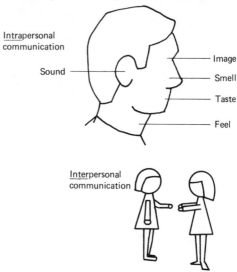

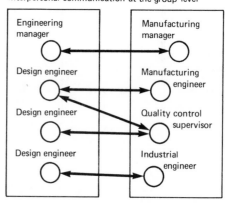

from the starting point of the individual's intrapersonal communication to intergroup contacts.

THE NATURE OF INTERPERSONAL COMMUNICATION

We have been discussing communication as if we all knew exactly what it is. It is now proper to check our mutual understandings. For instance, is communication a one-way process or a two-way process between two or more people? What are the possible channels of communication? What is the process of communication? What is communicated? Does communication occur between people and machines? between machines and machines? What are the basic purposes of interpersonal communication? Although we may not answer all of these questions here, we do want you to think about the many aspects of the communication process which are important to human resources management.

What is communication?

Interpersonal communication is the process by which one person transmits ideas, concepts, images, or sentiments to another. Not only is information exchanged, but the feelings and attitudes of the people involved are affected. Communication between people takes place when those involved attach significance to each other's behavior.

The basic objectives of communication

The basic objectives of interpersonal communication are to:

1. Inform.
2. Appraise.
3. Persuade.
4. Solicit information (feedback).

In work situations, the manager frequently informs a worker of new developments—techniques unknown to the worker—or both informs the worker and solicits the worker for information. All people in organizations constantly transmit appraisals of other people and work situations. Managers use communication to persuade subordinates to carry out certain tasks wholeheartedly. Subordinates use communication to persuade managers to accept proposals for programs. Much of daily communication is concerned with persuasion. Finally, problem-solving and conflict situations require one person to elicit information from another. From the first person's point of view, this is, in a sense, the opposite of informing.

What is "information"?

If you send a memo to a person in your company who doesn't read it, are the contents information? If your computer files are loaded with data, do those files contain information? If your mind is wandering so that you blocked out the words of the person talking to you, do those words constitute information?

For our purposes we will refer to such content as *data*. We *transmit* data. By information, we will mean data that affect our behavior, beliefs, or attitudes. We *communicate* information. A computer can only receive data, but it may *communicate information* to a manager who uses its output to make a decision. Two people who are talking and listening to each other are communicating.

EXHIBIT 11–4
Communicating information versus transmitting data

Communicating information = Affecting
behavior, opinions, attitudes

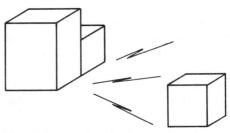

Transmitting data = Interchanging
signs that are having no impact on behavior

The quality of information

One of the biggest problems for managers and the rest of us is determining the quality of information. What we think we see and what we hear may be incomplete and distorted. The many ways that communication may be disrupted are covered later in the discussion of barriers to communication. Basically, however, the quality of information is affected by:

1. Reliability, or trustworthiness.
2. Precision, or the range of the possible error.
3. Accuracy, or the difference between what is communicated and the truth.
4. Bias, or consistent difference from the actual facts.
5. Validity, or the degree to which a statement represents what it is said to represent. For example, does a personnel selection test actually measure what it is claimed to measure?
6. Currency. How up-to-date is the information?
7. Redundancy. Is there a minimum of repetition of information?
8. Freedom from "noise." Is there little or much extraneous data in the message or in the communication process?

What's in a "message"?

As humans, we communicate ideas as a "message," or a spurt of information. For clear communication, particularly in writing and in more formal speaking, we should plan our messages. That is, we should consider:

1. *The number of ideas in our message.* If we wish to communicate only one idea, we are apt to have a high degree of success. If we attempt to communicate many, the receiver of our message may forget or confuse some of the ideas.

2. *The rate of information flow.* If we speak too rapidly, our listener may be unable to grasp what we are saying. Poor managers often try to keep up with every detail so that reports (messages) pile up and overload them. As managers, therefore, we must be selective about the kind of information we get so that we can absorb it in the time available.

3. *The relative importance of our ideas.* The organization of messages should make clear which ideas are most important. A sort of "priority for action" can thus be established.

4. *The coverage of each idea.* The coverage or detail given to each idea in a message must be considered. More important or

complex ideas usually require greater amplification than do less important or simpler ideas.

5. *The relationship of ideas.* Related ideas are usually grouped together. Alternatively, ideas may be presented in the sequence of the required action. Consider a manager discussing with a sales employee the tasks to be completed over the next three months. The manager could organize the discussion around products, customers, administrative reports, and pricing. Or, using the sequential approach, the manager could discuss plans for the areas and the customers to be covered, travel plans, the time to be spent with each customer, the products to emphasize with each customer, and daily reports.

EXHIBIT 11–5
Planning a message

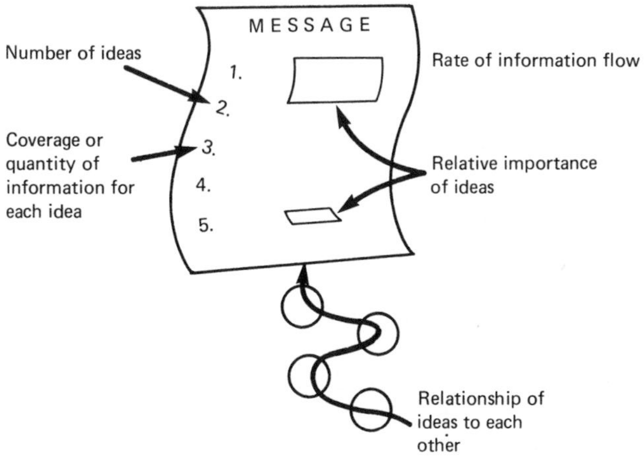

Psychological aspects of interpersonal communication

Without realizing what they are, we are all bound by psychological constraints. We also follow many cues in interpersonal communications without consciously thinking of them.

Personal filters and selective perception. We are each unique in the way that we construct the world outside ourselves. Our perceptions and our expectations about the world are based upon our past experiences and our conception of self. We selectively perceive or filter information. We tend to avoid information about occurrences which appear to be inconsistent with our beliefs about ourselves or the world. We also tend to forget such information or to discount it. Such filtering of information obviously distorts communication.

Verbal and nonverbal communication. What we say is usually not the whole message, and, in fact, may be the opposite of what we mean. Sarcasm is an illustration. How then do we fully communicate in interpersonal discussions?

We must view interpersonal communication as consisting of four parts: verbal + vocal + body movements + use of space. An example of communication that is, say, about 1 percent verbal + 99 percent vocal + no body movements + no use of space is the old recording by Stan Freberg which consisted of three minutes of

> John . . .
> Marsha . . .
> John . . .
> Marsha . . .

The variations in the emphasis, spacing, pitch, and volume of these two words caused several radio stations to refuse to broadcast the recording on the ground that it was too suggestive.

In face-to-face discussions we note the gestures, the arm and leg movements, and the total body movements of the individuals. Each culture has its own distinctive set of movements and meanings.[2] One of the most significant and complex body movements is mutual eye contact. Centering; the duration of eye contact; movement up, down, or sideways when eye contact is broken—all have important meanings.

Source credibility. Communicating with another person means leaving the security of one's own concepts and entering the experiential field of another. The degree to which this occurs depends upon the credibility of the other person. Former president Lyndon Johnson experienced a "credibility gap" in his explanations of the Vietnam War. Credibility depends upon trust, situation, and time.

Credibility is an extremely important concept in managing people. Too often, managers are unable or unwilling to deal with unpleasant topics in face-to-face discussions with employees. In such instances, the employee later learns the facts indirectly through the grapevine. Often a form of double-talk is employed in dealing with employees. A classic example of double-talk in the political arena may be drawn from Governor Nelson Rockefeller's statement of his position on Vietnam at a 1968 press conference:

> Surely, my position on Vietnam is very simple. And I feel this way. I haven't spoken on it before because I haven't felt there was any major contribution that I had to make at the time. I think our concepts as a nation, and that our actions have not kept pace with the changing conditions, and therefore our actions are not completely relevant

today to the realities of the magnitude of the complexity of the problems that we face in this conflict.

Power.   Power in communication is the potential of one person to influence another. The power of the corporation president or the capacity of a manager to exert strong sanctions will affect what the other person in a discussion says and how he or she listens. Power means the ability to determine the location, the time, and the length of a discussion. Both power and trust are bases for credibility.

When both discussants strive for power, conflict arises.[3] It should be the purpose of communication to prevent or curb conflict.

Listening.   If one person is talking and the other is hearing but not listening, little communication is taking place. In manager-subordinate interchanges, the subordinate is likely to listen carefully because of the power relationship. In fact, the subordinate is often oversensitive to each aspect of the manager's message.

On the other hand, the manager is often so intent on expressing his own ideas that he fails to listen to the subordinate. Listening is an active process. It consists of giving attention, of receiving stimuli from the sender, and finally, of perception, the assignment of meaning to whatever stimuli are received.

Physical aspects of interpersonal communication

North Americans demand more space about them than do the people of most countries. This is evident in the dispersion of residences, the size of offices, and finally, in the space maintained between two people who engage in conversation. Space is also maintained by using such barriers as furniture and by suppressing smells with deodorants and mouthwashes. We resent people who press against us or intrude on our sphere of privacy in conversation.

Another physical aspect of interpersonal communication is the orientation of the participants. Steinzor and later Bass and Klubek showed that two people sitting opposite each other tend to interact more than do two people seated side by side.[4]

Time aspects of interpersonal communication

Usually the manager or supervisor is under a time constraint that does not permit topics to be covered leisurely. In such circumstances, we often neglect courtesies and fail to listen to the messages that the other person is sending. This suggests that we should schedule discussions when we have adequate time or that we should limit the topics covered.

The time of day or the time of week selected for discussion affects the information received, as does the mood of the participants and the apparent importance of the meeting. For example, a manager who calls a meeting a few minutes before normal quitting time on Friday afternoon cannot expect full attention from participants.

Semantic aspects of interpersonal communication

Semantics is concerned with the relations among thought, language, and behavior. For semantics the meanings of words lie not in the words themselves but in our reactions to them. The same word may mean different things to different people. Thus such words as *scab, rate-buster,* and *management tool* arouse intense emotions among hourly union workers while producing little effect on professional workers.

Alfred Korzybski, the founder of general semantics, pointed out how, through built-in and simplistic mental processes, we have many misunderstandings in our communication.

Barriers to communication

The discussion above has introduced factors which affect communication. An understanding of those factors will guide you toward improved communication techniques. We may amplify further by identifying some specific ways in which barriers to communication may arise because of lack of such understanding. These ways, given in Exhibit 11–6, are generally self-explanatory. Since we have not grouped them according to the factors we have discussed, you may wish to test your understanding of the barriers by so grouping them.

EXHIBIT 11–6
Barriers to communication

1. Differences in perceptions of events in the world.
2. Misinterpretation of messages received.
3. Heightened emotions.
4. Laziness in trying to understand or transmit messages.
5. Resistance to change.
6. Failure to "listen" actively. Letting the mind wander or thinking about what *you* want to say.
7. Uncritically and mistakenly assuming that you understand what the speaker means.
8. Failure of the speaker or writer to recognize the situation and frame of reference of the listener or reader.
9. Cultural and social differences which affect the language, viewpoints, and values of the people who are attempting to communicate.
10. Confusing "facts" with inferences and sentiments.

EXHIBIT 11–6 *(continued)*

11. Failure to appraise motives. What is the other person really trying to accomplish?
12. Failure to obtain related information before interpreting the other person's meaning.
13. Overgeneralization or projection of the other person's meaning by listening to that person's first ideas and then jumping to conclusions.
14. Assuming that everything is either black or white. Many characteristics may assume a whole range of values.
15. Lack of feedback between people who are trying to communicate. Do you attempt to phrase the other person's ideas in your own words for checking?
16. Overcommunication so that you cannot identify the main ideas of the message.
17. Confusing words with concrete phenomena. The word *John* and the person John are not the same.
18. Inability of language and symbols to give some shadings of the meanings desired.
19. Use of "gobbledygook," *the ostentatious application of hypertechnical terms and oververbalization as an instrumentality of nugatory communication.*
20. Lack of organization and failure to emphasize ideas.
21. Conflict between verbal communication and behavioral signs. The receiver of the message may incorrectly interpret one or the other.
22. Interruptions to the communications process.
23. Outside "noise" or interference.
24. Distance between the sender and the receiver, which may reduce such aids to communication as the observation of behavior or the tone of voice.
25. Inappropriate channel of communication.
26. Time between origin of message and receipt of message.
27. Structure of the formal and informal organizations.
28. Status and other social barriers.
29. Number of people involved in the communication process.

MODELS OF COMMUNICATION

Models (diagrams and descriptions) help us to unify our knowledge and improve our understanding of a subject. A number of models have been developed which attempt to show relationships among the factors affecting interpersonal communication and/or to present the basic process.

In this connection, we will present a series of three models. The first model deals with the mechanics of transmitting a message. The second model (David K. Berlo model) relates sociopsychological and sensory aspects of communication in a framework of source, message, channel, and receiver. The third model delves further into the transfer of meaning as it relates to understanding and potential conflict between two individuals.

An early model of the communication process treated information from a statistical standpoint, without regard to semantic content.[5] Although this model dealt with electrical signals, it was extended to interpersonal communication. The basic model in Exhibit 11–7A presents the communication process and the "noise" that interferes with the process. Exhibit 11–7B expands the model to

EXHIBIT 11–7
Model of a communication system

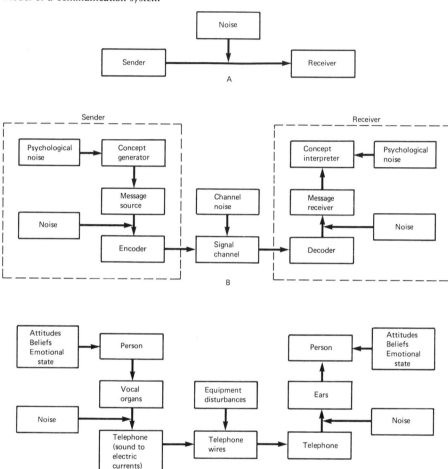

indicate that whoever generates a concept or receives a communication shapes it according to his or her background and emotional state. "Encoding" means converting an idea into a language. "Decoding" is, of course, the reverse process. Interfering noises throughout the system may distort communication. Exhibit 11–7C illustrates an application of this model.

David K. Berlo has given us a model which emphasizes the psychological factors in communication. A summary of the communication structure and process is shown in his presentation (Exhibit 11–8).

Joseph Luft has proposed a model which he calls the Johari Window model for interpersonal communication.[6] This suggests the

EXHIBIT 11–8
The Berlo model of communication

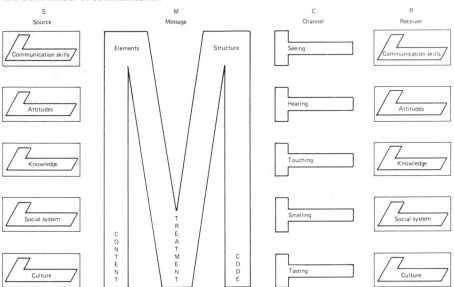

Source: Reprinted from *The Process of Communication: An Introduction to Theory and Practice* by David K. Berlo. Copyright © 1960 by Holt, Rinehart and Winston, Inc. Reprinted by permission of Holt, Rinehart and Winston, Inc.

more elaborate model in Exhibit 11–9, which shows the 16 possible states of awareness between two people. When both persons have an awareness or knowledge of a subject, this is the arena of the discussion. When one person knows something that the other does not know, the latter has a blind spot in the discussion. When either of the participants enters the discussion with incorrect facts or perceptions, this may well lead to conflict. Finally, if neither party is aware of certain information, we have an "unknown" area that will be excluded from communication.

From the systems view, then, we may represent the two-person discussion process as acting upon inputs (the knowledge and perceptions of each person) and yielding revised knowledge and perceptions, as shown in Exhibit 11–9B.

EXHIBIT 11–9
System of interpersonal communication

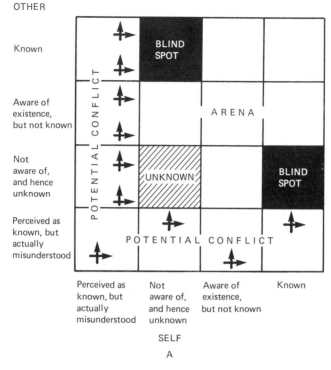

A

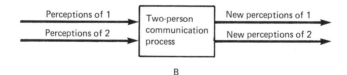

B

OBJECTIVES OF MANAGER-SUBORDINATE COMMUNICATION

The first step in designing a system is to set its objectives. After we set the objectives for the communication system, we may develop plans and make sure that all parts of the communication system are operating effectively. In the following discussion, we take up typical objectives or purposes of the person-to-person communication involved in managing human resources.

Communicating organizational objectives and the individual's responsibilities

When a new employee is first hired, he or she is usually given a brief orientation to the objectives and policies of the company. Someone from the human resources department may meet with a group of new employees or with a single new employee. Orientation literature is usually provided. Sometimes a series of company managers or staff people will make brief presentations.

The manager to whom the new employee is assigned will also seek to communicate information about the work group. Another objective will be to discuss the work to be performed by the new employee and the other members of the group.

Communicating policies, procedures, and practices

In order to ensure consistency in action and a unified sense of direction, the manager needs to communicate the company's policies, procedures, and practices. Although this information is usually available in manuals, it requires explanation and interpretation for most employees.

Providing employees with feedback and evaluation

To keep the human resource system going in the established direction, managers at every level must let their group members know how they are doing. If information on a person's performance versus plans is supplied, the person can usually correct his or her performance when things start to go wrong. For example, if a training director receives cost reports, attitude measurements of students and managers, and student examination results, the director may be able to revise programs to make them more efficient and effective. Chapter 13 deals with communicating during the appraisal process.

Providing employees with a sense of direction

The good manager will communicate to those in the work group a sense of mission, a feeling that the organization's objectives are important and that each individual should give his all. In sports, we sometimes see this esprit de corps when a theoretically weaker team beats a much stronger team. The toughest thing for a manager to do is to maintain a sense of mission in each employee over a long period of time.

Disciplining and other unpleasant topics

Communication between manager and subordinate has many positive objectives. Unfortunately, some objectives of communication in managing are "last resort" processes. Disciplining, demoting, or terminating an employee (for whatever reason) produces the unhappy hours.

Counseling employees

A more pleasant objective of communication in managing is that of counseling an individual. Here the objective is to help a person improve on the job or find solutions to career or personal problems. The manager or a specialist from the human resources department may perform the counseling function according to the employee's situation.

Hearing and resolving an employee's desires and grievances

Most workers desire control over their work and modification of their work situation. Such desires may be presented as proposals for which the employee simply seeks his or her manager's approval. In other cases, the employee may voice the desire as a complaint about a present situation and may or may not propose a solution. The source of the employee's grievance may be his or her manager or a third party. In all such cases, the manager and the employee should communicate fully to uncover the real problem and possible solutions.

Exit interviews

A major purpose of the exit interview, which is conducted when someone leaves the firm, is to uncover the attitudes and feelings of the interviewee toward the company and to diagnose organizational problems. This usually requires the nondirective interviewing technique which is discussed later in this chapter. It is also desirable that the employee who quits or is fired feel that he or she has been treated as fairly as possible. Such people may harm or enhance the reputation of the company through contact with other people.

GUIDES FOR IMPROVING TWO-WAY DISCUSSIONS
WITH EMPLOYEES

Since communication is a big subject, we can only give some guides to improving communication within the company. There are two basic steps. The first step is to give one person complete responsibility for the development of a company-wide program for communication improvement. The second step is to train managers and employees to communicate better both orally and in writing.

Develop a company-wide communications program

In a large company, an individual within the human resources department should be appointed to develop and maintain a communication program. The small company should probably use the services of a specialist in communication from a management consulting company to develop the program. Then an employee could be assigned part time to maintain it. The development of a communication program would consist of:

1. Reviewing organizational goals.
2. Auditing the present communication activities.
3. Establishing communication objectives.
4. Establishing communication policies.
5. Establishing communication activities.
6. Establishing communication modes.
7. Evaluating goal-related behavior.

The above company-wide broadcast program provides the backup system for face-to-face manager-subordinate discussions. The following are guides for holding effective discussions.

Build trust

Trust is not an instant gift. It is true that social standing, role, and power favor the development of trust. Generally, however, the manager must build a reputation for credibility over a period of time. Then, on the basis of trust, the subordinate will accept persuasion better and will also share his or her own ideas and feelings more honestly and freely.

On your side, *understand*, like, and trust your subordinate. Review, in your mind at least, all that you know about the person with whom you will be communicating. What is her or his education, work experience, background, and personality? How has she or he responded in similar conferences in the past? Since you depend on this person, you should review her or his strong points, those that caused you to hire the person. Prepare yourself to enter the discussion with an attitude of liking and trust.

Get the facts in advance

Each participant in a discussion should obtain as much information as is appropriate before the meeting. This prevents blind spots and areas of conflict, as shown in Exhibit 11–9.

Plan the discussion

As manager, you should jot down a plan of points to be covered and objectives to be reached in the discussion. If the discussion is to involve joint work on a technical problem, it may be worthwhile to send an agenda to the other person.

Note specifically what you hope to accomplish. Note the minimum satisfactory outcome.

Example. One of your subordinates has fallen behind in a project that she has taken. Your objectives are *(a)* to determine what her problems are, *(b)* to help her lay out a course of action that will overcome the problems, and *(c)* to arrange for such support or expertise as she will need for the next two weeks.

In planning discussions, such as interviews, plan *how* you will structure the interchange. Should your approach be "directive" or "nondirective"? In the directive approach, the manager (or interviewer) guides the interchange, seeks answers to specific questions, and gives advice. This approach is useful in covering routine matters, matters of fact, and reports of progress.

In the nondirective approach, the manager (or interviewer) seeks to uncover feelings or beliefs that the other party is reluctant to expose. In fact, a nondirective discussion may be used to help either party evolve or clarify thoughts that he or she was unaware of. If the manager has a specific objective in mind for the discussion, then the manager must stimulate the other person's thinking and responses by:

1. Asking questions and then listening without interruption or criticism until the other person has finished and remains silent for a time.
2. Making reflective comments, such as "Could you explain a little more?" "I see." "You feel that . . . ?" "Uh huh."

3. Observing the other person's facial expressions, body movements, tone of voice and inflections, and change of rate in speaking in order to determine points for probing questions.
4. Withholding criticism, judgments, and arguments.

Set a mutually agreeable time

If the matter at hand deals with a current work problem, you may call the employee into your office or visit his or her office immediately for a brief informal discussion. On the other hand, if a matter of importance affecting the employee's performance or career is at issue, the time and place should be chosen with care. Often layoffs, terminations, or other bad news is discussed late Friday afternoon so that the employee can adjust to the shock over the weekend. On the other hand, promotions may be discussed at any time unless there are serious side issues, such as transfers to another location.

In dealing with bad news, the manager should present and discuss possible alternative courses of action for the employee. He should reassure the employee by helping the employee to find a constructive solution to the problem. Adequate time must be allowed.

The lunch hour, after work hours, and Saturday mornings should be evaluated as possible times for meetings in different situations.

Set an appropriate meeting place

The place of the meeting and the physical setting have an important impact upon the way an interpersonal discussion will go. Casual topics should be discussed in convenient places—at the individual's work station, in the cafeteria, or even at the coffee machine.

More formal and serious subjects are usually taken up in the manager's office or a conference room. Correction interviews and evaluation interviews should be carried out in private and without interruption. Such topics as the promotion or transfer of an executive may be discussed at a restaurant, a country club, or a vacation spot.

Advise the employee in advance

Let the employee know the subject of the discussion far enough in advance for him to prepare himself technically or psychologically. If the discussion is to be on an unpleasant topic, however, it is sometimes better to just call the employee in and develop the discussion of the problem together.

Anticipate barriers

Check the list of possible barriers in Exhibit 11–6. Which are most likely to hamper your communication at the forthcoming meeting? How can you reduce these barriers?

Tell what and why

Good communication requires risk and the exposure of feelings. Tell the employee the problem as you see it, the alternatives that appear possible, and why you are recommending a particular course of action.

If you and the employee have developed mutual trust, encourage and help the employee (see Exhibit 11–9). What feedback has the employee received previously?[7]

Correctional and disciplinary interviews deserve special attention as adjustments to the malfunctioning of the human resource system. As much as possible, the worker should be given responsibility for corrective action. Therefore, the first such interview should be conducted to determine whether the employee is aware of the objectives, duties, or rules involved. If so, the discussion should center on the future action planned by the employee. The employee is not criticized. Rather, forward-looking action is discussed.[8]

If the employee does not take corrective action within a specified time, a second interview will be necessary. Has the employee been taking the corrective action previously agreed upon? Are other employees failing to cooperate or to provide required inputs, so that corrective action is not possible? Is the employee simply not competent or not trying? If following rules is the issue, did the employee again accidentally (forgetfully) or deliberately violate the rule? At this point, possible changes in the employee's position or possible disciplinary action may be identified. If the employee has deliberately or carelessly broken a rule for a second time, disciplinary action is called for. Such action should be objective, related to the particular individual, and consistent with the union contract if one exists. A record should always be kept of disciplinary interviews, and a contract expert from the human resources department should be present if it appears that disciplinary action will be required.

Listen and understand

Communication is a two-way process. As a manager, cultivate the skill of listening. Look at the other person, not out the window.

Why listening is hard work

Most people talk at a speed of about 125 words a minute. However, most of us think at a speed at least four times faster than this. So, we normally have about 400 words of thinking time to spare during every minute someone talks to us. It takes a lot of concentration to keep your thoughts from drifting during this spare time.

A good listener fights distractions. But it isn't easy. Experts tell us that good listening is hard work and is accompanied by faster heart action, a quicker circulation of the blood, and a small rise in bodily temperature.

Perhaps that explains why only 25% of the people who hear a formal talk are able to grasp the speaker's central idea.

The pay-off in communicating

The pay-off in communicating is paying close attention to *meaning* and not just words. The 500 most frequently used words have an average of 28 meanings each. The word "round" has 73 meanings.

 Southern Bell

Resist distractions. Give the other person a chance to marshal his or her ideas and to present them completely. Don't argue.

Don't evaluate what the other person says until there has been a full exchange of views. Judge the content and not the delivery. Be flexible; an idea that appears off target may be great with some modification.

Probe, question, and summarize in your own words what the other has said and ask whether he or she agrees that this was the idea presented. Use mirror questions, or signs indicating that you understand, that the speaker should continue.

Remember that nonverbal communication (body language) has a great influence on the other person. Make sure that your signs and expressions don't convey the opposite of active listening.

Summarize

At the end of the discussion, summarize the points of agreement and the action to be taken. Check to see whether the other person agrees with your summary. In some cases, notes should be prepared on the spot and initialed by both parties.

Terminate the discussion constructively

Complete the meeting courteously. Make constructive comments about the future or about possible future meetings. Even if there is substantial disagreement, offer to keep communications open by meeting again if this seems feasible.

Follow up

Whatever agreement, objectives, or action are agreed upon, put a note in your tickler file to follow up. This may call for another meeting and a person-to-person review. Without such a follow-up, the benefits of the meeting may slip away.

SUMMARY

Communication as a system, as a process, and as a skill has been reviewed in this chapter. The emphasis has been on interpersonal communication, particularly the manager-subordinate relationship. This is because such communication is usually the process that leads to the implementation of all the activities of human resources management.

This chapter began with a description of the communication process, including its role. This involved the presentation of definitions and models. The basic concepts were then used to present a set of guides or prescriptions for conducting effective two-person discussion.

CASE: THE CASE OF ANNE GREBLAD

Anne Greblad is the reference librarian of the City Public Library. In the last seven years she acquired considerable experience in developing library displays and in providing library service to the two local hospitals. She was considered to be one of the most capable workers at the library—until this year.

For several months Anne has been creating serious difficulties for Mrs. Kay, the associate director, because of her arbitrary, sullen disposition and her frequent critical "popping off" in the presence of other librarians. Mrs. Kay has felt that something had to be done because Anne's attitude has been damaging the morale of the other librarians. Friction has also been increasing between Anne and Mrs. Kay, and Anne's job efficiency has been adversely affected. Mrs. Kay has been unable to get at the problem herself, so she has told the library director that something has been bothering Anne but that she has been unable to find out what it was.

Mrs. Kay and the library director called Anne in for a conference after working hours on Saturday. They told Anne that they were concerned about her performance and were anxious to help.

At first, Anne belligerently blamed her colibrarians for their lack of cooperation. The director and Mrs. Kay continued to listen. Finally, the following conversation took place:

> **Director:** Anne, you used to be one of our most capable workers and did such an outstanding job in providing library service to our hospitals.
>
> **Anne:** I enjoyed this work when there was time to provide proper services, but that hasn't been possible since we went on this management by objectives kick. I was discussing this situation only last night with Tom in Acquisitions.
>
> **Mrs. Kay:** I explained to you earlier this year, Anne, that the purpose of the City Public Library has been expanded to provide books and information not only for the people in the city but for all residents of Howard County who wish to use its resources. Furthermore, we want to make information and material available to everyone within two days of the request.

Anne: The percentage of requests filled within this time limit will be low.

Director: Progress comes from establishing goals which exceed the routine requirements of your job.

Anne: I still think that a high priority should be given to providing library service to hospitals.

Director: I agree with you, Anne, but we do have to satisfy the overall objectives of the library.

QUESTIONS AND PROBLEMS

1. List company-wide or organization-wide programs that seek to improve communication among employees.

2. Discuss the use of communication in coordinating a specific project or task that you know of.

3. Discuss the role of communication for two people working on a project or problem versus its role for 1,000 people working on a project or problem.

4. Discuss the process of appraising the performance of the individual who receives reports directly versus the process of appraising the performance of the individual who receives all reports through his or her manager. Which communication system do you think would be more effective, and why?

5. Develop a diagram to show the flow of information upon the hiring of a new employee.

6. List all the ways that two people communicate with each other in business (written, face-to-face, and so on).

7. Distinguish between the intrapersonal and interpersonal communication systems.

8. Give examples drawn from business situations of each of the four basic objectives of communication.

9. Take an example of business information, such as the sales forecast, and discuss the likely quality of the information in terms of the eight characteristics of information covered in the chapter.

10. Give the substance of a recent conversation that you had in which the filters and perceptions of each party made communication difficult.

11. List five body gestures or positions that you have noticed people using when they talk, and give your interpretation of these gestures or positions.

12. Discuss the meanings and connotations of the terms *boss, manager,* and *leader.*

13. List the elements, the process, and the objectives of the Berlo model and the system model of communications.

14. Prepare a plan for discussing an employee's breach of a no-smoking rule and possible disciplinary action. Have another student play the role of the employee, and act out the meeting.

15. Play the role of manager in a discussion, with another student playing the role of a subordinate with a grievance. The grievance is that members of the work group keep hiding the subordinate's tools.

BIBLIOGRAPHY

Barker, Larry L. *Listening Behavior*. Englewood Cliffs, N.J.: Prentice-Hall, 1971.

Bensahel, Jane G. "Playing Roles to Convey Your Ideas." *International Management*, June 1973.

Civikly, Jean M. (ed.). *Messages: A Reader in Human Communication*. New York: Random House, 1974.

Clark, Tony, Bock, Doug, and Cornett, Mile. *Is That You Out There?* Columbus, Ohio: Charles E. Merrill Publishing Co., 1973.

DeVito, Joseph A. *Communication: Concepts and Processes*. Englewood Cliffs, N.J.: Prentice-Hall, 1971.

Farace, Richard V., and McDonald, Donald. "New Directions in the Study of Organizational Communication." *Personnel Psychology,* 1974.

Greenbaum, Howard H. "The Audit of Organizational Communication." *Academy of Management Journal,* December 1974.

Hall, Jay. "Communication Revisited." *California Management Review,* Spring 1973.

Harris, O. Jeff, Jr. *Managing People at Work*. Santa Barbara, Calif.: John Wiley & Sons, 1976.

Herold, David M., and Greller, Martin M. "Feedback: The Definition of a Construct." *Academy of Management Journal,* March 1977.

Huseman, Richard C., Lahiff, James M., and Hatfield, John D. *Interpersonal Communication in Organizations*. Boston: Holbrook Press, 1976.

Huseman, Richard C., Logue, Cal M., and Freshley, Dwight I. *Readings in Interpersonal and Organizational Communication.* 2d ed. Boston: Holbrook Press, 1975.

Kelly, Joe. *Organizational Behavior*. Homewood, Ill.: Richard D. Irwin, 1969. See chap. 11, "Communications."

Knapp, Mark L. *Nonverbal Communication in Human Interaction*. New York: Holt, Rinehart and Winston, 1972.

Kuhn, Alfred. *The Study of Society: A Unified Approach*. Homewood, Ill.: Richard D. Irwin, 1963. See part 2, "Communications."

Mortensen, C. David. *Communication: The Study of Human Interaction*. New York: McGraw-Hill Book Co., 1972.

Murdick, Robert G., and Ross, Joel E. *Information Systems for Modern Management.* 2d ed. Englewood Cliffs, N.J.: Prentice-Hall, 1975.

Pondy, L. R. "Organizational Conflict: Concepts and Models." In John M. Thomas and Warren G. Bennis (eds.). *Management of Change and Conflict*. Middlesex, England: Penguin Books, 1972.

Shulman, Arthur D.   "A Multichannel Transactional Model of Social Influence."
In Walter Nord (ed.). *Concepts and Controversy in Organizational Behavior.*
Pacific Palisades, Calif.: Goodyear Publishing Co., 1972.

Vardman, George T., and Vardman, Patricia Black. *Communication in Modern Organization.* New York: John Wiley & Sons, 1973.

NOTES

[1] See, for example, C. David Mortensen, *Communication: The Study of Human Interaction* (New York: McGraw-Hill Book Co., 1972), part 2, "The Intrapersonal System."

[2] For a technical discussion, see Merwyn A. Hayes, "Nonverbal Communication: Expression without Words," in Richard C. Huseman, Cal M. Logue, and Dwight I. Freshley (eds.), *Readings in Interpersonal and Organizational Communication,* 2d ed. (Boston: Holbrook Press, 1973).

[3] L. R. Pondy proposed five stages of conflict: latent, perceived, felt, manifest, and aftermath. See L. R. Pondy, "Organizational Conflict: Concepts and Models," in John M. Thomas and Warren G. Bennis (eds.), *Management of Change and Conflict* (Middlesex, England: Penguin Books, 1972).

[4] B. Steinzor, "The Spatial Factor in Face-to-Face Discussion Groups," *Journal of Abnormal and Social Psychology,* 45:552–555; and B. M. Bass and S. Klubeck, "Effects of Seating Arrangements in Leaderless Group Discussions," *Journal of Abnormal and Social Psychology,* 47:724–727.

[5] Claude E. Shannon and Warren Weaver, *The Mathematical Theory of Communication* (Urbana: University of Illinois Press, 1949); and Robert G. Murdick and Joel E. Ross, *Information Systems for Modern Management,* 2d ed. (Englewood Cliffs, N.J.: Prentice-Hall, 1975), especially pp. 447 and 453–56.

[6] Joseph Luft, *Of Human Interaction* (Palo Alto, Calif.: National Press Books, 1969); and Jay Hall, "Communication Revisited," *California Management Review,* Spring 1973.

[7] For a taxonomy of feedback events, see David M. Herold and Martin M. Greller, "Feedback: The Definition of a Construct," *Academy of Management Journal,* March 1977.

[8] For a good concise discussion of disciplinary interviews, see O. Jeff Harris, Jr., *Managing People at Work* (Santa Barbara, Calif.: Wiley /Hamilton, 1976), chap. 14, "When Disciplinary Action Becomes Necessary."

When you have finished studying
MANAGERIAL LEADERSHIP
you should be able to:

1. Explain why leadership is essential for the effective management of human resources.
2. Describe how the influence system provides the broad setting within which leadership occurs.
3. Differentiate among power, authority, and leadership.
4. Compare and contrast several important theories of leadership.
5. Describe how the leadership system involves these three basic elements: the leader, the followers, and the situation.
6. Show how effective leadership is affected by such variables as the external environment, the task, and the organization.
7. Point out several important implications of a contingency leadership theory for human resources management.

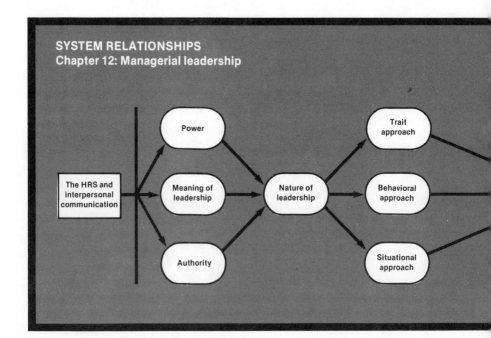

Leadership is essential for the effective management of human resources. An organization lacking in managerial leadership is destined to fail to meet its goals even if it possesses requisites for successful operation. From the systems view, leadership (1) provides "feedforward" control by shaping the nature and the quality of the inputs to the HRS and (2) determines the effectiveness of the system process. So vital is leadership to the organization that the organization will spend substantial amounts of money to search for leadership talent and to train managers in leadership skills.

In past years, it was assumed that leadership and management were synonymous. This is not necessarily so. Although an effective manager must be able to direct human resources

12

Managerial leadership

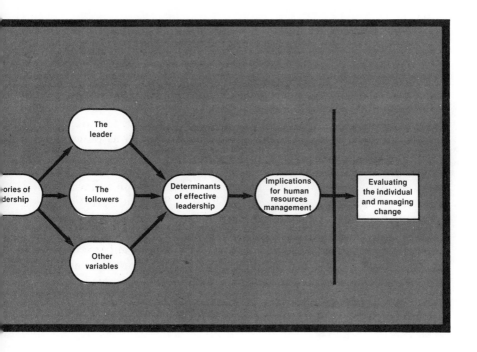

"How do you know the fault is in my 'leading'? Maybe the fault is in your 'following'!"

toward the organization's goals, a leader may not be a good overall manager. For example, although a charismatic leader may get his or her followers to work enthusiastically, there may be considerable inefficiency in organizational performance if the leader does a poor job in handling other managerial functions, such as planning. We shall also see that mere possession of a management title does not automatically imply leadership.

For decades, behavioral scientists and practitioners have studied leadership from a number of viewpoints. The end result has been many theories of leadership; some of these overlap, and others conflict. We shall see that no one behavioral theory of leadership is universally accepted. This chapter presents significant research findings that highlight both the theoretical and the practical aspects of leadership. Specifically, it discusses the nature of leadership, theories of leadership, leadership styles, and the determinants of effective leadership.

THE NATURE OF LEADERSHIP

Our discussion of leadership shall focus on leadership as a type of relationship among people. When we speak of leadership we are therefore discussing a situation in which a person influences the behavior of another person or a group of persons to produce some output. Influence, however, is exerted in many directions, for example, up and down the hierarchy in an organization and laterally in peer-group relationships.

The term *influence* is frequently used in connection with two other related terms: *power* and *authority.* Sometimes these terms are used interchangeably; at other times they are regarded as mutually exclusive concepts. Our approach will be to view influence as the all-inclusive concept which covers any means by which behavioral change is induced in individuals or groups. Such behavioral change may come through the use of power, authority, or leadership. We shall see that, as shown in Exhibit 12–1, power and/or

EXHIBIT 12–1
Power and authority underlie the ways leaders influence behavior

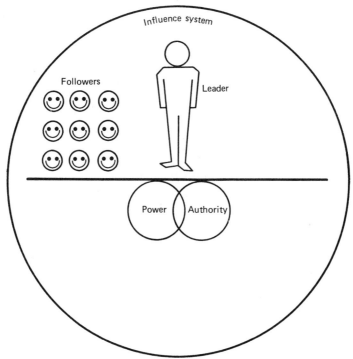

authority underlie the entire spectrum of the ways used to influence behavior. By examining these three concepts within the context of a human resource system, we will be better able to differentiate between the three and arrive at a more operational understanding of leadership.

Power

Power is the capacity to do or affect something, such as depriving an employee of some reward or inflicting some cost on an employee for nonperformance. There are two important characteristics of power: (1) it consists of an individual's capacity to influence another to do something that otherwise would not be done; (2) it is not an attribute of a given person.

To help in understanding the different uses and types of power, French and Raven designed a classification of power according to the type of power one person has over another person.[1] For French and Raven, the five bases of power are:

1. *Expert power.* One who can influence others on the basis of this type of power has some special skill, knowledge, or expertise which the follower accepts as greater than his or her own. An example would be the designer who follows the direction of the lead designer because the latter is well respected in his or her field.
2. *Referent power.* The individual who influences others on the basis of this power possesses certain traits that are admired by others. As a result of this admiration, the charismatic individual is able to influence the "admirers."
3. *Coercive power.* This is influence based upon fear. For example, an employee attempts to avoid some negative outcome (such as an official reprimand) that he perceives will occur from failure to meet the wishes of the superior.
4. *Reward power.* This is the opposite of coercive power. Here, the employee attempts to comply with the wishes of the superior. Compliance is perceived as leading to a monetary or psychological reward.
5. *Legitimate power.* This type of power is derived from the individual's position in the organizational hierarchy. Thus, workers follow orders because these "come from the boss", that is, they follow the directives of the manager because they "ought" to. We shall see that legitimate power is analogous to authority in the organization, whereby employees accept direction from the

manager because they accept the authority system when they choose to work for a firm.

Authority

Authority may be defined as the "legitimate" right to direct or influence the performance of others. Early writers on the subject of management perceived authority as the *right* and *power* to get performance from other persons. This view of authority held that the source of authority was at the top and flowed downward through the hierarchy. In more recent times, most behavioral scientists have held that authority stems from a willingness of followers to accept orders from others. For example, if an employee disagrees with an order given by the manager, the employee can circumvent that order in a number of ways without actually refusing to carry it out. Slowdowns, absenteeism, and sloppy work are just a few examples. This suggests that to be effective authority requires the consent of the employee.

We can see, therefore, that authority comes both from the top down and from the bottom up. Agreement must exist between leaders and followers. In a given situation, the authority and the *power* may reside with management, in which case the employee may be compelled to do as ordered. That is, the consequence of nonacceptance is so distasteful that the employee accepts the authority. In other situations, the employee may be in a position to exercise considerable influence over the way orders from above are followed and even over whether the orders are followed at all. Such might be the case where a powerful labor union exists.

Chester Barnard's "acceptance theory of authority" has helped to explain the limits placed on authority by the response of subordinates. According to this theory, there are orders "which are clearly unacceptable, that is, which certainly will not be obeyed; there is another group somewhat more or less on the neutral line . . . and a third group unquestionably acceptable."[2] In addition, there are many degrees of compliance to an order, ranging from enthusiasm to reluctant resignation.

The above discussion has at least two important applications for managing human resources. First, unless a directive falls within the "zone of acceptance," it will not be effective and the influence attempt fails. Second, formal authority is not absolute, and the subordinate's resistance to authority can show up in many ways short of direct refusal to comply with a request.

In summary, authority is a basis for influencing behavior in the human resource system. At the same time, it is not enough to ensure the desired response from subordinates. When greater reliance must be put on different means of influencing behavior, leadership becomes the important factor.

Leadership defined

Leadership has been defined in many ways by many different people. In general terms, leadership is the process of influencing others to act in order to accomplish certain goals. In more precise terms, leadership is "interpersonal influence, exercised in situations and directed, through the communication process, toward the attainment of a specified goal or goals."[3] Leadership always involves attempts by a person (leader) to influence the behavior of a follower (or followers) in a situation.

Effective leadership within the context of the human resource system may be defined as the influencing of individual and group behavior toward the optimal attainment of the enterprise's goals. The essence of leadership is found in the extent to which a manager can influence the behavior of peers or the actions of employees. If the manager can initiate action, induce others to engage in it, and direct the action toward goals, the manager is truly a leader.

We shall also extend our definition of the leader, as suggested by Katz and Kahn, to mean a person who exerts a significant amount of influence over and above that required to obtain routine compliance with the routine directives of an organization.[4] This is in sharp contrast to the bureaucrat who is concerned with doing routine activities efficiently. Accordingly, an effective leader is one who is able to go beyond expected role performance to realize more fully the potential of his or her position of influence. This chapter will also point out that effective leadership is a complex matter, involving the consideration of a wide variety of factors.

THEORIES OF LEADERSHIP

For as long as there have been leaders, people have been intrigued with the phenomenon of leadership. For centuries, writers and the general public believed that the great leaders were "great men," that such leaders were "born" and not "made" in terms of education and training.

An investigation of the numerous books dealing with leadership reveals that leadership has been heavily examined from the perspective of experience. Rather than scientific research, much of the literature is based on *how* or *why* someone was successful in "leading," with the writer suggesting that the panacea is to adopt that person's style of leadership.

During the past few decades, much time and money has been spent on attempts to determine the factors that make a leader effective. At this time, however, there are still no clear-cut guidelines for becoming a good leader. We do, however, have a number of useful theories which can help us understand leadership and become more effective leaders. We shall examine these theories under three general groupings: trait theories; the behavioral approach, or leadership styles; and situational theories.

Trait theories

A great deal of the early research was aimed at identifying those traits or characteristics which differentiated successful leaders from unsuccessful ones. Thus, most researchers tried to identify and measure intelligence, emotional, physical, and personal characteristics with little, if any, regard for situational factors, such as the nature of the group's task or the types of followers.

Reporting on a review of 12 leadership studies in the late 1940s, Stogdill found that intelligence, dependability, scholarship, responsibility, social participation, and socioeconomic status seemed to consistently differentiate leaders from nonleaders.[5] Another researcher during the same period, however, came to a different conclusion. He found that the "numerous studies of the personalities of leaders have failed to find any consistent pattern of traits which characterize leaders."[6]

Some interesting results were found in a later University of Minnesota study involving a sample of 468 managers from 13 companies. Leadership success was measured in terms of an effectiveness rating assigned by high-level managers. The more successful managers were found to be more intelligent and better educated and to demonstrate high motivation. They also preferred business-related activities and, in particular, preferred activities involving independent intensive thought with some risk. They were also more involved in activities and enjoyed relationships with people.[7] Although these results were fairly consistent, there were many exceptions. A number of successful managers did not have the characteristics mentioned, and the activity and people relationships were not found to exist in all 13 companies.

In more recent years, Ghiselli has found that the traits of supervisory ability, intelligence, and initiative related to success in managerial positions. He defined supervisory ability as the ability to direct the work of others, to organize and integrate activities so that the goal of the work group can be reached. Ghiselli claims that, of the three traits, supervisory ability and intelligence are the most important for managerial success.[8]

The astute reader will have recognized some limitations to the approach of the trait theories. For one thing, the theories overlook subordinates, who certainly must have an impact on the performance of the leader. Second, we do not know the relative importance of the desirable traits. Third, and most important, although we can see that successful leaders have certain traits, it is not clear whether the traits make the leader or whether the accomplishments of the leader make *the traits* noticeable.

Leadership styles: The behavioral approach

Another approach to understanding leadership concentrates on what the leader does and on how the leader behaves in conducting his or her leadership function. Trait theories explain leadership according to what the leader *is;* behavioral theories explain leadership according to what the leader *does.* Many behavioral theories advocate the effectiveness of one style of leadership over that of others. In this section we shall analyze several basic types of leadership behavior. We shall also see that individuals in leadership positions may follow contrasting approaches to leading people (see Exhibit 12–2).

Boss-centered and employee-centered leadership. Over the years, researchers examined two divergent styles of leading people, known as the boss-centered or autocratic style and the employee-centered or democratic style (see Exhibit 12–3). The difference between the two styles lies in the degree of authority used by the manager and in the amount of freedom available to the subordinate in making decisions. The leader actions shown on the right in Exhibit 12–3 characterize the manager who delegates decision-making authority.

The continuum in Exhibit 12–3 suggests that a number of leadership styles may be employed. According to this approach, the effective leader is one who can adapt his style to different kinds of situations. That is, he would delegate authority according to his own capabilities, his employees' abilities, and the goals to be accomplished.

The two-dimensional theory of leadership. As a result of extensive investigations undertaken by researchers at Ohio State Univer-

EXHIBIT 12–2
Contrasting approaches to leading

A Leader May Be:

Boss-centered (autocratic)	or	Employee-centered (democratic)
Production-oriented	or	Work-oriented
Task-oriented	or	Social-emotional
Initiating structure (planning, organizing, working through the organization structure)	or	Consideration (concern for the feelings of employees)
Directive	or	Permissive

sity, two dimensions of leadership behavior were identified. The two dimensions, initiating structure and consideration, were used to describe leader behavior in different types of organization settings.

Initiating structure, which is task oriented, emphasizes the needs of the organization. Consideration, which is more relationship oriented, stresses the needs of individual employees. Managers

EXHIBIT 12–3
The range of styles available to leaders

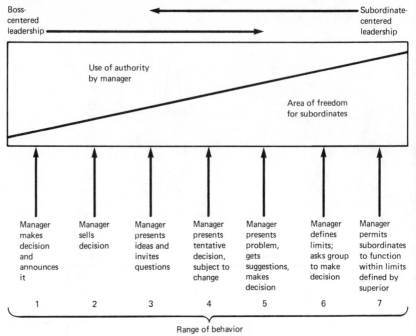

with high scores on the "initiating structure" dimension were those who structured their own role and those of their employees toward reaching preestablished goals. They were also active in planning work activities, scheduling work, and communicating pertinent information. High scores in "consideration" went to managers who developed a work atmosphere of mutual trust, respect for subordinates' ideas, and consideration of employees.

These two dimensions of leader behavior have been tested in several different studies with somewhat conflicting results. For example, foremen who were rated as most effective by their boss scored high on "initiating structure" and low on "consideration," whereas among managers in staff departments, this relationship was reversed. In general, it has been found that grievances, accidents, absenteeism, and turnover are likely to be higher among the employees of managers who are rated as high in "structure" and low in "consideration."

EXHIBIT 12–4
The managerial grid ®

Concern for people

High 9	1,9 Management Thoughtful attention to needs of people for satisfying relationships leads to a comfortable, friendly organization atmosphere and work tempo.						9,9 Management Work accomplishment is from committed people; interdependence through a "common stake" in organization purpose leads to relationships of trust and respect.
8							
7							
6							
5			5,5 Management Adequate organization performance is possible through balancing the necessity to get out work with maintaining morale of people at a satisfactory level.				
4							
3							
2							
1	1,1 Management Exertion of minimum effort to get required work done is appropriate to sustain organization membership.						9,1 Management Efficiency in operations results from arranging conditions of work in such a way that human elements interfere to a minimum degree.
Low							

1 Low   2   3   4   5   6   7   8   9 High
Concern for production

Source: The Managerial Grid® figure from *The Managerial Grid* by Robert R. Blake and Jane Srygley Mouton. Houston: Gulf Publishing Company, copyright © 1964, page 10. Reproduced by permission.

The managerial grid®.   The two dimensions of leadership have been set into a framework called the managerial grid, as seen in Exhibit 12–4. We can see that the two dimensions, "concern for production" and "concern for people," are similar to the "initiating structure" and "consideration" dimensions.

The grid helps to clarify how "concern for production" and "concern for people" are related and establishes a terminology for the styles of leadership found at five points on the grid, that is, at the four extremes and the center. The 1,1 style suggests little concern for either production or people, whereas the 9,1 style represents a strong emphasis on production and little concern for people. The 5,5 style suggests a compromise or middle-of-the-road attitude toward people and production. Finally, there is the 9,9, or ideal, style, in which the manager shows high concern for both people and production. This style is optimal in terms both of overall organizational results and the development of people.

While few leaders will ever achieve the 9,9 position on the grid, the effective manager will move toward it by improving whatever attitudes or skills are necessary to integrate employee needs and organizational needs with a team-building approach.

Situational theories

As more and more theories on leadership traits and styles developed, it became apparent that the traits or style required by an effective leader depended on the particular situation. Many of the situational theories suggest that the effective leader is one who is capable of adapting his or her style to deal with the situation at hand and the personality of the subordinates. Symbolically, the situational approach to leadership may be expressed as $L = f(LP, GP, S)$. That is, leadership is a function of the leader's personality, the group's personality, and the situation. This means that a successful leader in one situation, say, the dean of a business college, may not be as effective in another situation, for example, as the manager of a large industrial plant.

Fiedler's contingency theory. Based on many years of empirical research, Fred E. Fiedler developed the Leadership Contingency Model. He specified three important leadership dimensions as influencing the effectiveness of the leader:

1. *Leader-member relations.* This is the extent to which the leader "gets along" with the subordinates and the subordinates' degree of confidence in and loyalty to the leader.
2. *Task structure.* This refers to how routine and predictable the work group's task is. For example, well-defined jobs in which each aspect is spelled out have a high task structure.
3. *Position power.* This is the influence inherent in the position held by the leader. It includes the rewards and punishments associated with the position as well as the support the leader receives from his or her superiors and the overall organization.

The reader will notice that "leader-member relations" is much like the "consideration" (or relationship-oriented) concept previously discussed. Similarly, "task structure" is closely related to "initiating structure" (or task oriented). Fiedler, however, goes beyond these approaches by defining what characteristics of the situation are important in determining which leadership style is more effective. According to Fiedler's model, the situation variables determine the degree to which the leader is able to exert influence over his or her group. As seen in Exhibit 12–5, eight possible com-

EXHIBIT 12–5
Fiedler's perception of leadership styles

| Condition | Group situation | | | Leadership style correlating with productivity |
	Leader-member relations	Task structure	Position power	
1	Good	Structured	Strong	Directive
2	Good	Structured	Weak	Directive
3	Good	Unstructured	Strong	Directive
4	Good	Unstructured	Weak	Permissive
5	Moderately poor	Structured	Strong	Permissive
6	Moderately poor	Structured	Weak	No data
7	Moderately poor	Unstructured	Strong	No relationship found
8	Moderately poor	Unstructured	Weak	Directive

Source: F. Fiedler, *A Theory of Leadership Effectiveness* (New York: McGraw-Hill Book Co., 1967), p. 37.

binations of these three situation variables can occur. The most favorable situation for a leader is one in which he or she is well liked by the members, has a powerful position, and is directing a well-defined job. The most unfavorable situation is one in which the leader is disliked, has little position power, and directs workers in unstructured tasks—for example, an unpopular campaign manager leading a group of volunteers. Research evidence supports some, but not all, of Fiedler's predictions regarding the most effective approach for each of his eight conditions. In addition, other situational factors not considered by Fiedler may also affect performance.

The tridimensional leadership theory. Based on the work of William Reddin, Hersey and Blanchard developed a tridimensional leadership model. Like Fiedler, they recognize that a variety of styles may be effective or ineffective, depending upon the situation. While they also use the concepts of task and relationship, they differ by adding a third dimension—effectiveness. Exhibit 12–6 illustrates the ways in which the situation might affect the impact of various

EXHIBIT 12–6
The tridimensional model: Different combinations of relationship (considerate) style and task (structuring) style can be effective in some situations and not in others

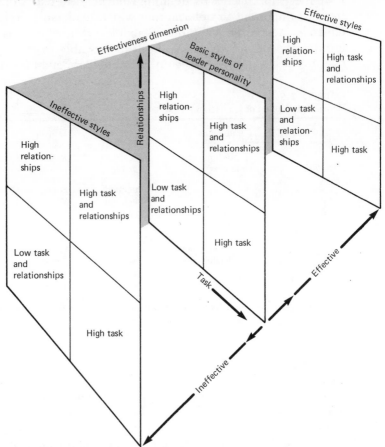

Source: Paul Hersey and Kenneth H. Blanchard, *Management of Organizational Behavior,* 2d ed., © 1972, pp. 84, 85. Reprinted by permission of Prentice-Hall, Inc., Englewood Cliffs, New Jersey.

leadership styles. For example, if applied in appropriate situations, high-task leadership may be perceived as providing the necessary structure. Conversely, if applied in inappropriate situations, it may be perceived as unpleasant or as indicating a lack of confidence in subordinates.

Although effectiveness appears to be an either/or situation in Exhibit 12–7, in reality it is a matter of degree. That is, any given

EXHIBIT 12–7
How the basic leader behavior styles are seen by others when they are effective and ineffective

Basic styles	Effective	Ineffective
High task	Often seen as knowing what he wants and as imposing his methods for accomplishing this without creating resentment	Often seen as having no confidence in others, unpleasant, and interested only in short-term output
High task and relationships	Often seen as a good motivator who sets high standards, treats everyone fairly, and prefers team management	Often seen as a person who tries to please everyone and therefore vacillates to avoid pressures in a situation
High relationships	Often seen as having implicit trust in people and as being primarily concerned with developing their talents	Often seen as primarily interested in harmony as "a good person," and as being unwilling to risk disruption of a relationship to accomplish a task
Low task and low relationships	Often seen as appropriately permitting his subordinates to decide how the work should be done and as playing only a minor part in their social interaction	Often seen as uninvolved and passive, as a "paper shuffler" who cares little about the task at hand or the people involved

Source: Paul Hersey and Kenneth H. Blanchard, *Management of Organizational Behavior*, 2d ed. (Englewood Cliffs, N.J.: Prentice-Hall, 1972), p. 84.

leadership style in a particular situation could fall somewhere on a continuum from very effective to very ineffective.

THE DETERMINANTS OF EFFECTIVE LEADERSHIP

We have seen that there is no universally accepted theory of leadership. What is considered to be effective leadership for one set of individuals, groups, and circumstances may be very ineffective leadership for other people or another situation. A contingency approach to leadership, therefore, appears to be a necessity. Within the contingency context, however, several useful generalizations can be made regarding effective leadership.

To begin with, we have seen earlier in this chapter that the influence system provides the broad setting within which leadership occurs. Power and/or authority underlie the entire spectrum of ways to influence behavior. It takes leadership, however, to obtain results which are "above the call of duty." The leadership system involves three basic elements—the leader, the follower, and the situation. In addition, leadership is affected by such important variables as the external environment, the task, and the organization.

The leader

Certain personality traits are helpful for effective managerial leadership, but are neither required nor sufficient. Above-average intelligence, initiative, and supervising ability are most important among traits identified. Effective leaders tend to be good listeners and to encourage meaningful two-way communication. They also typically exhibit a flexible personality as well as flexible leadership styles. That is, they are able to adjust to a particular individual or group in a particular situation and at a particular time. They recognize that effective leadership is a function of a complex combination of factors which are part of the broader human resource system. They know that effective leadership requires the integration of individual and organizational goals. This means that they have a high concern both for the objectives of the firm and for the goals of their followers. They believe that their followers' goals can be best attained through making contributions to the achievement of organizational objectives.

The personality of the leader will, of course, dictate a preference for a particular style of leadership. An aggressive, authoritarian manager would tend to be a more directive type of leader. On the other hand, a very democratic manager with a strong commitment to human values will probably use a more free-rein or participative leadership style. However, this does not mean that one style will always be more effective. For example, when subordinates prefer self-control and autonomy, the participative approach would be more effective. However, if the employees are dependent, avoid responsibility, and have a low commitment to group goals, a more directive style would be advisable.

The followers

We have seen that an appropriate leader is one who resembles the group in such things as values, attitudes, and personality. Although this does not mean that the characteristics of the leader must be the same as the characteristics of the group, it does suggest that a certain type of leader might not harmonize with a given group.

For example, if previous leaders of a group have been very directive and task oriented, this would have a major influence on that group's expectations regarding the type of leadership style for a new leader. A similar variable is the degree of homogeneity of the group. If the group is highly diverse and lacks common characteristics, a more directive leadership style might be more effective.

Exhibit 12–8 illustrates several group characteristics that influence the leader-follower relationship. Accordingly, situations with

EXHIBIT 12–8
Situational variables in leadership (leader and follower characteristics excluded)

	Group characteristics	
Quantity of interaction	Little	Extensive
Group unity	Conflict	Cooperation
Trust	Low	High
Membership	Heterogeneous	Homogeneous
Existing leadership roles	Directive	Free rein
Existing member roles	Obedience	Independence

Source: Adapted from Howard A. Carlisle, *Management: Concepts and Situations* (Chicago: Science Research Associates, 1976), pp. 505–6.

the characteristics identified on the left-hand side call for a more autocratic or directive leadership style, whereas situations with the characteristics identified on the right-hand side call for a participative or free-rein style.

Other variables

The tasks to be performed are an important determinant of effective leadership. Each job or position has specialized assignments and requirements associated with it. The fact that an individual has been an effective leader in one position does not mean that he will necessarily be effective in leading a group of workers performing different tasks. For example, the captain of the company's softball team may be very ineffective as sales manager. Similarly, we know that simple, repetitive tasks which provide few intrinsic rewards require a more directive leadership approach. On the other hand, a more supportive leader would be effective if the tasks to be accomplished were complex and intrinsically rewarding.

The characteristics of the organization are an equally important determinant of leadership effectiveness. Organizations may be private or public, large or small, highly structured or loosely organized, task centered or relationship oriented, economic oriented or social oriented. Too large a discrepancy between the personality of the leader and certain characteristics of the organization may result in ineffective leadership. A retired army general, for example, may be ineffective as a hospital administrator. The vice president of a large state university may be ineffective as the president of a small liberal arts college.

The characteristics of the environment external to the organization is another important determinant of leadership effectiveness. For example, a relatively authoritarian or directive leadership style may be effective in a business firm which is undergoing a financial crisis due to a severe business recession. Similarly, leadership must conform to the broader societal culture to be effective. This means, to take an extreme example, that a successful, democratic-oriented manager in the United States may be ineffective if he or she is transferred to a foreign country with a more authoritarian culture.

Implications of the contingency approach for human resources management

Howard M. Carlisle has pointed out several important implications of the contingency approach to leadership that are often contrary to current practices in human resources management:

> Organizations tend to restrict the criteria for selecting leaders to individuals who possess certain traits (aggressiveness, decisiveness, etc.) or who have demonstrated unusual technical expertise. However, these are only two factors that determine leadership effectiveness. This effectiveness is a function of many variables and conditions relating to the group and broader situational factors.
>
> No one leadership style should predominate throughout an organization. This sort of inbreeding is damaging, because different elements of the organization will display characteristics that call for different types of leaders.
>
> There is no one training approach to leadership because there is no one best style. Furthermore, attempts to change basic styles are often hazardous and always difficult. Leadership training should emphasize flexibility in behavior and skill in diagnosing situations.
>
> Selecting and capitalizing on effective leaders involves matching the skills, attitudes, values, and personality traits of the leader with the characteristics of members, organizational climate, and other variables. If a mismatch exists or changes are desired, rather than concentrating on changing the leader, more success will usually be achieved by modifying factors in the situation such as tasks, position power, organization structure, and other such variables.[9]

We wish to emphasize the last point by suggesting that, although leadership skills can be learned, it is difficult, if not nearly impossi-

ble, to change an individual's personality. As many human resources departments have found out, you cannot expect, for example, to change an autocratic, production-oriented foreman into a
participative, employee-oriented department manager. It may be
much more effective to adjust the situation than to attempt to recy-
cle the leader. Accordingly, the autocratic, production-oriented
foreman would be assigned to highly structured departments. The
participative, employee-oriented manager would be assigned to a
group whose work is less structured and more challenging. If possible, employees may be transferred to areas in which they would be
more compatible with the leader.

SUMMARY

Leadership is essential for the effective management of human
resources. A manager, however, is not necessarily a leader. The
essence of leadership is found in the extent to which a manager can
influence the behavior of peers or in the extent to which he or she
can influence the action of employees. If the manager can initiate
action, induce others to engage in it, and direct it toward goals, he or
she is a leader.

Effective leadership is a complex matter, involving consideration
of a wide variety of factors. Underlying the entire spectrum of ways
to influence behavior are power and authority. Both can be a basis
for influencing behavior in the human resource system. At the same
time, neither is sufficient to ensure effective cooperation. When
greater reliance must be placed on different ways of influencing
behavior, leadership becomes the important factor.

We examined some of the leading theories of leadership, under
the headings of traits, leadership styles, and the situation. We saw
that there is no universally accepted theory of leadership. A contingency approach to leadership is a necessity. Accordingly, effective
leadership must be viewed as a function of the leader, the followers,
and the situation. In addition, the external environment, the tasks to
be performed, and the organization must be considered. Within this
contingency context, however, several useful generalizations were
made regarding effective leadership. Finally, we examined the impact of a contingency approach to leadership on several current
practices in human resources management.

CASE: AN ADMINISTRATIVE ASSIGNMENT

You are a staff specialist in the Marketing Division of the XYZ
Consumer Products Corporation, which manufactures several re-

lated lines of health and beauty products. Each product is the sole responsibility of an individual product marketing department within the Marketing Division.

You report directly to the division director, and although your duties are quite varied, she has made it clear that you are expected to act primarily in a "troubleshooting" capacity. Although you have worked in the XYZ Corporation for ten years, you have been in the Marketing Division only one year and have recently been promoted to your present position of special assistant to the division director.

The division director has recently become quite concerned about the sales forecasts made by the various product marketing departments. The accuracy of these forecasts seems to have slipped badly over the last 18 months, leading to greatly increased costs in production, shipping, and order processing, as well as lost business and retailer complaints.

Although the accuracy of the forecasts varies across the departments, the problem is widespread. All of the product managers claim that they cannot improve their forecasts and that the decrease in accuracy is due to changing customer preferences or life-styles.

You have been assigned by your boss to get to the bottom of this difficulty and to eliminate it quickly. What will your strategy be (give specific actions and timetables)?

QUESTIONS AND PROBLEMS

1. Explain in what ways leadership is essential for the effective management of human resources.

2. Distinguish among the following concepts: (a) influence, (b) power, (c) authority, (d) leadership.

3. What is the relationship between leadership and power? What are the power bases upon which leaders may depend?

4. How does a leader differ from a manager or a bureaucrat?

5. Can anyone become a manager? Leader? Comment on the following statement: "Leaders are born, not made."

6. Identify three well-known leaders. Explain how they differ from nonleaders. Make a list of these leaders' common traits.

7. From your past experience, identify a leader who used an autocratic approach and one who used a democratic approach. List examples of follower behavior that was different for each approach. In which approach were you most productive?

8. What are some of the similarities (or differences) between Blake and Mouton's "managerial grid" and the Ohio State concepts of "initiating structure" and "consideration"?

9. Explain the central idea behind Fiedler's Leadership Contingency Model.
10. Based on your experiences, select three situations that required leadership. Prescribe (and justify) a leadership style for each situation.
11. What factors determine the particular style of leadership that should be used? Explain the effect of each factor upon the leadership style.
12. Outline several implications for the effective management of human resources that have been suggested by this chapter.

BIBLIOGRAPHY

Blake, Robert R., and Mouton, Jane S. *The Managerial Grid.* Houston: Gulf Publishing Co., 1964.

Bowers, David C., and Seashore, Stanley. "Predicting Organizational Effectiveness with a Four-Factor Theory of Leadership." *Administrative Science Quarterly,* April–June 1966.

Fiedler, Fred E. *A Theory of Leadership Effectiveness.* New York: McGraw-Hill Book Co., 1967.

Gibb, C. A. "Leadership," in Gardner Lindzey (ed.). *Handbook of Social Psychology.* Cambridge, Mass.: Addison-Wesley, 1964.

Green, Stephen G., et al. "Personality and Situational Effects on Leader Behavior," *Academy of Management Journal,* June 1976.

Hersey, Paul and Blanchard, Kenneth H. *Management of Organizational Behavior.* 2d ed. Englewood Cliffs, N.J.: Prentice-Hall, 1972.

Hunt, J. G. "Breakthrough in Leadership Research." *Personnel Administration,* September–October 1967.

Jones, John Paul. "Changing Patterns of Leadership." *Personnel,* March–April 1967.

Nash, A.N. *The Identification of Management Potential.* Dubuque, Iowa: William C. Brown, 1961.

Reddin, William J. "The 3-D Management Style Theory." *Training and Development Journal,* April 1967.

Rubin, Irwin M., and Goldman, Max. "An Open System Model of Leadership Performance." *Organizational Behavior and Human Performance,* May 1968.

Stinson, John E., and Johnson, Thomas W. "The Path-Goal Theory of Leadership: A Partial Test and Suggested Refinement." *Academy of Management Journal,* June 1975.

Stogdill, R. M., and Coons, A. E. (eds.). *Leader Behavior: Its Description and Measurement.* Columbus Bureau of Business Research, Ohio State University, 1957.

Tannenbaum, Robert, and Schmidt, Warren H. "How to Choose a Leadership Pattern." *Harvard Business Review,* March–April 1958.

Tannenbaum, Robert, et al. *Leadership and Organization: A Behavioral Science Approach.* New York: McGraw-Hill Book Co., 1961.

Van Fleet, James. *The 22 Biggest Mistakes Managers Make and How to Correct Them*. West Nyack, N.Y.: Parker Publishing, 1973.

Vroom, Victor, and Yetton, Philip. *Leadership and Decision Making*. Pittsburgh: University of Pittsburgh Press, 1973.

NOTES

[1] Adapted from J. R. C. French and Bertram Raven, "The Bases of Social Power," in Dorwin Cartwright and A. G. Zander (eds.), *Group Dynamics* (New York: Harper & Row, 1968), pp. 259–69.

[2] Chester I. Barnard, *The Function of the Executive* (Cambridge, Mass.: Harvard University Press, 1960), pp. 168–69.

[3] Robert Tannenbaum, Irving R. Weschler, and Fred Massarik, *Leadership and Organization: A Behavioral Science Approach* (New York: McGraw-Hill Book Co., 1961), p. 24.

[4] Daniel Katz and Robert L. Kahn, *The Social Psychology of Organizations* (New York: John Wiley & Sons, 1966), pp. 300–302.

[5] Ralph Stogdill, "Personal Factors Associated with Leadership," *Journal of Applied Psychology*, January 1948.

[6] C. Gibb, "Leadership," in G. Lindzey (ed.), *Handbook of Social Psychology*, vol. 2 (Reading, Mass.: Addison-Wesley, 1954).

[7] T. A. Mahoney, T. H. Jerdee, and A. N. Nash, "Predicting Managerial Effectiveness," *Personnel Psychology*, Summer 1960; and A. N. Nash, *The Identification of Management Potential* (Dubuque, Iowa: William C. Brown, 1961).

[8] Edwin C. Ghiselli, *Explorations in Managerial Talent* (Pacific Palisades, Calif.: Goodyear Publishing Co., 1971).

[9] Howard M. Carlisle, *Management: Concepts and Situations* (Chicago: Science Research Associates, 1976), pp. 514–15.

When you have completed studying
APPRAISING AND REQUITING FOR PERFORMANCE
you should be able to:

1. Describe several approaches to performance appraisal and indicate their advantages and disadvantages.
2. Custom-design a contingency-based approach to appraisal which best fits the needs and expectations of your own work group and organization.
3. Distinguish between hierarchical and participative approaches to appraisal and know when it is appropriate to use each.
4. Identify the theoretical and research basis for the MBO approach to performance appraisal.
5. Describe the desired relationship among performance, rewards, equity, and motivation.
6. Recognize the key motivational role of appraising and requiting for performance.
7. Implement a six-step process for appraising and requiting your subordinates.

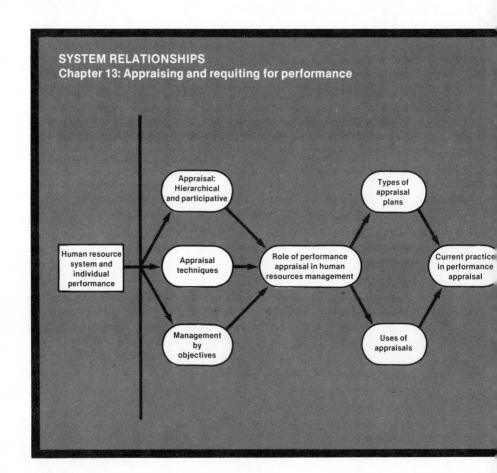

SYSTEM RELATIONSHIPS
Chapter 13: Appraising and requiting for performance

THE ROLE OF PERFORMANCE APPRAISAL

Appraising the performance of individuals and organizations is an inherent aspect of managing. Simply stated, it is impossible to make intelligent managerial decisions about individuals without measuring their performance in some manner. Hence, formal performance appraisal is as old as the concept of management and informal performance appraisal is as old as human history. Attempts at formal appraisal go

13

Appraising and requiting for performance

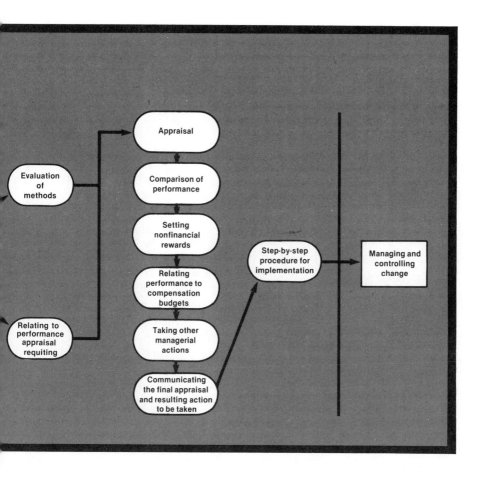

back many centuries, and in this century rigorous scientific studies of appraisal techniques and methods have a history of well over 50 years.

As indicated in Chapter 1, appraisal has a prominent role in human resources management. Appraisal and requiting (*requite* means to repay for a service, which involves rewarding good performance and penalizing nonperformance) are the two concluding steps of the human resources management process.

One of the outputs of the HRS (as shown in Exhibit 1–3) is individual performance. This chapter discusses the feedback of performance information, including appropriate rewards which affect the operation of the HRS.

Roles for line management and human resource specialists

The primary responsibility for appraising and requiting must be with line management. Top management must make the final policy decisions on the methods to be utilized, and managers at all levels must implement appraisal and requiting procedures. Nevertheless, there is often an important role for expert human resource staff advisers in keeping line management informed of new research findings and technology and in proposing alternative appraisal plans for the consideration of top management.

Uses of appraisals

Historically, appraisal has generally been used for administrative purposes, such as promotions and salary increases, and for individual development and motivation. Other frequent uses of appraisal information have been employee selection and placement, personnel planning, and organization planning. The relative emphasis on these uses of appraisal information has tended to shift over time. Early applications of performance appraisal in this country emphasized administrative uses of appraisal (that is, compensation and placement decisions). More recently, the emphasis has shifted toward a use of appraisal for both administrative and motivational purposes. This shift in emphasis has been a basic cause of the considerable controversy over the last 20 years concerning the most effective approaches and techniques for appraisal.

A recent study by Schuster and Kindall described the performance appraisal practices of *Fortune*'s 500 largest industrial corporations. Of the 403 companies responding to the survey, 316 (or 78 percent) reported the use of some type of formal performance appraisal plan. When asked about the uses to which appraisals were put, these 316 companies replied as shown in Exhibit 13–1. These

EXHIBIT 13–1
Uses of appraisals or ratings in 316 leading industrial corporations

	Responses	
Uses of appraisals	Number	Percent
Merit increases or bonuses	238	75.3
Counseling the ratee	278	88.0
Planning training or development for the ratee	270	85.4
Considering the ratee for promotion	266	84.2
Considering the retention or discharge of the ratee	184	58.2
Motivating the ratee to achieve higher levels of performance	269	85.1
Improving company planning	178	56.3
Other	28	8.9
Total companies reporting	316	

responses indicate that the vast majority of companies today attempt to use performance appraisals for both administrative and developmental-motivational purposes.[1]

Hierarchical versus participative approaches to appraisal

Until recently, almost all appraisal practices have been based on the implicit assumption that the superior is the person in the best position to judge the performance and behavior of his or her subordinates. Appraisals have thus emphasized the hierarchical relationship of superior and subordinate and have placed the superior in the position of "playing God" by passing judgment on the subordinate.

In this emphasis on passing judgment from above, the vast majority of the earlier appraisal approaches employed some form of trait rating. Basically, the trait rating approach requires the superior to evaluate, in some numerical or descriptive fashion, the subordinate's possession of certain personality and behavior traits. Two types of forms typically used for trait appraisal are shown in Exhibits 13–2 and 13–3.

As can be seen, trait appraisals often bear a striking resemblance to segments of grammar school report cards. In the 1960s, social science research revealed that this reliance on judgments from above may reduce the effectiveness of the appraisal process in achieving its motivational and developmental goals. For example, the work of Rensis Likert and others at the Social Science Research Center has shown that hierarchical control may lead to lower motivation and may restrict rather than encourage individual development. In contrast, these researchers assert that participative, supportive management tends to foster higher motivation and to encourage the development and personal growth of the employee.

EXHIBIT 13–2
Trait appraisal form

```
Rate the employee in the following traits, using this scale: 3—Excellent
                                                            2—Acceptable
                                                            1—Needs development
                                                            0—Not observed

Appearance                  _____    Ability to learn              _____
Self-confidence             _____    Accuracy                      _____
Ability to express self     _____    Meets deadlines               _____
Alertness                   _____    Health                        _____
Ambition                    _____    Enthusiasm                    _____
Initiative                  _____    Attitude and acceptance of
Energy                      _____       responsibility             _____
Knowledge of department     _____    Use of time                   _____
Contacts with superiors     _____    Organizes work to get a job
                 peers      _____       done                       _____
                 customers  _____    Independence                  _____
                                       Adaptability                  _____
                                       Maturity                      _____

                            Overall Evaluation

All factors considered, my overall evaluation of this employee is (circle one):

              1.  Outstanding
              2.  A good employee who should do well
              3.  A sound employee
              4.  An adequate but limited employee
              5.  Only just satisfactory

If reviewed, employee's reaction or comments:




Reviewed with employee by: _____  Date: _____
```

Research findings indicate that over the past several years a trend away from traditional trait-oriented performance appraisal and toward a more positive motivation-oriented approach has been developing in the field of human resources management. The origin of this new approach lies in the writings of commentators such as Peter Drucker and Douglas McGregor, who have suggested that a participative, motivation-oriented approach to appraisal should lead to higher performance levels than does the traditional trait-oriented approach.

The question of whether there might be such a conflict between hierarchical appraisal and motivation, however, was raised early in the history of performance appraisal. In 1926 Arthur Kornhauser presented the classical arguments in favor of conventional, numerical rating scales but also set forth a program for testing the usefulness of rating scales. To an amazing degree, he anticipated the later criticism of Likert, McGregor, and others. Kornhauser pointed out that the arguments in favor of rating scales were based on opinion and that scientific research would be required to determine whether psychological factors existed that would limit the usefulness of such ratings.[2] The effect of research by Likert, by Kay, Meyer, and French, and by Meyer and Walker has been to show that such psychological limiting factors do exist.[3]

The development of performance appraisal techniques

Changes in the work environment have also stimulated shifts in emphasis in performance appraisal. According to Whisler and Harper, the following changes have had a significant impact:

1. Shifts in the occupational structure toward higher skills.
2. The development of automation.
3. The increasing size of organizations.
4. Unionization.
5. The increase of staff activities.
6. Greater specialization in the roles of organization members, combined with increasing technical education.
7. Changes in the philosophy of management from scientific management to human relations, and then to quantitative decision techniques and overall corporate planning.[4]

In addition to the above, the movement toward greater decentralization and the creation of profit centers have had a major influence on performance appraisal practices.

The impact of these changes has been to reorient the emphasis of performance appraisal away from hierarchical judgment directed only toward controlling wages and salaries. The emphasis has recently shifted toward participation to stimulate motivation and development as well.

Essays and checklists. Some of the earliest formal appraisal plans used in this country employed open-ended essay appraisals or some form of adjective checklist. Because these approaches lacked objectivity and precision, the attention paid to psychometrics in the early 1920s led to the development of graphic rating scales.

Rating scales. These scales employed a list of traits, but in addition the rater was required to indicate his or her judgment of the amount of each trait possessed by the ratee by marking a point on a graphic scale (or continuum). The major technical flaw of this ap-

EXHIBIT 13–3
Employee performance review worksheet

Employee name	Department	Rated by	Date

Instructions:

1. Check the block beside each factor which contains the closest description of employee **with regard to that factor only.**
2. Enter rating points (0, 1, 2, 3) for each factor in the far right column.
3. Add the points in each section and divide the results by the figure shown. Round fractions as follows: 0.5–1.4 = 1; 1.5–2.4 = 2; 2.5–3 = 3.
4. Enter the "rating" on the rating card.

Quality

Factors	Poor—0	Fair—1	Good—2	Excellent—3	Rating points
Appearance of work	Work is generally sloppy and incomplete. Employee has little or no regard for appearance. Work must be redone often. ____	Some work is sloppy and incomplete. Employee tries to do acceptable work, but rework is required often enough to cause repeated reminders. ____	Work is generally neat and complete. Employee has pride in work. Rework seldom required. ____	Work is exceptionally neat, well organized, and complete. Employee has exceptional pride in work. Rework rarely required. ____	
Accuracy of work	Continuously makes errors. Makes no effort to check own work. Work must be checked 100 percent by others. ____	Frequently makes errors. Checks own work fairly often. Work must be checked 50 percent of the time by others. ____	Occasionally makes errors. Almost always checks own work for accuracy. Only spot checking required by others. ____	Rarely makes errors. Always checks own work. Little or no checking required by others. ____	
Supervision required	Constant direction required with little effect. ____	High degree of direction required to maintain level of quality. ____	Needs occasional direction to maintain a high level of quality. ____	Rarely requires direction to maintain outstanding level of quality. ____	

	Recommendations for improvement		Total points	
____ Has improved			Divided by	3
____ Little or no change			Rating	
____ Has regressed				

Quantity

Factors	Poor—0	Fair—1	Good—2	Excellent—3	Rating points
Volume	Volume of work is below acceptable level. ___	Volume of work meets minimal acceptable level. ___	Volume of work meets that of average worker. ___	Volume is exceptional, exceeding average requirements. ___	
Utilization of time	Frequently wastes time between assignments. ___	Occasionally wastes working time. ___	Wastes very little of available working time. ___	Utilizes working time to the fullest. ___	
Work pace	Work not organized; rarely meets deadlines. ___	Work is partially organized; frequently misses deadlines. ___	Work is well organized; occasionally misses deadlines. ___	Work is exceptionally well organized; rarely misses deadlines. ___	
Supervision required	Constant direction required to obtain quantity produced. ___	Frequent direction required to obtain quantity produced. ___	Occasional direction required to obtain quantity produced. ___	Rarely requires direction to obtain quantity produced. ___	

___ Has improved
___ Little or no change
___ Has regressed

Recommendations for improvement

Total points	
Divided by	4
Rating	

EXHIBIT 13–4
Essay appraisal form

Name _____   Position _____
Date of employment_____   Years in present position _____
Office _____   Previous position_____
Reports to_____

Performance, results, and methods—give production figures (be specific).

1. What has this person accomplished since the last appraisal? (Consider quantity
    and quality of work.)

2. How does this person go about getting his/her work done?

3. How well does this person work with people?

4. List outstanding personal qualifications or characteristics that help or hinder
    this person.

5. Recommended action to improve performance in present position.

The performance and personal qualification sections of this appraisal have been
discussed with the employee by:

Name _____   Position _____   Date_____
Approved _____

---

proach was that because of the "halo effect," most ratings tended to
cluster at either the high end or the low end of the scale.

The forced-distribution technique.   Since the failure to obtain a
distribution of ratings was seen as the primary flaw of appraisals,
attention shifted toward the development of methods to force a
normal distribution of appraisals around the average or mean performance of all members of the work group. This led to the
development of the forced-distribution technique. Although the
forced-distribution technique solved the technical distribution
problems, it foundered on the logical objection of raters that many
work groups did not reflect a normal distribution of individual
performance.

Further refinements.   Further technical refinements led to such
approaches as ranking (rating the members of a work group from
best to worst in the order of their relative performance), paired-
comparison (a refinement of the ranking method which involves the
systematic comparison of each member of a group with each of his

EXHIBIT 13–5
Graphic rating scale

Name _____

Division/Department_____   Present position _____

Instructions: Read carefully each of the factor descriptions. Judge the employee on
the basis of the work now being done. Consider each factor separately; do not let
your rating of one factor influence your rating of another factor. Rate each factor
by placing an x mark at the appropriate point along the line.

Ability to learn: Consider how quickly employee learns (ability
to retain instruction and information).
Outstanding _____ Poor

Initiative: Consider ingenuity (self-reliance and resourcefulness;
ability to know what needs to be done).
Outstanding _____ Poor

Job attitude: Consider the interest and enthusiasm shown.
Outstanding _____ Poor

Knowledge of job: Consider the knowledge of job and related
work.
Outstanding _____ Poor

Industry: Consider responsibility to duties (ability to apply time
and energy).
Outstanding _____ Poor

Quality of work: Consider accuracy of work regardless of volume
(ability to perform work efficiently).
Outstanding _____ Poor

Cooperation: Consider ability and willingness to work in har-
mony with and for others.
Outstanding _____ Poor

Personality: Consider ability to get along with co-workers (personal conduct, courtesy, tact, friendliness).
Outstanding _____ Poor

Appearance: Consider neatness, personal dress, and personal
habits.
Outstanding _____ Poor

or her peers in the group to produce the overall ranking), forced-
choice (a series of choices between equally positive and equally
negative descriptive phrases), and critical-incident (the systematic
recording, as they occur, of actual instances of significantly good or
significantly poor performance) techniques.

The critical-incident technique. Although these later approaches have been relatively successful in overcoming some of the
technical obstacles to appraisal, none of them has been widely
adopted, primarily because of various practical difficulties. For
example, the critical-incident technique has been shown to be relatively objective and reliable, but it is also prohibitively expensive
for many appraisal situations.

EXHIBIT 13–6
Forced distribution

Key:
1. Outstanding, exceptionally high level (top 5 percent)
2. Superior, exceeds the expected level (next 10 percent)
3. At the expected level (middle 70 percent)
4. Below the expected level (next 10 percent)
5. At a marginal level (bottom 5 percent)

I. Accountabilities (as listed in approved job description)	Performance

II. Work traits		Performance
Attitude:	Willingness to adjust to changes	
	Degree of interest and enthusiasm	
Communication:	Ability to convey ideas and plans	
	Written	
	Oral	
Cooperation:	Ability to work with and through others, including:	
	Supervisor	
	Peers	
	Subordinates	
	Government officials, educators, bankers, etc. . .	
Delegation:	Ability to effectively assign work to others	
Development:	Ability to develop attitudes, knowledge, and skills in:	
	Self	
	Subordinates	
Organization:	Ability to effectively organize time and effort on work assignments	
Forward planning:	Ability to plan ahead in order to meet changing needs	
Judgment:	Ability to arrive consistently at sound decisions . .	
Volume of work:	Ability to produce expected results in a given time	

III. Current overall performance

Having rated each accountability and work trait, please indicate what the employee's overall performance is in his or her present position.

1. _____Performs at an outstanding level (5 percent could be here)
2. _____Performs at a superior level (10 percent could be here)
3. _____Performs at the expected level (70 percent should be here)
4. _____Performs at below the expected level (10 percent could be here)
5. _____Performs at a marginal level (5 percent could be here)

EXHIBIT 13–7
Ranking scale

Consider all of your employees in terms of their total performance. Then select the one you would regard as having the best total performance. Put his or her name in Column I, below, on the first line, numbered 1. Next pick out the person having the worst total performance. Put his or her name at the bottom of Column II, on the line numbered 20. Now, from the *remaining* names, select the one having the best total performance. Put his or her name in the first column on line 2. Keep up this process until all names have been placed in the scale.

Column I (Best)	Column II (Worst)
1. _____	11. _____
2. _____	12. _____
3. _____	13. _____
4. _____	14. _____
5. _____	15. _____
6. _____	16. _____
7. _____	17. _____
8. _____	18. _____
9. _____	19. _____
10. _____	20. _____

EXHIBIT 13–8
Forced-choice method

Out of each set of five statements, check the one which best describes the employee and the one which least describes the employee.

	Best	Least
1. Would be very difficult to replace	_____	_____
Very valuable in a new operation	_____	_____
Alert to new opportunities for the company	_____	_____
Good for routine supervisory job	_____	_____
Tends to delegate things which will not reflect credit on him/her	_____	_____
2. Not willing to make decisions unless he/she has very complete information	_____	_____
Lets difficulties get him/her down	_____	_____
Makes snap judgments about people	_____	_____
Tries to run things his/her own way	_____	_____
Has not demonstrated up to now that he/she has the ability to progress further	_____	_____

EXHIBIT 13–9
Typical samples of critical incidents

Negative incidents			Positive incidents		
Date	Item	Incident	Date	Item	Incident
2/14	M	Customer complaint on rudeness	4/3	B	Covering duties of ill co-worker

Item M refers to Public Relations responsibility. Customer complained that employee was rude and abusive when customer criticized his handling of transaction.

Item B refers to Cooperation. Employee voluntarily took over critical duties of an ill co-worker for period of three days in addition to performing his regular duties. As a result, department was able to maintain its performance standards.

Profit performance measurement. Largely because of the many difficulties encountered with such rating programs, in the 1950s researchers and management experts began to devise a number of novel approaches as alternatives to conventional ratings. One of the important alternatives suggested was profit performance measurement. Under this approach, which was designed to evaluate the performance of profit center managers, a manager was to be judged almost solely on the basis of the profitability of the organization for which he or she was responsible. Further expanding the logic and application of this approach led to management by objectives.

Management by objectives

Peter Drucker proposed a new approach to performance appraisal, which he called "Management by Objectives and Self-Control." Drucker explains the concept as follows:

> Some of the most effective managers I know . . . have each of their subordinates write a "manager's letter" twice a year. In this letter to the superior, each manager first defines the objectives of his superior's job and of his own job as he sees them. He then sets down the performance standards which he believes are being applied to him. Next, he lists the things he must do himself to attain these goals—and the things within his own unit he considers the major obstacles. He lists the things his superior and the company do to help him and the things that hamper him. Finally, he outlines what he proposes to do during the next year to reach his goals. If his superior accepts this statement, the "manager's letter" becomes the charter under which the manager operates. The greatest advantage of Management by Objectives is perhaps that it makes it possible for a manager to control his own performance. Self-control means stronger motivation: a desire to do the best rather than just enough to get by. It means higher performance goals and broader vision. Even if Management by Objectives were

not necessary to give the enterprise the unity of direction and effort of a management team, it would be necessary to make possible management by self-control.[5]

Another major contributor to the development of contemporary performance appraisal practice was Douglas McGregor.[6] McGregor was concerned with the fact that most appraisal systems involved ratings of traits and personal qualities which he felt were highly unreliable. Besides, the use of such ratings produced two main difficulties:

1. The manager was uncomfortable about using them and resisted making appraisals.
2. It had a damaging effect on the motivation and development of the subordinate.

McGregor's criticism of trait rating was solidly supported by previous research in the social sciences. For example, Ronald Taft, a psychologist, had concluded from a survey of the extensive literature of research into human judgment that few individuals are qualified to judge the traits and aptitudes of others. Taft had found that ability to judge is a personality trait and that individuals vary widely in their ability to judge the traits and aptitudes of others.[7]

McGregor felt that Peter Drucker's concept of management by objectives offered an unusually promising framework within which to seek a solution to this problem, and he proposed a new approach to performance appraisal based upon Drucker's concept.

Building upon the logic of both Drucker and McGregor, Kindall and Gatza proposed a detailed plan for implementing a five-step performance appraisal program:

1. The individual discusses his job description with his superior, and they agree on the content of his job and relative importance of his major duties—the things he is paid to do and is accountable for.
2. The individual establishes performance targets for each of his responsibilities for the forthcoming period.
3. The individual meets with the superior to discuss the individual's target program.
4. Checkpoints are established for the evaluation of his progress; ways of measuring progress are selected.
5. The superior and subordinate meet at the end of the period to discuss the results of the subordinate's effort to meet the targets he had previously established.[8]

A typical set of forms used for the management by objectives approach to appraisal is shown in Exhibit 13–10. The forms used by

EXHIBIT 13–10
A.   **Review summary of objectives**

---

1.   The following items represent significant accomplishments (discuss as appropriate):

_____

2.   The following major items were not accomplished as planned (give reasons):

_____

3.   The following problems have been identified:

_____

4.   Additional comments:

_____

Review by _____   Date_____
Employee _____

                        Progress Review of Objectives

                                             Date _____

Objectives	Progress to Date	Problems	Suggested Action to Be Taken

_____

            (check one)   Manager's copy _____
                                         Employee's copy _____

EXHIBIT 13–10 *(continued)*
B. Bonus percents by grade and performance

Summary appraisal	Salary grade							
	10	11	12	13	14	15	16	17
Unusually high level of accomplishment on all targets. □ →	20–22.5%	33–37.5%	46–52.5%	65–75%	65–75%	78–90%	91–105%	104–120%
More than reasonable. Results against all targets were slightly better than normal expectations. □ →	17–19%	28–32%	39–45%	55–64%	55–64%	66–77%	77–90%	88–103%
Reasonable, normal achievement for managerial personnel. Did well on all the more important targets. □ →	14–16%	23–27%	32–38%	45–54%	45–54%	54–65%	63–76%	72–87%
Adequate performance against targets. However, achievement on the most important target could have been better. □ →	11–13%	18–22%	25–31%	35–44%	35–44%	42–53%	49–62%	56–71%
Results against several important targets could have been better. □ →	7.5–10%	12.5–17%	17.5–24%	25–34%	25–34%	30–41%	35–48%	40–55%
Failed to achieve minimum acceptable level of performance on all important targets. □ →	0	0	0	0	0	0	0	0

Bonus percent recommended: _____

different companies for this approach vary considerably, and some companies prefer to use only a blank sheet of paper. It will also be noted that the forms in Exhibit 13–10 emphasize an explicit relationship between the appraisal of performance against objectives and the determination of incentive bonuses. This direct tie between compensation and the accomplishment of objectives is not uncommon; however, some companies make the tie less explicit and prefer to use appraisal data only as an input to a separate compensation decision process.

A series of articles by Meyer, Kay, and French in the mid-1960s reported on General Electric's "Work Planning and Review" program, which was a major effort to apply the ideas of Drucker and

McGregor. The program included controlled research to compare the results of conventional appraisal with those of a management by objectives approach. The latter approach proved to be clearly superior for motivating and developing subordinates.[9]

Meyer, Kay, and French also concluded that the developmental and compensation uses of appraisal need to be clearly separated in time. More recently, Cummings and Schwab have emphasized the importance of clearly separating the evaluative and developmental purposes of appraisal.[10] They suggest that three types of appraisal systems be distinguished: (1) those designed to enhance development and growth; (2) those designed to maintain performance at acceptable levels; and (3) those designed to improve unacceptable performance. They conclude that all three systems are likely to be operating simultaneously in a particular organization and that a single individual will be appraised by more than one system in the course of his or her career.

CURRENT PRACTICE IN PERFORMANCE APPRAISAL

What appraisal techniques are being used at present by major American companies? Which employees are having their performance appraised? What are the primary current uses of appraisals? And most important, what effects do the answers to the last two questions have on the type of appraisal technique that is used in a particular company? Schuster and Kindall's recent research study, cited previously, provides some answers to these questions.

Types of plans

Exhibit 13–11 shows the types of appraisal plans used by the companies surveyed. Somewhat surprisingly, 106 companies (or 34.9 percent) indicated that they used only a management by objectives type of appraisal plan, and 75 companies (24.7 percent) indicated that they used a management by objectives type of plan for a part of the work force in combination with another type of appraisal plan. Thus, 181 companies (or 59.6 percent of those surveyed) said that management by objectives served as the basis of performance appraisal for at least a part of their work force. A total of 29 percent of the companies used some form of trait rating, and this was the only alternative besides MBO indicated by a significant number of companies. It seems clear that MBO is today by far the most common basis for performance appraisal in the largest industrial companies.

Of the companies having a management by objectives plan, 59.4 percent include all salaried employees in the plan, 17.9 percent

EXHIBIT 13–11
Appraisal plans used in 304 leading industrial corporations*

	Responses	
Type of plan used	Number	Percent
Number or descriptive rating of only one general item, "How well does the ratee perform his job?"	16	5.3%
Numerical or graphic trait ratings	27	8.9
Trait checklist	61	20.1
Forced-choice system of rating	11	3.6
Management by objectives	106	34.9
Other	8	2.6
Combination of management by objectives and another plan	75	24.7
Total	304	100.0%

* Twelve of the 316 respondents did not specify type of plan used.

include hourly employees, 70.8 percent include nonsupervisory salaried employees, 89.6 percent include first-level supervisors, and 97.2 percent include managers and executives. Thus, where MBO programs exist, they are almost always applied to managers and executives and they are applied with diminishing frequency to other groups at lower levels of the organization. The higher individuals are in the organization structure, the more likely is their performance to be appraised through use of a management by objectives approach.

There appears to be a clear difference in viewpoint regarding the primary goal of performance appraisal between companies which use management by objectives and companies which use other approaches. As seen in Exhibit 13–12, companies having an MBO approach to appraisal saw the principal purpose of the plan to be motivation of employees. Significantly, MBO is the only appraisal approach whose primary use is said to be motivation. Only 20 percent of the companies having a combination of MBO and some other appraisal approach said that motivation was the primary goal of their appraisal program; most of those companies used appraisals primarily to determine merit increases or bonuses. Companies having most other types of appraisal programs saw the principal use of the programs to be either in counseling or in determining merit increases and bonuses.

EVALUATION OF METHODS IN TERMS OF HUMAN RESOURCES MANAGEMENT OBJECTIVES

The tendency of current practice is to adopt a management by objectives approach to performance appraisal when higher level

EXHIBIT 13–12
Primary use of various types of appraisal plans

					Primary use of appraisals					
Type of plan	Not answered	Merit increases or bonuses	Counseling	Planning training or development	Promotion	Retention and discharge	Motivation	Improve company planning	Other	Total (rounded)
Overall performance	25.0%	50.0%	0.0%	12.5%	0.0%	0.0%	6.3%	6.3%	0.0%	100%
Traits:										
Numerical........	14.8	25.9	29.6	11.1	3.7	0.0	14.8	0.0	0.0	100
Descriptive	21.3	21.3	13.1	14.8	4.9	0.0	16.4	4.9	3.3	100
Forced-choice	45.5	9.1	0.0	9.1	9.1	18.2	9.1	0.0	0.0	100
MBO only	18.9	14.2	1.9	20.8	0.9	0.0	31.1	9.4	2.8	100
Other	25.0	25.0	0.0	12.5	0.0	0.0	25.0	12.5	0.0	100
MBO plus another	29.3	22.7	4.0	13.3	1.3	0.0	20.0	5.3	4.0	100
Total	39.0%	17.4%	5.5%	12.2%	2.0%	0.5%	16.6%	5.0%	2.0%	100%

managerial, professional, and technical personnel are to be appraised or when the making of compensation decisions is seen as only one purpose of appraisal along with development or motivation. When compensation decisions are seen as the primary aim of performance appraisal, or when less skilled blue-collar and clerical employees are primarily concerned, companies are more likely to adopt some form of trait appraisal.

The question of how far down in an organization the management by objectives approach should be applied is probably one that can best be answered by a particular company on the basis of the requirements and constraints of the organization; the content of jobs at different levels; the skills, attitudes, and expectations of individuals at different levels; and the management climate and traditions of the organization. No blanket conclusion on this issue can be made from research data, although companies have most often applied MBO to top-level management and to professional workers. They have been progressively less inclined to apply MBO at each successively lower level in the organization. There is theoretical support for this decision, in terms of job content and the skills and expectations of individuals; however, there has been no specific research finding that MBO is less successful at lower levels than at upper levels of organization.

The management climate

An important factor, often overlooked, is the management climate of the organization. To be effective, the type of appraisal plan adopted must be seen by all concerned as consistent with the basic assumptions and style of management prevalent in the organization. Management by objectives as an approach to appraisal works best within a climate which emphasizes participation and a high degree of mutual trust and confidence. Where management by direction and control is emphasized, and where there is less confidence in employees, more hierarchical appraisal methods (such as trait ratings or forced-choice techniques) are likely to be seen as more consistent with the overall management climate and may well be more effective.

Length of time in the job

Another important factor determining the most effective type of appraisal in a specific situation is the length of time the individual has been in the job. The appraisal technique that is most effective in measuring the performance of someone experienced in a position may be quite different from the technique that is most effective in appraising the performance of a beginner.

For reasons that will be obvious, MBO is most effective when the individual being measured has already mastered the basic requirements of the job. The appraisal of experienced persons focuses on the degree to which their performance goes beyond the basic job requirements and reflects their expansion of the job to fit their own potential. To the extent that the focus of appraisal is on measuring the individual's progress along the learning curve toward basic mastery of the job, more directive and hierarchical appraisal techniques, (such as trait ratings, ratings of performance characteristics, and ratings of overall performance) will perhaps be more appropriate. Among the factors that should be weighed in determining the most suitable appraisal approach are the incumbent's length of time on the job, age, previous experience, and evaluated potential.

As has been indicated, there are a number of factors which may be given consideration in an attempt to determine the most effective appraisal approach for a particular situation. And information about what other companies have done in specific situations can perhaps provide some guidance. So many interrelated factors must be considered, however, that prescriptive formulas are not feasible. Therefore, appraisal is an art rather than a science. In the last analysis, good judgment, assisted by knowledge of the practice and experience of other companies, remains the best guide to determining the appraisal technique that should be employed.

RELATING PERFORMANCE APPRAISAL TO REQUITING

The term *requiting* has been chosen by us to refer to the responsibilities of the individual manager for taking managerial action that will properly recognize and reward the performance of subordinates. The term is used to emphasize the central importance of the concept of equity (discussed in Chapter 7).

The managerial actions which may be taken to recognize and reward performance include praise (private and public), written commendation, published commendation, increased autonomy, change in job title, status symbols such as office space or furnishings, performance bonuses, salary increases, promotions in grade, increase in responsibilities, and various forms of supplementary compensation. In light of the contingency approach to rewards suggested in Chapter 7, however, it is most important to recognize the responsibility of the manager to match the rewards both with performance and with the perceptions and needs of the individual. Depending on the manager's analysis of the individual employee, the manager will wish to emphasize nonfinancial rewards, financial rewards, or a mixture of the two in order to "requite" each employee in such a way that (a) the employee will perceive the reward to relate equitably to his or her effort and accomplishment, and (b) the employee will perceive the reward to be the most attractive and motivating among the equal alternatives from which the manager selected.

In Chapter 7 it was emphasized that modern motivation theory (both reinforcement theory and expectancy-instrumentality theory) emphasizes the importance of a direct tie between performance and reward. For the reward to have the desired motivational impact, it is imperative that it be directly related to performance and that it be clearly perceived as such.[11] It was also pointed out in Chapter 7 that in order to be effective motivationally, rewards must be perceived by the recipients to be equitable in light of their inputs and outcomes (that is, results).

No matter how accurate, the appraisal is likely to be worthless unless it is followed by appropriate requiting action. Conversely, requiting can be effective only to the extent that it is based on an accurate appraisal. This underscores again the fact that performance evaluations must be both reliable and valid if they are to serve a useful motivational purpose.

Although the requiting responsibilities of the manager remain constant regardless of the approach to appraisal used, a considerable body of evidence indicates that, all things being equal, the management by objectives approach to appraisal is likely to result both in higher validity of the evaluation itself and in an increased perception of equity on the part of subordinates.[12] These would appear to be powerful arguments indeed in favor of adopting a management by objectives approach to appraisal whenever the situation makes such an approach feasible.

A recent research study by W. H. Mobley lends additional support to the conclusion that a direct relationship between the management by objectives process and the financial rewards system is desirable. The results are summarized by Mobley as follows:

> Due to the wide divergence of opinion on the value of linking MBO and merit compensation activities, 625 middle to top level managers were asked to indicate their perceptions of the relationship. The results of the study tend to reinforce the position that the arguments favoring linkage outweigh those against it.

EXHIBIT 13–13. Tying rewards to performance

Job description	Job evaluation	Establishing performance objectives	Performance appraisal	Effective communication	Requiting
Provides understanding of the objectives and content of a position	Determination of the salary level of the position in terms of the company salary structure	Determining objectives by which performance will later be evaluated	Determination of the degree to which the individual is achieving objectives	Giving each employee full understanding of the reward system	Recognition Increased responsibilities Performance bonus

Position guide
Broad function
Responsibilities
Relationships
Authority
Measure of accountability

Position evaluation plan

Description of factors and factor degrees

Position analysis (for individual position)

Supplementary information and data regarding the position required for adequate evaluation

Objectives

Objectives

Performance appraisal

Mutual understanding of
Work assignment
Evaluation of work
Performance
Appraisal
Basis of compensation
Promotion opportunities

Personal discussions

Salary range

Salary $

1 2 3 4 5 6 7 8 etc.
Position level

Paycheck

Promotion
Fringes
Perquisites

To the extent that pay is a valued reward, linking it, along with other desirable rewards to performance, should enhance motivation and performance. Evidence supporting this proposition has been summarized by Lawler. [see Chapter 7]

One argument for establishing a link between the MBO process and merit compensation, Mobley points out, is that "it permits establishment of the performance-reward contingency suggested by reinforcement and expectancy-instrumentality theories of motivation and performance."[13]

STEP-BY-STEP PROCEDURE FOR THE IMPLEMENTATION OF A PERFORMANCE APPRAISAL SYSTEM

The preceding part of this chapter has been conceptual in nature. We have described in principle an approach to appraising and requiting for performance that is consistent both with the systems approach for managing human resources taken throughout this book and with what is known about human motivation. Although a "cookbook" recipe is inappropriate for a contingency-based approach to managing, there is practical utility in providing some step-by-step guidelines for the manager. We are therefore detailing a six-step process through which each manager may discharge responsibilities for appraising and requiting performance. The steps in this process are as follows:

1. Appraisal.
2. Comparison of performance.
3. Setting nonfinancial rewards.
4. Relating performance to compensation budgets.
5. Taking other managerial actions.
6. Communicating the final appraisal and the action to be taken.

Appraisal

As indicated previously, a number of very different approaches to the appraisal process may be taken. Regardless of the specific format used (whether trait rating, critical incident, MBO, or something in between), however, and regardless of whether the basic approach is hierarchical or participative, two elements are essential to an effective appraisal.

The *first* element is that some of the data for the appraisal must come from the subordinate. Clearly, this will be especially true for MBO-based appraisals, in which a great deal of the data will come from subordinates. Even in the most hierarchical type of appraisal, however, it is important that the subordinate be given an opportunity to provide data on his or her performance. This is so because the subordinate may often be aware of performance elements not known to the superior. A minimal perception of equity by the subordinate requires that the superior take all relevant data into account in arriving at the appraisal.

The *second* essential element of the appraisal is a face-to-face conference at which the subordinate has an opportunity to present his perception of his performance, to comment on the superior's preliminary appraisal, and to supply additional data which he feels has been omitted in the superior's appraisal. Again, the purpose of the face-to-face meeting is both to increase the validity of the appraisal and to increase the employee's perception of equity.

Comparison of performance

The next step in the appraising and requiting process is for the manager to compare the individual subordinate's performance with accepted standards of performance. If an MBO process is being used, this step involves comparing achievement with objectives. If other procedures are being used, it involves comparing the individual's performance with the job description. How does the individual's performance compare with the performance expected of a typical employee at this individual's position in grade? If the particular individual is currently at the midpoint in his or her salary grade, is the performance about what would be expected at that stage, is it far in excess of what would be expected, or is it about what one would expect from a beginner rather than a seasoned employee.

Finally, the manager will want to compare on a person-to-person basis individuals who are in the same or very similar jobs and/or individuals who are at approximately the same salary grade and position within grade even though their specific duties may vary. This step will be absolutely essential in situations where the rewards available to the manager are inadequate. Even in the rare circumstances in which ample rewards are available, the manager will want to make appropriate person-to-person comparisons in order to ensure that all individuals are being rewarded equitably in relation to their relative performance (that is, inputs and contribution).

Setting nonfinancial rewards

Having completed the preliminary appraisal, the fact-finding conference with the subordinate, and the comparison of the subordinate's performance to the subordinate's position description and position in grade and to the performance of other employees, the manager must decide on the appropriate reward mix for each subordinate.

The manager's first step in making that decision is to consider what nonfinancial rewards will be equitable in terms of each individual's performance, motivating in terms of each individual's needs, and feasible given the traditions and managerial practices of the particular organization. The many different types of nonfinancial rewards available to the manager have been discussed in Chapter 7. They include such things as recognition, increased responsibility, greater freedom and autonomy, and praise.

We recommend that nonfinancial rewards be considered first simply in order to ensure that these rewards (which are often neglected) are given proper consideration. Also, nonfinancial rewards often prove to be less expensive options.

Relating performance to compensation budgets

In ideal circumstances the manager will have sufficient resources to award each subordinate whatever increase in compensation appears to be appropriate in order to equitably reward the subordinate for performance in light of the subordinate's job description, position, and salary grade, and of the performance of other individuals. In such situations the manager has a relatively simple job. The manager merely determines the appropriate increase in compensation (and/or the appropriate performance bonus) for each individual. These increases and bonuses are then added together to determine the total compensation increases and bonus expenditures for the year.

Of course, the organization may have policy guidelines and limitations which determine the maximum amounts that may be awarded. The organization may set an absolute limit (such as 20 percent) as the largest salary increase that may be awarded, regardless of circumstances. Or, there may be guidelines which say that individuals may receive increases of up to 20 percent if they are below the midpoint of a salary grade but that increases for individuals above the midpoint of the salary grade are limited to 10 percent. Whatever the policy constraints are, the manager will naturally have to abide by them. In our example, however, there are no budget limits on the total amount that the manager may spend on salary increases and/or bonuses for all subordinates.

Although ideal in theory, this degree of freedom and flexibility rarely occurs in practice. It is far more likely that in specific situations managers will be constrained not only by policy limits but also by a compensation budget which sets absolute limits on the total amount which they may award to all subordinates. Often this amount will be less (sometimes far less) than their appraisal and comparison has led them to believe would be appropriate if "equitable" salary action were taken for each individual subordinate. In this fairly common set of circumstances, managers are then called upon to take the additional step of determining how to allocate an inadequate compensation budget to requite the performance of their subordinates.

Although seldom emphasized in texts on appraisal and compensation, this step is perhaps the most difficult one for the manager. The previous steps in this process, though technically demanding, can lead to what the manager perceives as the "right" solution. Unfortunately, at this step of relating performance to the budget for financial rewards the manager for the first time is required to aim for something less than an optimum solution. Now, the manager must recognize that all subordinates cannot receive the treatment which he or she has determined to be equitable; instead, *the manager must aim at minimizing inequity*.

There are no magic formulas for handling this dilemma, although, clearly, person-to-person comparisons are now called for in earnest. In addition to making even more searching person-to-person comparisons than may have been necessary before, the manager will also want to rethink the opportunities for nonfinancial rewards. After this has been done, a variety of techniques may be considered, including the following:

1. Treating everyone equally by reducing all "equitable" compensation actions by the same percentage.
2. Giving preference to the individuals whose performance is most outstanding and reducing the increases of the individuals whose performance is marginally satisfactory.
3. Awarding all subordinates some minimum percentage increase, then allocating increases above that minimum on a person-to-person comparison basis.
4. Some combination of these approaches.

Although it has not been possible to suggest any perfect solutions to this dilemma, it should be pointed out that performing this step with extreme care and precision is critical if employees are to perceive their compensation to be equitable. It is bad enough that due to extraneous constraints beyond the employees' control they will not receive the rewards that their manager determined to be appropriate in relation to their performance. If employees also feel that they are receiving an inequitable share of the inadequate rewards, motivationally this would be the last straw.

Taking other managerial actions

After deciding on an allocation of both nonfinancial and financial rewards, managers should turn their attention to such other actions as promotion, demotion, transfer, and training. These activities have been discussed elsewhere in this book, but are referred to here to emphasize the fact that they should flow directly from and be directly related to the results of performance appraisal. Moreover, they are a part of the total requiting process, and as such they should be a part of what is reported to the individual employee as being the reward for his or her contributions.

Communicating the final appraisal and the action to be taken

The final step in the appraising and requiting process is communication of the final appraisal and action taken by the manager to each individual subordinate. It is not sufficient for the manager to casually comment to the subordinate that, following the fact-finding conference, adjustments were made in the preliminary appraisal. And it is clearly not sufficient that the subordinate find out about the compensation action taken when he or she receives the next paycheck or a bonus check.

Whether the news is good or bad, it is absolutely essential from the standpoint of the subordinate's perception of equity and motivation that the manager communicate clearly in a private, quiet conference and in detail the action which he or she has taken and the specific reasons for it. The whole complex and demanding process of appraising and requiting for performance comes to fruition at this step. Depending on how well the communication job is done, the opportunity to create a sense of equity and to strengthen motivation is either realized or is lost. It is not too strong to say that all of the other steps in the appraising and requiting process lead up to this.

At this step more than at any other the manager has the opportunity to emphasize the direct tie between individual performance and the rewards received. Here (and only here) can the payoff to the manager and the organization occur in terms of motivation and perception of equity.

For all of these reasons, managers should consider this conference with each individual subordinate to be one of their most important responsibilities. This mental set will lead managers to provide the appropriate amount of time, to make sure that the subordinate is in a receptive mood, to prepare themselves very carefully for the conference, and to listen carefully and respond alertly to what is said.

SUMMARY

This chapter has emphasized a contingency-based approach to appraisal which recognizes the usefulness of a broad spectrum of appraisal techniques, ranging from hierarchical trait appraisals to highly participative management by objectives approaches. Which approach is best will depend on the particular situation, including the subordinates (their experiences, expectations, and abilities), the manager and his or her capabilities, and the traditions, climate, style, and policies of the organization. Each of the different forms of appraisal has unique advantages and drawbacks.

Although no one approach to appraisal is clearly best for all situations, an impressive accumulation of research evidence indicates that, for purposes of perceived equity and motivation, the management by objectives approach has a great deal of potential. This is because the MBO approach emphasizes a direct tie between performance and reward.

The critical importance of appraising and requiting for performance as the final step in the human resources management process was emphasized throughout the chapter. From the standpoint of motivating future organizational performance, the whole process of managing human resources effectively comes to fruition at the step of appraising and requiting for performance. If this step is performed badly, all the preceding steps in the process lose their value.

Finally, a six-step implementation process provided specific guidelines that would enable individual managers to discharge their responsibilities in appraising and requiting for performance: (1) appraisal, (2) comparison of performance, (3) setting nonfinancial rewards, (4) relating performance to compensation (5) taking other managerial actions, and (6) communicating the final appraisal and the action to be taken.

CASE: A MATTER OF MONEY

How would you utilize a salary increase budget of $5,000 (7.5 percent of total payroll) to reward the employees in Table A? You do not have to spend the full budget, but under no circumstances may you exceed it. In your opinion, all of these individuals were properly paid in relationship to their relative performance and seniority one year (12 months) ago, when you last adjusted their compensation. The rate of inflation last year was 6.5 percent.

TABLE A
A matter of money

Name	Present salary	Title	Salary grade	Years in department	Performance	Personal circumstances
John Mason	$15,000	Analyst	6	5	Acceptable. Has missed several important deadlines, but this may not have been his fault.	Married. Large family dependent on him as sole support.
G. W. Jones	$13,000	Analyst	6	2	Outstanding. Sometimes a bit "pushy" in making requests and suggestions about the department.	Single. No dependents. Has no pressing need for money. Reported to lead a rather "wild" life outside the office.
Jane Boston	$12,000	Junior analyst	5	8	Consistently an excellent performer, though she has not been assigned the full range of duties of an analyst. Dependable. Often initiates improvements in work methods.	Married. Husband is a successful architect. Children in high school.
Ralph Schmidt	$16,000	Senior analyst	7	15	Acceptable. Few original contributions recently. Seems to be a "plodder." Content to get by with minimum performance and participation.	Married. Financially pressed because he has two children in college (one plans to go on to medical school).
Hillary Johnson	$11,000	Junior analyst	5	6	Acceptable volume, but continues to make costly mistakes. Has repeatedly been warned about this over the last years.	Single. Has a dependent mother who is chronically ill.

QUESTIONS AND PROBLEMS

1. "Employees should be concerned only with their own compensation. What others are paid is none of their business." Discuss.

2. Describe and distinguish among the following approaches to appraisal:

    a. Adjective checklist.   d. Forced choice.
    b. Rating scale.   e. Critical incident.
    c. Forced distribution.   f. MBO.

3. Discuss the advantages and disadvantages of each of the above approaches. Describe situations in which each approach might be particularly appropriate.

4. Outline a performance appraisal plan for a small public accounting firm consisting of 3 supervising partners, 15 staff accountants, and 6 clerical workers.

5. What is meant by the term *equity* within the context of performance appraisal and compensation?

6. What is the relationship among rewards, equity, and motivation?

7. Discuss the role which appraising and requiting for performance plays within the overall process of managing human resources.

8. Discuss the six-step implementation process for appraising and requiting. Comment meaningfully on the efficacy of each step and the hoped-for end result.

BIBLIOGRAPHY

Beer, M., and Gerry, G. J. "Pay Systems Preferences and Their Correlates." Paper presented at American Psychological Association Convention, San Francisco, August 1968.

Belcher, David W. *Compensation Administration*. Englewood Cliffs, N.J.: Prentice-Hall, 1974.

Campbell, John P., et al. "The Development and Evaluation of Behaviorally Based Rating Scales." *Journal of Applied Psychology,* February 1973.

Carroll, S. J., Jr., and Tosi, H. L., Jr. "Goal Characteristics and Personality Factors in a Management by Objectives Program." *Administrative Science Quarterly,* September 1970.

Cummings, Larry L., and Scott, W. E., Jr. (eds.). *Readings in Organizational Behavior and Human Performance*. Homewood, Ill.: Richard D. Irwin, 1969.

Cummings, Larry L., and Schwab, Donald P. *Performance in Organizations: Determinants and Appraisal*. Glenview, Ill.: Scott, Foresman and Company, 1974.

Downey, H. K., Helbriezel, D. and Slocum, J. W., Jr. "Congruence between Individual Needs, Organizational Climate, Job Satisfaction, and Performance." *Academy of Management Journal,* March 1975.

Drucker, Peter R. *Management: Its Tasks, Responsibilities, Challenges.* New York: Harper & Row, 1974.

Drucker, Peter R. *Managing for Results.* New York: Harper & Row, 1964.

Drucker, Peter R. *The Practice of Management.* New York: Harper & Row, 1954.

Dunnette, Marvin D. (ed.). *Handbook of Industrial and Organizational Psychology.* Chicago: Rand McNally, 1976.

Evans, W. A. "Pay for Performance—Fact or Fable?" *Personnel Journal,* September 1970.

Finn, R. H., and Sang, M. Lee. "Salary Equity: Its Determination, Analysis, and Correlates." *Journal of Applied Psychology,* August 1972.

Flanagan, J. C. "The Critical Incident Technique." *Psychological Bulletin,* July 1954.

Flanagan, J. C., and Burns, R. K. "The Employee Performance Record: A New Appraisal and Development Tool." *Harvard Business Review,* September–October 1955.

Ford, R. N. *Motivation through the Work Itself.* New York: American Management Association, 1969.

Foulkes, F. *Creating More Meaningful Work.* New York: Macmillan Co., 1969.

Foundation for Research on Human Behavior. *Performance Appraisals—Effects on Employees and Their Behavior.* Ann Arbor, Mich.: Foundation for Research on Human Behavior, 1963.

French, J. R. P., Kay, E., and Meyer, H. H. "Participation and the Appraisal System." *Human Relations,* February 1966.

French, W. *The Personnel Management Process.* 3d ed. Boston: Houghton Mifflin, 1974.

Freyd, M. "The Graphic Rating Scale." *Journal of Educational Psychology,* February 1923.

Galbraith, J. R., and Cummings, L. L. "An Empirical Investigation of the Motivational Determinants of Task Performance: Interactive Effects between Instrumentality-Valence and Motivation-Ability. *Organizational Behavior and Human Performance,* August 1967.

Ghiselli, E. E. *Explorations in Managerial Talent.* Pacific Palisades, Calif.: Goodyear Publishing Co., Winter 1971.

Ghiselli, E. E. "Some Motivational Factors in the Success of Managers." *Personnel Psychology,* 1968.

Giles, B. A., and Barrett, G. V. "The Utility of Merit Increases." *Journal of Applied Psychology,* April 1971.

Greene, C. N. "Causal Connections among Managers' Merit Pay, Job Satisfaction, and Performance." *Journal of Applied Psychology,* August 1973.

Greiner, J. M. "Employee Incentives in Local Government: Monetary Performance Rewards." *Labor-Management Relations Service Newsletter,* National League of Cities, Fall 1973.

Hackman, J. R., and Lawler, E. E., III. "Employee Reactions to Job Characteristics." *Journal of Applied Psychology,* June 1971.

Hinrichs, J. R. "Correlates of Employee Evaluations of Pay Increases." *Journal of Applied Psychology*, December 1969.

Hollmann, Robert W. "Supportive Organizational Climate and Managerial Assessment of MBO Effectiveness." *Academy of Management Journal*, December 1976.

Howell, M. A., and Newman, S. H. "The Development of a Supervisory Appraisal Form for the Federal Merit Promotion Program." *Public Personnel Review*, July 1971.

Hughes, C. L. *Goal Setting*. New York: American Management Association, 1965.

Hulin, C. L. "Sources of Variation in Job and Life Satisfaction: The Role of Community and Job-Related Variables." *Journal of Applied Psychology*, August 1969.

Jacobs, L., and Saccardi, V. "The Relative Importance and Interaction of Past, Present, and Future Performance on Raises." Unpublished graduate paper, University of Maryland, Spring 1973.

Jacques, E. *Equitable Payment*. New York: John Wiley & Sons, 1961.

Japlonsky, S. F., and De Vries, D. L. "Operant Conditioning Principles Extrapolated to the Theory of Management." *Organizational Behavior and Human Performance*, April 1972.

Kay, E., Meyer, H. H., and French, J. R. P. "Effects of Threat on a Performance Appraisal Interview." *Journal of Applied Psychology*, October 1965.

Kellogg M. S. *What to Do about Performance Appraisal*. New York: American Management Association, 1965.

Kindall, A. F., and Gatza, J. "Positive Program for Performance Appraisal." *Harvard Business Review*, November–December 1963.

Kirkpatrick, Donald L. "MBO and Salary Administration." *Training and Development Journal*, September 1973.

Kline, S. M., and Maher, J. R. "Education Level and Satisfaction with Pay." *Personnel Psychology*, Summer 1966.

Kohn, M. L., and Schooler, C. "Class, Occupation, and Orientation." *American Sociological Review*, October 1969.

Kornhauser, Arthur W. "What Are Rating Scales Good For?" *Journal of Personnel Research*, September 1926.

Lawler, E. E., III. "Managers' Attitudes toward How Their Pay Is and Should Be Determined." *Journal of Applied Psychology*, August 1966.

Lawler, E. E., III. *Pay and Organization Effectiveness: A Psychological View*. New York: McGraw-Hill Book Co., 1971.

Lawler, E. E., III, and Suttle, J. L. "Expectancy Theory and Job Behavior." *Organizational Behavior and Human Performance*, June 1973.

Lawsche, C. H., Kephart, N. C., and McCormick, E. J. "The Paired-Comparison Technique for Rating Performance of Industrial Employees." *Journal of Applied Psychology*, February 1949.

Locke, E. A. "The Nature and Consequences of Job Satisfaction." In M. Dunnette (ed.). *Handbook of Industrial and Organizational Psychology.* Chicago: Rand McNally, 1976.

Locke, E. A. "Satisfiers and Dissatisfiers among White Collar and Blue Collar Employees." *Journal of Applied Psychology,* 1973.

Locke, E. A. "Toward a Theory of Task Motivation and Incentives." *Organizational Behavior and Human Performance,* May 1968.

Luthans, F., and Kreitner, R. "Organizational Behavior Modification." *Public Personnel Management,* June 1973.

McGregor, D. "An Uneasy Look at Performance Appraisal." *Harvard Business Review,* May–June 1957.

Meyer, H. "Cobwebs in Plans to Pay Creative People." *Compensation Review,* 1971.

Meyer, H., Kay, E., and French, J. R. P. "Split Roles in Performance Appraisal." *Harvard Business Review,* January–February 1965.

Meyer, H. H., and Walker, W. B. "A Study of Factors Relating to the Effectiveness of a Performance Appraisal Program." *Personnel Psychology,* Autumn 1961.

Miner, J. B. *The Management Process.* New York: Macmillan Co., 1973.

Miner, J. B., and Dachler, H. P. "Personnel Attitudes and Motivation." *Annual Review of Psychology,* 1973.

Miner, J. B., and Nash, Allan N. *Personnel and Labor Relations: An Evolutionary Approach.* New York: Macmillan Co., 1973.

Mobley, W. H. "The Link between MBO and Merit Compensation." *Personnel Journal,* June 1974.

Norrgard, D. L. "The Public Pay Plan: Some New Approaches." *Public Personnel Review,* April 1971.

Opshal, R. L., and Dunnette, M. D. "The Role of Financial Compensation in Industrial Motivation." *Psychological Bulletin,* August 1966.

Patten, Thomas H. "Linking Financial Reports to Employee Performance: The Role of OD and MBO." *Human Resources Management,* Winter 1976.

Penzer, W. M. "Educational Level and Satisfaction with Pay: An Attempted Replication." *Personnel Psychology,* Summer 1969.

Porter, L. W., and Lawler, E. E., III. *Managerial Attitudes and Performance.* Homewood, Ill.: Irwin-Dorsey, 1968.

Pritchard, R. D. "Equity Theory: A Review and Critique." *Organizational Behavior and Human Performance,* May 1969.

Pritchard, R. D., Dunnette, M. D., and Jorgenson, D. O. "Effects of Perception of Equity and Inequity on Worker Performance and Satisfaction." *Journal of Applied Psychology,* February 1972.

Redling, Edward T. "The Determinants of Management Compensation." *Personnel Journal,* August 1972.

Richardson, M. W. "Forced Choice Performance Records." *Personnel,* November 1949.

Roche, W. J., and MacKinnon, J. K. "Motivating People with Meaningful Work." *Harvard Business Review*, May–June 1970.

Schuster, Fred, and Kindall, Alva F. "Management by Objectives—Where We Stand." *Human Resources Management*, Spring 1974.

Schuster, J. R., Clark, B., and Rogers, M. "Testing Portions of the Porter and Lawler Model regarding the Motivational Role of Pay." *Journal of Applied Psychology*, June 1971.

Slocum, John W., Jr. "Motivation in Managerial Levels: Relationship of Need Satisfaction to Job Performance." *Journal of Applied Psychology*, August 1971.

Smith, P. C., Kendall, L. M., and Hulin, C. L. *The Measure of Satisfaction in Work and Retirement*. Chicago: Rand McNally, 1969.

Smith, R. A. "Achieving Flexibility in Compensation Administration." *Compensation Review*, 1970.

Starcevich, Matt M. "Job Factor Importance for Job Satisfaction and Dissatisfaction across Different Occupational Levels." *Journal of Applied Psychology*, December 1972.

Taft, Ronald. "The Ability to Judge People." *Psychological Bulletin*, January 1955.

Thompson, P. A., and Dalton, G. W. "Performance Appraisal: Managers Beware." *Harvard Business Review*, January–February 1970.

Wernimont, P. F., and Fitzpatrick, S. "The Meaning of Money." *Journal of Applied Psychology*, June 1972.

Wood, Donald A. "Background Characteristics and Work Values Distinguishing Satisfaction Levels among Engineers." *Journal of Applied Psychology*, December 1971.

Yukl, G., Wexley, K. N., and Seymore, J. D. "Effectiveness of Pay Incentives under Variable Ratio and Continuous Reinforcement Schedules." *Journal of Applied Psychology*, February 1972.

NOTES

[1] Fred Schuster and Alva F. Kindall, "Management by Objectives—Where We Stand," *Human Resource Management*, Spring 1974.

[2] Arthur Kornhauser, "What Are Rating Scales Good For?" *Journal of Personnel Research*, September 1926.

[3] Rensis Likert, *New Patterns of Management* (New York: McGraw-Hill Book Co., 1961); E. Kay, H. H. Meyer, and J. R. P. French, "Effects of Threat in a Performance Appraisal Interview," *Journal of Applied Psychology*, October 1965; Herbert Meyer and W. B. Walker, "A Study of Factors Relating to the Effectiveness of a Performance Appraisal Program," *Personnel Psychology*, Autumn 1961; H. K. Downey, D. Helbriezel, and J. W. Slocum, Jr., "Congruence between Individual Needs, Organizational Climate, Job Satisfaction, and Performance," *Academy of Management Journal*, March 1975); and Marvin D. Dunnette (ed.), *Handbook of Industrial and Organizational Psychology* (Chicago: Rand McNally, 1976).

[4] Thomas Whisler and S. F. Harper, *Performance Appraisal Research and Practice* (New York: Holt, Rinehart and Winston, 1962).

[5] Peter F. Drucker, *Management: Its Tasks, Responsibilities, Challenges* (New York: Harper & Row, 1974), pp. 438–39.

[6] Douglas McGregor, "An Uneasy Look at Performance Appraisal," *Harvard Business Review*, May–June 1957.

[7] Ronald Taft, "The Ability to Judge People," *Psychological Bulletin*, January 1955; and Robert W. Hollmann, "Supportive Organizational Climate and Managerial Assessment of MBO Effectiveness," *Academy of Management Journal*, December 1976.

[8] Alva F. Kindall and J. Gatza, "Positive Program for Performance Appraisal," *Harvard Business Review*, November–December 1963. Copyright © 1963 by the President and Fellows of Harvard College; all rights reserved.

[9] H. H. Meyer, E. Kay, and J. R. P. French, "Split Roles in Performance Appraisal," *Harvard Business Review*, January–February 1965.

[10] Larry L. Cummings and Donald P. Schwab, *Performance in Organizations: Determinants and Appraisal* (Glenview, Ill.: Scott, Foresman and Company, 1973).

[11] Thomas H. Patten, "Linking Financial Reports to Employee Performance: The Roles of OD and MBO," *Human Resource Management*, Winter 1976; Dale E. Melin, "Compensation by Objectives," unpublished paper, 1975; and Donald L. Kirkpatrick, "MBO and Salary Administration," *Training and Development Journal*, September 1973.

[12] David W. Belcher, *Compensation Administration* (Englewood Cliffs, N.J.: Prentice-Hall, 1974).

[13] W. H. Mobley, "The Link between MBO and Merit Compensation," *Personnel Journal*, June 1974.

When you have finished studying
MANAGING BY OBJECTIVES
you should be able to:

1. Show why MBO represents a process for tying together all of a manager's responsibilities rather than an *additional* task.
2. Differentiate among the planning, implementation, and control aspects of MBO.
3. Describe how MBO evolved as a management process designed to help line managers apply behavioral science knowledge about employee motivation and performance.
4. Show how MBO fits into the total system concept of human resources management.
5. Write achievable performance objectives which are demanding, specific, and measurable and have target dates.
6. Implement a complete six-step MBO process to plan, motivate, and control the performance of your subordinates.

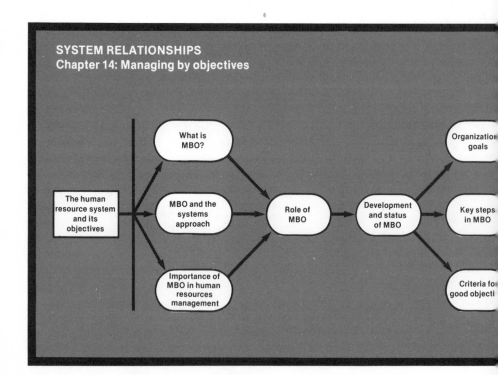

SYSTEM RELATIONSHIPS
Chapter 14: Managing by objectives

14

Managing by objectives

MBO has been referred to throughout the previous chapters of this book, especially the chapters dealing with planning, appraisal, and compensation. Why has MBO received unparalleled attention among practicing managers, and why does it have such a prominent role in this text on human resources management?

What is MBO?

Unlike many management "programs" which become temporary fads, MBO is not a gimmick or just another set of forms which is added to the work

Management by Objectives is probably the most pervasive management idea of the last quarter century, and certainly the most widely touted.[1]
Stephen Singular

It's still a spreading concept, but the important thing is not that it is spreading but that it is not being done well.[2]
Harold Koontz

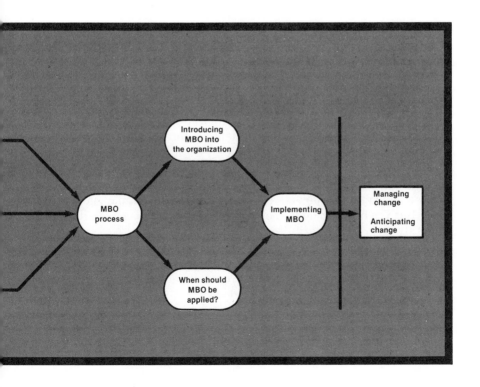

load of a manager. Rather, MBO represents a fundamental approach to managing that permeates the entire organization and covers the full range of each manager's responsibilities. MBO represents a systems approach which helps the manager to integrate his or her performance into a common set of organizational objectives.

At the same time, the whole process of managing by objectives is totally consistent with our knowledge of human behavior and with the managerial practices recommended throughout this book for the motivation of human resources.

MBO thus represents a way to tie everything together—both the traditional practices for effectively managing physical resources and our most modern practices for effectively managing human resources. As was recently stated by one management observer, "MBO is not just another pretty face on the management scene. It is a technique based on real planning and thought and is, most agree, the best theoretical management program ever conceived."[3]

Although (as mentioned in the previous chapter) management by objectives provides a very effective basis for performance appraisal and compensation, its functions are far broader. MBO also figured prominently in our discussion of long-range planning. In addition, MBO is relevant for implementation and control as well as planning.

MBO and the systems approach

In short, it is our view that MBO is the ideal management tool for making operational the total system approach to the effective management of human resources that has been emphasized throughout this book. For this reason we delayed the detailed treatment of the management by objectives process until the more specific responsibilities of human resources management had been introduced. Also for this reason we now devote an entire chapter to the process of managing by objectives—not as an additional management duty, but as a broad-gauged tool which can assist managers in discharging all of their responsibilities.

Just why MBO should be so widely acclaimed as a management tool and why we give it such a prominent role in this text can best be explained perhaps by first indicating briefly the basic stages in the MBO process:

1. The establishment and publication of clearly stated, precise, and measurable corporate objectives, and the successive establishment of divisional, departmental, and unit objectives. At

each step down through the organization, care is taken to make sure that the objectives of each unit and each individual are within the framework of the larger organizations of which they are a part (see Exhibit 14–1).

2. The periodic initiation by the employee of a set of written personal performance goals or targets.

3. Discussion of the goals between the employee and his or her superior, followed by mutual agreement on a set of goals to which the employee is committed.

4. Periodic review by the employee and his or her superior to determine the extent to which goals previously set have been met or exceeded.

EXHIBIT 14–1
The integration of objectives

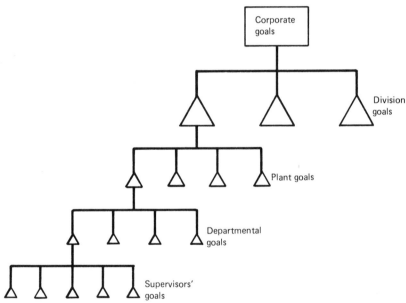

The importance of MBO in human resources management

As can be inferred from this brief description of the process, MBO seems to derive its unique potency from a number of different sources. First of all, the planning process alone assures that the organization will have clearly stated objectives, that these will be commonly understood throughout the organization, and that the objectives of each subunit and individual will be directed toward accomplishing corporate objectives. Although this process represents nothing more than good management, in many organizations it is introduced when the organization begins a formal MBO process. This alone would make MBO worthwhile.

Second, MBO gives every individual in the organization an opportunity for more involvement in and more control over his or her own work. This is the source of MBO's motivational potential. Each individual has an open invitation to propose how he or she can best contribute to the accomplishment of organizational objectives. Behavioral research has, of course, told us for some time that it would be desirable motivationally for individuals to have more involvement in and more control over their work. The unique contribution of MBO is to provide a practical tool for marrying this motivational objective with the realistic necessity of achieving corporate goals.

A third contribution of the MBO process to the effective management of human resources is that it provides an ideal control mechanism. Since precise objectives are stated in advance for the total organization, each unit in the organization, and each individual, it is necessary to merely compare results with objectives to evaluate performance and to identify needed corrective action.

The final unique contribution of the MBO process is that it provides the ideal basis for creating and demonstrating a direct tie between performance and rewards. Doing this has already been described as a critical element in the motivation of human resources.

MBO and the systems view

Let us now see how the management by objectives process underlies the human resources management system as reflected in Exhibit 1–3. The human resources management system begins with organizational objectives as the sole input. The exhibit next shows the processes of organization planning, staffing, and modification of the environment in order to serve those objectives, and appraisal and requiting as the end steps in the human resources management process.

THE DEVELOPMENT AND STATUS OF THE MBO CONCEPT

When Peter Drucker coined the phrase *management by objectives*, his concept described an overall approach to management, which included setting corporate goals and objectives, departmental goals directed toward achieving corporate goals, and individual goals directed toward meeting departmental goals. Performance appraisal was considered by Drucker to be an important aspect— but only an aspect—of the overall management by objectives approach.

The MBO concept, however, was first popularized by social scientists and others primarily interested in personnel administration and motivation. For this reason, the early literature on management by objectives, which appeared in the 1950s and the early 1960s, was heavily oriented toward the use of MBO in performance appraisal.

More recently, the term *management by objectives* has been widely used by many authors of diverse orientations. As a result, a variety of ideas (some quite conflicting) have been referred to as management by objectives.

We believe that these three central questions underlie the various viewpoints and thus provide a convenient framework for analysis:

Should goal setting proceed from the top of the organization downward, or from the bottom of the organization upward?

Should management by objectives be viewed primarily as a process for motivation or as a process for control?

How much emphasis should be placed on the individual's participation in setting his or her own objectives?

Setting goals from the top down means that, first, overall organizational objectives are determined. Then, within these overall objectives, specific departmental objectives are determined, and finally, within the departmental objectives, individual objectives are determined. Hughes, Granger, and Odiorne have expounded the logical necessity of the top-down approach and criticized earlier writers such as McGregor for failing to make this point explicit.[4]

The second issue, on which writers have been more sharply divided, is the emphasis on motivation as opposed to control. McGregor, for example, has said:

A sounder approach, which places the major responsibility on the subordinate for establishing performance goals and appraising progress toward them, avoids the major weaknesses of the old plan and benefits the organization by stimulating the development of the subordinate. It is true that more managerial skill and the investment of a considerable amount of time are required, but the greater motivation and the more effective development of subordinates can justify these added costs.[5]

Finally, the third issue on which widely divergent views have been expressed is the question of participation by the individual subordinate in setting performance goals. As previously indicated, the original MBO concept placed major emphasis on the importance of individual participation in goal setting as a key source of motivation. It can be said, in fact, that the initiation of objectives by the individual to be appraised is the basic element of the approach. For example, McGregor emphasizes that:

> this approach calls on the subordinate to establish short-term performance goals *for himself*. The superior enters the process actively only after the subordinate has *(a)* done a good deal of thinking about his job, *(b)* made a careful assessment of his own strengths and weaknesses, and *(c)* formulated some specific plans to accomplish his goals. The superior's role is to help the man relate his self-appraisal, his "targets," and his plans for the ensuing period to the realities of the organization.[6]

On the other hand, other writers emphasize the superior's role in assigning or directing performance objectives. Odiorne states that participation in individual goal setting may *sometimes* be beneficial, but in no sense does participation play a critical role in his concept of management by objectives.[7] In fact, he criticizes Drucker and McGregor for their emphasis on participation.

Although Odiorne's statement is essentially accurate with regard to the research evidence concerning the effects of participation, it is important to keep firmly in mind that it is the participative and self-control aspects of MBO which create the potential for increased motivation; thus these aspects are vital if motivation is seen as a major objective of an MBO program.

THE MANAGEMENT BY OBJECTIVES PROCESS

The MBO process was described earlier as consisting of four basic stages. In analyzing this process in more detail, it will be helpful to distinguish at this point between the stage which takes place as a part of the overall corporate-wide MBO process and the stages which take place as a part of the interaction between each individual and his or her own manager.

Organizational goals

As previously indicated, the first stage in the MBO process is to establish goals for the total organization. These goals must be established by the top policymaking body, usually the board of directors. Whether or not the president and other top executives are asked to participate in establishing corporate goals depends upon the policies and traditions of the organization. Once these goals are established, they are disseminated throughout the organization to the widest degree that is deemed acceptable.

From the standpoint of organization-wide motivation and commitment it is highly desirable that corporate goals be transmitted to every member of the organization. Although this is theoretically desirable, in some situations the top executives may feel that because of some external constraint—for example, competitive reasons or the company's relationship with a labor union—limitations must be placed on the publication of corporate objectives. Clearly, this measure should be taken reluctantly since limiting the understanding of organizational purpose automatically creates limits to commitment and motivation.

Once corporate objectives have been established, they *must* be transmitted at least to the chief executives of the next lower organizational level, for example, divisional vice presidents. These divisional chief executives, usually in consultation with their immediate subordinates, must then determine the overall objectives for their subunit. An example of departmental goals is shown in Exhibit 14–2.

Two important criteria must be kept in mind in setting objectives at this subunit level and at each succeeding level: (1) The subunit

EXHIBIT 14–2
Performance goals: Department 10—Blanking

1. Improve production labor cost to 90 percent efficiency.
2. Decrease the number of jobs run on estimated standards to 35 percent.
3. Increase efficiency for 37–1 time to 85 percent.
4. Maintain 100 percent efficiency on indirect labor costs.
5. Contribute a minimum of $5,000 toward the M.I.P. goal.
6. Maintain production standards at a 95 percent minimum efficiency level.
7. Control departmental variable expense budget within the planned limits.
8. Work with all departments to raise delivery as promised to a 30 percent minimum on flat releases.
9. Control returned goods to a maximum of 2 percent of net shipments.
10. Conduct a monthly safety patrol on the tenth day of each month and forward a copy of the report to the superintendent.
11. Initiate a preventive maintenance program on the primary blanking presses.
12. Work with plant engineering to rearrange the blanking areas to enable two machine operations in press group 3B.
13. Continue tool history cards and install this program on an additional 40 dies during 1978.
14. Complete the installation of Wintress controls and add probes to an additional 25 dies during 1978.

objectives must be totally consistent with the overall corporate objectives and must fit within the framework of the corporate objectives—that is, they must contribute to the achievement of the corporate objectives. (2) The total of all objectives at the division level must be equal to the total corporate objectives. Obviously, if this is not so, there is no way that the corporate objectives can be achieved.

It is the responsibility of the manager at each level to coordinate and integrate the objectives of all units immediately subordinate to him or her so as to ensure the complete coverage and congruence of goals. To the extent that a preliminary analysis indicates gaps, corporate goals must be adjusted downward or divisional goals must be modified or expanded.

This procedure of transmitting goals from the larger unit to the units at the next organizational level, followed by the setting of goals at the next lower level, then proceeds downward in the organization, exactly following the sequence of an organization chart, until objectives have been set for the smallest unit in the organization.

Key steps in the MBO process between the individual and the manager

When objectives have been set for each organizational unit, the next stage in the MBO process involves the establishment of individual objectives for each employee. Exhibit 14–3 illustrates the steps of this process for managing individual objectives.

EXHIBIT 14–3
Key steps in managing individual objectives in an MBO program

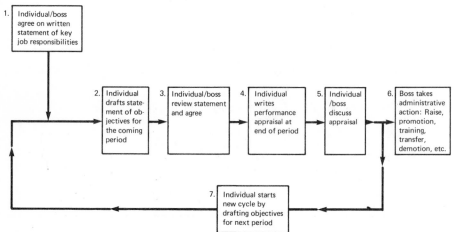

This one-to-one MBO process involving each individual and his or her manager may be thought of as occurring between the first-line supervisor and each subordinate. However, it should also be recognized that this process is equally applicable to the relationship between each individual and his or her manager at every level in the organization. This process takes place between each divisional vice president and his or her manager, the president; it takes place between each department manager and his or her manager, the divisional vice president; and so forth at each level of the organization. The *process* is precisely the same at all levels.

1. **Write key job responsibilities.** As indicated in Exhibit 14–3, the MBO process begins with an agreement between the individual and the boss on a *written* statement of key job responsibilities. Emphasis is placed on having the statement in writing because experience has shown that otherwise both parties tend to believe that they have a common understanding and then, when forced to be very specific, usually discover that they do not.

If an organization already has position descriptions that are accurate, up-to-date, and complete, these will meet the requirement for the agreed-upon statement of key job responsibilities. However, it should be pointed out that only rarely do organizations really have accurate, up-to-date, and complete job descriptions.

For this reason emphasis is placed on determining whether or not such a written statement exists before proceeding farther. Since everything else in the MBO process depends upon the validity of this written statement of responsibilities, unless there is assurance that it exists, all further work should be suspended until agreement is achieved.

2. **Draft statement of objectives.** In the second step of the MBO process, each individual *drafts* a statement of objectives for the coming period. This does not mean that the boss has abdicated the responsibility for having the final determination of the subordinate's assignments. The boss must boss, and he or she has the final responsibility for approving all subordinates' objectives, but this responsibility is exercised at a later step.

Emphasis is placed on the drafting of the statement of objectives by the individual because this is the major source of the motivational opportunities inherent in MBO. This is the individual's opportunity to show what he or she can contribute to the achievement of organizational objectives. Often the individual will see a potential for contributions that would not occur to the boss. Often the individual can suggest better ways of doing things or new things to be done which will aid in the achievement of corporate objectives.

In short, this is the individual's opportunity to make use of his complete potential (to "self-actualize"). At this step the reins which have constrained human performance can be thrown off—and therein lies the secret of the increased performance which can come from a successful use of MBO.

The individual should be instructed to make certain that the objectives drafted jibe with the organizational objectives and contribute to their achievement. But he or she should also be encouraged to think big, to think in terms of the overall purposes of the position and how his or her talent and abilities may be used most effectively to contribute to organizational purposes. In short, the individual should be encouraged to throw off the blinders of past experience and to brainstorm additional contributions that he or she would like to make if given the opportunity.

At this step the individual should also be encouraged to discuss those things which are needed from the boss or other areas of the organization in order to fully achieve his or her potential contribution to the organization.

Although it is certainly true that all individuals will not respond positively to this challenge, experience shows that in most organizations the majority will. Moreover, if there is a central message in this book's approach to effective human resources management, it is that we should always work toward the *highest common denominator* (to challenge the best employees), rather than limit our management practices to the potential of the lowest common denominator.

Those who lack motivation will contribute little in any case; but the advantage of MBO is that it challenges and encourages the most talented and most highly motivated individuals to maximize their contribution to the organization.

3. **Manager: Review draft of objectives.** The next step of the MBO process involves the manager's review of each subordinate's draft of objectives. This is followed by discussion between the two to revise the objectives as necessary and reach final agreement on a written statement. Hopefully, in most cases this discussion will lead to a true meeting of minds. But when it does not, the boss must act like a boss.

At the end of this step, objectives must be produced which the boss honestly believes are challenging and represent what he or she regards as acceptable performance. In some cases, the final objectives may have to be dictated; but in practice this will usually turn out to be a rarer circumstance than might be supposed.

Experience shows that subordinates are far more likely to be overly ambitious and to set impossible objectives than they are to underestimate their potential or to try to get away with trivial objectives. In reality, one of the manager's toughest jobs turns out to be persuading subordinates to set objectives that are realistically attainable within the constraints of the situation (including the probability of unexpected and unpredictable obstacles).

Setting objectives that are demanding and challenging, but also feasible, turns out to be one of the critical skills óf effective MBO and one of the toughest to acquire. The only effective means for acquiring this skill seem to be sincere effort and a lot of practice on the part of both the individual and a supportive boss.

4. Draft own performance appraisal. The next step in the MBO process occurs at the end of the performance period. At this time the individual again takes the initiative by drafting the performance appraisal. This performance period, incidentally, can vary widely among organizations and sometimes within an organization. Some organizations write and evaluate objectives annually; others do so on a monthly basis. By far the most common period of time for objectives, however, is six months. The next most common period is one year.

The best time period for objectives depends upon the climate and operations of the particular organization. The only important requirement is that the period selected should fit the operations, the environment, and the administrative policies of the business.

If the MBO process is operating well, drafting the performance appraisal is a very simple and straightforward step. Since specific and measurable objectives were set at the beginning of the period, and since performance data are available on accomplishments, all that is required is to match up the accomplishments with the objectives. The performance appraisal merely reports the facts, along with a brief explanation of the reasons for the results.

Although simple to describe (and, in fact, simple to do), this step nevertheless involves two things which are often not present in an organization until the implementation of management by objectives.

First, this step requires that factual data which measure and evaluate the accomplishment of objectives be available. Frequently such data (in sufficient detail to permit the easy evaluation of objective accomplishment) are not available prior to MBO. This means that in order to make MBO operational, new control data and reports must be generated.

Each objective set should have matching control data to evaluate its accomplishment. Where such data are not already available in the organization, or where they are not available in the appropriate form, they must be created or modified.

Second, this step requires that the necessary data be in the hands of the individual performer. This often means providing data to individuals who have not previously received them.

Providing feedback data on performance during the performance period so that the individual performer may adjust his or her performance in time to achieve objectives by the end of the period is not really a new concept. In fact, it is wholly consistent with the most traditional forms of scientific management. What is new is that this concept must be operational if MBO is to be effective.

Aside from its necessity for MBO, the provision of feedback data to enable the individual to adjust his or her performance is a highly valuable procedure in its own right. After the fact it does little good to tell a person that he or she has failed. What is helpful is to let the person know that he or she is in trouble before the opportunity to change the performance and create the desired results has been lost.

At the end of this fourth step, the individual will have drafted a document which says, in effect, "I accomplished the following objectives, and here is how, and I failed to accomplish the following objectives, and here is why."

5. Discuss the appraisal. The next step in the MBO process involves the discussion of the draft appraisal by the boss and the subordinate. Frequently the boss will have little to do at this step except agree with the appraisal, perhaps add some content, and question a few minor details. Nevertheless, at this step too the boss may have to be a boss.

If the boss feels that the self-appraisal has been slipshod or that it glosses over failures, it is his or her responsibility to say so and to demand a more complete evaluation from the subordinate. Finally, if a complete appraisal is not forthcoming from the subordinate, it is the boss's job to provide one.

Again, experience shows that this degree of direction is rarely required. This is particularly true because of the factual nature of the MBO process. It should be remembered that we are dealing with specific and measurable objectives, and with factual data reporting the extent to which they have been accomplished. Since "facts are facts," there is little room for opinion or disagreement. Objectives have either been achieved or they have not been achieved, and there is usually little room for debate. This fact alone makes MBO highly desirable to a manager.

6. **Manager: Take action based on discussion.** Although shown in Exhibit 14–3 as off line, the next logical step in the MBO process is for the manager to take the administrative action for each individual subordinate which is appropriate in light of his or her performance. Such action includes increases in compensation, bonuses, promotion, training, demotion, transfer, and so on.

As has been indicated in Chapter 13, it is critical from the standpoint of motivation and perceived equity that all such administrative actions be directly related to individual performance and directly proportionate to such performance. Although these objectives are neither new nor dependent on the MBO process, MBO permits the objectives to be achieved more readily.

Since performance is measured much more precisely under MBO than under other management systems, MBO facilitates tying compensation and other rewards directly to performance. Moreover, the use of the MBO process throughout the organization makes it obvious that the accomplishment of objectives should be the only basis for rewards. Thus MBO sets the proper climate for a direct tie between performance and compensation.

Finally, the widespread perception of equity throughout the organization is enhanced both by the factual nature of appraisals and by the fact that each individual sets his own objectives and makes his own appraisal. There is much less opportunity under this system for an individual to feel that an unfair evaluation has been received. Failure to achieve objectives and receive rewards is laid squarely on the shoulders of the individual.

Step 6 is shown off line because, although it follows logically from the appraisal in Step 5, in a particular organization administrative action may not take place immediately after the appraisal. This is not important. What is important is that each individual perceive the administrative action to be a direct outgrowth of the accomplishment of objectives (that is, "equitable").

7. **Start new MBO cycle.** The final step in the MBO process, following immediately after the appraisal discussion, requires that the individual start off a new MBO cycle by drafting his or her objectives for the next period. Inherent in this step is a review of the written statement of key job responsibilities. If these have changed, the written statement should be changed; however, in many instances the key responsibilities will not change at each cycle of the MBO process. After any necessary revision of the statement of job responsibilities, the individual continues from Step 2 in the process.

The criteria for good objectives

In describing the management by objectives process, we have skipped lightly over the question of what constitutes good objectives for making the process operational. This has been done because it is easier to understand the criteria for good objectives after understanding the purposes and steps in the process. We turn our attention now, however, to a closer analysis of objectives.

It was mentioned earlier that setting objectives is the most difficult part of the MBO process. This is due only in part to the necessity for striking a balance among objectives that are acceptable both to the individual and to the manager and also fall within the context of overall corporate objectives.

Another dimension of the challenge grows from the technical difficulty of establishing objectives that are specific and clear, as well as measurable. As indicated in Exhibit 14–4, we recommend

EXHIBIT 14–4
Checklist for good
MBO objectives

√**Demanding** but **possible**

√**Specific** and **clear**

√**Measurable** (quantified)

√**Target dates set**

four criteria for satisfactory MBO objectives: (1) objectives should be demanding but possible; (2) they should be specific and clear; (3) they should be measurable (that is, quantified whenever possible), and (4) they should each include a definite target date. These criteria are equally applicable to corporate objectives, unit objectives, and individual objectives. The whole MBO process is based on the assumption that objectives will meet these standards.

For example, unless objectives are specific and clear, it will not be easy to evaluate accomplishments, as described in Step 5, and the lack of opportunity for disagreement in that step will not be realized. If objectives are not measurable, even the best-intentioned individual will have difficulty in evaluating their achievement. Clearly, if target dates are not set, there is no way to finally determine that failure has occurred.

1. Demanding but possible. The reason for suggesting that objectives be both demanding and possible is psychological. Objectives which are not demanding, which do not stretch the individual to give his or her best performance, are not motivating. By the same token, impossible objectives are not motivating either.

Some managers operate on this basis: "I'll set unrealistically high targets, and even though they can't be achieved, the performance forthcoming will be better than I'd have gotten otherwise." Experience shows this approach to be fallacious. In fact, rational people respond by being discouraged and unmotivated, since they recognize that the target set cannot be achieved. Thus, for objectives to call forth maximum motivation and performance, they must be demanding, but they must be also recognized as achievable if the individual exerts his or her best effort.

2. Specific and clear. One important caution is very much in order at this point. When faced with the task of setting objectives for the first time, most individuals begin by believing that many of their responsibilities cannot be stated specifically. On closer analysis (and with much hard work), this usually turns out to be an erroneous impression. More often than not, creative thought can suggest ways to state objectives in very specific, clear, and quantified terms, even though at first they may have seemed quite intangible.

3. Quantified. For example, executives often believe at first glance that such responsibilities as "public relations" are intangible and cannot be quantified. Executives with public relations responsibilities may be tempted to draft an objective which says, "I will improve the public relations of my unit over the next six months." This is a very poor objective from the standpoint of the MBO process, since it is so unclear and unmeasurable that no one will ever be able to decide whether or not it was achieved.

On the other hand, more careful study shows that public relations can be quantified. For example, an objective may be written which states that "public relations will be improved over the next six months as measured in the following ways: (1) Complaint letters from the general public will be reduced from an average of six per month to an average of two per month. (2) A sample attitude survey of the public will be conducted on a periodic basis, and the overall index of the organization's public image will improve by a factor of at least 25 percent over the period measured."

4. Target dates set. It is obvious that there is no way to determine that an objective has been missed unless a specific completion date has been clearly established.

Although careful analysis and study is undeniably required to develop skill in setting objectives which meet the indicated criteria, we have yet to find a case in which setting such objectives was really impossible for a particular job. If necessary, most people can be challenged and stimulated to creatively set measurable, specific, clear, demanding, and target-dated objectives if this question is posed to them: "If you really don't think it is possible to measure the contributions of your job in a quantitative way, how can you be sure that you are really contributing anything to the organization? Moreover, how can you be sure that the job needs to exist at all? If we can't measure the contributions of the job, maybe there aren't any, and maybe we don't need the job."

IMPLEMENTING MANAGEMENT BY OBJECTIVES

The difficulty confronting the organization which undertakes to implement management by objectives for the first time has been summed up rather well by Dale McConkey: "There are two primary reasons for the failure of MBO. The first is adoption in ignorance, and the second is implementation in haste. MBO works, but it takes time and competent implementation."[8]

This is a realistic assessment, because the implementation of MBO involves a fundamental restructuring of assumptions held within an organization about human behavior and the potential of human resources, as well as a restructuring of communication and management systems.[9] When top management attempts to use MBO as anything less extensive or fundamental to the organization, the results are predictably disastrous.

To be successful, a company must nurture its MBO program through the faltering initial years and must take a long-range view. You can't just plug MBO in mechanically. Union Carbide, for example, admits that it took five years to get its MBO program operating and ten years to make it successful.

The future, however, is in the direction of MBO because MBO fits so well with other current developments both inside and outside the world of business. People are more educated now. They expect and demand more from their jobs than money. Managers want to have more impact on their own careers and on the goals of the organization. Management by objectives hasn't worked where the organization hasn't evolved to the point of accepting it. But we are 80 percent of the way there, and by the 1980s most companies will want to use MBO.

It also seems clear that in most organizations there are some jobs to which MBO is not applicable. This includes all jobs which are lacking in opportunity for creativity, innovation, and individual control (for example, typical assembly line jobs, though some management jobs are just as restrictive). In such situations, about the best we can do is try to apply some of Frederick Herzberg's concepts of job enrichment so that opportunities for creativity, initiative, and individual control are increased. The successful application of job enrichment concepts will lead to new opportunities for applying management by objectives to enlarged jobs.

Introducing MBO to the organization

The first priority in introducing a management by objectives approach should be to make certain that top management has a full understanding of the MBO concept, the underlying philosophy, and the demands that such an approach will make on the organization and its managers.

Once commitment at the top level has been achieved, these executives should be involved, to the maximum extent possible, in introducing the concept to their immediate subordinates and to the organization, and in conducting the training to develop skill in setting objectives and reviewing accomplishment.

In many organizations, it will be preferable to introduce MBO on a pilot basis in one or two divisions that appear most ready to accept the concept. Which divisions to select will depend on the interests and management styles of the top division management team as well as on the tasks typically performed in the various divisions. Jobs which have measurable results, provide opportunity for individual initiative, and include some nonrepetitive, innovative aspects seem particularly well suited to the management by objectives approach. Thus, divisions typically containing many such jobs present especially appropriate environments for the initial introduction of MBO.

Although a high level of top management participation in introducing the approach is crucial, there is considerable evidence that top management should be supported by a massive training effort—particularly training which emphasizes skill practice through such devices as role playing, case discussion, and simulation. This requires sophisticated and technically expert training resources. When such resources are not present within the organization, the help of outside consultants can be extremely useful.

Based on the results of research, it appears highly desirable to establish at the outset a formal procedure for measuring the impact of MBO on such criteria as productivity, profitability, morale, and turnover. In addition to providing feedback which will be useful in modifying the approach or providing additional support where needed, measurement communicates top management's commitment to, and interest in, the management by objectives program. Such measurement could be established by comparing "experimental" MBO plants or units with a matched "control" (a similar plant doing similar work) that does not use MBO. Where this is not feasible, consistent measurements of particular criteria can be made before and after the adoption of MBO.

It is also desirable to set up a definite procedure and timing for the formal review of objectives, as well as administrative machinery

EXHIBIT 14–5
Typical form to record objectives

Performance Objectives

Date prepared: _____

Employee: _____   Manager: _____

Job description (responsibilities): _____

_____

_____

Objectives	Achievement measures: Due dates	Priorities

to ensure that such review takes place. Although the administrative machinery will necessarily concentrate on formal reviews, emphasis should also be placed on the value and importance of more frequent informal reviews.

Where should MBO be applied?

The question of how far down in an organization the management by objectives approach should be applied can best be answered on the basis of the requirements and constraints of the organization; the content of jobs at different levels; the skills, at-

EXHIBIT 14–6
An alternate form to record objectives

Objectives for _____ (year)	
Submitted by: _____	Title: _____
Department/Division: _____	Supervisor: _____
Job description (responsibilities): _____ _____ _____	

Target (ranked importance __ and weight % __)	Performance criteria (measurements, target, date)

Review dates	Progress and results
Final (January)	

titudes, and expectations of individuals at different levels; and the management climate of the organization.

Although companies have most often applied MBO to jobs in top-level management, and have been progressively less inclined to apply it at each successively lower level in the organization, there is no research finding to suggest that MBO has been less successful at lower levels than at upper levels.

Finally, one question which is commonly raised by organizations and individuals embarking on MBO is: "What kinds of forms should we use for stating objectives and reporting on the accomplishment of objectives?" In fact, entirely too much attention has been given to the design of forms to support MBO. It is the substance of the process which is really significant and not the paperwork, which at best can provide only weak support. Some of the most successful applications of MBO use no forms at all. Objectives and their accomplishment are recorded in memo form on a blank sheet of paper.

Nevertheless, some managers feel that forms are helpful as a guide to drafting and evaluating objectives. For this reason two alternative sets of forms are shown in Exhibits 14–5 and 14–6. Either of these forms, or a blank sheet of paper, can serve equally well to support the necessary record keeping of an otherwise carefully planned and implemented MBO program.

SUMMARY

Almost half of the *Fortune* 500 largest industrial corporations claim to have adopted management by objectives. On the other hand, it seems clear that many of these MBO programs are superficial at best, and some may represent attempts at manipulation.[10]

Although there is wide latitude in the seriousness with which top managements have viewed MBO, it is considerably beyond the stage of being a management fad, since in some companies it appears to represent a permanent and significant change in the basic approach to management.

There is convincing evidence that when MBO is viewed principally as a "personnel program" or another management gimmick, it meets with resistance, is given minimal middle-management support, and has little, if any, effect. There is also evidence that when MBO has top management support and is viewed as a new approach to management whose goal is the greater commitment and involvement of the entire work force, MBO can have (and frequently does have) a significant influence on the organization.[11] This influence has most often been felt in such areas as motivation, commitment, and morale. In fewer instances, MBO has been seen as having a direct influence on productivity and profitability.

To be successful, management by objectives requires a change in the approach to managing (toward a more participative emphasis that pushes responsibility downward in the organization), top management support and participation, and the learning of new skills and attitudes.

For these reasons, it is not an easy approach to implement. Superficial efforts to introduce MBO as a new "personnel program" do not make any impact on results. Even those companies which have made the most serious and wholehearted attempts to introduce management by objectives have encountered problems and have found the task a long and difficult one.

Typically, several years are required to disseminate real understanding of the MBO approach throughout the company and to give managers and subordinates sufficient training and practice in setting objectives and evaluating accomplishments. The most crucial factor in determining the outcome of a management by objectives approach is the commitment and daily involvement of top management.

CASE: MBO ROLE PLAY

Establish six to ten specific performance objectives for a 12-month period in your current job. (If you are not employed, establish objectives for a job you know well.) Remember to consider the criteria for good objectives.

After a 15-minutes period for drafting objectives, the class will be divided into pairs of "supervisors" and "subordinates" for role-playing the objectives review and approval interview session.

CASE: DELTA CORPORATION

Bill Joiner studied carefully the draft of performance objectives he had just received in the mail from one of his new sales representatives, Ralph Stone. He pondered what steps he should take next and wondered just what approach he should take in reviewing the objectives with Stone.

Bill Joiner was the Florida district sales manager for Delta Corporation, a national distributor of construction tools and equipment. Joiner's primary responsibility was the supervision of a seven-member field sales force covering the state of Florida.

Stone had just joined Delta two months earlier. This would

therefore be the first time that Joiner would go through a cycle of the MBO program with him. At Delta, subordinates drafted new objectives and reviewed them with their superiors every six months.

Bill remembered that the company had stressed the importance of mutual understanding and agreement between the subordinate and the superior as the keystone of the MBO program. He wondered what action he should take in response to Ralph Stone's first attempt at drafting objectives (see Figure A).

FIGURE A
Management by objectives work sheet

Name: Ralph Stone	Department: Florida District Sales
Title: Field Sales Representative	Supervisor: Wm. Joiner

	Objectives	*Target date for completion*
1.	To significantly increase the market share of the Delta product line in my territory.	Continuing
2.	To develop additional contacts within my present customers' organizations as well as prospect for new business with firms that we do not now service.	Daily
3.	To strengthen my knowledge of the Delta product line.	As soon as possible
4.	To achieve a total sales volume of $326,000 for all products this quarter.	June 30
5.	To improve customer relations.	Continuing
6.	To develop my management potential by completing at least one evening course this year at Florida Atlantic University.	December 31

QUESTIONS AND PROBLEMS

1. "MBO is the best theoretical management program ever conceived." Do you agree or disagree? Why?

2. "MBO is good in theory, but I just don't have enough time left after my other managerial duties to go through the process with my subordinates." Comment on this statement.

3. In what ways may MBO be said to integrate all of a manager's responsibilities for utilizing human resources?

4. Describe the relationship of behavioral science research and the evolution of MBO as a management tool.

5. Discuss and distinguish the planning, implementation, and control aspects of MBO.

6. Imagine that you are the personnel director of a major department store chain consisting of 20 stores of varying sizes. Draft performance objectives for your own job for the next six-month period. Be sure the objectives meet the criteria for good objectives discussed in this chapter.

7. Describe and discuss the six-step process for managing by objectives.

8. Contact a number of large companies and organizations in your area to find out whether they use MBO. Present a summary of the experiences with and the results obtained from MBO programs by those organizations using them.

BIBLIOGRAPHY

Carroll, S. J., Jr., and Tosi, H. L., Jr. "Goal Characteristics and Personality Factors in a Management by Objectives Program." *Administrative Science Quarterly,* September 1970.

Carroll, S. J., Jr., and Tosi, H. L., Jr. *Management by Objectives: Applications and Research.* New York: Macmillan Co., 1973.

Chesser, R. J. "MBO as a Behavioral System: A Focus on Change Relationships and Inferences of Causality." Unpublished doctoral dissertation, Michigan State University, 1970.

Dean, J. "Profit Performance Measurement of Division Managers." *Controller,* September 1957.

Drucker, Peter R. "Managing for Business Effectiveness." *Harvard Business Review,* May–June 1963.

Drucker, Peter R. *Managing for Results.* New York: Harper & Row, 1964.

Drucker, Peter R. *The Practice of Management.* New York: Harper & Row, 1954.

Fay, P. P., and Beach, D. N. "Management by Objectives Evaluated," *Personnel Journal,* October 1974.

French, J. R. P., Kay, E., and Meyer, H. H. "Participation and the Appraisal System." *Human Relations,* February 1966.

French, W., and Bell, Cecil. *Organizational Development.* Englewood Cliffs, N.J.: Prentice-Hall, 1973.

Hollmann, Robert W. "Supportive Organizational Climate and Managerial Assessment of MBO Effectiveness." *Academy of Management Journal,* December 1976.

Howell, Robert A. "A Fresh Look at Management by Objectives." *Business Horizons,* Fall 1967.

Howell, Robert A. "Management by Objectives—Should It Be Applied?" Unpublished doctoral dissertation, Harvard University, 1966.

Howell, Robert A. "Managing by Objectives—A Three Stage System." *Business Horizons,* February 1970.

Hughes, C. L. *Goal Setting.* New York: American Management Association, 1965.

Ivancevich, J. M. "Changes in Performance in a Management by Objectives Program." *Administrative Science Quarterly,* December 1974.

Ivancevich, J. M. "A Longitudinal Assessment of Management by Objectives." *Administrative Science Quarterly,* March 1972.

Kay E., Meyer, H. H., and French, J. R. P. "Effects of Threat in a Performance Appraisal Interview." *Journal of Applied Psychology,* October 1965.

Kindall, A. F., and Gatza, J. "Positive Program for Performance Appraisal." *Harvard Business Review,* November–December 1963.

Kleber, Thomas P. "The Six Hardest Areas to Manage by Objectives." *Personnel Journal,* August 1972.

Koontz, Harold. "Shortcomings and Pitfalls in Managing by Objectives." *Management by Objectives,* January 1972.

Lasagna, John B. "Make Your MBO Pragmatic." *Harvard Business Review,* November–December 1971.

Levinson, Harry. "Management by Whose Objectives?" *Harvard Business Review,* July–August 1970.

McGregor, D. *The Human Side of Enterprise.* New York: McGraw-Hill Book Co., 1960.

McGregor, D. "An Uneasy Look at Performance Appraisal." *Harvard Business Review,* May–June, 1957.

Mali, Paul. *Managing by Objectives.* New York: Wiley-Interscience, 1972.

Meyer, J. H., Kay, E., and French, J. R. P. "Split Roles in Performance Appraisal." *Harvard Business Review,* January–February 1965.

Murdick, Robert G. "MIS for MBO." *Journal of Systems Management,* March 1977.

Odiorne, G. S. *Management by Objectives—A System of Management Leadership.* New York: Pitman Publishing Corp., 1965.

Odiorne, G. S. "Management by Objectives and the Phenomenon of Goals Displacement." *Human Resources Management,* Spring 1974.

Owens, J. "The Values and Pitfalls of MBO." *Michigan Business Review,* July 1974.

Patton, Thomas H. "OD, MBO, and the R/P Systems." *Personnel Administration,* March–April 1972.

Raia, Anthony. *Managing by Objectives.* Glenview, Ill.: Scott, Foresman and Company, 1974.

Schuster, Fred E. "Management by Objectives—What and Why?" *Personnel Administrator,* November–December 1972.

Schuster, Fred E., and Kindall, A. F. "Management by Objectives—Where We Stand Today." *Human Resource Management,* Spring 1974.

Singular, S. "Has MBO Failed?" *MBA,* October 1975.

Strauss, George. "Management by Objectives: A Critical View." *Training and Development Journal,* April 1972.

Tosi, Henri L., Rizzo, John R., and Carroll, Stephen J. "Setting Goals in Management by Objectives." *California Management Review,* Summer 1970.

Vroom, Victor H. "Some Personality Determinants of the Effects of Participation." *Journal of Abnormal and Social Psychology,* November 1959.

Wikstrom, Walter S. *Managing by and with Objectives.* Studies in Personnel Policy No. 212. New York: National Industrial Conference Board, 1968.

NOTES

[1] S. Singular, "Has MBO Failed?" *MBA*, October 1975, pp. 47–50.

[2] Harold Koontz, interviewed in "Has MBO Failed?" p. 50.

[3] Singular, "Has MBO Failed?"

[4] C. L. Hughes, *Goal Setting* (New York: American Management Association, 1965); C. H. Granger, "The Hierarchy of Objectives," *Harvard Business Review,* May–June 1964; G. S. Odiorne, *Management by Objectives—A System of Management Leadership* (New York: Pitman Publishing Corp., 1965); D. McGregor, "An Uneasy Look at Performance Appraisal," *Harvard Business Review,* May–June 1957; and R. G. Murdick, "MIS for MBO," *Journal of Systems Management,* March 1977.

[5] McGregor, "An Uneasy Look at Performance Appraisal," Harvard Business Review, May–June, 1957, pp. 89–94.

[6] Ibid.

[7] George Odiorne, *Management by Objectives;* and Anthony P. Raia, *Managing by Objectives* (Glenview, Ill.: Scott, Foresman and Company, 1974).

[8] S. Singular, "Has MBO Failed?" pp. 47–50.

[9] Robert W. Hollmann, "Supportive Organizational Climate and Managerial Assessment of MBO Effectiveness," *Academy of Management Journal,* December 1976.

[10] Fred E. Schuster and A. F. Kindall, "Management by Objectives—Where We Stand Today," *Human Resource Management,* Spring 1974.

[11] J. M. Ivancevich, "Changes in Performance in a Management by Objectives Program," *Administrative Science Quarterly,* December 1974; J. Owens, "The Values and Pitfalls of MBO," *Michigan Business Review,* July 1974; and P. P. Fay and D. N. Beach, "Management by Objectives Evaluated," *Personnel Journal,* October 1974.

When you have completed studying
**MANAGING CHANGE IN THE HUMAN
RESOURCE SYSTEM**
you should be able to:

1. Explain how each manager must be concerned with introducing four types of changes in the human resource system.
2. Describe how a change affects the human resource system.
3. Describe the impact of change upon the individual.
4. List several ways in which the manager can stimulate creativity and change.
5. Classify and explain the major causes for resistance to change.
6. List the steps that the manager involved in any type of change goes through and the corresponding undesirable reactions.
7. Explain how the manager can avoid resistance to change.
8. Identify ways in which resistance to change can be overcome in the human resource system.

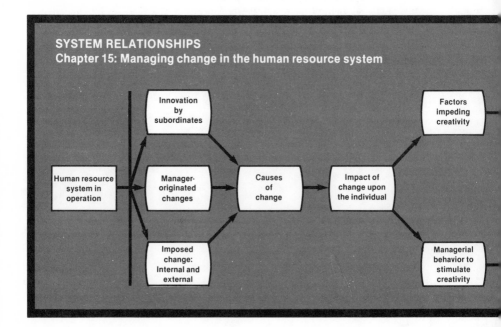

SYSTEM RELATIONSHIPS
Chapter 15: Managing change in the human resource system

In the past 100 years, the worldwide use of energy increased 1,000-fold.

In the past 100 years, the speed of communication increased 10,000,000-fold.

The number of scientific journals is doubling every 15 years.

In the 12th century the population of the world was doubling at the rate of every 600 years; now it is doubling every 30 years.

The $10 bill of today will be the first-class postage stamp of 1990.

The creation of artificial life is projected for the year 2000.

15

Managing change in the human resource system

The new is constantly replacing the old. We live in a world of change. Our way of life was founded on change, and the continuation of the organization at which we work, as well as our very society, depends upon change. In fact, one of the most important mea-

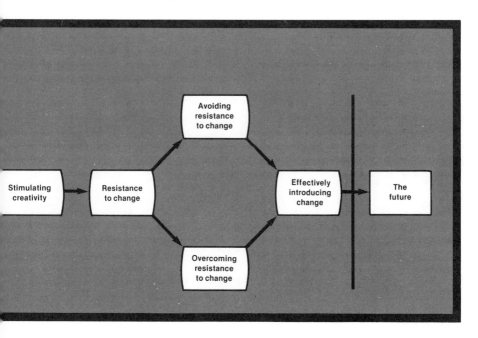

Stimulating creativity → Resistance to change → Avoiding resistance to change → Effectively introducing change → The future

Overcoming resistance to change

sures of a firm's success is its ability to change. At the same time, problems caused by change have been among the most common management headaches since organizations have been in existence.

Every member of the organization is affected by changes in all the human resource subsystems discussed in earlier chapters as well as by innovations introduced by his or her own manager. It is the function of the manager to work with each subordinate to obtain acceptance of new directions and commitment to change. In this chapter we tell how this is accomplished.[1]

Change has no beginning and no end. It is a continuous process. This does not mean that everything needs changing all the time. It would be foolish for the manager to advocate change simply for the sake of change. Certain customs, policies, and practices in any organization need to be retained. Managers must be able to assume that tomorrow many things are going to be essentially the same as they are today. Continuity is as important to the success of a firm as is change.

Thus, the manager is faced with two opposing forces: one emphasizing the need for stability, the other emphasizing the need for change. As suggested in Exhibit 15–1, the successful manager at-

EXHIBIT 15–1
Continuum of organization change and stability

Source: From *Management: The Individual, The Organization, The Process* by Gerald H. Graham: © 1975 by Wadsworth Publishing Company, Inc., Belmont, California 94002. Reprinted by permission of the publisher.

tempts to achieve a balance between change and stability. The equilibrium sought is some sort of healthy, desirable planned change. For in most organizations, externally or internally imposed change necessitates that the manager either manage change or be the victim of random, uncontrolled change. At the same time, unnecessary change may be both disruptive to the human resource system and counterproductive to the goals of the organization.

Far too often, the manager suffers from "tunnel vision," whereby only the desired change is seen; the broader impact of the change on the people involved is blocked out. Consider, for example, the manager who is introducing a new office layout on the basis of expected cost savings. The tunnel-vision view neglects the impact of the change on the people in the office. The breakup of social groups and working relationships cannot be ignored.

If the effect of an innovation or a change on the human resource system is not evaluated and provided for, the expected payoff from a change may never be achieved. Further confusing to the manager is the fact that employees may resist a change even when it is in their apparent self-interest to go along with the change. Why? Maybe the employees fear the uncertainties of the change; maybe they have a vested interest in the old way. Whatever the reason, the manager must expect some resistance as a normal part of the change process.

The reader will recall that some aspects of change in the human resource system have already been covered in Chapter 5, "Organization Development." In that chapter, however, we dealt exclusively with change to raise the level of performance of the total organization. In this chapter we will view the management of change at the manager-employee level. Specifically, we will examine the nature of change, the stimulation of change, and resistance to change. Most important, we will discuss how the manager can effectively deal with employees when introducing change.

CAUSES OF CHANGE

Each manager, from the president down to the foreman or the first-level supervisor, must be concerned with introducing four types of changes in his or her organization:

1. Innovations by subordinates.
2. Changes which the manager originates.
3. Changes imposed by higher level managers (the board of directors, in the case of the president).
4. Changes imposed by the environment.

The last two causes of change stated above are beyond the manager's control, yet he or she must work with subordinates to respond effectively. The effect of any change caused by the above factors is, generally, a change in the individual manager's portion of the total human resource system. Such changes, as shown in Exhibit 15–2, affect the formal organization, the informal organization, roles, the

EXHIBIT 15–2
Causes of change in the HRS

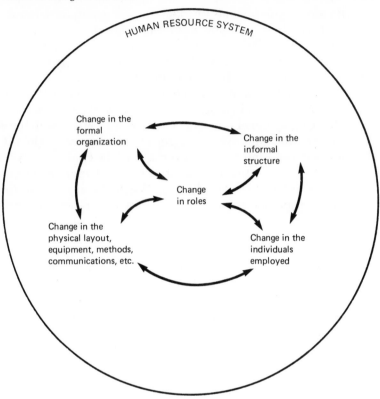

attitudes of individuals, and possibly physical factors such as
equipment, the processing of work, the plant or office layout.

Innovations by subordinates

Among the greatest unrealized outputs of human resources are
the bottled-up ideas and the suppressed creativity of the individual
employees. Creativity and innovation become introduced in three
ways. First, in progressive companies, managers are strongly urged
to stimulate productive, creative thinking by subordinates. Texas
Instruments is an example of a company that actively pursues this
policy.

Second, new employees often press forward with new ideas, particularly before the employees become "socialized."[2]

Third, highly creative employees are also creative in beating the system. When they come up with a good idea, they find ways to get through, under, over, or around bureaucratic obstacles.

Innovation by the subordinate is the arena in which the manager may exercise the most positive influence in furthering both organizational and individual goals. This opportunity to make the maximum contribution they can is what workers frequently want most from their jobs.[3]

And finally, as young people become employed, they bring with them new sets of values that affect organizational goals and objectives. This poses new issues for managers who are tied into past values and attitudes. One such issue is corporate social responsibility. Others include the use of "pot," the greater informality of dress, the demand for greater freedom and responsibility at work, and the decline of materialistic demands relative to work satisfaction.

Changes which the manager originates

The manager exercises most control over changes which he or she originates. That is, the manager may introduce such changes gradually, vary the timing, modify them, or even withdraw them if this seems appropriate. The manager also has the advantage of being able to obtain ready acceptance by evolving needed changes with the participation of subordinates.

Imposed changes

Almost daily the manager must introduce changes to individual subordinates which are imposed by higher management or the environment. Consider such examples of internally imposed changes as:

1. Changes in the requirements for transfers or promotions.
2. Changes in work rules or work hours.
3. The introduction of a female or black manager.
4. A new procedure for reporting or preparing reports.
5. Speedup in the production line or change in the product mix.
6. The transfer of some employees to a new work station or location.
7. Change from a manual procedure to an automatic process.
8. Change to a new incentive system or compensation plan.

Some inputs from the environment which require change within a particular manager's organization and operations are:

1. New laws or government regulations.
2. Technological advances.
3. Personnel turnover.
4. Changes in the environment.
5. Computerization of operations.
6. Competition.
7. Materials shortages.
8. Changing values and aspirations.
9. Business cycles.

To illustrate further, technological innovation, such as the introduction of a large-scale computer, produces a new organization structure, new positions, and new interpersonal relationships. New conflicts over responsibilities often arise and produce shifts in organizational patterns and roles. As another example, the almost total automation of some automobile assembly lines affect workers and their behavior. The new skills of operating complex control equipment and the job insecurity caused by this automation affect the managing of human resources.

THE IMPACT OF CHANGE ON THE INDIVIDUAL

The objective of the manager should be to make change a stimulating experience that motivates the worker. In the case of innovation proposed by an employee and encouraged by the manager, this is not difficult. At least the individual originating ideas and then seeing them implemented will be positively affected. Others in the organization may or may not be unless the manager communicates favorably with them.

Other types of changes, even relatively minor and limited ones, tend to produce stress in employees. It is not, however, the complexity and extent of the changes that determine the amount of stress introduced. Experience and research suggest that the degree of stress created by a change and the amount of resistance to the change frequently bear little relationship to the nature of the change.[4] For reasons we shall discuss, a minor change introduced by the manager may meet with considerable opposition.

Gardner and Moore long ago found that "the cost in employee feelings of anxiety and insecurity and the loss of productive energies and efficiency, engendered by changes affecting the well-being and status of employees, are significant items of human and economic expense."[5] It is surprising, therefore, that many managers still view adaptation to a work change as an individual problem which the employee must work out alone.

We should note that all stress or resistance to change is not necessarily undesirable. A complete lack of resistance to change would indicate apathy or an unfavorable organizational climate. It may be that the employees are so dominated by the manager, or so fearful of reprimand, that they are unwilling to express legitimate concern.

We should also recognize that most changes cause some tension and anxiety in the individual. Resistance is basically a reaction to such tension and anxiety. But the ways in which the individual reacts vary widely, depending on such factors as the individual personality, the perceived situation, and past experiences with similar changes.

STIMULATING CREATIVITY AND CHANGE

The manager who continually looks for better ways to do things, who seeks to make subordinates more productive through innovative contributions, is greatly in demand. Such a manager must recognize that he or she is not the only source of good ideas; in fact, he may be the least creative person in his organization. In the latter case, it is extremely important that he draw upon the ideas of subordinates.

In order to stimulate creativity, the manager must be aware of factors that impede creativity and of the behavior that he or she should adopt in order to stimulate the creativity of subordinates.

Factors which impede creativity

In most organizations, there are basic reasons for resistance to change, as discussed in the following section. As a result, tradition and habit dominate the cognitive requirements for change. The absurdities that may arise as a result of such passive behavior are illustrated in Exhibit 15–3. We do not have to look long in any company to find practices that just grew and remained unchanged many years later.

Generally, an autocratic or bureaucratic managerial style tends to suppress creativity. We also find creativity impeded because some managers take credit for the good ideas of their subordinates. In many companies creativity is limited or misdirected because subordinates are not kept informed of the organization's objectives. As a

EXHIBIT 15–3
When old habits stifle creativity

Path of the Calf *

"One day through the primeval wood
A calf walked home as good calves should;
But made a trail all bent askew,
A crooked trail as all calves do.
Since then three hundred years have fled,
And I infer the calf is dead.
But still he left behind his trail,
And thereby hangs my moral tale.
The trail was taken up next day
By a lone dog that passed that way;
And then a wise bellwether sheep
Pursued the trail o'er vale and steep,
And drew the flock behind him, too,
As good bellwethers always do.
And from that day o'er hill and glade,
Through those old woods a path was made.

The years passed on in swiftness fleet,
The road became a village street;
And this, before men were aware,
A city's crowded thoroughfare.
And soon the central street was this
Of a renowned metropolis;
And men two centuries and a half
Trod in the footsteps of that calf.
Each day a hundred thousand more
Followed the calf who went before
And o'er his crooked journey went
The traffic of a continent.
A hundred thousand men were led
By one calf near three centuries dead.
They followed still his crooked way,
And lost one hundred years a day;
For thus such reverence is lent
To well established precedent."

* Partial quotation from
Path of the Calf —
(by Samuel Walter Foss,
written in 1895).

Source: *General Electric Review* APD–135B (undated).

result they become discouraged when their suggestions are rejected as inappropriate.

In total, we may say that the manager impedes creativity by failing to establish a climate for creativity. As director of the Center for Creativity and Mental Health at the University of Chicago,

Morris A. Stein made an eight-year study of the factors affecting creative performance. He found that the role of environment is a significant and measurable factor in creative productivity.

Managerial behavior that will stimulate creativity

As a result of several empirical studies, Joel D. Goldhar, Louis K. Bragaw, and Jules J. Schwartz found that there are at least six identifiable characteristics of environments which stimulate technical innovation:

1. Easy access to information.
2. Free flow of information both in and out of the organization.
3. Rewards for sharing, seeking, and utilizing new (externally developed) information.
4. Rewards for risk taking.
5. Rewards for accepting and adapting to change.
6. Encouragement of mobility and interpersonal contacts.[6]

In line with the above research and that of Morris Stein, we may establish certain behavior for the manager to follow in person-to-person contact with subordinates.

Discuss the creative process with each subordinate. Make each person aware that creativity involves the constant search for needs, gathering relevant data, piling up alternative solutions, incubation (putting the problem aside to "hatch"), illumination (the sudden solution), and verification.

Challenge the subordinate. When a subordinate proposes a solution, challenge him or her to suggest three or more. "Brainstorm" with the subordinate after this to come up with even more. Suspend evaluation and criticism until all solutions are in.

Set an example by constantly questioning old ideas. In face-to-face discussions about long-established practices, ask subordinates, "Why do we do it this way?" "Can we find a better way?" Keep stimulating subordinates to question the old and to seek new and better ways.

Encourage subordinates to discuss problems, ideas, and changes with one another. Ask subordinates to get the ideas of their associates. Encourage informal get-togethers of small groups. Encourage preliminary memos of new ideas. Hold weekly staff meetings.

"Plant" one of your most highly creative people at each meeting. One creative person on a committee or at a meeting will stimulate others and set a model for them.

Give credit. Be careful to give appropriate credit for each useful idea. This may vary from an acknowledgment in a private meeting with the employee (in the case of a small contribution) to a newspaper story and management commendation or award for a very valuable idea.

Assign individuals to special task forces. Task forces are established to find new solutions so that creativity is actively and continuously encouraged.

Rotate people into new jobs. New situations arouse new thinking. Often, an untrained person may ask questions that lead to new solutions.

Develop open-ended position descriptions. Let the employee make up, and vary from time to time, a part of his or her own position description. Marian Kellogg rose to become vice president of General Electric by creating jobs for herself that never existed before.

Make idea creation part of the appraisal process. When employees see that you value their full mental effort beyond the standard job, they will seek the associated rewards.

RESISTANCE TO CHANGE

It should be noted at the outset that not all change is resisted. In fact, some changes are welcomed—the consumer looks forward to new fashions in clothing; the secretarial pool welcomes its new office equipment; and the worker eagerly awaits the "change of scene" during a two-week vacation. We can see that it is not change itself which causes resistance, but the *meaning of change* for the people involved. There is little resistance to change in a company in which the previous outcomes of changes have been positive. On the other hand, change will be opposed if the outcome is viewed as negative or uncertain. Of course, some changes are so trivial that they are not resisted.

Two other generalizations regarding resistance to change should be noted. First, the fact that an individual is well educated or highly intelligent does not mean that he or she will be less resistant to a necessary, logical change introduced by the manager. In fact, a highly educated employee is likely to come up with more rationalizations for *not* making a change.[7] Second, although we are focusing on the difficulty faced by managers in effecting change, it is not unusual to find that the manager is the obstacle to change. It would appear that managers are frequently reluctant to change because of the strong commitment they have to current activities and to programs that they initiated.

One of the functions of the human resources department is to work with line managers to *avoid* resistance before such opposition can form. As our above discussion has suggested, there are numerous causes of resistance to change. The identification of likely areas of resistance is not quite the massive task that it may at first appear to be. The reasons for resistance to change are limited and may be grouped as follows.

Economic reasons

A major change may be feared by an individual because of the possibility of demotion, reduced salary or wages, or termination. Employees may fear that work will be shifted to other plants or be subcontracted. Speedup on the assembly line, reduced work hours, or lower piece rates may also be feared.

Personal reasons

Individuals may fear a change because they will have new, unknown responsibilities. Or their jobs may become narrower and more specialized. In either case, their personal insecurity creates resistance to change.

Many people in a company possess years of experience in their area of work. They do not wish to learn new skills or are afraid that they will not be able to. New techniques pose the threat of personal obsolescence.

Some people feel that any change implies that their present performance has been inadequate. Some workers may fear that they will have to work much harder after a change has been implemented.

Status symbols, such as who reports to whom, office location, or the reputation of an organization component, may be lost in a reorganization. People value these and many other symbols highly, and hence may resist the change.

People may resent increased control in some areas of their work despite increased responsibility in other areas. Similarly, workers may resent the fact that they did not have a part in the change decision ("No one asked me what I thought about it").

Social reasons

Organization change may break longtime social relationships developed on the job. This means that adjustment to new people and new social relationships must be faced. New roles and norms within a new group must be evolved. To people who prefer stable relationships, such change will be feared and opposed.

An employee who does not participate in the changes affecting relationships with others may resent change. Similarly, employees are likely to oppose change which threatens their group status.

Workers may perceive changes as benefiting the company at the expense of themselves and their friends. "Any time a change is made around here, you can bet it's the worker who gets the shaft."

Political reasons

At the executive level, change may mean shifts in power and the realignment of power cliques. The unions representing organized production, clerical, and some professional workers may fear that changes will reduce the informally developed power of these groups in some plants or offices. When an assembly line is automated, an entire union may be threatened, even though the employees are retained by transferring them to jobs outside the bargaining unit.

Finally, a change introduced by staff departments is frequently resisted by the line people who must carry it out. As one manager explained the difference between line and staff departments:

"Staff tells line what to do.
Line tells staff where to go."

EFFECTIVELY INTRODUCING CHANGE

The manager involved in any type of change goes through four steps:

1. Recognizes that a change is necessary or desirable.
2. Determines the ideal change.
3. Decides how to implement the change.
4. Introduces the most practical form of the ideal change.

Each of these steps can produce an undesirable reaction or a particular resistance from the employee:

1. To the very idea of a change.
2. To the intended change.
3. To the method of implementing the change.
4. To the changed state itself.

The effective manager will keep these four areas of possible resistance in mind in trying to *avoid* resistance before it develops.

Overcoming resistance once it has developed is more difficult, and therefore, though necessary, a poor, secondary course of action. Let us see what the individual manager can do to successfully introduce change into the human resource system.

Avoiding resistance to change

Successful managers need to understand why change is resisted (discussed earlier in this chapter) and to be familiar with the change process and techniques (covered in Chapter 5). Given this background, managers should recognize that though they are typically the change agents, the employees control the final decision to accept or reject. This is because the employees are the ones who actually implement the proposed change. Based on this premise, several practical guides become apparent.

Develop two-way communication. The intended change, its benefits to the worker, and the method of implementation should be communicated to those affected as far in advance as possible. Lack of clear communication leaves room for distorted interpretation of facts and intentions. As we have seen in Chapter 11, "Communicating," if a vacuum develops in the grapevine, a rumor will develop to fill it. The rumor tends to foster uncertainty and dwells on the negative. Resistance may arise because of such distortions.

If the change to be introduced originated from an outside consultant or a staff department, uncertainty and mistrust are likely to be even greater. Effective communication becomes even more critical in such cases. It is also a good practice to encourage questions from the employees regarding the intended change. If the change will have a major impact on the employees, the manager might hold meetings of small groups, since such meetings are more conducive to questions and discussion.

Provide opportunity for ego-involvement. Individuals are less likely to resist decisions for change which they have participated in making. A study by Gruenfeld and Foltman, for example, found that supervisors who had been integrated and identified with the group responsible for a change were more likely to accept and encourage the change than were supervisors who had not been involved.[8]

Sometimes participation in a change may not be possible or desirable, as in the introduction of a new product where an information leak to a competitor could be disastrous. When ego-involvement is possible, however, resistance to a change may be avoided if the individuals who will be affected by the change are given the opportunity to voice their own ideas and opinions.

Research also suggests that if participation is to be effective, it must be perceived as "legitimate" in the eyes of the employees. That is, if participation is to facilitate change, the workers must consider their involvement as "right and proper" as well as relevant to the problem at hand.[9]

Gain support for the change. The manager who tries to mislead or deceive his or her employees will create mistrust and thus increase tension and resistance to change. An effective manager will attempt to create an atmosphere of trust by being open and frank in dealing with subordinates.

We have seen that fear of economic loss and fear of economic insecurity are important reasons for resisting change. A worker may fear that the phasing out of a product or service will affect his or her earnings or chance for promotion. To avoid resistance, some sort of protection will have to be given to this employee. For example, it has become common in union contracts for management to guarantee that no one will be displaced by technological change. This means handling all reductions in human resources through attrition rather than termination; allowing voluntary transfers to other work areas or locations; and retraining those displaced by the change. A formal grievance procedure may give the employee a feeling of security that any inequities resulting from change can be resolved. If change will result in the termination of selected employees, a termination policy based on seniority or some other equitable system must be developed and communicated. This will alleviate the problem of having everyone think that "*I* will be fired."

Another effective technique is to allow workers to share in the benefits resulting from a change. Those who go along with the change should be rewarded.

Of course, such guarantees and rewards will be expensive. They will appear even more expensive if the purpose of the change was to reduce costs. On the other hand, the short-run cost of avoiding resistance may far outweigh the long-run cost of attempting to overcome such resistance.

Provide a creative climate. We all drift into habit patterns that we repeat over and over again with no thought of doing otherwise. Habit is easy, comfortable, and safe; however, it must be continually challenged if we are to strengthen our ability to accept change.

A number of industrial firms believe that if change is to be readily accepted, an environment which stimulates ideas and creativity must be developed. For example, General Motors, U.S. Steel, and General Electric long ago inaugurated creative training programs. General Electric, to illustrate, sponsors a 13-week course in creative engineering for each engineer in which methods and attitudes of creativity are covered and actual engineering problems are solved.

What does this mean for the individual manager? It means that if he or she can provide an atmosphere in which ideas and creativity flourish, resistance to change can be avoided.

Overcoming resistance to change

Under the threat of a change, the individual translates tension and anxiety into resistive behavior of some kind. In some instances, this behavior is immediately attributable to the change; in other instances, the behavior does not appear to be related to the change ("I just can't figure out why Jim's been acting so peculiar"). Either way, the resistive behavior is likely to manifest itself in one of the following forms:

1. Openly expressed opposition—slowdowns, strikes, sabotage, an increase in grievances, more complaints, refusals to comply or to provide information, voluntary quits.
2. Indirectly expressed opposition—a greater interest in unionization, greater competition, less friendliness, a sudden increase in complaints about working conditions, an increase in discrimination charges, conforming to the letter rather than the spirit of a directive, a greater number of mistakes, more waste.
3. Unconscious hostility—an increase in accidents, lower morale, more tardiness and absenteeism, sullenness and uncommunicativeness, psychosomatic illnesses, alcoholism.

Regardless of the form of the resistance, action must be taken quickly to reduce it. Let us see how this may be accomplished.

Determine the causal factor. We can see that the manager is not necessarily dealing with objective behavior when people resist change. There may be a need for a venting of supercharged emotions before rational problem solving can take place. These emotions will be much more intense if the change takes place in an organization which lacks trust and two-way communication.

The manager must find out why the employee perceives the change as a threat. This means going beyond the employee's surface reason and examining the change as it affects the employee and his or her relationships with others. The attitude of the group as well as the sentiments of the informal leaders of the group can cause resistance to a change. It will therefore be helpful to seek out the informal leader in order to discuss why the change is perceived as a threat and what can be done about this.

Adjust "driving" and "opposing" forces.   As discussed earlier people resist change for a number of reasons. There are also, however, a number of reasons why people may want change. Some of these reasons are:

1. The desire for better methods of work.
2. The desire for an improved or upgraded job.
3. The desire for a new manager.
4. The desire for less control.
5. The incentives offered.
6. A climate encouraging continuing change.
7. The pressure of authority.
8. Recognition of the need for change in order to keep the company competitive.
9. Awareness of the organization's communication problems and of its lack of cooperation and clarity of purpose.

If a change has been implemented but is meeting with considerable resistance, action must be taken quickly to reduce that resistance. The general approach is to increase the pressures which favor change (driving forces) and to decrease the pressures which oppose change (see Exhibit 15–4).

Provide leadership and support.   We have seen in Chapter 12 that the effective leader adapts his or her leadership style to the

EXHIBIT 15–4
Driving forces and opposing forces of change in the organization

Driving forces		Opposing forces
Desire for better ways	→	← Economic loss
Improved job	→	
New manager	→	
Less control	→	← Personal reasons
Incentives	→ HRS	
Expectations of change	→	
Pressure of authority	→ Change	
Recognized need for change	←	← Social reasons
Awareness of communication problems, lack of cooperation, and lack of objectives	→	← Political reasons

EXHIBIT 15–5
Different approaches used in dealing with a disruptive worker

High-task manager	High-relationships manager	Behavior modification manager
Manager reaction: "This worker is going to be a troublemaker. This behavior must be stopped!"	"Oh, dear, I hope I can get them interacting and happy."	"Feels Tony needs to learn to cope in positive ways to replace aggressive behavior!" Separates conflicting workers without hostility or comment.
Supervisor-subordinate interaction: "Hey, you. Knock it off! We don't allow fighting around here," said with coldness or anger.	"How would you both like to give me a hand on a job over here?"	Manager watches for any positive behavior he can immediately reinforce. Supervisor sets limits on some behavior and carefully ignores others.
Worker reaction: Tony builds resentment and hostility. Next few days, behavior becomes more aggressive.	Tony finds he can get attention of supervisor by being disruptive because the supervisor wants to be "understanding." He causes trouble and watches supervisor's reaction. Supervisor pays more and more attention as his behavior gets worse. Disruptive behavior reinforced.	Tony finds the supervisor appreciates good things about him. Wants to gain his respect. Supervisor strategy: 1. Watches for any occurrences of positive behavior to reinforce. 2. Decides which new behaviors Tony needs to learn first. 3. Plans strategy to get desired behavior. 4. Attempts to better understand Tony in an effort to use incentives appropriate for his need structure. 5. Uses the incentives to reinforce behavior Tony needs to learn. 6. Continues to evaluate to make sure incentives are still appropriate since the appropriate incentives tend to change with time.
Outcome: Tony feels disliked by supervisor. Self-image deteriorates as he attempts to defend ego from assaults. Becomes more hostile and aggressive or withdrawn. Avoids supervisor and learning tasks.	Tony's aggressiveness remains. Becomes more obnoxious as other workers withdraw. Creates incidents to get attention and to get assigned to those jobs he wants. Does not learn. No friends. Low self-image covered by bravado.	Outcome in two or three weeks. Tony's work and acceptance by other members of his work group continue to improve. Builds new self-image on basis of new behavior he has learned. Hostile and aggressive behavior toward other employees stops. Begins to have a sense of accomplishment. Inner needs and feelings start to change. Aggressiveness used in constructive ways. Has friends and becomes a positive rather than a disruptive influence on his work group.

Source: Paul Hersey and Kenneth H. Blanchard, "The Management of Change." Reproduced by special permission from the January–February–March 1972 *Training and Development Journal.* Copyright 1972 by The American Society for Training and Development, Inc.

needs of the followers and of the situation at hand. This means, for example, that if a change results in overt resistance, different approaches could be used in dealing with the disruptive worker. Exhibit 15–5 shows the different approaches (along with the expected reactions and outcomes) used by three different types of managers.

In some cases the manager will have to engage in implicit or explicit bargaining with subordinates regarding those modifications in the changes which the subordinates feel to be justified. At the same time the manager must exercise firm, but fair, leadership in underscoring his or her belief in the fundamental necessity of the change. This may require corrective interviews and possible disciplinary action against any workers who continue to obstruct the change.

Experience shows that the resistance to change usually diminishes as people develop the knowledge and skills they need in order to perform successfully in the new situation. Thus, the manager should determine whether the affected employees have the necessary support to perform adequately. If additional training or knowledge is suggested, the manager might ask the human resources department to provide training sessions, courses, or workshops as required.

SUMMARY

The survival of the organization at which we work depends upon change. At the same time, problems caused by change have been among the most common management headaches since organizations have been in existence. In Chapter 5 we covered change at the macro level by focusing exclusively on changes made in the total organization in order to raise its level of performance. In this chapter we examined change at the manager-employee level. Specifically, we examined the nature of change, resistance to it, and how the manager can effectively deal with employees when introducing change.

All change is not resisted; nor is all resistance to change necessarily undesirable. Resistance to change is basically a reaction to the tension and anxiety caused by change. The reasons for resistance to change may be economic, personal, social, or political. The effective manager will keep these four areas of possible resistance in mind when trying to *avoid* resistance before it develops. *Overcoming* resistance once it has developed is a more difficult, but poor, secondary course of action.

One function of the human resources department is to work with line managers to avoid resistance before it can form. Practical steps that the manager should utilize include the following:

1. Develop two-way communication.
2. Provide opportunities for ego-involvement in the change.
3. Gain support for the change.
4. Provide a creative climate.

If resistance to a change takes place, action must be taken quickly to reduce it. We have seen how this can be accomplished by determining the causal factor, adjusting the "driving" and "opposing" forces, and providing the proper leadership and support.

CASE: ORDER PROCESSING

It had been six months since Mr. Spear, the newly hired manager of management information systems, had arrived on the scene. Ms. Dawn Adams recalled his first visit to her office. She had shown him the work flow of her order processing organization.

Six clerks received purchase orders and sales orders by mail and orders from salespersons over the telephone. Two other clerks checked records and divided these orders into "new customer" and "old customer" groups to be logged in a record journal and then checked for credit. Six more clerks edited the orders to see whether they were complete in terms of customer information and correct in terms of stock numbers and product descriptions. Finally, three typists transferred the order information onto a standard company form for transmission to product planning and control.

Most of Ms. Adams' employees were men and women in their 40s and 50s who had worked for the company for an average of 11 years. When they were interviewed by the MIS staff analysts, they had appeared quite agitated.

Ms. Adams had just met with Mr. Spear to go over his recommended change in her order processing operation. The changes included both system changes and computerization of most of the operation. This meant that a number of personnel would have to be trained in such computer-related skills as card punching and output checking. About eight people would have to be transferred to other sections of the company.

Ms. Adams considered calling her entire group together and informing the group as a whole of the new proposal, which was logical, economical, and certain to be implemented by management. On the other hand, she envisioned weeping men and women. Should she meet with each of her subordinates individually to provide reassurance and point out the advantages of the change to the subordinate? She was aware that after one or two people had been in her office, all of the others would get the news informally without the personal reassurances.

What were *all* the causes of resistance to this change going to be, and how could Ms. Adams overcome them?

QUESTIONS AND PROBLEMS

1. Describe specific ways in which changes in the following would affect the individual manager's job:
   a. A new layout for the office.
   b. Earlier retirement.
   c. The recent hiring of several black supervisors under the firm's affirmative action program.
2. Assume that you are a manager in a company having a strong union. Identify a specific change, and draw up a detailed plan showing how you would implement the change.
3. A computer is going to be installed in the ABC Company. What role would the human resources department play in implementing such a change? What role would the line manager play?
4. Of the four types of changes a manager may have to introduce, which is likely to create the most problems in the human resource system? Why?
5. What is the relationship between the complexity and the degree of change and the acceptance of change? Can you cite a minor change which met with considerable resistance? a major change which was enthusiastically accepted?
6. Discuss what the individual manager can do to stimulate creativity and change.
7. Is resistance to change to be expected? Why do people resist change?
8. What can be done to reduce or overcome resistance to change?
9. What do the previous chapters on communicating and leadership suggest to you concerning ways to *avoid* resistance to change?

BIBLIOGRAPHY

Dalton, Gene W., Lawrence, Paul R., and Greiner, Larry. *Organizational Change and Development*. Homewood, Ill.: Richard D. Irwin, 1970.

Davis, Keith. *Human Relations at Work*. 3d ed. New York: McGraw-Hill Book Co., 1967. See chap. 23, "Managing Change."

Goetz, Billy E., and Zimmerer, Thomas W. "New Employees: An Investment in Innovative Thinking." *Advanced Management Journal*, Autumn 1975.

Goldhar, Joel D., Bragaw, Louis K., and Schwartz, Jules J. "Information Flows, Management Styles, and Technological Innovation." *IEEE Transactions on Engineering Management,* February 1976.

Graham, Gerald H. *Management.* Belmont, Calif.: Wadsworth Publishing Co., 1975. See chap. 22, "Managing Change."

Harvey, Donald F., and Brown, Donald R. *An Experiential Approach to Organization Development.* Englewood Cliffs, N.J.: Prentice-Hall, 1976.

Hunt, John W. *The Restless Organization.* Sydney, Australia: John Wiley & Sons, 1972.

Kelley, George. "Seducing the Elites: The Politics of Decision Making in Organizational Networks." *Academy of Management Review,* July 1976.

Lawrence, Paul. "How to Deal with Resistance to Change." *Harvard Business Review,* January–February 1969.

Massie, Joseph L., and Douglas, John. *Managing: A Contemporary Introduction.* Englewood Cliffs, N.J.: Prentice-Hall, 1973. See chap. 8, "The Management of Change."

Morgan, John S. *Managing Change.* New York: McGraw-Hill Book Co., 1972.

O'Connell, Jeremiah. *Managing Organizational Innovation.* Homewood, Ill.: Richard D. Irwin, 1968.

Pierce, Jon L., and Delbecq, Andre L. "Organizational Structure, Individual Attitudes, and Innovation." *Academy of Management Review,* January 1977.

Skibbins, Gerald J. *Organizational Evolution.* New York: AMACOM, 1974.

Sokalik, Stanley L. *The Personnel Process: Line and Staff Dimensions in Managing People at Work.* Scranton, Pa.: International Textbook Co., 1970. See chap. 16, "Effecting Change: The Personnel Process under Stress."

Strauss, George, and Sayles, Leonard R. *Personnel: The Human Problems of Management.* 3d ed. Englewood Cliffs, N.J.: Prentice-Hall, 1972. See chap. 12, "Introducing Change."

Tosi, Henry L., and Hammer, W. Clay. *Organizational Behavior and Management: A Contingency Approach.* Chicago: St. Clair Press, 1974.

Weaver, Charles N. "What Workers Want Most from Their Jobs." *Personnel,* May–June 1976.

NOTES

[1] Donald F. Harvey and Donald R. Brown, *An Experiential Approach to Organization Development* (Englewood Cliffs, N.J.: Prentice-Hall, 1976).

[2] Billy E. Goetz and Thomas W. Zimmerer, "New Employees: An Investment in Innovative Thinking," *Advanced Management Journal,* Autumn 1975.

[3] Charles N. Weaver, "What Workers Want Most from Their Jobs," *Personnel,* May–June 1976.

[4] For example, see Stanley L. Sokalik, *The Personnel Process: Line and Staff Dimensions in Managing People at Work* (Scranton, Pa.: International Textbook Co., 1970), pp. 410–11.

[5] Burleigh B. Gardner and David G. Moore, *Human Relations in Industry*, 4th ed. (Homewood, Ill.: Richard D. Irwin, 1964), p. 465.

[6] Joel D. Goldhar, Louis K. Bragaw, and Jules J. Schwartz, "Information Flows, Management Styles, and Technological Innovation," *IEEE Transactions on Engineering Management*, February 1976.

[7] Keith Davis, *Human Relations at Work*, 3d ed. (New York: McGraw-Hill Book Co., 1967), pp. 393–95.

[8] L. W. Gruenfeld and F. F. Foltman, "Relationship among Supervisors' Integration, Satisfaction, and Acceptance of a Technological Change," *Journal of Applied Psychology*, February 1967.

[9] John R. P. French, Jr. et al., "An Experiment on Participation in a Norwegian Factory," *Human Relations*, February 1960; and M. Sashkin, "Participation in Organization: A Contingency Analysis," paper presented at the Michigan Psychological Association meeting, Eastern Michigan University, April 5, 1974.

PART IV

HUMAN RESOURCES IN THE CHANGING ENVIRONMENT

When you have completed studying
FUTURE CHALLENGES AND RESPONSE
you should be able to:

1. Identify four major areas of change which are likely to affect human resources management significantly.
2. Identify the factors which are producing change in the four major areas.
3. Write an essay on the changes in human resources management that may be required to deal with these change factors.
4. Outline a plan for a human resources organization of five to ten years hence.

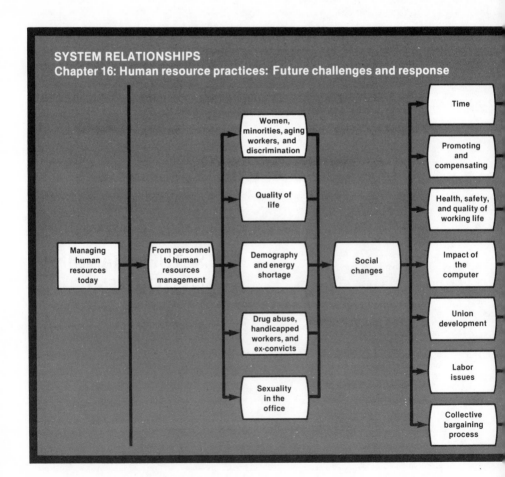

SYSTEM RELATIONSHIPS
Chapter 16: Human resource practices: Future challenges and response

The essence of managing is to prepare for the future rather than back into it. The manager of human resources in an organization must start preparations now to cope with changes anticipated over the next five to ten years. Changes are occurring at such a rate and magnitude as to challenge the most creative managers.

To cope with change, we must anticipate likely "futures of the world." The future world is determined by fundamental trends, the responses of

16

Future challenges and response

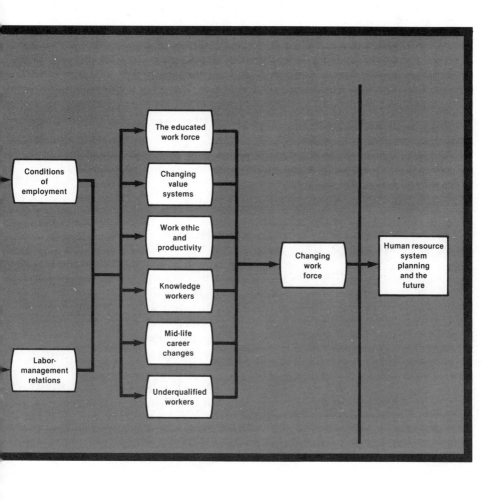

governments to world events, and changes in the values and behavior of people.

The development of descriptions of the future has been carried out by a variety of people from cartoonists and novelists to scientists. Such descriptions are often called "scenarios." The basis for such scenarios may be imagination, extrapolation of trends, modeling the world with the aid of systems analysis and the computer, or special processes involving panels of experts. Our peering into the future rests on our interpretation of trends and the views of experts.[1]

The purpose of this chapter is to suggest specific changes that we may expect in the human resource system and possible responses by management. Different experts in the human resource field will probably have somewhat different visions of the future. The manager can only try to prepare for several of the more likely possibilities.

We cover a variety of topics in this chapter and attempt to answer three questions in each case:

What is the present situation?

What are the likely coming changes?

How may these changes affect the management of human resources?

Our intent is to evoke discussion and to stimulate the reader to think about the future.

FROM PERSONNEL ADMINISTRATION TO HUMAN RESOURCES MANAGEMENT

We believe that the personnel department as it exists in 1979 will no longer exist in the late 1980s in any but the smallest organizations. We predict that specialists in human resources management (the staff experts in the human resources area) will either take on a radically different role than that currently performed by the typical personnel department or that they will cease to exist as a staff organization.

Although we have stressed throughout this book the responsibility of *line* managers for the management of human resources, we believe nevertheless that there is a parallel important role for staff expertise. Human resource experts will be needed to serve as internal consultants to line management in areas of growing technical difficulty, such as selection, motivation, organization development, compensation, and management by objectives.

In the 1980s and beyond, the staff specialists in human resources management will be called on less and less for routine maintenance functions, such as record keeping and orientation and training programs, but will be in increasing demand as a source of expert advice and counsel for busy line managers. This role can be assumed by human resource specialists only if they are willing to assume it, and only if they become as technically expert in managing human resources as the organization's accountants and finance officers are technically expert in their function. The day of the washed-up production manager as "personnel director" is rapidly coming to an end. The real experts in human resources management will be recognized as major contributors to the performance of their organizations.

Fundamental trends

To summarize briefly, among the fundamental trends which we believe will provide increased importance to the human resources management function are the following:

1. The increasing realization of top management that in an era of declining productivity human resources *really* are the organization's most important asset. Top management will expect human resources specialists to be more proactive in solving the real management problems of the company, and will come to expect a more meaningful *bottom-line* contribution from them.
2. Severe pressure on the economy springing from declining productivity in the United States coexistent with rapidly increasing productivity in Japan, West Germany, and other competing economies.
3. Radical social changes in the American culture which have led to a new set of values among Americans generally and specifically among members of the work force.
4. The rising expectations of members of the work force with regard to the possibilities for satisfying higher level needs as well as lower level needs at the workplace. Coupled with this are an increasing resistance to the role of authority and an increasing desire for participation in decision making, control over job factors, and a voice in how the organization is run.

5. The flood of legislation in the 1960s and 70s (particularly OSHA and equal opportunity legislation).

The changing role of human resource specialists

Because of the changes in management philosophy and the environment discussed above, we foresee the following radical changes in the role of specialists in human resources management.

1. These specialists will tend less and less to be individuals who spend their entire careers in human resources management. An increasing proportion of human resource specialists will be managers who spend a part of their career assigned to the specialized function of managing human resources. Often these will be seen as key developmental assignments for high-potential executives who are being groomed for top management positions. This trend will develop because of the increasing realization that human resources management is an integral function of line management and therefore an important training step for executives who are being developed for high general management positions. The human resources management function will be looked upon increasingly as a profit center in the organization, with opportunity for generating incremental profit; thus it will command the best executive talent that the organization has to offer. Although we believe that this phenomenon will occur much more extensively over the next 25 years, there is evidence that such a trend has already developed. In the early 1970s more and more organizations began promoting their top personnel executives to general management positions. At the same time, more and more up-and-coming "hotshots" began to receive development assignments in human resources management. We believe that we have only begun to see the tip of the iceberg; what is now worthy of comment will be commonplace by the 1980s. By 1985 we believe that it will be no more unusual for the vice president of human resources to become a company president than it would be for the vice president of marketing, the vice president of production, or the vice president of finance.

2. As the human resource department takes on its new role as internal consultant to line management, we believe that some specialists will also take on the role of staff behavioral scientist. Their key duties will include bringing the latest ideas from research and theory in the behavioral sciences to the organization and translating those ideas for line executives in very practical and operational terms. The human resource department will be charged with introducing the latest scientific techniques for effectively managing

human resources, just as the research and development organization is charged with bringing the latest developments of technology into the organization. The human resources management specialist will be viewed as a member of the total management team, as an internal consultant to all levels of management, and as a source of expertise.

3. Because both of the above developments call for vastly higher skills (both general management skills and technical skills in the behavioral sciences), human resource specialists will be much better educated and more experienced than they typically are at present. Advanced degrees in general management (MBA degrees) or advanced degrees in the behavioral sciences will become commonplace. Perhaps the very best human resource specialists will combine MBA degrees with advanced degrees in the behavioral sciences.

4. Vastly increased attention will be paid to fitting the various subfunctions of human resources management to organizational objectives. A systems view will require that the organization's overall objectives (especially its profit objectives) be the starting point for the development of all strategies for the management of human resources. It will increasingly be recognized that the only purpose of the subfunctions of human resources management is to serve the achievement of overall organizational objectives.

5. Certain subfunctions of human resources management will tend to receive disproportionately greater emphasis in the last 25 years of the 20th century. Among the functions which we see growing dramatically in importance are organization development, work force planning, compensation planning and administration, and management by objectives. These will be the key subfunctions of human resources management in the 1980s because they have the greatest potential for contributing to increased profits. At the same time, much less attention will be paid to routine record keeping, lower level training unrelated to organizational objectives, and employee services.

Finally, underlying all of the above changes will be the assumption of a contingency approach to managing human resources. The contingency approach departs from the assumption that all people have the same needs and expectations and that they can therefore be managed in the same way. It assumes that people are quite different in terms of the needs which motivate them, the managerial styles and policies to which they will respond, and the kinds of organizational environment in which they can be most effective.

SOCIAL CHANGES

Women at work

Women constitute slightly under 50 percent of the labor force; yet they constitute only about 5 percent of the managers. Generally, they hold lower-paying stereotyped positions in business. As marriages become equalized relationships, more women will be able to engage in lifetime careers. In addition, the number of women attending colleges of business administration will increase greatly over the next ten years. As the pool of competent people increases, the quality and productivity of the work force will tend to increase significantly.[2]

Organization development programs directed at changing the attitudes of both men and women are a possible response by management. Managements may also establish day-care centers at the plant to relieve the stress on both husband and wife with regard to the care of preschool children.

Discrimination at work

Most objective measures indicate that blacks have made substantial gains during the past decade in terms of income, promotion and employment opportunities, and skills. At the same time, a great many career opportunities are now being opened to women and all but the subtle discriminatory barriers are disappearing. Thus, although equal employment opportunities for women and minority groups will remain important problems, emphasis will shift to discrimination based on age.

We can expect the state and federal regulatory agencies to change their emphasis from a preoccupation with overt discrimination to correcting the more deep-rooted procedures which have perpetrated inequality. This will mean more challenges to the traditional selection and promotion methods of all organizations. It will also mean more action from the regulatory agencies to require individual firms to establish specific goals and quotas for certain age groups, females, and members of minority groups. This, in turn, will result in growing resentment among the white males who are bypassed for employment and/or promotion. Lawsuits and charges of reverse discrimination can be expected.

This means that unless human resources departments devise ways of increasing job opportunities for minority, female, and older workers, they will face challenges to their traditional selection,

training, and promotion practices. At the same time, all human resources managers must devise ways of handling the resentment that
will develop among those employees who are negatively affected
by these new antidiscrimination policies.

The quality of life

It is generally conceded that the quality of life is deteriorating.
Inflation, pollution, overpopulation, crime, and the stress due to the
complexity of modern life are all contributing factors. Instead of the
rugged individualist, we find the nervous citizen who views the
employer as arbiter of his or her fate.[3] Workers will face increasing
frustration and resentment over unfulfilled expectations with regard
to life outside the workplace.

Although the human resources specialist and management are
limited in their power to reduce most frustrations off the job, they
can seek more ways to reduce frustrations on the job. Possible responses include making greater efforts toward job enrichment, de-
voting greater attention to the encouragement and recognition of
each individual, and arranging work tasks to bring about more social interaction on the job.

Drug abuse, alcoholism, handicapped workers, and ex-convicts

There are today a number of small groups or organizations which
are concerned with rehabilitating people who have special employment problems. These people are drug abusers (including alcoholics), handicapped workers, or ex-convicts. The National Alcohol Council estimates that 6 percent of the nation's work force
suffers from some kind of alcohol or drug abuse problem and that
another 4 percent suffers from some kind of physical or mental dis-
order that affects job performance. There are over 10 million "troubled" workers. The cost to business is *10 billion* dollars annually.

The percentage of alcoholics is likely to remain about the same.
On the other hand, as our country becomes more health-conscious,
the social use of alcohol may decline slightly. Further, as programs
improve, abusers may be rehabilitated at an earlier stage. Offsetting
this decrease will be the growing number of people who turn to
alcohol for relief from the declining quality of life.

Drugs may be classified as sedative-hypnotic, psychedelic, central nervous system stimulant, and narcotic. With ever increasing
tension and competition for jobs, the first group, tranquilizers, and
the third group, "pep pills," will probably become more common.

The use of narcotics, which receives so much attention because of its impact on individual behavior, will probably start to decrease in the next few years. This is because the large number of hard-drug addicts who returned from Vietnam are turning increasingly to sedative-hypnotic drugs.

Some companies, notably Kemper Insurance Company, have long-standing alcoholic rehabilitation programs. Kemper currently has a program to aid former drug addicts. Such programs generally consist of sensitizing all managers to these problems, early detection, professional help, and indicating company concern for the welfare of the individual. It is made clear to the worker (or manager) that the responsibility for cure, and job retention, lies with him or her. Agencies such as the National Institute of Alcohol Abuse and Alcoholism provide assistance to companies in starting programs.

A much smaller group of people now receiving concentrated attention by government and business are the physically handicapped. New regulations have recently been issued by the Labor Department under Section 503 of the Vocational Rehabilitation Act of 1973 to spur the employment of handicapped workers.

A serious problem exists with regard to ex-convicts. Companies which have programs do not seek publicity. Companies do not show such past history in the individual's personnel record in order to protect the worker. Generally, ex-convicts have a difficult time finding employment despite the government agencies which provide assistance.

It will be advantageous for business if companies take the initiative in developing programs for the rehabilitation and employment of such problem workers. If they do not, we expect that laws will be strengthened and government regulations issued to *require* affirmative action and constant reporting.

Demography and the energy shortage

Our population has grown rapidly in the past and will continue to grow at a slower rate. People have spread out from the center of cities. The automobile has become a necessary means for getting to work. Because of our government's failure to inform the American people of the seriousness of the energy shortage and because of efforts to hide the shortage through regulated low prices for gasoline, a crisis is in the offing.

The general public is having difficulty in understanding that a serious energy shortage will occur within the next three to ten years. Mass transit within urban areas will increase slowly, but most industry is located at a distance from residential areas. The development of electric- or alcohol-powered automobiles is a possibility for the future.

To cope with these problems, work force planning and site location should be closely related. Large companies may be able to establish themselves centrally to residential communities. If heavy industry can clean itself up, avoid pollution, and increase the beautification of plants, it may be able to locate near residential areas. Companies may have to become involved with local governments in developing mass transit from city to plants.

Aged workers

Currently most companies have a mandatory retirement age which is often overruled for chief executive officers. Retirement at age 65 is required in most companies, although the retirement age may vary from 62 to 70 years of age.

The Age Discrimination in Employment Act has been increasingly enforced. The act covers private employers of 20 or more people and public and labor organizations. It protects people who are at least 40 years old but under 65 from age discrimination.

The trend is toward greater government pressure to prevent age discrimination. In the future, pressure will develop to do away with mandatory retirement age limits.

Human resources managers should be developing criteria to differentiate between adequate and inadequate job performance. Companies cannot afford to retain slow, senile workers, but they also cannot afford to lose alert, intelligent, and highly experienced people because of age barriers.

Sexuality in the office

Two unrelated problems that are now becoming apparent are sexual harassment and the existence of homosexuals in business.

Women in business have long been forced to bear up quietly under the pat, pinch, or proposition. Often, sexual harassment has been practically a condition of employment. At present, in some states, women may file a complaint with the state against sexual harassment. Few do, however, because such cases are difficult to prove.

With women's rights and better education of women on how to handle sexual harassment, this indignity will decline somewhat. On the other hand, as more women rise to positions of power, males may find themselves facing the same type of harassment.

Management will have to stop closing its eyes to such practices. Policies may be formulated in writing. Serious action, including the careful investigation of complaints and protection for the victims, may be instituted. Penalties and sanctions may be levied against offenders.

Studies have produced conflicting results as to the prevalence of homosexuality. For example, in a study of 5,600 executives by Harry J. Johnson, 4.4 percent revealed themselves as homosexuals.[4] On the other hand, Richard Zoglin's article "The Homosexual Executive" estimated the percentage of gay managers as ranging from 10 percent to 20 percent.[5] Many homosexuals fear that they may lose their jobs or be barred from promotion. They frequently live a double life, having wives and children. Research on homosexual women in industry is essentially nonexistent.[6]

As sexual identities and roles are explored, and society comes to accept the presence of homosexuals, such persons will have less to fear. As long as their behavior does not influence accepted work roles, homosexuals will no longer need to suffer the tensions of secrecy and potential blackmail.

THE CONDITIONS OF EMPLOYMENT

Time

Reduction in time spent on the job will continue to be the trend. In 1910, the average employee worked 54 hours per week. Today, the five-day, 40-hour workweek is standard. In New York City, the workday is generally 9 A.M. to 5 P.M. In some isolated industries, such as rubber, the workweek is 32 to 35 hours.

Because we will be able to satisfy the majority of society's material needs with fewer and fewer workers, it is likely that the workweek will be further reduced within the next ten years. In addition, as women achieve equality with men, it is possible that workweeks will be shortened so that more people can be employed and husbands and wives may spend more time together.

"Flexitime," an innovation more common in Europe but receiving considerable attention in the United States and Canada, will probably increase in the next decade. Flexitime allows each employee to work the required number of hours within a range of time. It is built around a central core of hours during the middle of the business day, when all employees are expected to be present. Starting and quitting times are set by workers to meet their own needs. For example, swingers who stay up late at night might come to work at

10 A.M. They would take a shorter lunch break and work extra time at the end of the normal day. Other employees might like to take a longer lunch break, and perhaps squeeze in a few sets of tennis. They would start earlier and finish later than the normal hours. Although complex administrative problems may increase, employee cooperation to date has surprised many opponents of flexitime.

Because people wish to have larger blocks of time for recreation, over 200 firms in the United States have gone to four ten-hour days per week with mixed results. Such plans will probably precede four-day weeks with fewer hours per day.

As more workers get more time off, however, their desire for goods and services will increase, and boredom will become a problem for many. Therefore, we anticipate that moonlighting (holding down two jobs) will increase. The restraining forces will be the severe competition for most jobs. However, skilled workers and managers will not find this a great obstacle.

At the executive level, leaves of absence for professional development purposes are being tried by larger companies. The executive may work for the federal government or return to school for an advanced degree. Shorter leaves of several months are granted so that executives can attend advanced management programs. Such "sabbaticals" broaden and recharge the individual. By 1985, this practice will be very common, and it will be necessary for the human resources manager to develop policies that will bring about the practice, assure fairness to individuals, and guide the company in utilizing this benefit to the mutual advantage of the person and the company.

Compensation

Because compensation comes in so many forms, the human resources manager of the future faces a great challenge. Many forms of compensation may provide greater rewards to the employee than they cost the company. A highly paid executive may perceive several days off per month or a long vacation as more valuable than a raise which costs the company the same amount, for example, and Christmas or vacation bonuses may have more impact than does the equivalent in salary spread throughout the year. On the other hand, the company may pay out large amounts in salary and fringe benefits that do not represent great rewards in the minds of the employees.

The concept of flexi-compensation, in which compensation is

tailored to each individual's desires, may expand in the future. For example, an older worker might prefer to give up a birthday as a paid holiday in exchange for more health insurance. Younger employees might like "maternity leaves" for new fathers. An infinite number of combinations is possible, given a complex benefit structure. Because of the complexity of such policies, the human resource staff will need to become deeply involved in this task.

The impact of the computer

The impact that the computer will have on business operations in the next ten years is beyond the imagination of most people. The present rate of increase in computer miniaturization, speed, and storage capacity will revolutionize organization and processes within companies. Managers will become systems oriented and will participate as partners with systems designers. The master-servant relationship of today's hierarchical organization will fade considerably as people play out their roles in systems where a large proportion of decisions will be programmed.

The development of special-purpose and general-purpose process computers for the factory will relieve humans of much of the dull routine of monitoring automatic machines.

The human resources manager should be looking forward to the need for having and training systems designers, people with a broad knowledge of various areas of business. Fewer unskilled workers will be required, and jobs will demand more creativity.

Objectivity in selecting, promoting, compensating

Over the years sophisticated tools for selecting, promoting, and compensating employees have been developed. Many companies are not aware of these tools, and many more prefer not to use them. It is common for companies to select, promote, and compensate people on the basis of friendships or political arrangements within the organization.

We predict, however, that the need for increased productivity and civil rights laws will lead to the adoption of more scientific approaches to selecting and rewarding personnel. It will be essential to fit people better to jobs and to fit better people to the better jobs. With the increased education of managers and the development of the systems approach to managing, the incompetent manager or functional worker will soon be uncovered. This is because management by objectives and the evaluation of performance against established objectives will be increasingly applied as measurement tools.

Health and safety

Much has been accomplished in providing a safe workplace for the employee. Unfortunately, however, the rise in the frequency of work injuries that began in the 1960s has not been reversed. Although most *Fortune* 500 firms now have excellent accident prevention and safety engineering programs, many small and medium-sized employers are facing a rising accident rate.

The Occupational Safety and Health Act of 1970 was passed in order to make the working environment safer. Both employees and employers will need to learn of the intent and the procedures of the new regulations, which are still undergoing modification. Public employees, once considered outside the purview of such laws, are now covered. Members of the human resources department will become the in-house experts on safety and occupational health.

The impact of the employee's job upon mental health is just becoming recognized. There is growing awareness by some corporate managements that they have a stake in the "whole person" not just in the employee's physical being. We expect that this awareness will lead to such things as corporate alcoholic and drug abuse programs. Accordingly, organization-wide programs of information and education concerning the dimensions of these problems need to be established. Provision must be made for professional services. Supervisors and managers at all levels must be given training so that they can carry out their responsibilities under such programs.

The quality of working life

The quality of working life will improve slightly for people on production lines. This will be the result of greater automation and job enrichment. The nature of continuous production will, however, make progress slow. Shorter workweeks will improve the quality of the total working life.

In white-collar jobs, greater team effort, more interaction among employees, increased emphasis on creativity and responsibility, and computerization of more and more routine, repetitive work will make work life much more interesting to employees.

The challenge to the HR manager is to stay at the forefront and encourage management to participate in this trend. Failure to adapt early will mean the loss of good employees and problems with the remaining employees, who will be trying to protect themselves against change.

LABOR-MANAGEMENT RELATIONS

Union membership

Although many projections suggest that union membership will decline as a proportion of the total labor force, certain areas of the labor force will become more unionized.[7] Some experts predict that the labor movement in this country will die out as a result of more white-collar jobs, more female employees, more educated workers, higher standards of living, and better management practices. Most experts, however, see union growth as being on the verge of a tremendous leap forward as teachers, police officers, government employees, clerical workers, nurses, and other professionals and paraprofessionals begin to organize.

For example, according to a 1976 study by the Conference Board, a private business research group, 40 percent of all salaried non-managerial professionals are now represented by collective bargaining agents, as compared to 25 percent of the labor force as a whole. Union leaders feel that this trend will continue for a number of reasons. For one thing, by 1980 more workers will be employed in white-collar jobs than in all other occupational groups combined. By 1985, the growth rate in white-collar occupations is expected to include a 34 percent increase among clerical workers, a 30 percent increase among professional and technical workers, and a 28 percent increase among service workers. Another reason underlying pro-union attitudes among white-collar workers, especially professional employees, is concern with job and wage security during uncertain economic periods. Seniority provisions and cost-of-living escalator clauses have even gained in appeal with professionals as they become more susceptible to layoffs and as inflation erodes their purchasing power.

Labor issues

The labor unions themselves are likely to face increased internal conflict and strife as younger members and leaders challenge older leaders. The younger workers, with different values and more education, are likely to be more demanding and to be concerned with different issues. For example, pension programs, which have been gaining since the 1950s, will decline in importance, and other benefits, such as company-financed training programs, will be emphasized. The new union members will be less interested in seniority for job upgrading, and instead will push for programs which will allow them to adjust to change and to upgrade themselves. Unions will also put more pressure on management to enrich jobs and to give more attention to social issues, such as ecology.

A trend is developing toward fewer but larger labor unions. A broader union structure, with fewer unions, results in more financial and political power. This facilitates union organizing activities. The development of broad-base unions will also reduce jurisdictional disputes among unions and make the unions more adaptive to technological change. We are also likely to see the Auto Workers and the Teamsters reaffiliate with the AFL–CIO. When this occurs, the labor movement will have even more political clout. Thus, as the federal government increases its control over employment matters, the AFL–CIO, with its added strength, will expand its political activity in order to obtain favorable labor laws and regulations.

The collective bargaining process

It is well known that in the past the collective bargaining process has often been marked by prolonged and violent strikes as well as other forms of hostile behavior. In more recent times, labor relations have improved considerably. An overwhelming number of contracts are settled without stalemates and strikes. When strikes have taken place, incidents of violence have decreased significantly. Furthermore, instead of resorting to open warfare in order to settle disputes over the interpretation of existing contracts, the unions and management have reached equitable settlements through the grievance and arbitration procedures.

Regardless of what may be said to the press during contract negotiations, there is growing evidence that a feeling of mutual respect and trust exists between many union officials and management. In addition, more and more companies have changed their emphasis from "breaking" the union to seeing how to get along with it on a day-to-day basis.

At the same time, the unions are recognizing that, since no business firm is an island, future wage and benefit increases hinge on productivity increases. We will probably be hearing more about productivity bargaining, and unions will probably be urging their members to find new ways to increase output to ward off foreign competition. More and more union leaders will realize that in the last analysis the future of employees depends upon the economic survival and the prosperity of the business.

It is unlikely that the lawmakers will pass any restrictions on free collective bargaining, such as compulsory arbitration. Although conflict and disruption will still occur, management and the unions are likely to voluntarily agree to have third parties resolve such incidents. At the same time, more private and public organizations will hire qualified professional staffs to handle the technical aspects of union-management relations, such as contract negotiations. These human resource specialists will also play an important role in advising and training line managers on labor relations matters.

CHANGES IN THE ECONOMY AND PROBLEMS OF PRODUCTIVITY

In the early 1970s a number of simultaneous profound changes in the business environment called unprecedented attention to the importance of the human resources management function. These environmental pressures included a major recession for the entire United States, vastly increased foreign competition in many of America's traditional markets (including such high-technology areas as electronics and computers), and a halt for the first time in the steady rise of productivity per worker-hour. These three environmental pressures were interrelated and tended to reinforce one another, but they were also to some extent independent.

Although these environmental forces all seemed to hit at once in the early 1970s, the pressures had been building for years. Furthermore, these forces will continue to push industry in essentially the same direction for at least the next 20 years. Thus, we predict that they will continue to play an important role in calling attention to and increasing the importance of the human resources management function for the remainder of the 20th century.

The decline in the rate of productivity gains

A serious slippage in the rate of increase in productivity per worker-hour began in the mid-1960s. During the 1960s the rate of increase in productivity in the United States was in the vicinity of 3 percent per year. Although this was lower than the historical average in the United States, and far lower than that of any of the rapidly industrializing competing nations, such as Japan and West Germany, the 3 percent figure in the 60s was generally viewed as a problem to be solved rather than as an impending disaster.

Toward the end of the 60s, however, the rate of increase slowed even more, and it was near zero by 1973. It again fell sharply in 1974, resulting in an unprecedented *decline* in productivity per worker-hour. Although the severity of the decline may have been due *in part* to the severe recession under way in 1974, the long-range trend makes it obvious that declining productivity is a long-term problem.

With improvement in the economy in 1975, the output per worker-hour leveled off to about a zero change. Meanwhile, the output per worker-hour of Japan and West Germany has continued to increase, making the United States less and less able to compete in many of its traditional markets.

Increasing attention to productivity

A U.S. productivity center has recently been created, and several states have created productivity commissions to encourage the joint participation of management and labor in efforts to improve the quality of work. One of the early states to set up such a joint productivity commission was Ohio.

Although the 1974–75 recession seems to have contributed to the decrease in worker-hour productivity, the long-term downward trend appears to have more fundamental causes. A number of studies, such as the 1973 Department of Health, Education, and Welfare study *Work in America*, edited by Elliot Richardson, and a 1973 report of the American Assembly Seminar conducted by Columbia University, have pointed to the quality of working life and the lack of fundamental satisfaction in jobs as the underlying causes of the productivity crisis.

Both reports concluded that major changes are taking place in American life which present both a threat and an opportunity in relation to industrial productivity. The consensus of both reports was that a major part of the solution to this problem must lie in a massive attempt to restructure and improve the quality of working life and to give workers increasing opportunities to satisfy such higher level needs as recognition, participation, autonomy, responsibility, and self-development.

Some data are now available on early experimental attempts—including attempts at job enrichment—by companies to improve productivity through improving the quality of work life. Among the organizations whose efforts appear to be having significant success are General Motors, Travelers Insurance, Texas Instruments, American Telephone and Telegraph, Kaiser Aluminum, Xerox, and Motorola.

Productivity and the quality of working life

As a result of the growing interest in the quality of working life and the environmental press of foreign competition, much greater attention will be paid over the next 25 years to the key role of the human resources management function in improving productivity through improvements in the quality of working life. We predict, therefore, that such techniques as organization development, job enrichment, and management by objectives will continue to receive ever greater attention from top management.

For the same reasons, we believe that more and more workers will demand participation and some degree of control in the important managerial decisions which affect them. We also predict that more and more top managers will see the wisdom of reacting to such demands creatively by finding ways to match organizational policy and objectives to individual needs.

Because of the increased attention to the quality of working life, we predict optimistically that over the next 25 years a significantly higher portion of the work force will be motivated and committed to their work. We believe that increasing proportions of the work force will come to find their work satisfying and rewarding, as more and more organizations are forced by environmental press to create enriched jobs and to provide increased participation in decision making and a more satisfying work climate.

The measurement of productivity

We also predict that more attention will be paid to the measurement of productivity by executives at all levels. More attention and effort will be directed toward the refinement of techniques for measuring and improving productivity. More and more, both corporate and individual objectives will tend to reflect specific productivity targets.

If drastic change in the direction of more effective management of human resources is not forthcoming, America will simply fail to compete effectively in the world marketplace and will lose its position of industrial leadership. We do not believe that our society will allow this to happen.

THE CHANGING WORK FORCE—WHERE HAVE ALL THE ROBOTS GONE?

The educated work force

It is widely recognized that the culture and the social order of the United States have undergone radical changes during the decade of the 1960s and the early 1970s. These widespread changes have been documented in an earlier section of this chapter. Not surprisingly, since the work force is merely a portion of the total society, these changes in the society at large have been reflected in changes among the work force.

Since more people in our society are graduating from high school, going to college, and receiving advanced degrees every year, the work force is made up increasingly of highly educated and sophisticated employees. An increasing number of professional employees are receiving advanced degrees. Equally important is the fact that more first-level supervisors have college degrees and that most blue-collar workers just joining the work force have high school diplomas or some college.

Moreover, the work force is becoming more knowledgeable and more sophisticated because of its exposure to the media. This is both an advantage and a challenge to management. As a society becomes better informed and more sophisticated, it also tends to become more critical, less accepting of authority, and more cynical.

This change in attitude has clearly been reflected in the work force. Workers, particularly younger workers, are increasingly inclined to challenge management's judgment, increasingly cynical about the decisions made by superiors, and increasingly resistant to authority. Whether we are referring to executives, middle and firstline managers, or blue-collar workers, it is generally true that the "organization man" of the 50s has given way to the rebel of the 70s.

We believe that this change is a direct result of higher levels of education and sophistication, and thus represents more an opportunity than a threat to management, if the change can be properly understood and defined. We say it is an opportunity because higher quality human resources are potentially more productive human resources, if they can be directed toward the organization's purpose. Managers will need to consult more with employees on decisions which affect the employees' activities.

Changing value systems

It should be anticipated that one of the complexities of managing human resources over the next 25 years will be the problem of dealing with a work force with more rapidly changing values. By and large, younger workers have reflected the changed values of society at large more quickly. As compared to older workers, they are more distrustful of authority and more cynical, and they expect more satisfaction of higher level needs from their work. Older workers tend to reflect more the earlier values of society and are therefore more inclined to be "organization men," to accept authority, and to seek primarily the satisfaction of lower level needs at work.

A specific research study done by Altinus and Tersine supports this statement.[8] The study investigated the job satisfaction level of young blue-collar workers. The perceptions and satisfactions of the young were quite different from those of their older counterparts. The younger workers were found to be significantly lower in satisfaction with the work itself and in total work satisfaction. The study also concluded that younger workers tend to try to meet higher level needs on the job, whereas older workers consider social factors on the job more important.

Although different segments of the work force will need to be managed differently for some time to come, it also appears to be true that there is a steady and continuing shift in the values of the total work force toward less acceptance of authority, greater cynicism, increased desire for participation in decision making, and increased desire to satisfy higher level needs at the job. This overall shift is due in part to the retirement of older workers and the influx of younger workers and in part to the changing values of the older workers themselves.

Thus, one complication for the human resources manager of the 1970s and 1980s will be the need to deal with the different values and motivations of different segments of the work force. This is, of course, only another example of the need for the contingency approach to management policy and practice which has been stressed throughout this book.

The work ethic and productivity

One cause of the drop in worker-hour productivity in recent years (discussed in an earlier section of this chapter) may well be that jobs and human resources management practices have not kept pace with the changing values and expectations of the work force.

For example, in the important Department of Health, Education, and Welfare report entitled *Work in America*, Elliot Richardson concludes that "the design of jobs appears to be lagging markedly behind the enormous gains in educational attainments of the work force, and the elevation in credentials required of the worker has not been accompanied by an elevation in the content of work. If anything, it is more routine and bureaucratized, leaving less to the imagination and control of the worker."[9]

An important change in the values of the work force during the 1970s has been a general decline in the work ethic. There was a time when most people in our culture believed that work was inherently good and took great pride in their work. They felt that work had meaning and value in its own right. This cultural belief has sometimes been referred to as the Protestant ethic, and it has been said to have originated in the Puritan notion that work represents an opportunity to earn salvation and that success symbolizes the attainment of salvation.

It has been suggested by some that the loss of pride in work is due to the increasing size of organizations, the increasing remoteness of the end product, and the increasing specialization of work. We believe that this is true because the increasing size and depersonalization of organizations, the increasing remoteness of the end product, and the increasing specialization of work all lead to lowered opportunities to satisfy higher level needs at work. The result of these trends has been to reduce motivation and therefore productivity. The only solution is to change the design of jobs so that there is a real opportunity to obtain a sense of accomplishment and pride from the work itself.

The shift of the work force to knowledge workers

Another important change in the work force which impacts management strategy for managing human resources is the shifting balance between manual workers and knowledge workers. During the early 1970s the U.S. economy passed a significant milestone when manual workers were outnumbered for the very first time in any society by knowledge workers, whose work depends on mental skills rather than physical skills and whose productivity is directly related to formal education. As Peter Drucker has pointed out, "This historic shift in the nature of work makes Theory Y a necessity. The knowledge worker simply does not produce under Theory X. Knowledge has to be self-directed; the knowledge worker has to take responsibility."[10]

Another fundamental change is the tendency for larger and larger portions of the work force to identify primarily with their profession or occupation rather than with their employer. As the level of training increases, it seems to follow naturally that workers begin to identify themselves as members of a particular professional or occupational group. They become more loyal to the norms and values of that professional or occupational group than to their individual employers.

This has at least two immediate results. First of all, the work force is more mobile, due in part to the weakening of the ties with a particular employer. Another result is what Herbert Meyer refers to as the increased tendency toward "whistle blowing." Meyer means by this the tendency of both the worker and the executive to call public attention to the actions of the employer when they feel that these actions violate their professional or ethical standards.[11] Although this phenomenon has received relatively little attention, we believe that it may well represent a "sleeper" in terms of its future significance to management. The increased tendency of members of the work force to look for, to find, and then to publicize errors of judgment or violations of law underscores dramatically the importance of making absolutely certain that everything the organization does in managing its human resources is in accordance with the laws regulating human resources.

Mid-life career changing

Related to all of the above changes is the increasing frequency of mid-life career changes. It is becoming common for both managers and blue-collar workers to make dramatic shifts in their career pattern. Executives enter the priesthood; engineers and scientists go into small businesses unrelated to their technical training; and blue-collar workers leave their trade to go to college and a new professional career. Undoubtedly, the increased frequency of mid-life career changes is due to a number of underlying factors already discussed, including increased affluence, increased education and sophistication, and increased awareness of higher level needs.

The increased acceptance of mid-life career changes combined with the greater knowledge requirements of most occupations has led to the rapid development of a new view of education as a lifetime pursuit. The rapid development of company-sponsored training and development programs, the increased attendance of both blue-collar and managerial workers in part-time college courses while employed, and the pursuit of advanced degrees in the evening by experienced executives, all attest to the dramatic change in the attitude of the work force toward lifetime education. Education is going to be an expensive investment for most companies—expensive in terms of the provision of educational opportunities as well as expensive in terms of worker time.

We predict that this trend will increase in intensity. By the end of the 1980s, most members of the work force will no longer make a distinction between education and their employment. Virtually all members of the work force (from the blue-collar level on up to the chief executive) will simply take it for granted that they will go to school part time while they are working. Moreover, we believe that self-education through individual reading programs will grow in significance.

This points to the need for human resources management specialists who will pay increased attention to the development of quality materials for individual education and to the development of formal programs. These programs may consist of increased opportunities for in-company training as well as university programs outside the company.

We believe that finding a viable strategy for providing increased lifetime education opportunities will be an inevitable requirement for companies that wish to remain competitive and to attract the best human resources. But it will also make imperative the development of a parallel strategy to reduce turnover, since turnover will increasingly represent the loss of an investment.

Underqualified workers

We believe that another very probable development over the last quarter of the 20th century will be increased incentives (and later increased pressure) for business organizations to employ and train underqualified and disadvantaged members of the work force. Whether the organization elects to wait for social pressure to force such programs or whether it elects to exhibit social leadership by creating such programs voluntarily, we predict that over the next 25 years most managers of human resources will find it necessary to create programs for a growing proportion of the work force which will come into the company underqualified for entry-level jobs, without either the basic intellectual skills or social skills which employers today take for granted.

A report of the American Assembly Seminar sponsored by Columbia University in May 1976 to consider "Manpower Goals for American Democracy" strongly reflected the growing conviction that employment is a right of all members of our society (whether or not prequalified) and that the provision of employment opportunities to unqualified individuals is a social obligation of employers.

Among the many far-reaching proposals for extending employment opportunities to people currently considered unemployable, this report called for programs to encourage employers in both the private and the public sector to employ and train "underqualified" members of the work force, with the training to be partly subsidized by society (that is, government). Whether or not such programs are ever created, the conclusions of this assembly reflect a new assumption that employers are obligated to utilize all elements of the potential work force, not merely the most employable. This view will represent a major challenge to human resources managers, who will be called upon to devise programs to satisfy these new demands.

QUESTIONS AND PROBLEMS

1. We have covered the managing of human resources today. Why should we be concerned about the environmental and behavioral characteristics of our society five to ten years hence?

2. a. Can we "forecast the future"?
    b. How do we structure the future?

3. a. What is the major overall change in the philosophy and practice of human resource administration which is anticipated in the next few years?
    b. Describe trends which you believe substantiate your view.

4. Social changes are occurring at a very rapid rate in modern society. These have a tremendous impact on both individual behavior and the managing of people. List the social changes covered in this chapter, and develop additional important changes that you may identify from reading and personal observation.

5. Discuss the public responsibility of corporations in areas relating to social change, such as discrimination, rehabilitation, and other areas mentioned in the text.

6. Discuss the possible impact of the exhaustion of oil resources on business organization, employment, and human resources management.

7. Estimate how many hours the average workday would be if unemployment were reduced to zero by sharing the work now available among the entire labor force.

8. Discuss the pros and cons of flexitime from:
    a. The company's viewpoint.
    b. Your career viewpoint.

9. The computer has made possible powerful management information systems (MIS) to aid managers in planning, controlling, and decision making. On the

basis of library research, prepare a short paper discussing the role of MIS for human resources management.

10. Discuss the quality of working life that you would like in a job that you might obtain.

11. Discuss possible labor-management scenarios of the future.

12. a. What factors appear to be affecting current productivity trends in the United States?

b. Discuss why you believe that productivity will be higher, the same, or lower in the United States ten years from now.

13. a. Is it possible that within ten years the work force will be divided into two large groups—the educated and the uneducated?

b. Give the pros and cons for your conclusion.

c. "We are producing an overeducated society." Discuss this statement in terms of human resources management.

14. Why is there a shift of the work force towards a higher and higher proportion of knowledge workers?

15. As society becomes more and more complex and all jobs require more skill, there may be a growing number of hard-core unemployables. These are people with little education and limited mental ability. What solutions can you propose to absorb these people into the productive work force?

16. We have studied human resources in business as a system. How do you relate each change discussed in this chapter to Exhibit 1–3?

17. In your opinion, will the total human resource system work to effect successful responses to the challenges described in this chapter? Explain and illustrate your answer.

BIBLIOGRAPHY

Altinus, Cyrus, and Tersine, Richard. "Chronological Age and Job Satisfaction: The Young Blue Collar Worker," *Academy of Management Journal,* March 1973.

Benedict, Clyde. "A Personnel Perspective—Today." *Personnel Administrator,* November 1975.

Bloom, Gordon F., and Northrup, Herbert R. *Economics of Labor Relations.* 8th ed. Homewood, Ill.: Richard D. Irwin, 1977. See chap. 24, "Some Labor Problems of the Future."

Bower, Catherine D. "Alcoholism: Industry's $9 Billion Headache." *Personnel Administrator,* January 1975.

Bradlove, Mary. "Despite Much Hoopla, Few Women Capture Companies' Top Jobs." *Wall Street Journal,* April 18, 1974.

Burack, Elmer H., and Miller, Edwin L. "The Personnel Function in Transition." *California Management Review,* Spring 1976.

"The Cash Deterrent to Discrimination." *Business Week,* April 20, 1974.

Chapman, J. Brad, and Ottemann, Robert. "Employee Preference for Various

Compensation and Fringe Benefit Options." *Personnel Administrator,* November 1975.

Coleman, Charles J. "Personnel: The Changing Function." *Public Personnel Management,* May–June 1973.

Decker, Louis R., and Peed, Daniel A. "Affirmative Action for the Handicapped." *Personnel,* May–June 1976.

Dillon, John S. "A New Role for Personnel: Monitoring Super Change." *Personnel Administrator,* November 1975.

Drucker, Peter F. "Beyond Stick and Carrot: Hysteria over the Work Ethic." *Psychology Today,* November 1973.

Dyer, Frederick C., and Ford, Chris W. "Training the Handicapped: Now It's Their Turn for Affirmative Action." *Personnel Journal,* April 1976.

England, George W., Dhingra, O. P., Agarwal, Maresh C. *The Manager and the Man.* Kent, Ohio: Comparative Administration Research Institute of the Center for Business and Economic Research, Kent State University 1974.

"Executive Sabbaticals—A 'Fringe' That Pays Double Dividends." *U.S. News & World Report,* January 20, 1975.

Flatermayer, Edmund. "Ever Increasing Affluence Is Less of a Sure Thing." *Fortune,* April 1975.

Flowers, Vincent S., et al. *Managerial Values for Working.* New York: AMACOM, 1975.

Follmann, Joseph F., Jr. *Alcoholics and Business: Problems, Costs, Solutions.* New York: AMACOM, 1976.

Foulkes, Fred K. "The Expanding Role of the Personnel Function." *Harvard Business Review,* March–April 1975.

The Future of Collective Bargaining. BNA–ASPA Bulletin to Management. Washington, D.C.: Bureau of National Affairs, Inc., February 10, 1972.

Graham, Victoria. "When a Pinch Becomes a Problem," *Miami Herald,* January 5, 1976.

Huffman, Eileen B. *Unionization of Professional Societies.* Report No. 690, New York: Conference Board, 1976.

International City Management Association. *Guide to Productivity Improvement Projects.* Washington, D.C.: National Center for Productivity and Quality of Working Life, July 1976.

Johnson, Rossall J. "The Personnel Administrator of the 1970's." *Personnel Journal,* April 1971.

Leavitt, Harold J., and Whisler, Thomas L. "Management in the 1980's." *Harvard Business Review,* November–December 1958.

McFarland, Dalton E. *Company Officers Assess the Personnel Function.* AMA Research Study 79. New York: American Management Association, 1967.

Manpower Goals for American Democracy. Report of the American Assembly Seminar, Columbia University, 1976.

Marshall, F. Ray, et al. *Labor Economics.* 3d ed. Homewood, Ill.: Richard D. Irwin, 1976. See chap. 23, "Labor Issues of the Future."

Mee, John S. "The Manager of the Future." *Business Horizons,* June 1973.

Meyer, Herbert E. "Personnel Directors Are the New Corporate Heroes." *Fortune,* February 1976.

Miner, John B. *The Human Constraint: The Coming Shortage of Managerial Talent.* Washington, D.C.: BNA Books, 1974.

Mullally, John J. "Moonlighting? Even Managers Do It." *Industry Week,* June 21, 1976.

Myers, Susan S., and Myers, M. Scott. "Adapting to the New Work Ethic." *Business Quarterly,* Winter 1973.

National Commission on Productivity and Work Quality: *A National Policy for Productivity Improvement.* Washington, D.C.: National Center for Productivity and Quality of Working Life, July 1976.

Polk, Barbara Bovee. "Male Power and the Women's Movement." *Journal of Applied Behavioral Science,* July–September 1974.

Reardon, Robert W. "Help for the Troubled Worker in a Small Company." *Personnel,* January–February 1976.

Ross, Joel E. *Managing Productivity.* Reston, Va.: Reston Publishing Co., 1977.

Somers, Gerald G. (ed.). *The Next Twenty-Five Years of Industrial Relations.* Madison, Wis.: Industrial Relations Research Association, 1973.

Special Task Force to the Secretary of Health, Education, and Welfare. *Work in America.* Cambridge, Mass.: MIT Press, 1973.

Stanton, Erwin S. "Last Chance for Personnel to Come of Age." *Personnel Administrator,* November 1975.

Tarnowieski, Dale. *The Changing Success Ethic.* New York: AMACOM, 1973.

Toffler, Alvin. *Future Shock.* New York: Bantam Books, 1970.

Walton, Richard E. "Quality of Working Life: What Is It?" *Sloan Management Review,* Fall 1973.

"White Males Complain They Are Now Victims of Job Discrimination." *Wall Street Journal,* February 28, 1974.

Whyte, William H. *The Organization Man.* New York: Simon and Schuster, 1956.

Williams, Richard L., and Moffat, Gene H. (eds.). *Occupational Alcoholism Programs.* Springfield, Ill.: Charles C Thomas, 1975.

NOTES

[1] You may wish to look at examples of "futures" forecasting in *Technological Forecasting and Social Change* (a journal); Alvin Toffler, *Future Shock* (New York: Random House, 1970); and Dennis L. Meadows, *Dynamics of Growth in a Finite World* (Cambridge Mass.: Wright-Allen Press, 1974).

[2] "Women Hold Few Top Federal Jobs," *Miami Herald,* July 26, 1976.

[3] "Americans Fearful They've Lost Control of Life, Surveys Say," *Miami Herald,*

April 3, 1974. See also surveys conducted in 1968 and 1973 by Daniel Yankelovich, Inc., for the Institute of Life Insurance.

[4] Harry J. Johnson, *Executive Life Styles* (New York: Thomas Y. Crowell, 1974).

[5] Richard Zoglin, "The Homosexual Executive," *MBA*, July–August 1974.

[6] Lesbianism in the general population is discussed in Shere Hite, *The Hite Report* (New York: Macmillan Co., 1976).

[7] See Arthur A. Sloane and Fred Whitney, *Labor Relations*, 3d ed. (Englewood Cliffs, N.J.: Prentice-Hall, 1977), pp. 492–93.

[8] Cyrus Altinus and Richard Tersine, "Chronological Age and Job Satisfaction: The Young Blue Collar Worker," *Academy of Management Journal*, March 1973.

[9] Special Task Force to the Secretary of Health, Education, and Welfare. *Work in America:* Cambridge, Mass.: MIT Press, 1973.

[10] Peter F. Drucker, "Beyond Stick and Carrot: Hysteria over the Work Ethic," *Psychology Today*, November 1973, pp. 87–92.

[11] Herbert E. Meyer, "Personnel Directors Are the New Corporate Heroes," *Fortune*, February 1976.

INDEX

Index

This book has been set in 10 point and 9 point Caledonia, leaded 2 points. Part numbers and chapter titles are in 18 point Optima; part titles in 14 point Optima; and chapter numbers in 36 point Optima. The size of the type page is 29 (maximum) × 44¼ picas.